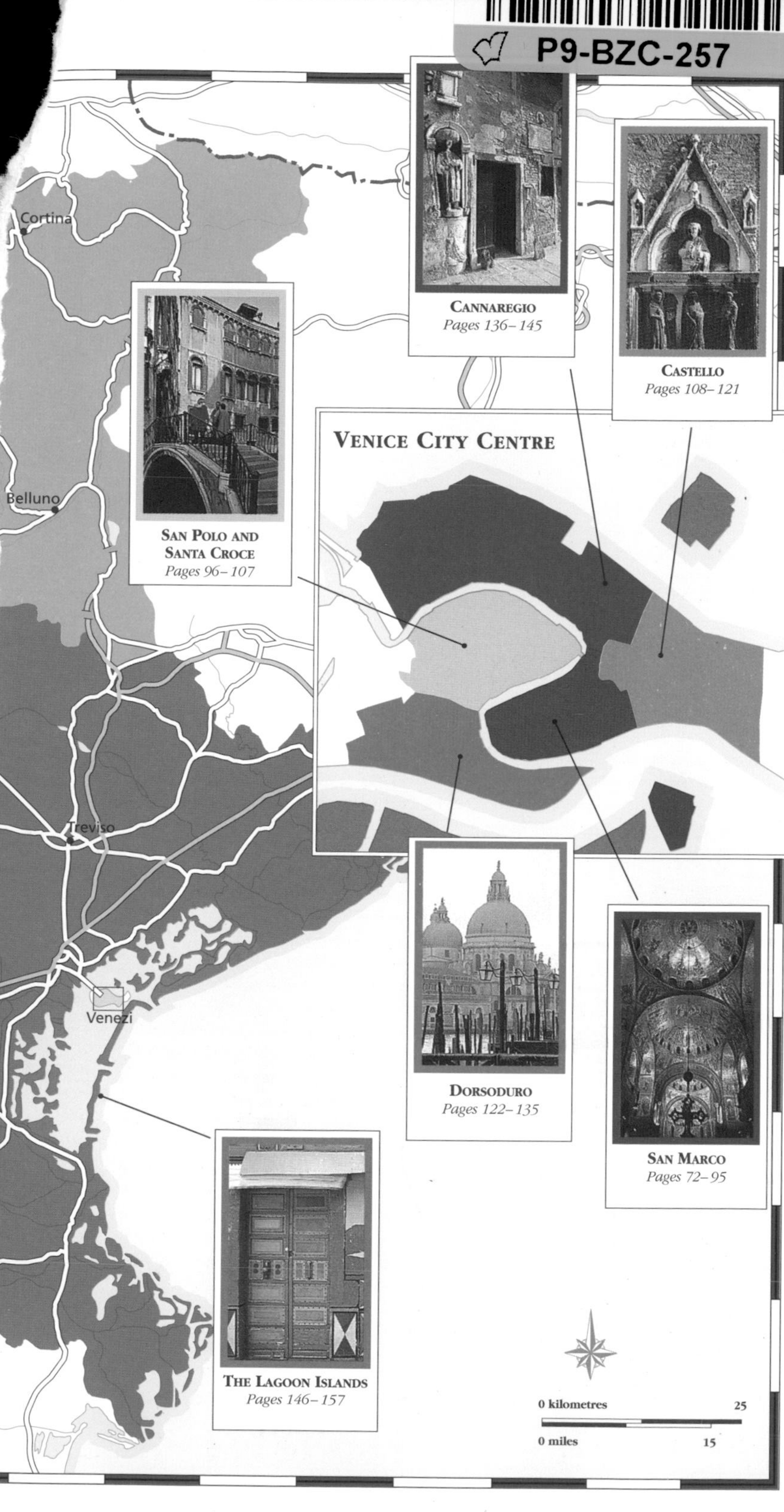
Cortina
Belluno
Treviso
Venezi
Cannaregio
Pages 136–145
Castello
Pages 108–121
Venice City Centre
San Polo and
Santa Croce
Pages 96–107
Dorsoduro
Pages 122–135
San Marco
Pages 72–95
The Lagoon Islands
Pages 146–157
0 kilometres
25
0 miles
15

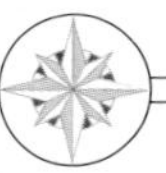

EYEWITNESS TRAVEL GUIDES

VENICE & THE VENETO

TAXI n. 176

EYEWITNESS TRAVEL GUIDES

VENICE & THE VENETO

Main contributors:
SUSIE BOULTON
CHRISTOPHER CATLING

LONDON, NEW YORK,
MELBOURNE, MUNICH AND DELHI
www.dk.com

Produced by Pardoe Blacker Publishing Limited, Lingfield, Surrey
PROJECT EDITOR Caroline Ball
ART EDITOR Simon Blacker
EDITORS Jo Bourne, Molly Perham, Linda Williams
DESIGNERS Kelvin Barratt, Dawn Brend, Jon Eland,
Nick Raven, Steve Rowling
MAP CO-ORDINATORS Simon Farbrother, David Pugh
PICTURE RESEARCH Jill De Cet

CONTRIBUTOR (TRAVELLERS' NEEDS) Sally Roy

MAPS Phil Rose, Jennifer Skelley, Jane Hanson
(Lovell Johns Ltd, Oxford UK)
Street Finder maps based upon digital data, adapted
with permission from L.A.C. (Italy)

PHOTOGRAPHERS John Heseltine (Venice), Roger Moss (Veneto)

ILLUSTRATORS Arcana Studios, Donati Giudici Associati srl,
Robbie Polley, Simon Roulstone

Reproduced by Colourscan, Singapore
Printed and bound in China by Toppan Printing Co., (Shenzhen Ltd)

First American Edition, 1995
04 05 10 9

Published in the United States by
DK Publishing, Inc.,
375 Hudson Street, New York, New York 10014
**Reprinted with revisions 1995,
1997 (twice), 1998, 1999, 2000, 2001, 2002, 2003, 2004**

Published in Great Britain by Dorling Kindersley Limited.

ISSN 1542-1554
ISBN 0-7894-9574-0

THROUGHOUT THIS BOOK, FLOORS ARE REFERRED TO IN ACCORDANCE WITH EUROPEAN USAGE, I.E., THE "FIRST FLOOR" IS THE FLOOR ABOVE GROUND LEVEL.

The information in this Dorling Kindersley Travel Guide is checked annually. Every effort has been made to ensure that this book is as up-to-date as possible at the time of going to press. Some details, however, such as telephone numbers, opening hours, prices, gallery hanging arrangements and travel information are liable to change. The publishers cannot accept responsibility for any consequences arising from the use of this book, nor for any material on third party websites, and cannot guarantee that any website address in this book will be a suitable source of travel information. We value the views and suggestions of our readers very highly. Please write to: Publisher, DK Eyewitness Travel Guides, Dorling Kindersley, 80 Strand, London WC2R 0RL, Great Britain.

CONTENTS

The Venetian explorer Marco Polo

INTRODUCING VENICE AND THE VENETO

Palazzo Pisani Moretta on the Grand Canal

Venice Area by Area

The Rialto Bridge, on the Grand Canal

Veronese's *Passion and Virtue* in the Villa Barbaro at Masèr

The Veneto Area by Area

The medieval Palio dei Dieci Comuni at Montagnana

Travellers' Needs

Survival Guide

Anguilla in umido

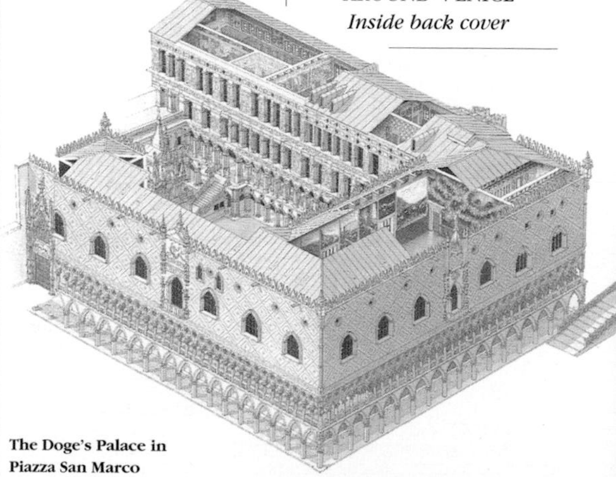

The Doge's Palace in Piazza San Marco

How to Use this Guide

This guide helps you get the most from your stay in Venice and the Veneto. It provides both expert recommendations and detailed practical information. *Introducing Venice and the Veneto* maps the region and sets it in its historical and cultural context. *Venice Area by Area* and *The Veneto Area by Area* describe the important sights, with maps, pictures and detailed illustrations. Suggestions for food, drink, accommodation, shopping and entertainment are in *Travellers' Needs*, and the *Survival Guide* has tips on everything from the Italian telephone system to travelling around Venice by *vaporetto*.

Venice Area by Area

The city has been divided into five sightseeing areas. The lagoon islands make up a sixth area. Each area has its own chapter, which opens with a list of the sights described. All the sights are numbered and plotted on an *Area Map*. The detailed information for each sight is presented in numerical order, making it easy to locate within the chapter.

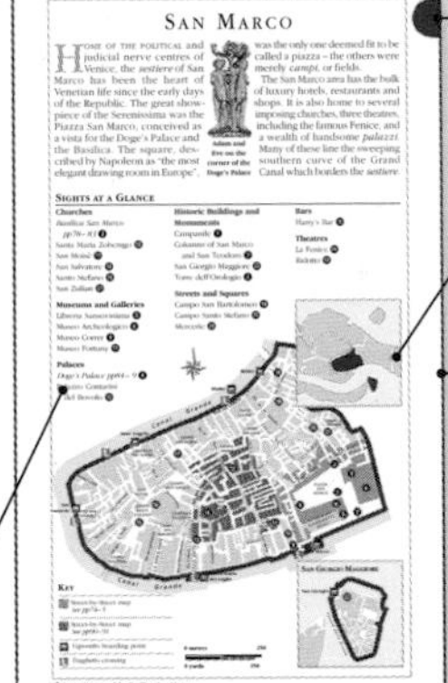

Each area of Venice can be quickly identified by its colour coding.

A locator map shows where you are in relation to other areas of the city.

Sights at a Glance lists the chapter's sights by category: Churches; Museums and Galleries; Historic Buildings; Palaces; Streets, Bridges and Squares.

1 Area Map
For easy reference, the sights are numbered and located on a map. The sights are also shown on the Venice Street Finder *on pages 280–89.*

2 Street-by-Street Map
This gives a bird's eye view of the heart of each sightseeing area.

Stars indicate the sights that no visitor should miss.

A suggested route for a walk covers the more interesting streets in the area.

3 Detailed information on each sight
All the sights in Venice are described individually. Addresses, telephone numbers, nearest vaporetto *stop, opening hours and information on admission charges are also provided.*

1 **Introduction**
The landscape, history and character of each region is described here, showing how the area has developed over the centuries and what it offers to the visitor today.

THE VENETO AREA BY AREA
In this book, the Veneto has been divided into three regions, each of which has a separate chapter. The most interesting sights to visit have been numbered on a *Pictorial Map.*

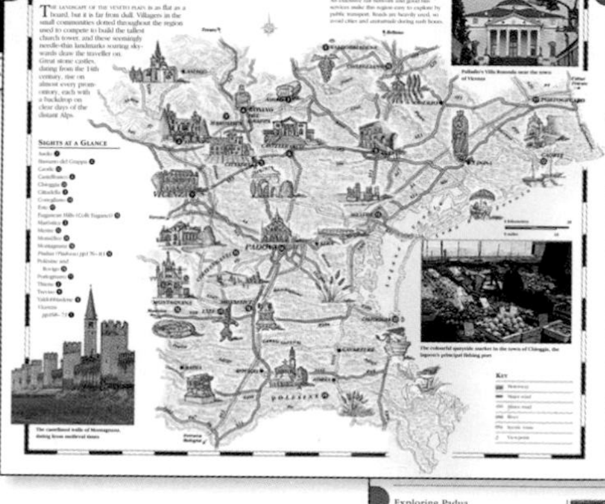

Each area of the Veneto can be quickly identified by its colour coding.

2 **Pictorial Map**
This shows the road network and gives an illustrated overview of the whole region. All the sights are numbered and there are also useful tips on getting around the region by car, bus and train.

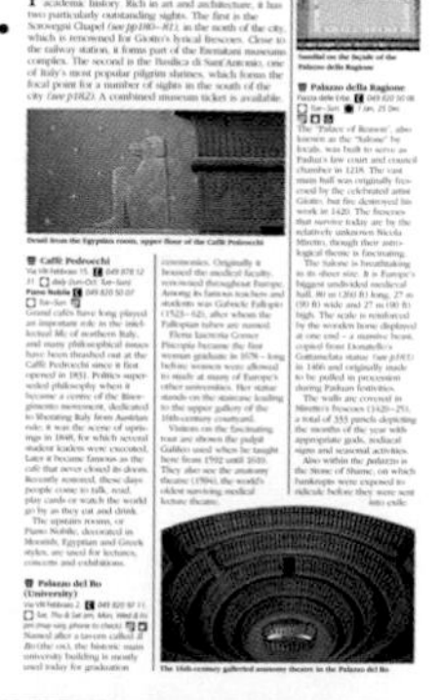

3 **Detailed information on each sight**
All the important towns and other places to visit are described individually. They are listed in order, following the numbering on the Pictorial Map. *Within each town or city, there is detailed information on important buildings and other sights.*

Stars indicate the best features and works of art.

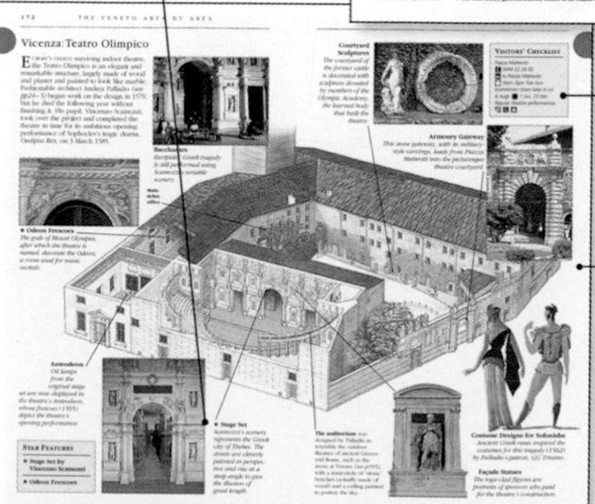

For all the top sights, a Visitors' Checklist provides the practical information you will need to plan your visit.

4 **The top sights**
These are given two or more full pages. Historic buildings are dissected to reveal their interiors; museums and galleries have colour-coded floorplans to help you locate the most interesting exhibits.

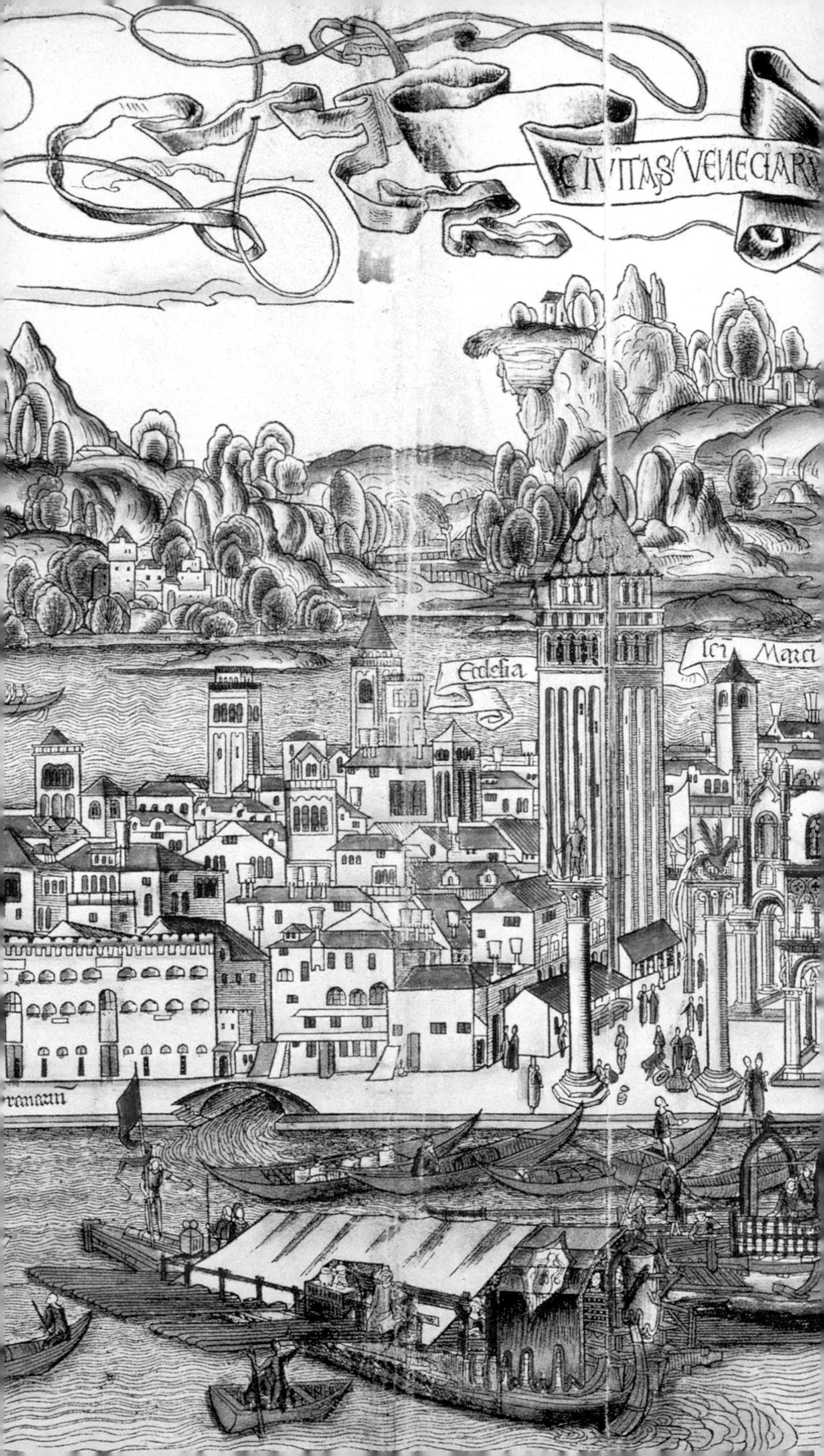
CIVITAS VENECIARV
Ecclesia
sci Marci

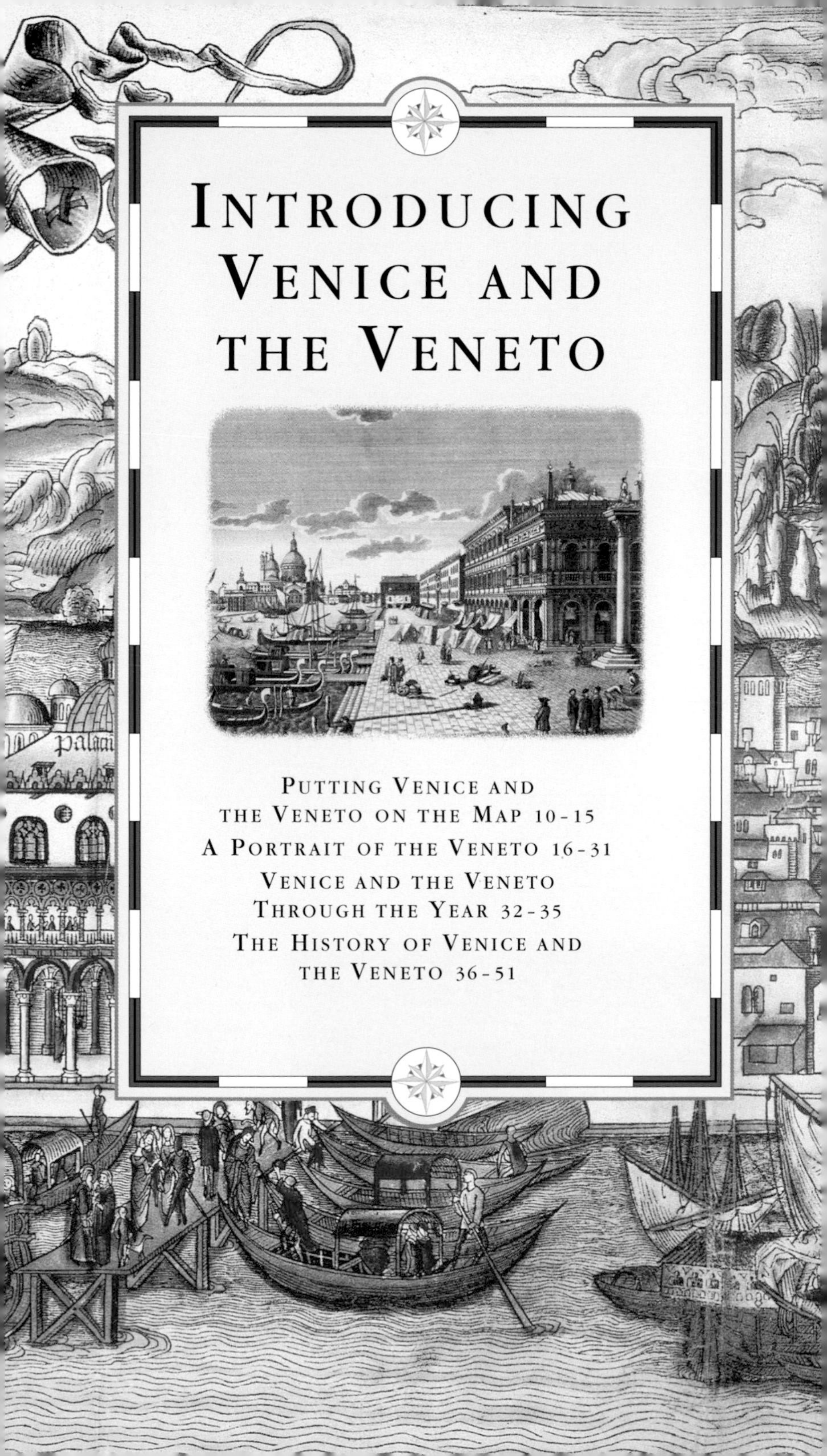

Introducing Venice and the Veneto

Putting Venice and the Veneto on the Map

THE VENETO LIES in the northernmost sector of Italy, and stretches from the Dolomite mountains in the north to the flatlands of the Venetian lagoon in the south. One of the most prosperous regions of Italy, the Veneto covers an area of 47,562 sq km (18,364 sq miles), and has a population of 4.5 million. Rail and road links with the rest of Europe are excellent, and three international airports serve the region: Valerio Catullo in Verona, Marco Polo on the edge of the lagoon, and Treviso.

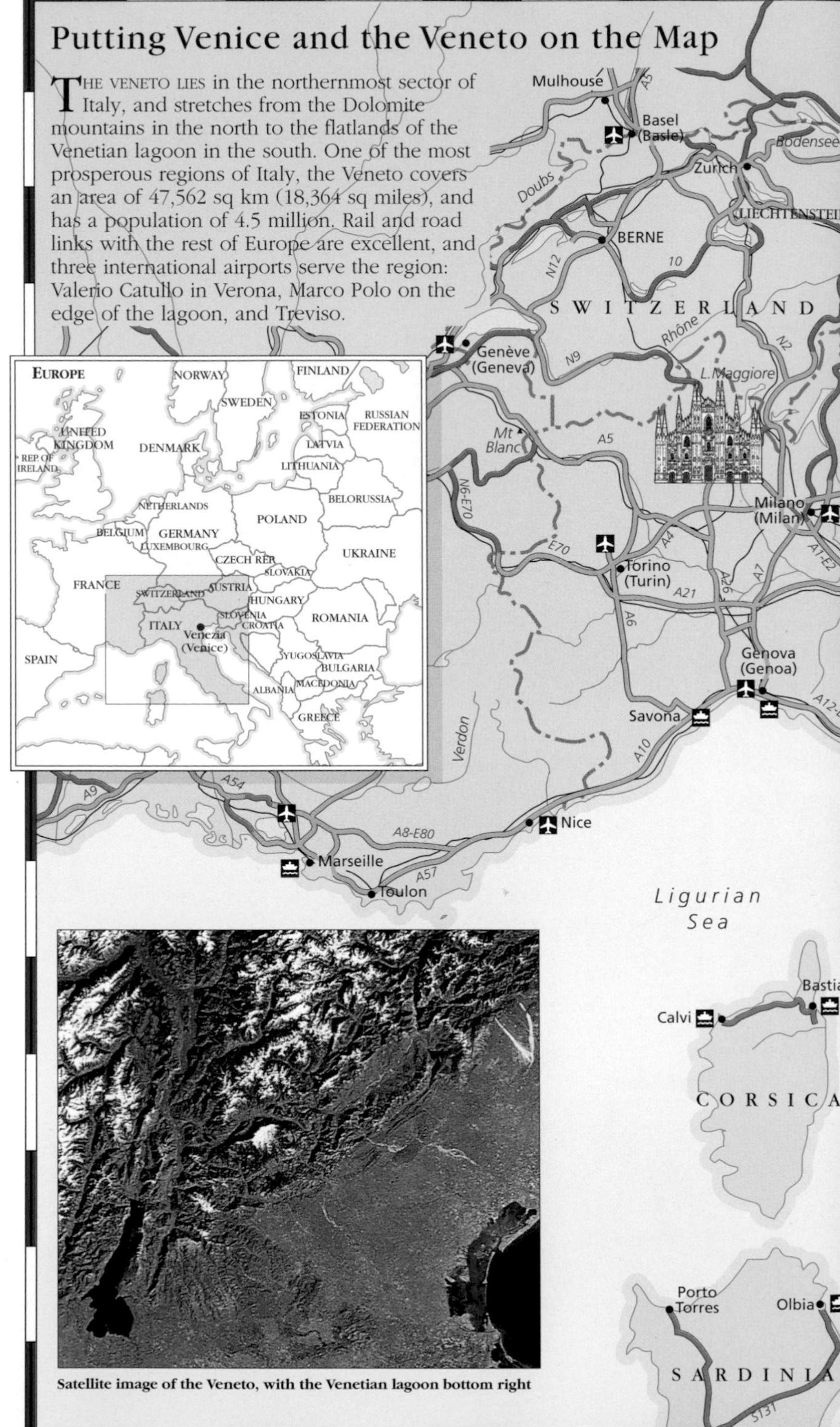

Satellite image of the Veneto, with the Venetian lagoon bottom right

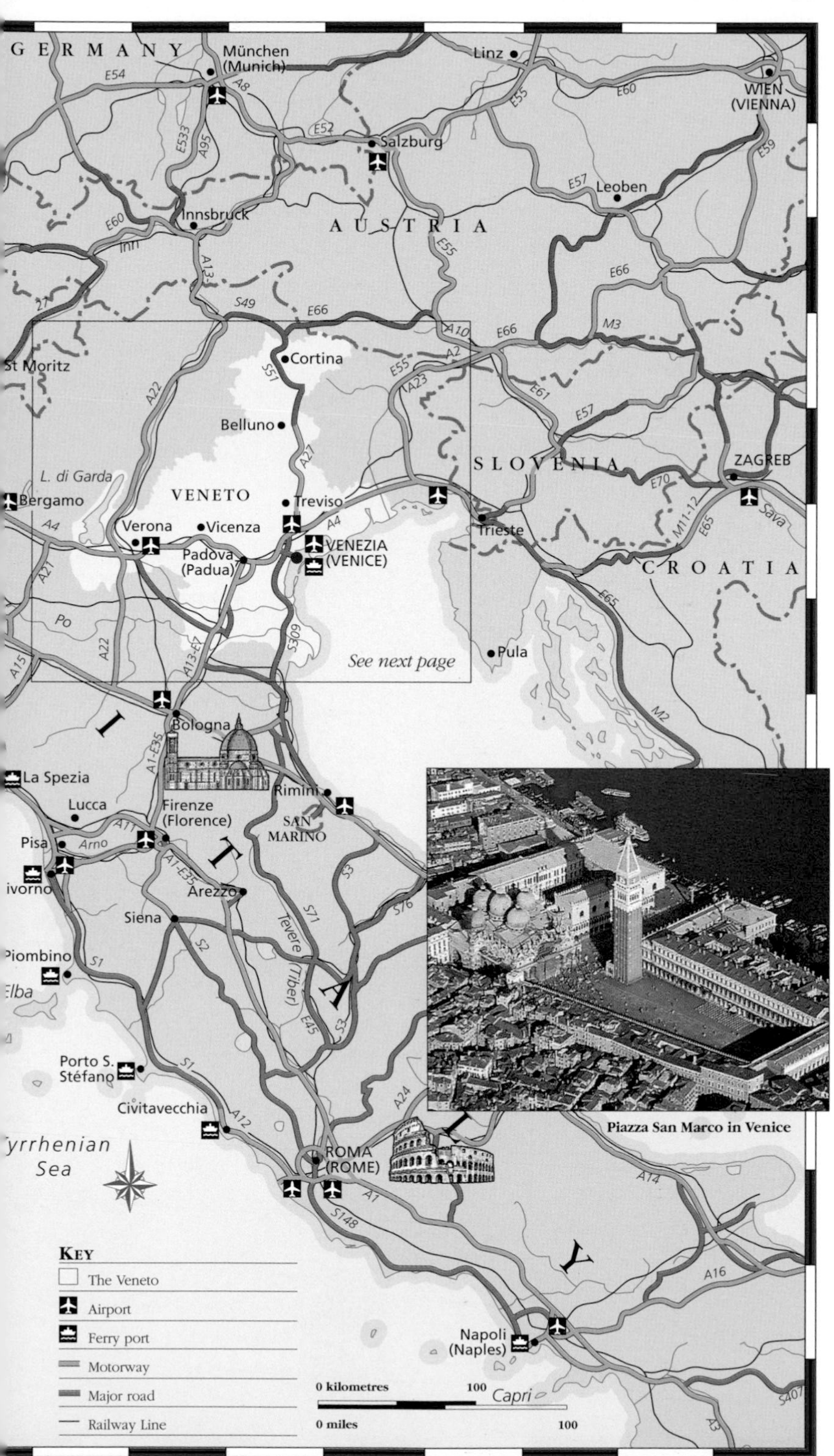

Piazza San Marco in Venice

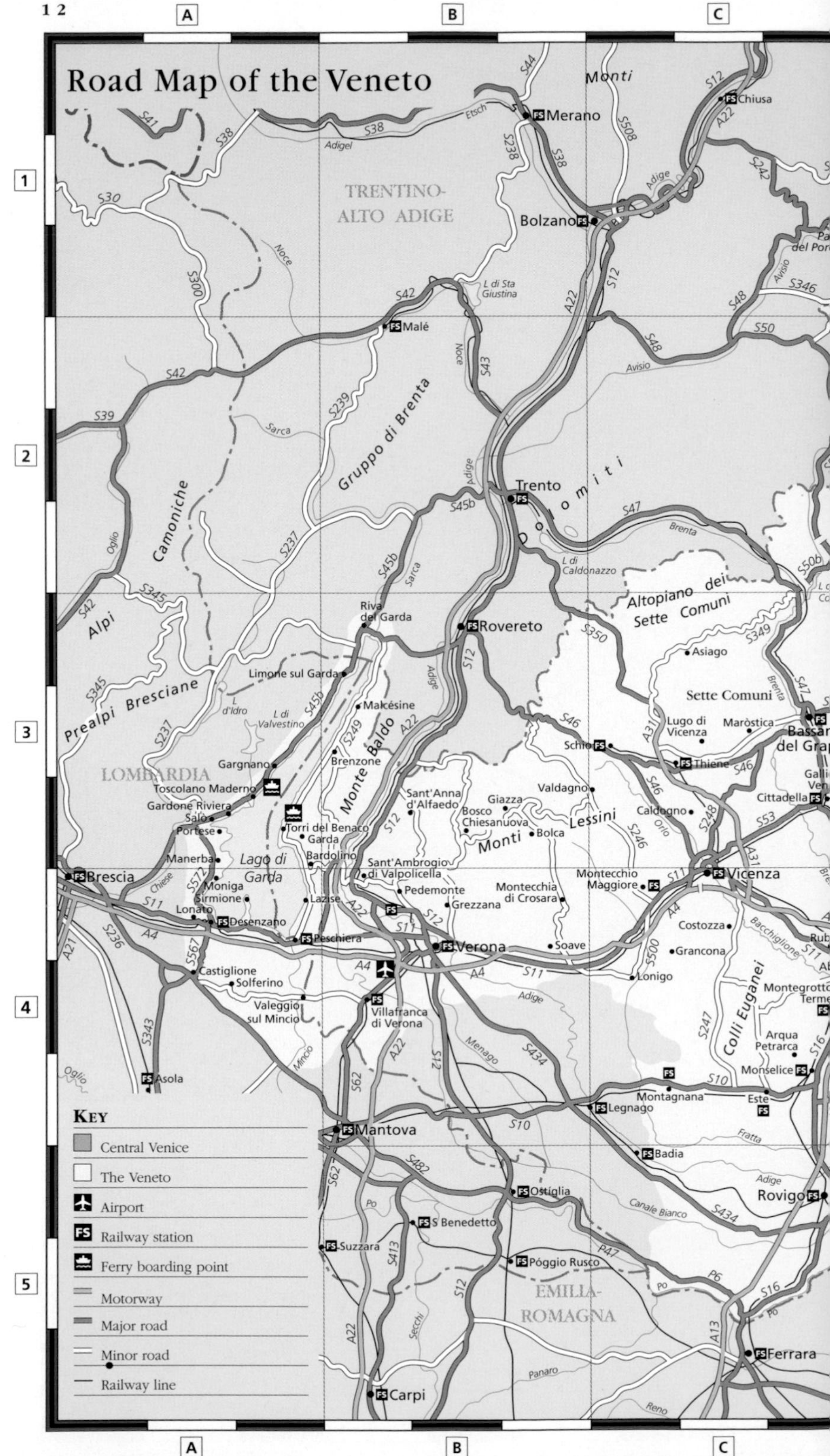
A
B
C
1
2
3
4
5
Road Map of the Veneto
TRENTINO-ALTO ADIGE
LOMBARDIA
EMILIA-ROMAGNA
Merano
Chiusa
Bolzano
Malé
L di Sta Giustina
Gruppo di Brenta
Dolomiti
Trento
Monti
Alpi Camoniche
Prealpi Bresciane
Riva del Garda
Rovereto
L di Caldonazzo
Altopiano dei Sette Comuni
Asiago
Sette Comuni
Limone sul Garda
L d'Idro
L di Valvestino
Malcésine
Monte Baldo
Brenzone
Gargnano
Toscolano Maderno
Gardone Riviera
Salò
Portese
Torri del Benaco
Garda
Bardolino
Manerba
Lago di Garda
Moniga
Sirmione
Lonato
Desenzano
Lazise
Peschiera
Brescia
Sant'Anna d'Alfaedo
Bosco Chiesanuova
Giazza
Monti Lessini
Bolca
Valdagno
Schio
Thiene
Lugo di Vicenza
Maròstica
Caldogno
Cittadella
Sant'Ambrogio di Valpolicella
Pedemonte
Grezzana
Montecchia di Crosara
Montecchio Maggiore
Vicenza
Verona
Soave
Costozza
Grancona
Lonigo
Colli Euganei
Castiglione
Solferino
Valeggio sul Mincio
Villafranca di Verona
Asola
Montegrotto Terme
Arqua Petrarca
Monselice
Montagnana
Este
Legnago
Mantova
Badia
Ostíglia
Rovigo
S Benedetto
Suzzara
Póggio Rusco
Ferrara
Carpi
Adige
Brenta
Sarca
Noce
Oglio
Chiese
Mincio
Po
Menago
Fratta
Canale Bianco
Secchi
Panaro
Reno
Bacchiglione
Avisio
Etsch
S12
S38
S42
S45b
S47
S11
S10
S434
A4
A22
A31
A13
KEY
Central Venice
The Veneto
Airport
Railway station
Ferry boarding point
Motorway
Major road
Minor road
Railway line

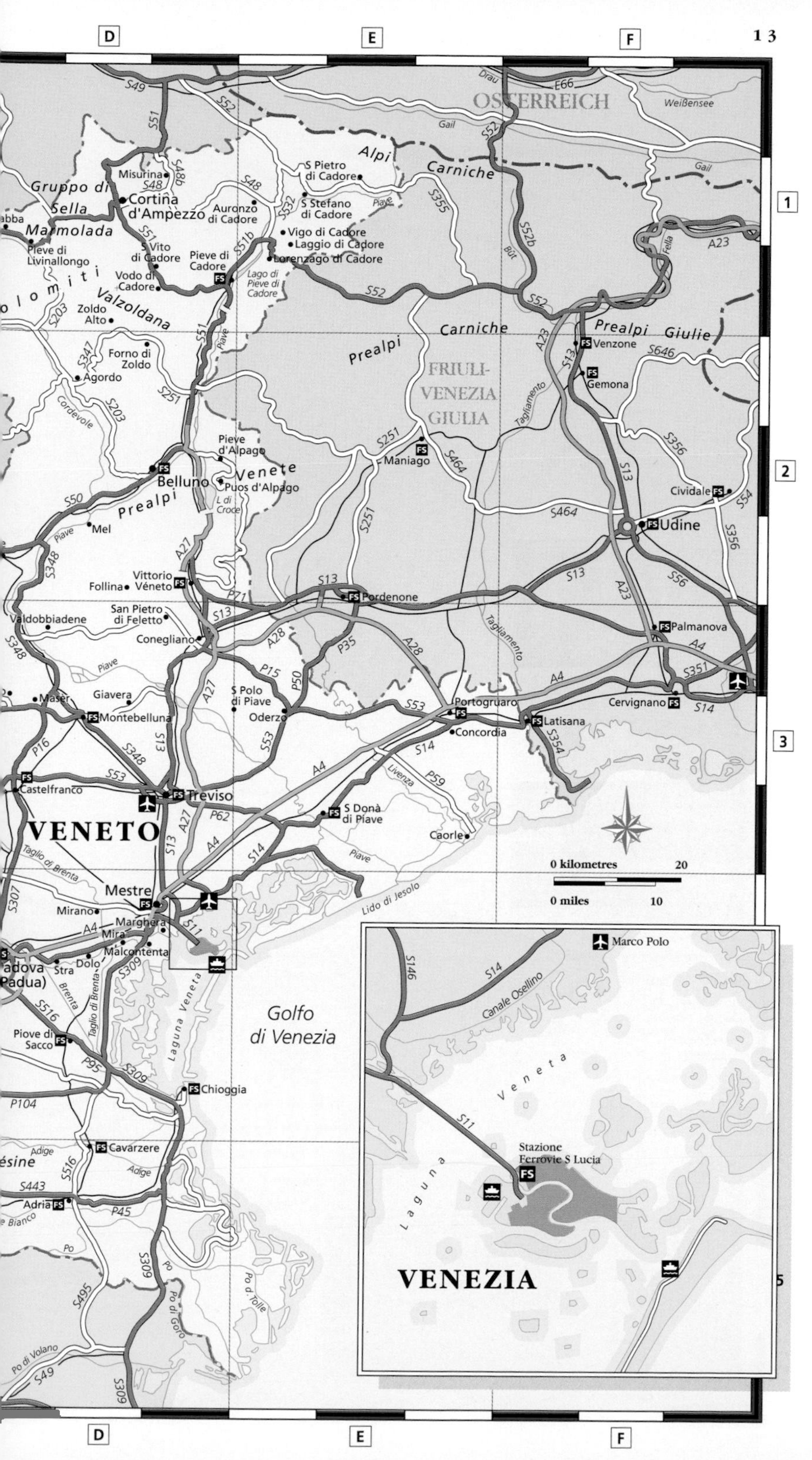
D
E
F
1
2
3
OSTERREICH
Weißensee
Drau
E66
Gail
S49
S51
S52
Alpi
Carniche
S Pietro di Cadore
Misurina
S48b
S48
Gruppo di Sella
Cortina d'Ampezzo
Auronzo di Cadore
S Stefano di Cadore
S355
S52b
Piave
Marmolada
Pieve di Livinallongo
S Vito di Cadore
Pieve di Cadore
S51b
Vigo di Cadore
Laggio di Cadore
Lorenzago di Cadore
Lago di Pieve di Cadore
Fella
A23
Büt
Vodo di Cadore
Dolomiti
Valzoldana
Zoldo Alto
S203
S52
Carniche
Prealpi Giulie
Venzone
S646
Forno di Zoldo
S347
Agordo
Prealpi
FRIULI-VENEZIA GIULIA
S13
Gemona
Tagliamento
S251
Cordevole
S203
Pieve d'Alpago
S251
Maniago
S464
S356
Belluno
Puos d'Alpago
Prealpi Venete
L di Croce
Cividale
S54
S50
S464
Udine
Mel
S251
S356
S348
A27
Vittorio Véneto
Follina
S13
S56
A23
P71
Pordenone
Valdobbiadene
San Pietro di Feletto
S13
Conegliano
A28
Palmanova
S348
P35
A28
Tagliamento
A4
Piave
P15
P50
S351
Maser
Giavera
S Polo di Piave
Oderzo
A27
S53
Portogruaro
A4
Cervignano
S14
Montebelluna
Latisana
Concordia
S348
S13
S53
S14
S354
P16
S53
A4
Livenza
P59
Castelfranco
Treviso
S Donà di Piave
VENETO
A27
P62
S13
A4
S14
Caorle
Piave
Taglio di Brenta
0 kilometres 20
0 miles 10
Mestre
S307
Mirano
Lido di Jesolo
A4
Marghera
Mira
S11
Malcontenta
Dolo
Padova (Padua)
Stra
S309
Brenta
Laguna Veneta
S516
Golfo di Venezia
Taglio di Brenta
Piove di Sacco
P95
S309
Chioggia
P104
Adige
Cavarzere
Adige
S516
S443
Adria
P45
Po
S309
Po
Po d. Tolle
S495
Po di Goro
Po di Volano
S49
S309
Marco Polo
S146
S14
Canale Osellino
Laguna Veneta
S11
Stazione Ferrovie S Lucia
VENEZIA
FS

Central Venice

VENICE IS DIVIDED into six ancient administrative districts or *sestieri*. The areas described in this book for the most part follow the *sestieri* boundaries, with San Polo and Santa Croce combined. Visitors usually start with the Piazza San Marco, heading for the Doge's Palace and the breathtaking basilica, but each district has its own distinct character, and time spent exploring each will be fully rewarded.

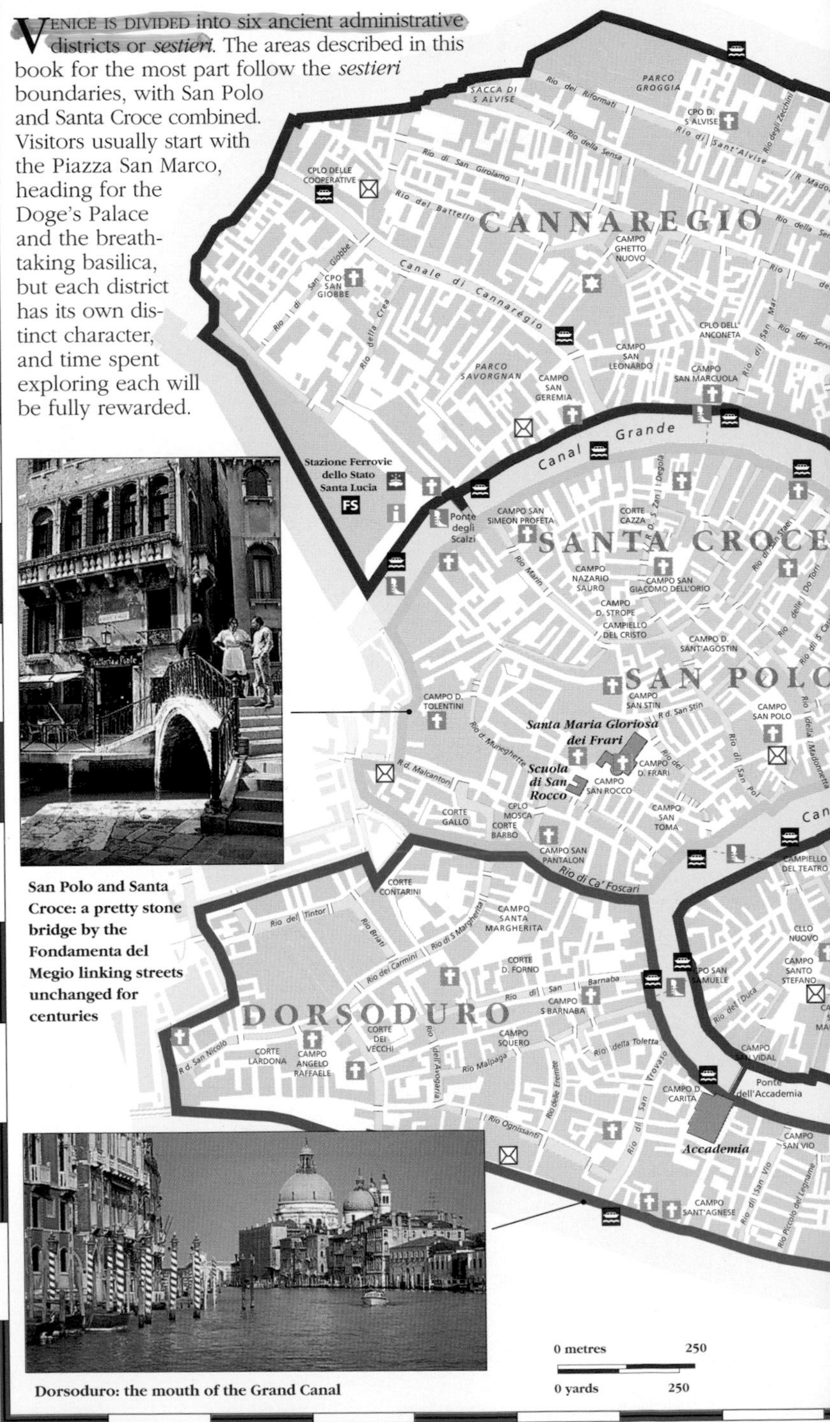

San Polo and Santa Croce: a pretty stone bridge by the Fondamenta del Megio linking streets unchanged for centuries

Dorsoduro: the mouth of the Grand Canal

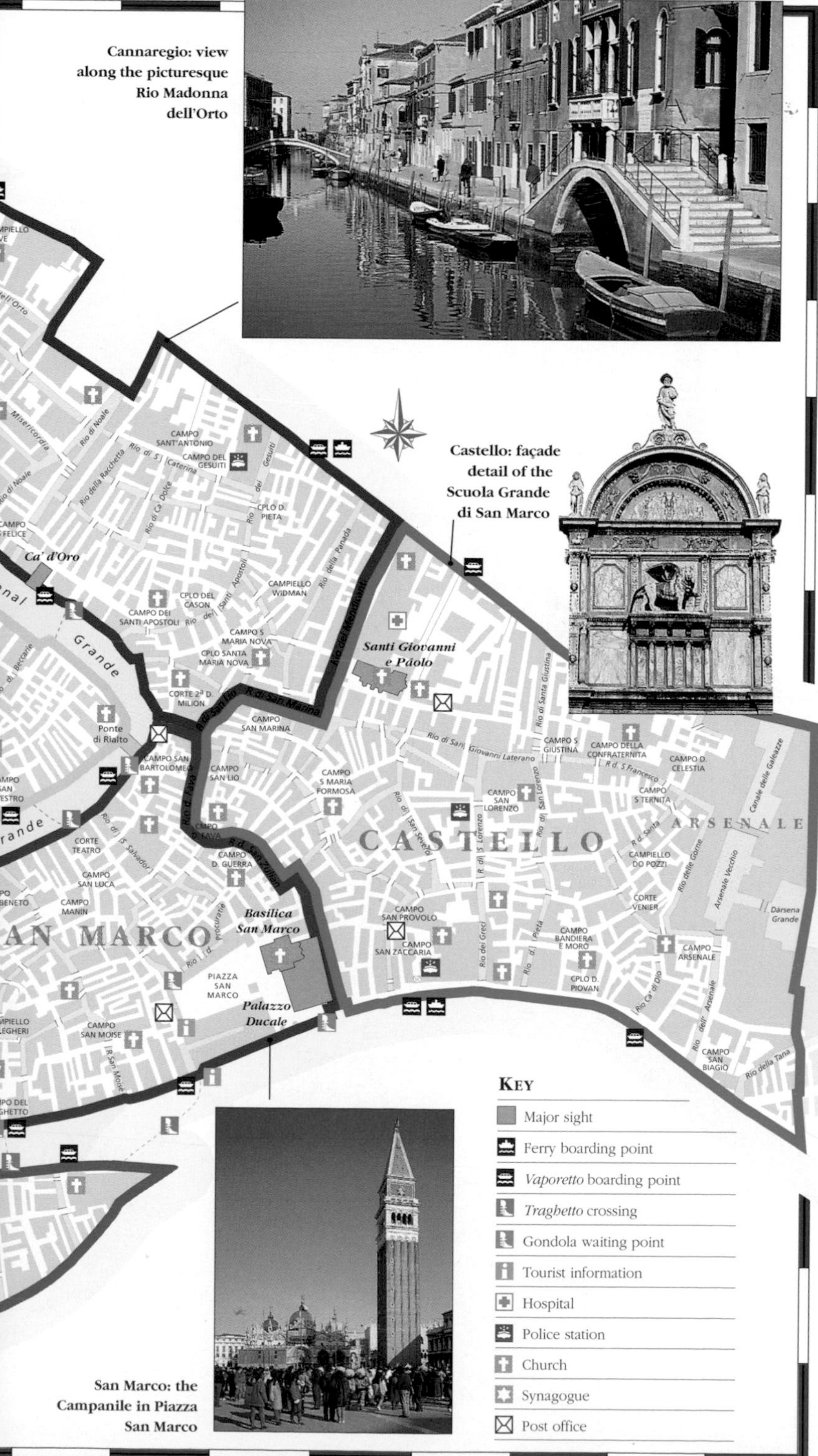

Cannaregio: view along the picturesque Rio Madonna dell'Orto

Castello: façade detail of the Scuola Grande di San Marco

San Marco: the Campanile in Piazza San Marco

KEY

- Major sight
- Ferry boarding point
- *Vaporetto* boarding point
- *Traghetto* crossing
- Gondola waiting point
- Tourist information
- Hospital
- Police station
- Church
- Synagogue
- Post office

A Portrait of the Veneto

VENICE AND THE VENETO FORM, on the face of it, an unlikely partnership. Venice is a romantic tourist city frozen in time, the Veneto a forward-thinking and cosmopolitan part of the new Europe. Yet the commercial dynamism of the mainland cities is a direct legacy of the Old Lady of the Lagoon who, in her prime, ruled much of the Mediterranean.

Venice is one of the few cities in the world that can truly be described as unique. It survives against all the odds, built on a series of low mud banks amid the tidal waters of the Adriatic and regularly subject to floods. Once a powerful commercial and naval force in the Mediterranean, Venice has found a new role. Her *palazzi* have become shops, hotels and apartments, her warehouses have been transformed into museums and her convents have been turned into centres for art restoration. Yet little of the essential fabric of Venice has altered in 200 years. A prewar guide to the city is just as useful today as when it was published, a rare occurrence on a continent scarred by the aerial bombing of World War II and the demands of postwar development. More than 12 million visitors a year succumb to the magic of this improbable city whose streets are full of water and where the past has more meaning than the present.

The lion of St Mark, symbol of imperial Venice

For all this Venice has had a price to pay. So desirable is a Venetian apartment that rents are beyond the means of the Venetians themselves. Many of the city's apartments are owned by wealthy foreigners who use them perhaps for two or three weeks a year – unlit windows at night are indicative of absent owners.

Children attending their first communion at Monte Berico, outside Vicenza

◁ Venice's Carnival, an historic celebration revived in 1979

An elderly Venetian in an ageing Venice

In 1997 the population of the city was 68,600 (compared with 150,000 in 1950), but in 2001 the numbers rose for the first time since the 1950s. The average age of the Venetian population is nearly 50. One reason the city shuts down so early at night is that the waiters, cooks and shop assistants all have to catch the last train home across the causeway to Mestre.

Mestre, by contrast, is a bustling city of 180,000 inhabitants, with a busy oil terminal and an expanding industrial base, as well as some of the liveliest discos in Italy. Governed by the same mayor and city council, Mestre and Venice have been described as the ugliest city in the world married to the most beautiful. Yet Mestre, founded by Venetians who foresaw a day when development land would run out in the lagoon, is simply an extension of the same entrepreneurial spirit that characterized mercantile Venice in her heyday, a spirit that is now typical of the region as a whole.

Fruit seller in Sirmione, on Lake Garda

One move to inject new life into Venice entails reconverting former industrial sites such as the abattoir and the cotton mill, which have become university premises. A flour mill is currently being transformed into a convention centre.

The Industrious North

The creativity and industry of the people of the Veneto contradict all the clichés about the irrationality and indolence of the Italian character. For a tiny area, with a population of 4.5 million, the Veneto is remarkably productive. Many world-renowned companies have manufacturing bases in the area, from Jacuzzi Europe and Zanussi, to

Benetton shop in Treviso

Benetton, Olivetti and Iveco Ford. As a result, poverty is rare, and the region has progressed from its prewar agricultural base to a modern manufacturing and distribution economy.

Unencumbered by the rest of Italy, the three northern regions of Piedmont, Lombardy and Veneto alone would qualify for membership of the G10 group of the world's richest nations, a fact exploited by the region's politicians in separatist calls for independence from Rome. Coldshouldering the rest of the Italian peninsula, the Veneto looks east to Slovenia for an example of a small state that has recently achieved independence, and north to Germany as a model of political federalism and sound economic management.

Valle di Cadore in the Dolomites, close to the Austrian border

Despite the ferocity of battles fought against them down the ages, the people in the north of the Veneto have a close relationship with their Teutonic neighbours. Today, German signs, food and language can be easily found in the towns around Lake Garda and the Dolomites. Here, the pretty Tyrolean farmsteads and onion-domed churches are a marked contrast to the isolated fishing communities of the lagoon, where Venice's maritime heritage is still evident. Between these two extremes, however, the cities of the Veneto plain, with their wealth of culture, provide a more typical view of Italian life.

Traditional Venetian rowing

Italian Tradition

Padua is a perfect example of the *città salotto*, a city built like a salon on a human scale, where the streets are an extension of the home and where the doorless Caffè Pedrocchi is treated like the city's main square. Here Paduans come to drink coffee or write a letter, read a newspaper or talk to friends. Just like the salons of old, the café provides a meeting place for intellectual discourse and entertainment.

It is not just the Paduans who treat their streets and squares like so many corridors and rooms in one vast communal palace. After 5pm crowds throng Verona's Via Mazzini, taking part in the evening stroll, the *passeggiata*. Against the backdrop of the Roman arena or medieval *palazzi* they argue, swap gossip, forge alliances and strike deals. Younger strollers dress to impress, while young mothers bring their babies out to be admired. For all their modernity, the people of the Veneto still understand the powerful part played by ancient rituals such as this in cementing a strong sense of community.

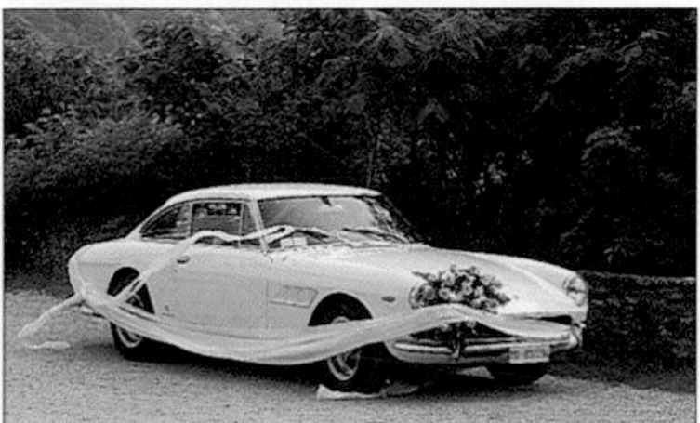
Wedding Ferrari decorated with typical Italian style

The Building of Venice

VENICE IS BUILT on a patchwork of more than 100 low-lying islands in the middle of a swampy lagoon. To overcome these extremely challenging conditions, early Venetian builders evolved construction techniques unique to the city, building with impermeable stone supported by larchwood rafts and timber piles. This method proved effective and most Venetian buildings are remarkably robust, many having stood for at least 400 years. By 1500 the city had taken on much of its present shape and only in the 20th century has further building begun to alter the outline.

Campo Santa Maria Mater Domini *is a typical medieval square, with its central wellhead and its business-like landward façades – decoration on buildings was usually reserved for the canal façades.*

Pinewood piles *were driven 7.5 m (25 ft) into the ground before building work could begin. They rest on the solid* caranto *(compressed clay) layer at the bottom of the lagoon.*

Campaniles often lean because of compaction of the underlying subsoil.

Istrian stone, a type of marble, was used to create damp-proof foundations.

Bricks

Closely packed piles do not rot in the waterlogged subsoil because there is no free oxygen, vital for microbes that cause decay.

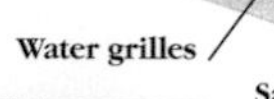

Water grilles

Sand acting as a filter

The well was the source of the fresh water supply. Rainwater was channelled through pavement grilles into a clay-lined cistern filled with sand to act as a filter.

Ornate wellheads, *such as this one in the Doge's Palace courtyard photographed in the late 19th century, indicate the importance of a reliable water supply for the survival of the community. Strict laws protected the purity of the source, prohibiting "beasts, unwashed pots and unclean hands".*

The Campanile Foundations

When the Campanile in the Piazza San Marco *(see p76)* collapsed in 1902, the ancient pilings, underpinning the 98.5-m high (323-ft) landmark, were found to be in excellent condition, after 1,000 years in the ground. Like the Campanile, all buildings in Venice are supported on slender oak and pine piles, harvested in the forests of the northern Veneto and floated downriver to the Venetian lagoon. Once driven through the lagoon subsoil, they create an immensely strong and flexible foundation. Even so, there is a limit to how much weight the piles can carry – the Campanile, its height having been increased several times, simply grew too tall and collapsed. When the tower was rebuilt, timber foundations were again used, but this time more than double the size.

Strengthening the Campanile foundations

***Palazzo* roofs**, built of light, glazed tiles, had gutters to channel rainwater to the well.

Façades were built of lightweight rose-coloured bricks, sometimes left bare, sometimes weatherproofed with plaster.

Bridges *were often privately owned and tolls were charged for their use. Originally, none had railings, creating a night-time hazard for the unwary in the dark streets.*

High water level

Low water level

Accumulated rubbish is regularly removed by dredging to prevent the canal silting up.

Sand and clay

Caranto is compacted clay and sand in alternate layers, which provides a stable base for building.

The Campo (Santa Maria Mater Domini)

The fabric of Venice is made up of scores of self-contained island communities, linked by bridges to neighbouring islands. Each has its own water supply, church and belltower, centred on a *campo* (square), once the focus of commercial life. *Palazzi*, with shops and warehouses at ground floor level, border the *campo* which is connected to workshops and humbler houses by a maze of side alleys.

The Venetian Palazzo

Baroque statue

VENETIAN HOUSES EVOLVED to meet the needs of a city without roads. Visitors usually arrived by boat, so the façade facing the canal was given lavish architectural treatment, while the landward side, which was accessible from a square or alley, was rarely so ornate. Most Venetian houses were built with three storeys, with kitchens located on the ground floor for ready access to water, or in the attic to enable cooking smells to escape. Typically, a *palazzo* served as a warehouse and business premises, as well as a family home, reflecting the city's mercantile character.

Renaissance doorcase with lion

Byzantine (12th and 13th Centuries)

The earliest surviving private *palazzi* in Venice date from the 13th century and reflect the architectural influence of the Byzantine world. Façades are recognizable by their ground-floor arcades and arched open galleries which run the entire length of the first floor. Simple motifs feature leaves or palm trees.

Byzantine roundel, Fondaco dei Turchi

The Byzantine arcades of the Fondaco dei Turchi (built 1225)

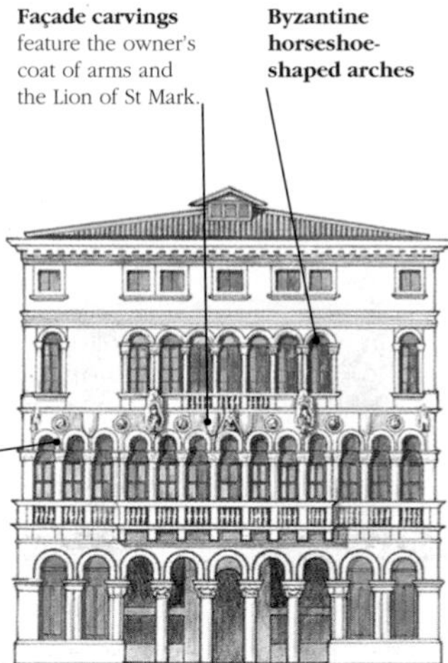
Façade carvings feature the owner's coat of arms and the Lion of St Mark.

Byzantine horseshoe-shaped arches

Cushion capitals have only simple motifs.

Palazzo Loredan (see p64) *has an elegant ground floor arcade and first floor gallery typical of a 13th-century Byzantine palace.*

Gothic (13th to mid-15th Centuries)

Elaborate Gothic *palazzi* are more numerous than any other style in Venice. Most famous of all is the Doge's Palace *(see pp82–3)*, with elegant arches in Istrian stone and fine tracery which give the façade a delicate, lace-like appearance. This style, emulated throughout the city, can be identified through its use of pointed arches and carved window heads.

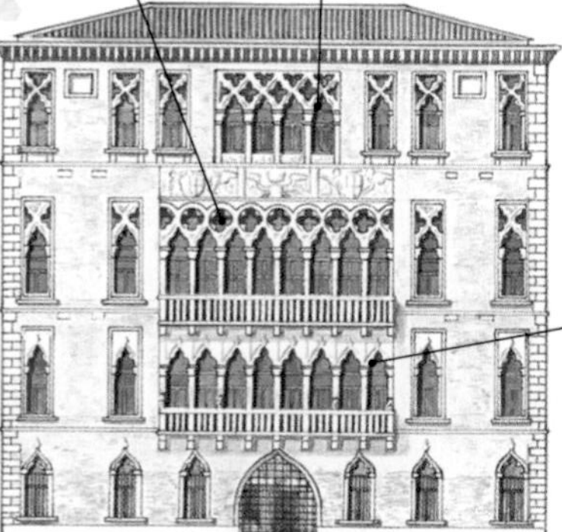
The interlacing ribs of pointed ogee arches create a delicate tracery.

Trefoil "three leaved" window heads are typically Gothic.

Gothic capitals are adorned with foliage, animals and faces.

Palazzo Foscari (see p66) *is a fine example of the 15th-century Venetian Gothic style, with its finely carved white Istrian stone façade and pointed arches.*

Quatrefoil patterns on elegant gallery windows

Gothic capitals (Doge's Palace)

Renaissance (15th and 16th Centuries)

Houses of the Renaissance period were often built in sandstone rather than traditional Venetian brick. The new style was based on Classical architecture, with emphasis on harmonious proportions and symmetry. The new decorative language, borrowing motifs from ancient Rome and Greece, typically incorporated fluted columns, Corinthian capitals and semi-circular arches.

Bold projecting roof cornices are a feature of Renaissance architecture.

Theatrical masks serve as keystones to window arches.

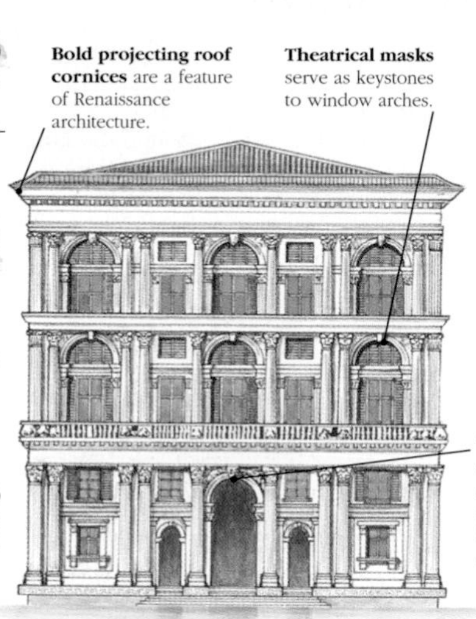

Palazzo Grimani (see p64) *has lavish stone carving which none but the wealthy could afford; massive foundations were constructed to bear the incredible weight.*

Corinthian pilasters on the portal to San Giovanni Evangelista

The Venetian door, a very popular Renaissance motif, has a rounded central arch flanked by narrower side openings. This combination was also used for windows.

Baroque (17th Century)

Venetian Baroque has its roots in the Renaissance Classical style but is far more exuberant. Revelling in bold ornamentation that leaves no surface uncarved, garlands, swags, cherubs, grotesque masks and rosettes animate the main façades of buildings such as the 17th-century Ca' Pesaro.

Semi-circular window head of Palazzo Balbi with two lights and spandrel decorated with a circle.

Cherubs and plumed heads are carved into Baroque stone window heads.

Recessed windows and column clusters create an interesting play of light and shadow.

Massive blocks with deep ridges give solidity to the lower walls.

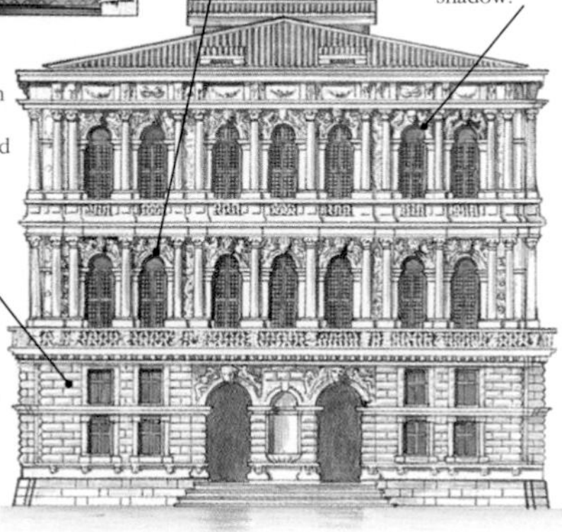

Ca' Pesaro (see p62) *is an example of Baroque experimentation, with its flat façade broken into a three-dimensional stone pattern of deep recesses and strong projections.*

Baroque cartouche

The Venetian House

The layout of a typical *palazzo* (often called Ca', short for *casa*, or house) has changed little over the centuries, despite the very different styles of external decoration.

Attic rooms were reserved for servants.

Courtyards took the place of gardens.

The upper floor housed the family.

The *piano nobile* (grand floor), often lavishly decorated, was used to entertain visitors.

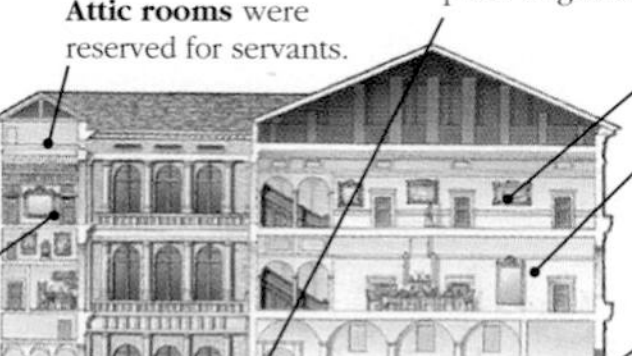

Offices, used for storing business records, evolved into libraries.

The ground floor storerooms and offices were used for the transaction of business.

The Villas of Palladio

Andrea Palladio

When it became fashionable in the 16th century for wealthy Venetians to acquire rural estates on the mainland, many turned to the prolific architect, Andrea Palladio (1508–80) for the design of their villas. Inspired by ancient Roman prototypes, described by authors such as Vitruvius and Virgil, Palladio provided his clients with elegant buildings in which the pursuit of pleasure could be combined with the functions of a working farm. Palladio's designs were widely imitated and continue to inspire architects to this day.

The façade *is symmetrical; dovecotes and stables in the wings balance the central block.*

The Room of the Little Dog *is ornate and lavishly decorated with frescoes by Veronese. Look closely to see the detail of a spaniel in one of the panels.*

The Nymphaeum *combines utility with art; the same spring that feeds the statue-lined pool also supplies water to the villa.*

Key

- Crociera
- Bacchus Room
- Room of the Tribunal of Love
- Hall of Olympus
- Room of the Little Dog
- Room of the Oil Lamp
- Nymphaeum
- Non-exhibition space

The Villa Barbaro

Palladio and Veronese worked closely to create this splendid villa (commissioned in 1555, *see p167*). Lively frescoes of false balconies, doors, windows and rural views create the illusion of greater space, perfectly complementing Palladio's light, airy rooms.

Development of the Villa

Palladio experimented with many different designs which he published in his influential *Quattro Libri (Four Books)* in 1570, illustrating the astonishing fertility of his mind and his ability to create endless variations on the Classical Roman style.

The portico statues reflect Palladio's study of ancient Roman buildings.

The pedimented pavilion is all that survives of Palladio's ambitious design; the main residence was never built.

Stables and storerooms

Villa Thiene (1546), now the town hall, Quinto Vicentino

The Hall of Olympus *shows Giustiniana, mistress of the house and wife of Venetian ambassador Marcantonio Barbaro, with her youngest son, wetnurse and family pets.*

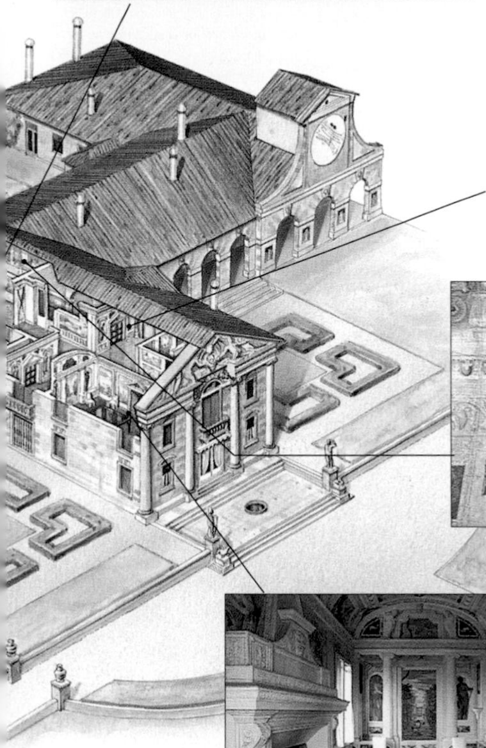

In the Crociera*, the cross-shaped central hall, servants peer round false doors, while imaginary landscapes blur the boundary between the house interior and the garden.*

The Room of the Oil Lamp *symbolizes virtuous behaviour; here Strength, with the club, leans on Truth, with the mirror.*

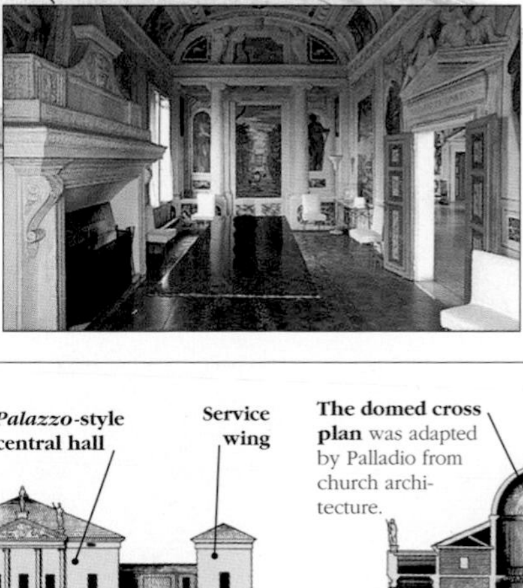

The Bacchus Room*, with its winemaking scenes and chimneypiece carved with the figure of Abundance, reflects the bucolic ideal of the villa as a place of good living and plenty.*

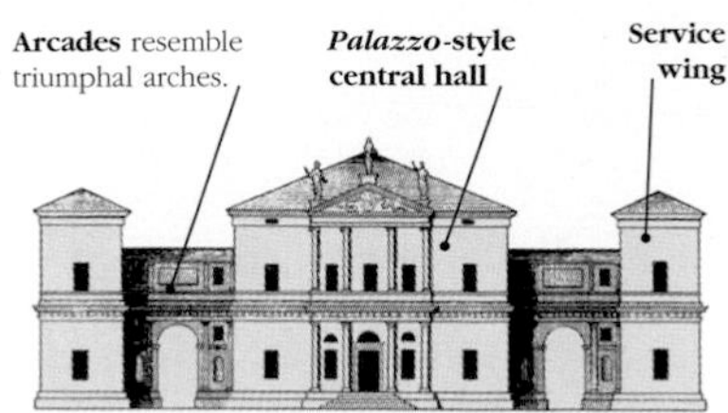
Arcades resemble triumphal arches.
***Palazzo*-style central hall**
Service wing

Villa Pisani (1555), Montagnana ***(see p184)***

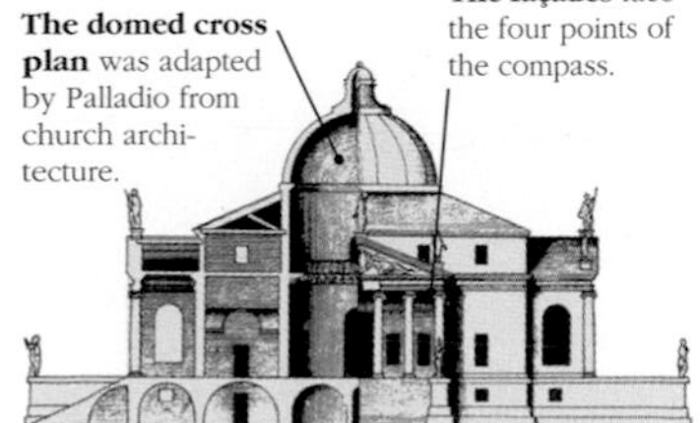
The domed cross plan was adapted by Palladio from church architecture.
The façades face the four points of the compass.

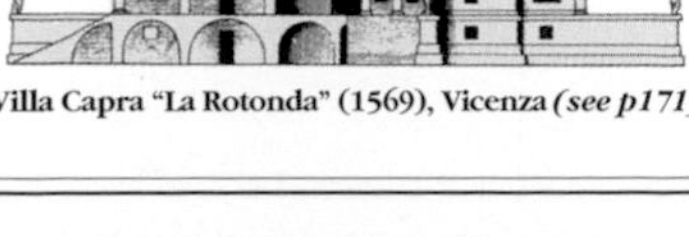

Villa Capra "La Rotonda" (1569), Vicenza ***(see p171)***

Styles in Venetian Art

Venetian art grew out of the Byzantine tradition of iconographic art, designed to inspire religious awe. Because of the trade links between Venice and Constantinople, capital of Byzantium, the Eastern influence lasted longer here than elsewhere in Italy. Andrea Mantegna introduced the Renaissance style to the Veneto in the 1460s, and his brother-in-law Giovanni Bellini became Venice's leading painter. In the early 16th century Venetian artists began to develop their own style, in which soft shading and dramatic use of light distinguishes the works of Venetian masters Titian, Giorgione, Tintoretto and Veronese. The development of this characteristic Venetian style, which the prolific but lesser known artists of the Baroque and Rococo periods continued, can be seen in the chronological arrangement of the Accademia *(see p130–33).*

Detail from Veneziano's *Coronation of the Virgin*

The Last Judgment *(12th century) from Torcello: in the damp climate, mosaics, not frescoes, were used to decorate Venetian churches.*

Byzantine Gothic

Paolo Veneziano is credited with the move from grand-scale mosaics to more intimate altarpieces. His painting mixes idealized figures with the hair-styles, costumes and textiles familiar to 14th-century Venetians. The typically lavish use of jewel colours and gold, symbol of purity, can also be seen in the work of Veneziano's pupil (and namesake) Lorenzo, and in the gilded warrior angels of Guariento *(see p179).*

Veneziano's entire dazzling polyptych *(1325) of which this is the centrepiece, is in the Accademia* (see p132).

Paolo Veneziano's *Coronation of the Virgin*

The Madonna's gentle face *reinforces the courtly refinement of Veneziano's work.*

The composition and colours reflect the style of the early Byzantine icons which influenced the artist.

Arabesque patterns on the tunics reflect Moorish influence.

Musicians like these played at grand ceremonies in San Marco.

Timeline of Venetian Artists

1356–72 (active)	Lorenzo Veneziano
1338–c.1368	Guariento
1430–1516	Giovanni Bellini
1431–1506	Andrea Mantegna
1415–84	Antonio Vivarini
1483–1539	Giovanni Pordenone
1450–1526	Vittore Carpaccio
1480–1528	Palma il Vecchio
1480–1556	Lorenzo Lotto
1395–1455	Antonio Pisanello
1400–71	Jacopo Bellini
1321–62 (active)	Paolo Veneziano
1429–1507	Gentile Bellini
1432–99	Bartolomeo Vivarini
1441–1507	Alvise Vivarini
1467–1510	"Il Morto da Feltre"
1477–1510	Giorgione
1487–1576	Titian

1300 | 1350 | 1400 | 1450

Byzantine Gothic **Early Renaissance**

EARLY RENAISSANCE

Renaissance artists were fascinated by Classical sculpture and developed new techniques of perspective and shading to give their figures a three-dimensional look. Using egg-based tempera gave crisp lines and bold blocks of colour, but with little tonal gradation. The Bellini family dominated art in Renaissance Venice, and Giovanni, who studied anatomy for greater accuracy in his work, portrays the feelings of his subjects through their facial expressions.

In Bellini's 1488 Frari altarpiece*, the Madonna is flanked by Saints Peter, Nicholas, Benedict and Mark* (see p102).

Illusionistic details *fool the eye: the real moulding copies the painted one.*

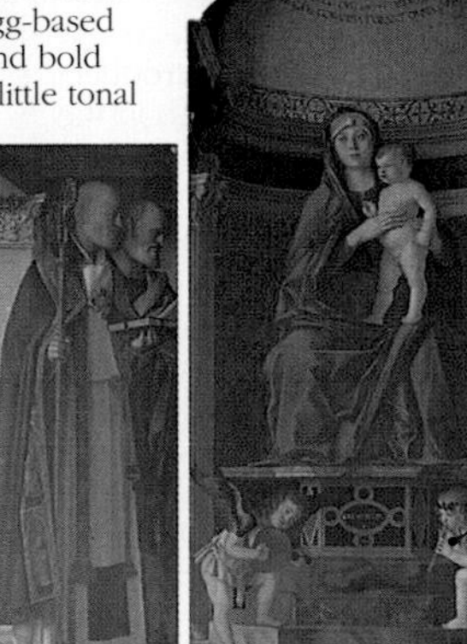

St Benedict carries the Benedictine book of monastic rule.

Musical cherubs playing at the feet of the Virgin are a Bellini trademark; music was a symbol of order and harmony.

Giovanni Bellini's *Madonna and Child with Saints*

HIGH RENAISSANCE

Oil-based paints, developed in the late 15th century, liberated artists. This new medium enabled them to create more fluid effects, an advantage Titian exploited fully. The increasingly expressive use of light by Titian and contemporaries resulted in a distinctive Venetian style, leading to Tintoretto's masterly combination of light and shade *(see p106–7).*

Titian began this Madonna *in 1519 for the Pesaro family altar in the great Frari church* (see p102), *after his* Assumption *was hung above the high altar.*

Titian's *Madonna di Ca' Pesaro*

The Virgin is placed off centre, contrary to a centuries-old rule, but Titian's theatrical use of light ensures that she remains the focus of attention.

Saint Peter looks down at Venetian nobleman Jacopo Pesaro, who kneels to give thanks to the Virgin.

Members of the Pesaro family*, Titian's patrons, attend the Virgin; Lunardo Pesaro, gazing outwards, was heir to the family fortune.*

1500–71 Paris Bordone

1518–94 Tintoretto

1600–38 Francesco Maffei

1712–93 Francesco Guardi

1707–88 Francesco Zuccarelli

1708–85 Pietro Longhi

1696–1770 Giambattista Tiepolo

1500	1550	1600	1650	1700

1548–1628 Palma il Giovane

1528–88 Paolo Veronese

1517–92 Jacopo Bassano

1581–1644 Bernardo Strozzi

1675–1758 Rosalba Carriera

1676–1729 Marco Ricci

1697–1768 Canaletto

1727–1804 Giandomenico Tiepolo

☐ **High Renaissance** ☐ **Baroque, Rococo & Later Artists**

Gondolas and Gondoliers

Hippocampus (sea horse) ornament

GONDOLIERS ARE PART of the symbolism and mythology of Venice. Local legend has it that they are born with webbed feet to help them walk on water. Their intimate knowledge of the city's waterways is passed down from father to son (this is still very much a male preserve). The gondola, with its slim hull and flat underside, is perfectly adapted to negotiating narrow, shallow canals. Once essential for the transport of goods from the markets to the *palazzi*, gondolas today are largely pleasure craft and a trip on one is an essential part of the Venetian experience *(see p276)*. It gives an entirely different perspective on the city, gliding past grand palatial homes, using a form of transport that dates back over 1,000 years.

Squero San Trovaso (see p129) *is the oldest of Venice's five surviving* squeri *(boatyards). Here, new wood is seasoned, while skilled craftsmen build new gondolas and repair some of the 400 craft in use.*

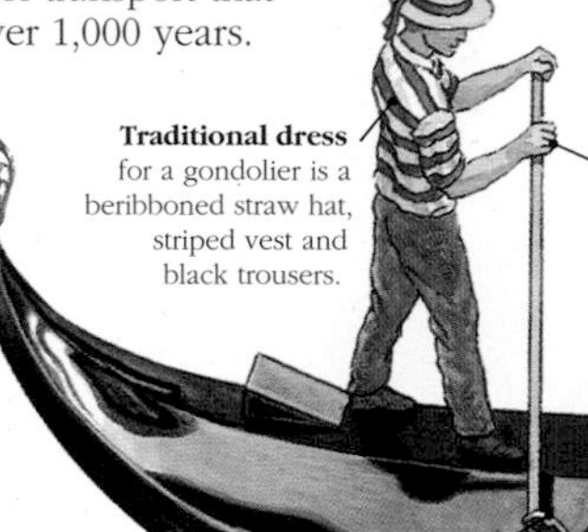

Traditional dress for a gondolier is a beribboned straw hat, striped vest and black trousers.

The gondolier, unusually for an oarsman, stands upright and pushes on the oar to row the boat in the direction he is facing.

Passengers sit on upholstered cushions and low stools.

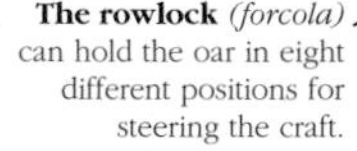

The rowlock *(forcola)* can hold the oar in eight different positions for steering the craft.

The oar has a ribbed blade.

The asymmetrical shape *of the gondola counteracts the force of the oar. Without the leftward curve to the prow, 24 cm (9.5 inches) wider on the left than the right, the boat would go round in circles.*

CONTINUING A TRADITION

Gondolas are hand-crafted from nine woods – beech, cherry, elm, fir, larch, lime, mahogany, oak and walnut – using techniques established in the 1880s. A new gondola takes three months to build and costs £10,000.

GONDOLA DECORATION

Black pitch, or tar, was originally used to make gondolas watertight. In time this sombre colour gave way to bright paintwork and rich carpets, but such displays of wealth were banned in 1562. Today all except ceremonial gondolas are black, ornamented only with their *ferro*, and a golden hippocampus on either side. For special occasions such as weddings, the *felze* (the traditional black canopy) and garlands of flowers appear, while funeral craft, now seldom seen, have gilded angels.

Ceremonial gondolas

Upper Reaches of the Grand Canal *(c.1738) is one of many paintings by Canaletto to capture the everyday life of gondoliers and their craft. Since they were first recorded in 1094, gondolas have been a Venetian institution, inspiring writers, artists and musicians.*

Races and parades *are part of the fun during Venice regattas. Professional gondoliers race in pairs or in teams of six, using boats specially designed for competition. Many amateur gondoliers also participate in the events.*

The *ferro* serves to balance the weight of the rower. Its metal teeth symbolize the six *sestieri* of Venice, beneath a doge's cap.

Seven layers of black lacquer give the gondola its gloss.

The main frame is built of oak.

More than 280 separate pieces of wood are used in constructing a gondola.

Mooring posts *and channel markers feature prominently in the crowded waterways of Venice. The posts may be topped with a family crest, to indicate a private mooring.*

Funeral gondola approaching S Michele ***(see p149)***

Wedding gondola

Venetian Masks and the Carnival

Flamboyant Carnival costume

THE VENETIAN GIFT for intrigue comes into its own during the Carnival, a vibrant, playful festival preceding the abstinence of Lent *(see p32)*. Masks and costume play a key role in this anonymous world; social divisions are dissolved, participants delight in playing practical jokes, and anything goes. The tradition of Carnival in Venice began in the 11th century and reached its peak of popularity and outrageousness in the 18th century. Industrialization left little leisure time and Carnival fell into decline, but was successfully revived in 1979.

Modern Carnival Revellers
Since 1979, each year sees more lavish costumes and impromptu celebrations.

The Plague Doctor
This sinister Carnival garb is based on the medieval doctor's beaked face-protector and black gown, worn as a precaution against plague.

Laws forbidding the wearing of costly lace were suspended at Carnival.

The high spirits of Venetian women scandalized many foreign observers.

TRADITIONAL MASK CELEBRATION

Carnival in the 18th century began with a series of balls in the Piazza San Marco, as in this fresco on the walls of Quadri's famous café in the square *(see p74)*.

Gambling at the Ridotto
Fortunes were squandered every night of Carnival at the state-run casino depicted in Guardi's painting (c.1768).

Street Entertainers
Musicians and comedians attract the crowds in the piazza San Marco.

The satyr-like profile of this dancer hints that he is the devil in disguise.

Columbine
A classic Carnival figure, Columbine wears lace and an apron, but no mask.

Making a Mask

Many masks, and the characters they represent, are deeply rooted in Venetian history. Though instantly recognizable by such features as the beaked nose of the Plague Doctor, each character can be interpreted in a style that is unique to its maker, making each piece a true work of art.

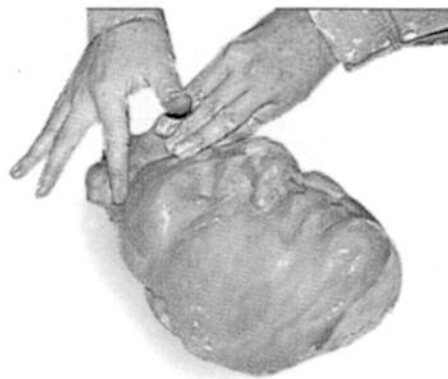

① ***The form of the mask*** *is first modelled out of clay. Then a plaster of Paris mould is made using the fired clay sculpture as a pattern.*

② ***Papier mâché paste,*** *made from a pulpy fibrous mixture of rags and paper dipped in glue, is used to make the mask itself.*

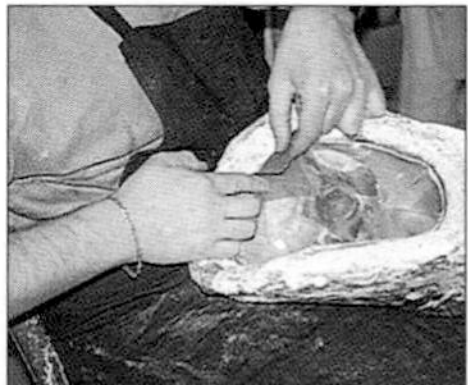

③ ***To shape the mask****, papier mâché paste is pushed into the plaster mould, then put aside to set. It becomes hard yet flexible as it dries..*

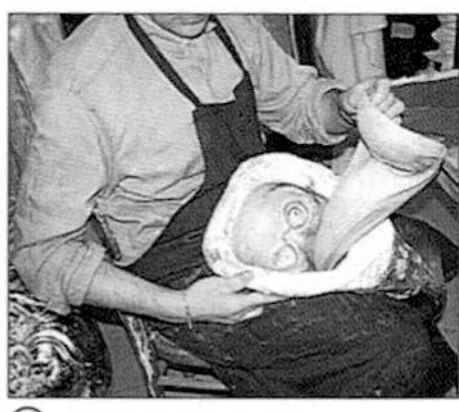

④ ***The size, or glue,*** *used to make the papier mâché gives the mask a smooth, shiny surface, similar to porcelain, when it is extracted.*

⑤ ***An abrasive polish*** *is used to buff the surface of the mask, which is then ready to receive the white base coat.*

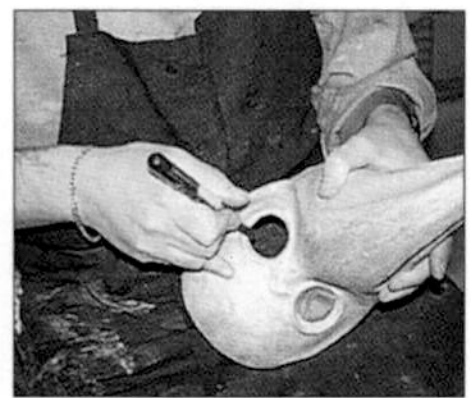

⑥ ***Cutting the eye holes*** *and other features requires the mask maker to have a steady hand.*

⑦ ***The features*** *are painted on the mask and the final touches are added with a few clever brushstrokes.*

⑧ ***The finished mask*** *is ready to wear at the Carnival or to hang on a wall – the perfect Venetian souvenir.*

VENICE AND THE VENETO THROUGH THE YEAR

VENICE IS A CITY that can be enjoyed at all times of the year. Even winter's mists add to the city's romantic appeal, though clear blue skies and balmy weather make spring and autumn the best times to go. This is especially true if you combine a visit to Venice with a tour of the Veneto, where villa gardens and alpine meadows put on a colourful display from the beginning of April. Autumn sees the beech, birch and chestnut trees of the region turn every shade of red and gold. In summer the waters of Lake Garda, fed by melted snow from the Alps, serve to moderate the heat. Winters are mild, allowing some of the crops typical of the southern Mediterranean, like lemons and oranges, to grow.

Festive flag throwers in Feltre

Winter in the delta of the River Po

WINTER

ONCE A QUIET time of year, winter now brings an increasing number of visitors to the city of Venice, especially over Christmas, New Year and Carnival. Many a day that begins wet and overcast ends in a blaze of colour – the kind of sunset reflected off rain-washed buildings that Canaletto liked to paint. In the resorts of the Venetian Dolomites, popular for winter sports, the conditions are perfect for skiing from early December throughout the winter months.

DECEMBER

Nativity. Churches all over Venice and the Veneto mount elaborate Nativity scenes in the days leading up to Christmas. Attending mass is a moving experience at this time, even for non-Christians.

Canto della Stella. In Desenzano, on Lake Garda *(see p204)*, Christmas is marked by open-air processions called *Canto della Stella*, literally "singing to the stars".

JANUARY

Epiphany *(6 Jan)*. Children of the Veneto get another stocking full of presents at Epiphany, supposedly brought by the old witch Befania (also known as Befana, Refana or Berolon). She forgot about Christmas, according to the story, because she was too busy cleaning her house. Good children traditionally get sweets, but naughty children get cinders from her hearth. Images of the witch appear in cake-shop windows, along with evil-looking biscuits made to resemble charcoal.

FEBRUARY

Carnival *(ten days up to Shrove Tuesday)*. The pre-Lent festival of Carnevale *(see p30)*, which means "farewell to meat", is celebrated throughout the Veneto. First held in Venice in the 11th century, it consisted of two months of revelry every year. Carnival fell into decline during the 18th century, but was revived in 1979 with such success that the causeway has to be closed at times to prevent overcrowding in the city.

Today the ten-day festival is mainly an excuse for donning a mask and costume and parading around the city. Various events are organized for which the Tourist Board will have details, but anyone can buy a mask and participate while watching the gorgeous costumes on show in the Piazza San Marco *(see pp74–5)*.

Bacanal del Gnoco *(last Fri of Carnival)*. Traditional masked procession in Verona, with groups from foreign countries and allegorical floats from the Verona area. Masked balls are held in the town's squares.

Masked revellers at the Carnival

Sunshine Chart
Few days are entirely without sunshine in Venice and the Veneto. The amount of sunshine progressively builds up to mid-summer, when it is dangerous to venture out without adequate skin protection.

Spring wisteria in Verona's Giardini Giusti *(see p203)*

SPRING

THIS IS THE SEASON when many fine gardens all over the Veneto and round Lake Garda come into their own. As the snow melts, there is time to catch the brief glory of the alpine meadows and the region's nature reserves, renowned for rare orchids and gentians. Verona holds its annual cherry market and many other towns celebrate the arrival of early crops.

MARCH

La Vecia *(mid-Lent).* Gardone and Gargnano, villages on Lake Garda *(see p204)*, play host to festivals of great antiquity, when the effigy of an old woman is burnt on a bonfire. The so-called Hag's Trials are an echo of the darker side of medieval life.
Su e zo per i ponti *(second Sun in Mar).* A marathon-style race in Venice. Participants run or walk through the city's streets *su e zo per i ponti* (up and down the bridges).

APRIL

Festa di San Marco *(25 Apr).* The feast of St Mark, patron saint of Venice, is marked by a gondola race across St Mark's Basin between Sant' Elena *(see p121)* and Punta della Dogana *(see p135).* On this occasion, it is traditional for Venetian men to give their wives or lovers a red rose.

MAY

Festa della Sparesea *(1 May).* Festival and regatta for the new season's asparagus held on Cavallino, in the lagoon, where the crop is grown.

Spring produce in the Rialto's vegetable market

La Sensa *(Sun after Ascension Day).* The ceremony of Venice's Marriage with the Sea draws huge crowds, as it has every year since Doge Pietro Orseolo established the custom in AD 1000. Once the ceremony was marked with all the pomp that the doge and his courtiers could muster. Today the words: "We wed thee, O Sea, in token of true and lasting dominion" are spoken by a local dignitary who then casts a laurel crown and ring into the sea.

Celebrating La Sensa, Venice's annual Marriage with the Sea

Vogalonga *(Sun following La Sensa).* Hundreds of boats take part in the Vogalonga (the "Long Row") from the Piazza San Marco to Burano *(see p150)* and back – a distance of 32 km (20 miles).
Festa Medioevale del vino Soave Bianco Soave *(16 May).* Sumptuous medieval-style celebration of the investiture of the Castillian of Suavia. There is a procession with a historical theme, music in the town square, theatrical performances and displays of various sports.
Valpollicellore *(9 May).* Festival of local wine, with exhibitions, in Cellore d'Illasi.

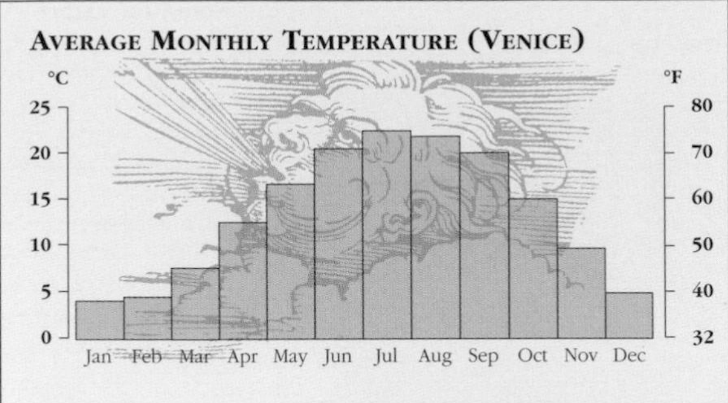

Temperature Chart
Summers in Venice can be unbearably humid, while winters can bring the occasional snowfall. Temperatures in the Dolomites are considerably lower, with snow and freezing conditions from November to March.

SUMMER

SUMMER BRINGS the crowds to Venice. Queues for museums and popular sites are long, and hotels are frequently fully booked. Avoid visiting the city during the school holidays (mid-Jul–end Aug). Verona, too, will be full of opera lovers attending the famous festival, but elsewhere in the Veneto it is possible to escape the crowds and enjoy the spectacular countryside.

JUNE

Sagra di Sant'Antonio *(13 Jun).* The Feast of St Anthony has been celebrated in Padua for centuries. The day is marked by a lively fair in Prato della Valle *(see p183).*
Biennale *(Jun–Oct).* The world's biggest contemporary art exhibition takes place in Venice in odd-numbered years *(see p256).*
Festa di Santi Pietro e Paolo *(end Jun).* The feast day of Saints Peter and Paul is celebrated in many towns with fairs and musical festivals.
Regata dei 500 x 2 *(third Sun in Jun).* Adriatic Classic sailing regatta from Caorle *(see p175).*

Exhibit by Japanese artist Yayoi Kusama at the Biennale

Boats for hire at Sirmione on Lake Garda

JULY

Opera Festival *(Jul–Sep).* Verona's renowned opera festival overlaps with the equally famous **Shakespeare Festival**, providing culture lovers with a feast of music, drama, opera and dance in the stimulating setting of the Roman Arena and the city's churches *(see pp256–7).*
Festa del Redentore *(third Sun in Jul).* The city of Venice commemorates its deliverance from the plague of 1576. An impressive bridge of boats stretches across the Giudecca Canal so that people can walk to the Redentore church to attend mass. On the Saturday night, crowds line the Zattere or row their boats into the lagoon to watch a spectacular firework display *(see p154).*
Sardellata al Pal del Vo *(late Jul).* Moonlit sardine fishing displays on Lake Garda at Pal del Vo. Boats are illuminated and decorated, and the catch is cooked and distributed to guests and participants.

AUGUST

Village Festivals. The official holiday month is marked by local festivals throughout the Veneto, giving visitors the chance to sample food and wines and see local costume and dance. Around Lake Garda these are often accompanied by firework displays and races in boats like large gondolas.
Palio di Feltre *(first weekend in Aug).* Medieval games, horse-racing and feasts commemorate Feltre's inclusion in the Venetian empire *(see p219).*
Festa dell'Assunta *(8–16 Aug).* Spectacular nine-day celebration in Vittorio Veneto *(see p219).* The colourful festivities feature dance, poetry, cabaret and music competitions.

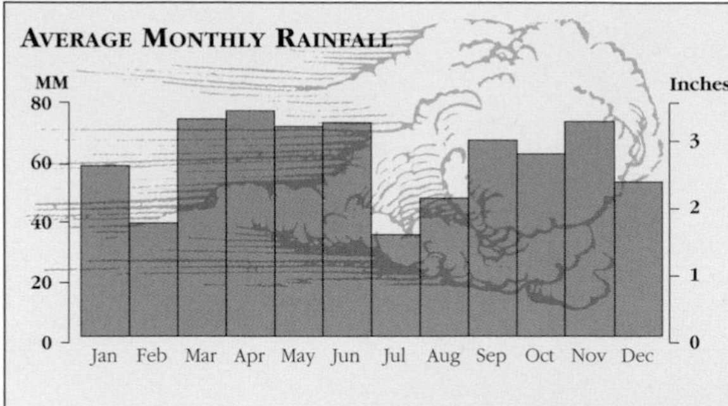

Rainfall Chart
The mountains and sea combine to give Venice and the Veneto higher rainfall than is normal in the rest of Italy, with the possibility of rain on just about any day of the year. The driest months are February and July.

AUTUMN

EXPECT TO SEE a profusion of market stalls selling a huge range of wild fungi as soon as the climatic conditions are right for them to grow. Local people go on expeditions to harvest them, and mushroom dishes will also feature high on the restaurant menus along with game. Another feature of autumn is the grape harvest, a busy time of year in the wine-producing regions of Soave, Bardolino and Valpolicella *(see pp208–9).*

Grapes ripening in the Bardolino area

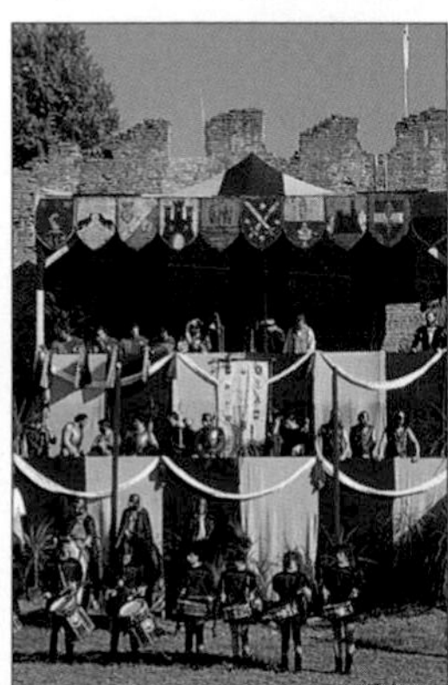

Medieval costume at Montagnana's Palio dei Dieci Comuni

SEPTEMBER

Venice Film Festival *(early Sep).* The International Film Festival attracts an array of filmstars and paparazzi to the Lido *(see p157).*
Regata Storica *(first Sun in Sep).* Gondoliers and other boatsmen compete in a regatta which starts with an historic pageant down the Grand Canal.
Partita a Scacchi *(second weekend in Sep, in even-numbered years).* Maròstica's chequerboard main square hosts a human chess game in medieval costume *(see p166).*
Palio dei Dieci Comuni *(first Sun in Sep).* The liberation of the town of Montagnana is celebrated with a pageant and horse race *(see p184).*

OCTOBER

Bardolino Grape Festival *(first weekend in Oct).* A festival that celebrates the completion of the harvest.
Festa del Mosto *(first weekend in Oct).* The Feast of the Must on Sant'Erasmo, the market-garden island in the lagoon *(see p149).*
Venice Marathon *(mid-Oct).* This run starts on the Brenta Riviera and finishes in Venice.

NOVEMBER

Festa della Salute *(21 Nov).* Deliverance from the plague is celebrated with the erection of a pontoon bridge across the Grand Canal to La Salute *(see p135).* Venetians light candles in the church to give thanks for a year's good health.

PUBLIC HOLIDAYS

New Year (1 Jan)
Epiphany (6 Jan)
Easter Monday (variable)
Liberation Day (25 Apr)
Labour Day (1 May)
Assumption (15 Aug)
All Saints (1 Nov)
Immaculate Conception (8 Dec)
Christmas Day (25 Dec)
Santo Stefano (26 Dec)

Rowers practising for the Regata Storica

THE HISTORY OF VENICE AND THE VENETO

THE WINGED LION of St Mark is a familiar sight to anyone travelling in the Veneto. Mounted on top of tall columns in the central square of Vicenza, Verona, Chioggia and elsewhere, it is a sign that these cities were once part of the proud Venetian empire. The fact that the lion was never torn down as a hated symbol of oppression is a credit to the benign nature of Venetian authority.

Doge Giovanni Mocenigo (1478–85)

In the 6th century AD, Venice had been no more than a collection of small villages in a swampy lagoon. By the 13th century she ruled Byzantium and, in 1508, the pope, the kings of France and Spain and the Holy Roman Emperor felt compelled to join forces to stop the advances of this powerful empire. As the League of Cambrai, their combined armies sacked the cities of the Veneto, including those such as Vicenza which had initially sided with the League. Venetian territorial expansion was halted, but she continued to dominate the Eastern Mediterranean for another 200 years.

The Venetian system of government came as close to democracy as anyone was to devise until the 19th century, and it stood the city and its empire in good stead until the bumptious figure of Napoleon Bonaparte dared to intrude in 1797. But by then Venice had become a byword for decadence and decline, the essential mercantile instinct that had created and sustained the Serene Republic for so long having been extinguished. As though exhausted by 1,376 years of independent existence, the ruling doge and his Grand Council simply resigned, but their legacy lives on, to fascinate visitors with its extraordinary beauty and remarkable history.

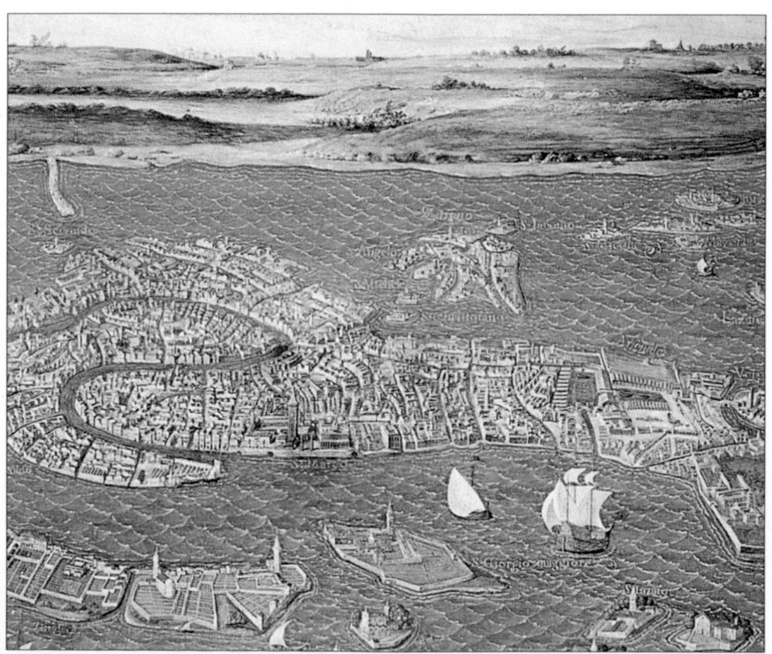

A map dated 1550, showing how little Venice has changed in nearly 500 years

◁ **Tintoretto's *Triumph of Doge Nicolò da Ponte* (1580–84), Sala del Maggior Consiglio, Doge's Palace**

Roman Veneto

THE VENETO TAKES ITS NAME from the Veneti, the pre-Roman inhabitants of the region, whose territory fell to the superior military might of the Romans in the 3rd century BC. Verona was then built as a base for the thrusting and ambitious Roman army which swept northwards over the Alps to conquer much of modern France and Germany. While the Roman empire remained intact the Veneto prospered, but the region bore the brunt of fierce and destructive barbarian attacks that began in the 4th century AD. Riddled by in-fighting and the split between Rome and Constantinople, the imperial administration began to crumble.

A Roman bust in Vicenza

Horsemen in Roman Army
Goths, Huns and Vandals served as mercenaries in the Roman cavalry but later turned to plunder.

Horse-Drawn Carriage
Finds from the region show the technological skills and luxurious lifestyles of the inhabitants.

The Forum (market square)

The Arena was completed in AD 30 to entertain the troops stationed in Verona. It could hold 30,000 spectators.

Chariot Racing
A pre-Roman chariot in Adria's museum (see p185) *suggests the Romans adopted the sport from their predecessors.*

VERONA

Securely fortified and moated by the River Adige, Roman Verona was divided into square blocks (*insulae* or "islands"). The Forum has since been filled in by medieval palaces, but several landmarks are still discernible today *(see p192).*

TIMELINE

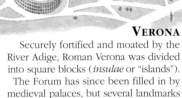

6th century BC Veneto region occupied by the Euganei and the Veneti

87 BC Catullus, Roman love poet, born in Verona

89 BC The citizens of Verona, Padua, Vicenza, Este and Treviso granted full rights of Roman citizenship

600 BC	500	400	300	200	10

3rd century BC Veneto conquered by the Romans. The Veneti and Euganei adopt Roman culture and lose their separate identities

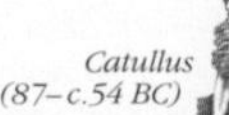

Catullus (87–c.54 BC)

Hunting in the Lagoon
The wild lagoon, future site of Venice, attracted fishermen and huntsmen in pursuit of game and wildfowl. It also became a place of refuge during raids by Huns and Goths.

The theatre, built in the 1st century BC, is still used for open-air performances *(see p256)*.

Two arches of the Ponte Romano *(see p202)* survive intact.

Gladiators
Bloodthirsty citizens flocked to the gladiatorial contests in which prisoners of war, criminals and Christian martyrs were put to the sword.

Where to See Roman Veneto

Verona *(p192)* has the highest concentration of Roman sites in the region; the archaeological museum *(p202)* is full of fine mosaics and sculptures, and Castelvecchio *(p193)* has some very rare early Christian glass and silver. Good museums can also be found at Este *(p184)*, Adria, Treviso *(p174)* and Portogruaro, situated near Concordia *(p175)*.

***This fine mosaic** of a nightingale in Treviso Museum is from Trevisium, the town's Roman predecessor.*

***Verona's Arena** is an awe-inspiring home for the city's opera festival, despite the loss of its outer wall to earthquakes.*

AD 100 The Arena, Verona's amphitheatre, is built. Near Eastern merchants bring Christianity to the region

360 The Roman Empire's northern borders under attack from Slavic and Teutonic tribes

401 Led by Alaric, the Goths invade northern Italy; the Veneto bears the brunt of the attack

Fierce Visigoth

AD 1 | 100 | 200 | 300 | 400

59 BC Livy, Roman historian, born in Padua

313 Constantine the Great grants official status to Christianity

331 Constantinople takes over from Rome as capital of the Roman Empire

395 Roman Empire splits into eastern and western halves

410 Alaric succeeds in sacking Rome itself, but dies the same year

The Birth of Venice

9th-century Venetian coin

FLEEING THE GOTHS, who were systematically looting and burning their way southwards to Rome, the people of the Veneto sought refuge among the wild and uninhabited islands of their marshy coast. There they formed villages, and from the ashes of the Roman past rose the city of Venice (founded, as tradition has it, in AD 421). Exploiting its easily defended maritime position, important trade links with Byzantium were created. Venice proclaimed its brash self-confidence by brazenly stealing the relics of St Mark the Evangelist from Alexandria, in Egypt.

Early Venetian Settlements
The Rialto Bridge (from Rivo Alto, or "high bank") marks the spot of one of many early settlements.

San Marco as it was before 14th-century rebuilding.

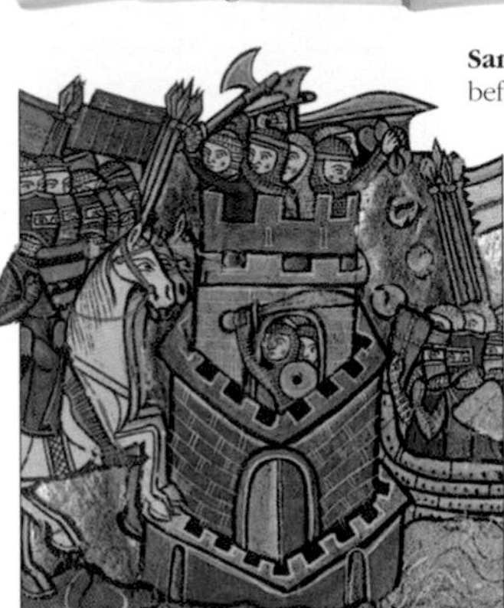
The First Crusade *(1095–9)*
Venice cunningly used the Crusades to her advantage, gaining valuable trading rights in captured cities such as Antioch and Tripoli.

The Bishop of Altino
The cathedral at Torcello was founded in AD 639, when Altino's bishop led a mass exodus to the lagoon island, fleeing Lombardic invaders.

THE ARRIVAL OF THE RELICS
This 13th-century mosaic from the façade of San Marco depicts the body of St Mark being carried into the newly built basilica for reburial in AD 832. By securing the relics of such an important saint, Venice signalled its ambition to be considered one of the foremost cities in Christendom, on a par with Rome.

TIMELINE

421 Venice founded, traditionally – and conveniently – on St Mark's Day, 25 April

452 Attila the Hun invades Italy and plunders the Veneto

570 The Lombards' first invasion of northern Italy; beginning of mass migration from the cities of the Veneto to lagoon islands

726 First documented doge, Orso Ipato

Charlemagne (742–814)

400 | 500 | 600 | 700 | 8

So-called "Attila's throne" in Torcello

552 Totila the Goth invades Italy and destroys many towns in the Veneto

639 Torcello cathedral founded

697 According to legend, Paoluccio Anafesta is elected first doge

774 Charlemagne invited to drive Lombards from Italy

800 Charlemagne is crowned first Holy Roman Emperor by Pope Leo III

Diplomacy
Strategically placed between the powers of Rome and Byzantium, Venice was continually exerting her powers of diplomacy. Here, Doge Ziani receives Holy Roman Emperor Frederick I, whom he reconciled with Pope Alexander III in 1177.

Looting the remains of St Mark from Alexandria was seen as an act of anti-Moslem piety.

The doge and his entourage are wearing Byzantine-style caps and robes.

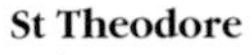

St Theodore
The Byzantine emperor nominated Theodore as the patron saint of Venice. Venice chose St Mark instead, an act of defiance against Byzantine rule.

Where to See Early Venice

The cathedral at Torcello *(pp152–3)* is the oldest surviving building in Venice, and the Basilica San Marco *(pp78–83)* has many period treasures. Early Venetian coins are in the Correr Museum *(p77)*. The original statue of St Theodore is in the Doge's Palace courtyard.

***Torcello cathedral's** jewel-like mosaics (11th century) are masterpieces of Byzantine art, probably the work of craftsmen from Constantinople.*

***The Pala d'Oro**, St Mark's 10th-century altarpiece, shows merchants bringing St Mark's plundered relics to Venice.*

814 First Venetian coins minted; work begins on first Doge's Palace

832 First Basilica San Marco completed

1171 Six districts *(sestieri)* of Venice established

1095 First Crusade; Venice provides ships and supplies

1120 Verona's San Zeno church begun

1173 First Rialto Bridge built

1177 Emperor Frederick I Barbarossa agrees to peace terms with Pope Alexander III

900 | 1000 | 1100 | 1200

888 King Berengar I of Italy chooses Verona as his seat

828 Venetian merchants steal body of St Mark from Alexandria

1128 First street lighting in Venice

1000 Doge Pietro Orseolo rids the Adriatic of pirates, commemorated by the first Marriage of Venice to the Sea ceremony

1202 Venice diverts the Fourth Crusade to its own ends, the conquest of Byzantium

The Growth of the Empire

During the Middle Ages, Venice expanded in power and influence throughout the eastern Mediterranean, culminating in the conquest of Byzantium in 1204. At home, in contrast to the fractional strife of most of the area, Venice enjoyed a uniquely ordered administration headed by the doge, an elected leader whose powers were carefully defined by the Venetian constitution. Real power lay with the Council of Ten and the 2,000 or so members of the Grand Council, from whose number the doge and his advisers were elected.

The doge's hat, the *zogia*

Bocca di Leone
Such letterboxes were used to report crimes anonymously and were often abused (p89).

Doge Enrico Dandolo boldly led the attack on Constantinople, despite being over 90 and completely blind.

Cangrande I
Founder of the Veronese Scaligeri dynasty (see p207)*, Cangrande I ("Big Dog") typified the totalitarian rule of most Italian cities.*

Marco Polo in China
Renowned Venetian merchant, Marco Polo (see p143) *spent over 20 years at the court of Kublai Khan.*

Siege of Constantinople

Facing financial difficulties, the leaders of the Fourth Crusade agreed to attack the capital of Byzantium, as payment for warships supplied by Venice. The city fell in 1204, leaving Venice ruler of Byzantium.

Timeline

1200 | 1250 | 1300 | 1350

1204 Conquest of Constantinople; Venice's plunder includes four bronze horses

1222 University of Padua founded

1260 Scaligeri family rules Verona

1271–95 Marco Polo's journey to China

1284 Gold ducats first minted in Venice

1301 Dante, exiled from his native Florence, is welcomed to Verona by the Scaligeri rulers

1304–13 Giotto paints the Scrovegni Chapel frescoes *(pp180–81)* in Padua

1309 Present Doge's Palace begun

1310 The Venetian Constitution is passed; Council of Ten formed

1325 The names of Venice's ruling families are fixed and inscribed in the Golden Book

1348–9 Black Death plague kills half Venice's population

The Four Horses of San Marco

Decapitation
Doge Marin Falier was beheaded in 1355 for plotting to become absolute ruler of Venice. His execution was a warning to future doges.

Imperial treasures and ancient buildings were lost when the 900-year-old city was looted and burned.

Electing the Doge
This pointer was used for counting votes during dogal elections, using a convoluted system designed to prevent candidates bribing their way to power.

Troops scaled the fortifications from galleys moored against the city walls.

Queen of Cyprus
Venice shamelessly gained Cyprus in 1489 by arranging for Caterina Cornaro, from one of Venice's noblest families, to marry the island's king, then poisoning him.

WHERE TO SEE IMPERIAL VENICE

The Doge's Palace combines ceremonial splendour and the grimmer business of imprisonment and torture *(pp84–9)*. Aspects of the constitution are on display in the Correr Museum *(p77)*. A *bocca di leone* survives on the Zattere *(p129)*.

***Many doges** are commemorated by Renaissance-style monuments in the church of Santi Giovanni e Paolo* (pp116–17).

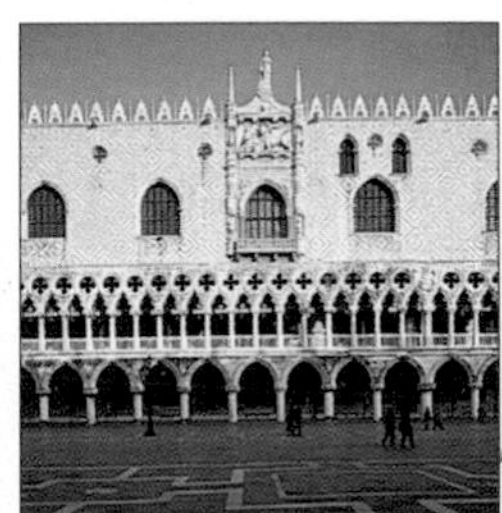

***Meetings of the Grand Council**, dominated by the merchant class, were held in the Sala del Maggior Consiglio* (p87) *in the Doge's Palace.*

Battle of Chioggia

1380 Battle of Chioggia: Venice defeats Genoa to win undisputed maritime supremacy in the Adriatic and Mediterranean

1400

1430 Giovanni Bellini born, greatest of the artistic family

1450

1453 Constantinople falls to the Turks; Venice's empire reaches its zenith

1489 Cyprus ceded to Venice by Queen Caterina Cornaro

1500

1508 Andrea Palladio, architect, born in Padua

1518 Titian's *Assumption* hung in Frari *(p102)*

Titian (1487–1576)

The Queen of the Adriatic

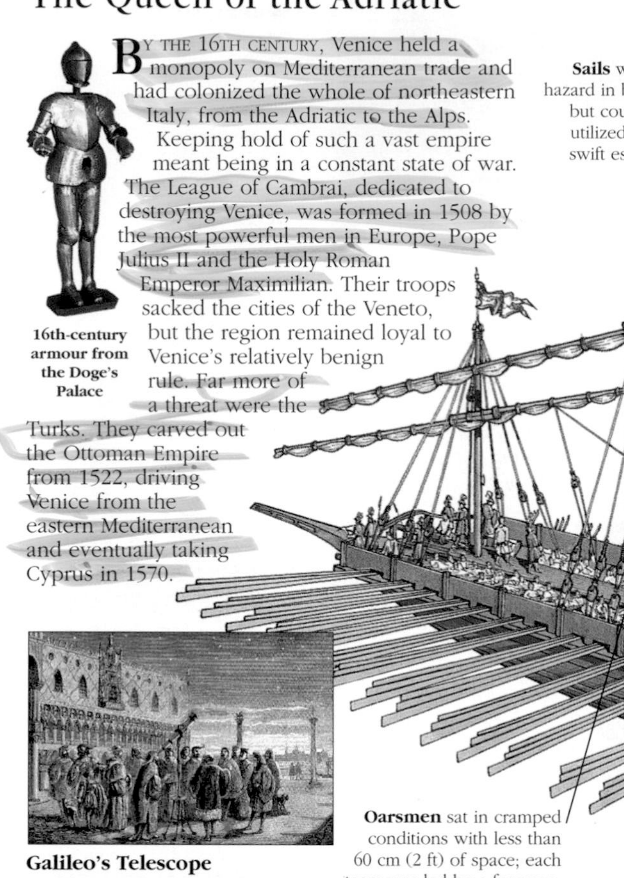
Sails were a hazard in battle, but could be utilized for a swift escape.
Oarsmen sat in cramped conditions with less than 60 cm (2 ft) of space; each team was led by a foreman.

By the 16th century, Venice held a monopoly on Mediterranean trade and had colonized the whole of northeastern Italy, from the Adriatic to the Alps. Keeping hold of such a vast empire meant being in a constant state of war. The League of Cambrai, dedicated to destroying Venice, was formed in 1508 by the most powerful men in Europe, Pope Julius II and the Holy Roman Emperor Maximilian. Their troops sacked the cities of the Veneto, but the region remained loyal to Venice's relatively benign rule. Far more of a threat were the Turks. They carved out the Ottoman Empire from 1522, driving Venice from the eastern Mediterranean and eventually taking Cyprus in 1570.

16th-century armour from the Doge's Palace

Galileo's Telescope
Galileo, professor at Padua University from 1592 to 1610, demonstrated his telescope to Doge Leonardo Donà in 1609.

Battle of Lepanto
Venice led the combined forces of the Christian world in this bloody victory over the Turks, fought in 1571.

Timeline

- **1501** Doge Leonardo Loredan, great diplomat, begins 20-year rule
- **1514** Fire destroys the original timber Rialto Bridge
- **1516** Jews confined to the Venetian Ghetto. End of League of Cambrai wars
- **1518** Tintoretto born
- **1528** Paolo Veronese born
- **1529** Death of Luigi da Porto of Vicenza, author of the story of Romeo and Juliet
- **1570** Cyprus lost to the Turks
- **1571** Battle of Lepanto: decisive victory for the western fleet, led by Venice, over the Turks
- **1577** Palladio designs the Redentore church *(p154)* to mark the end of the plague that took 51,000 lives
- **1585** First performance at Vicenza's Teatro Olimpico *(p172)*
- **1592** Galileo appointed professor of mathematics at Padua University
- **1595** Shakespeare's *Romeo and Juliet*

1500 | 1550 | 1600

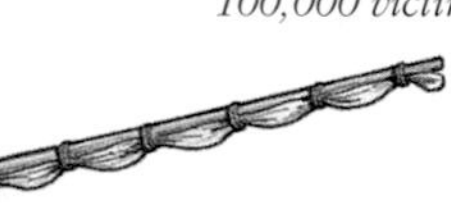

Celebrating the End of the Plague
More deadly than any opposing army, plague hit Venice in 1575 and again in 1630, carrying off Titian among its 100,000 victims.

Where to See Maritime Venice

The triumph of Venice over the sea is celebrated in the Museo Storico Navale *(p118).* For a glimpse of the extensive and disused Arsenale shipyard in Castello, take a trip on *vaporetto* route No. 41, 42, 51 or 52 *(p275).*

***Arsenale lions**, plundered from Piraeus in 1687, guard the forbidding gates of the Arsenale shipyard* (p119).

***Santa Maria della Salute** was built in thanksgiving for deliverance from the 1630 plague* (p135).

The Venice Arsenale
Venice was at the forefront of maritime construction. Her heavily defended shipyards were capable of turning out warships at the rate of one a day.

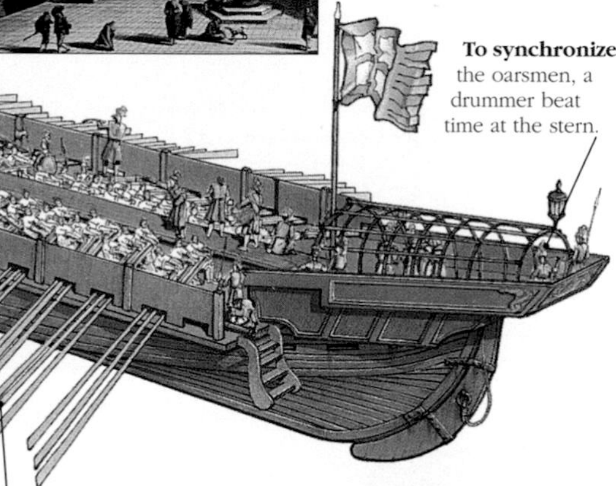

To synchronize the oarsmen, a drummer beat time at the stern.

The trireme was so named because the oars were grouped in threes. Each trireme had up to 150 oars.

Venetian Trireme

Venetian naval supremacy was based on the swift and highly manoeuvrable trireme, used to sink enemy ships by means of its pointed battering ram and its bow-mounted cannon.

onteverdi (1567–1643)

1613 Monteverdi appointed choirmaster at Basilica San Marco

1630 Plague strikes Venice again, reducing the city's population to 102,243, its smallest for 250 years

1650

1669 Venice loses Crete to the Turks

1678 Elena Piscopia receives doctorate from Padua University, the first woman in the world ever to be awarded a degree *(p178)*

Elena Piscopia (1646–84)

1700

1703 Vivaldi joins La Pietà as musical director

1708 In a bitter winter, the lagoon freezes over and Venetians can walk to the mainland

1718 Venetian maritime empire ends with the surrender of Morea to the Turks

Glorious Decadence

Casanova, the Venetian libertine

NO LONGER A MAJOR POWER, 18th-century Venice became a byword for decadence, as aristocratic Venetians frittered away their inherited wealth in lavish parties and gambling. All this crumbled in 1797 when the city was besieged by Napoleon, who demanded the abdication of the doge. Napoleon granted the city to his opponents, the Austrians, whose often authoritarian rule drove many people of the Veneto to join the vanguard of the revolutionary Risorgimento. This movement, led in Venice by Daniele Manin, was dedicated to creating a free and united Italy, a dream not fully realized until 1870, four years after Venice was freed from Austrian rule.

The State-Run Casino
The notorious Ridotto, open to anyone wearing a mask, closed in 1774 as many Venetians had bankrupted themselves.

Gambling fever so gripped the city that gaming tables were set up between the columns in the Piazza.

Caffè Pedrocchi
Several intellectuals who had used this lavishly decorated café (see p178) *in Padua as their base, were executed for leading a revolt against Austrian rule in 1831.*

IMPERIAL RITUAL
Canaletto's *St Mark's Basin on Ascension Day* (c.1733) captures the empty splendour of Venice on the eve of her demise. The doge's gold and scarlet barge has been launched for the annual ceremony of Venice's Marriage to the Sea.

The Horses of St Mark
Among the art treasures looted by Napoleon were the Four Horses of St Mark, symbols of Venetian liberty. The horses were returned in 1815.

TIMELINE

1720 Caffè Florian opens in Venice *(p246)*

1725 Casanova born in Venice

1752 Completion of sea walls protecting the lagoon entrances

1755 Casanova imprisoned in Doge's Palace

1757 Canova, Neo-Classical sculptor, born in Venice

1775 Caffè Quadri *(p246)* opens in Venice

1789 The Dolomites named after Déodat Dolomieu (1750–1801)

1790 Venetian opera house, La Fenice, opens

1797 Napoleon invades the Veneto; Doge Lodovico Manin abdicates; Venetian Republic ends

1798 Napoleon grants Venice and its territories to his Austrian allies in return for Lombardy

1720 | 1770

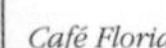

Café Florian

Antonio Vivaldi *(1678–1741) Fashionable Venetians flocked to hear the red-haired priest's latest compositions, performed by the orphan girls of La Pietà. Vivaldi's most famous work,* The Four Seasons *(1725), was a great success throughout Europe.*

The Bucintoro, the doge's ceremonial barge

Sumptuary laws, passed in 1562, decreed that all Venetian gondolas must be black to prevent lavish displays of wealth.

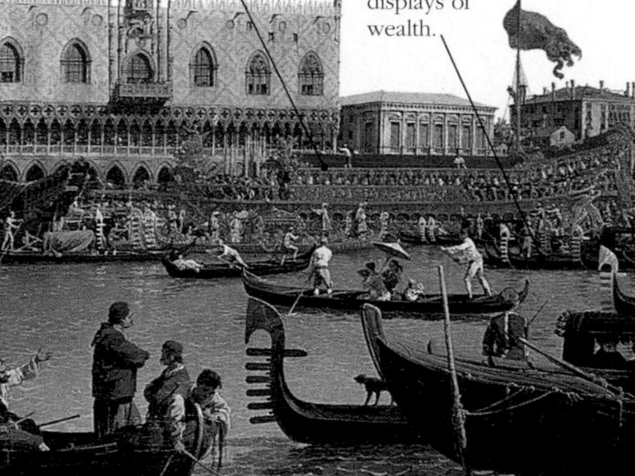

No Longer an Island

Venice lost its isolation in 1846 when a causeway joined the city to the mainland and the Italian rail network.

Where to See 18th-Century Venice

The Museo Storico Navale *(p118)* displays a beautifully crafted model of the Bucintoro and its original banner. Vivaldi concerts are a regular feature at La Pietà church *(p112)*. Paintings by Guardi, Canaletto and Longhi capture the spirit of the age and are found in the Accademia *(pp130–3)*, Correr Museum and Ca' Rezzonico *(p126)*.

***Fortunes were spent** on opulent wigs, jewels and clothing for costume balls and the theatre. This high-heeled shoe is in the Correr Museum* (p77).

***The comic antics** of Harlequin and Pantaloon at La Fenice* (p93) *ensured the popularity of the theatre with Venetians.*

1804 Napoleon crowned King of Italy and takes back Venice

1814–15 Austrians drive French from Venice; Congress of Vienna returns the Veneto to Austria

Daniele Manin (1804–57)

1859 Second War of Italian Independence; after Battle of Solferino, Red Cross founded

1861 Vittorio Emanuele crowned King of Italy

1820 | **1870**

1818 Byron swims up the Grand Canal

1846 Venetian rail causeway links the city to the mainland for the first time

1848 First Italian War of Independence. Venice revolts against Austrian rule

1853 Ruskin publishes *The Stones of Venice*

1849 Hunger and disease force Venetian rebels, led by Daniele Manin, to surrender

1866 Venice and Veneto freed from Austrian rule

Venice in Vogue

FROM BEING AN INTROVERTED and unchanging city, Venice developed with remarkable speed. The opening of the Suez Canal in 1869 brought new prosperity; a new harbour was built for ocean-going ships and Venice became a favourite embarkation point for colonial administrators and rich Europeans travelling east. The fashion for sea-bathing and patronage by wealthy socialites reawakened interest in the city, and the founding of the Biennale attracted Europe's leading artists, who expressed their enthusiasm for the city in novels, paintings and music.

Peggy Guggenheim *(1898–1979)*
Patron of the avant garde, Peggy Guggenheim brought her outstanding art collection (see p134) *to Venice in 1949.*

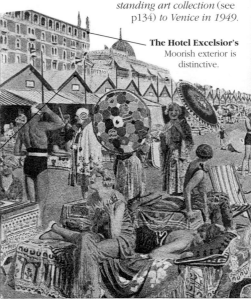

The Hotel Excelsior's Moorish exterior is distinctive.

Bathing huts, designed for modesty in the 1920s, are still a feature of the Lido.

Igor Stravinsky *(1882– 1971)*
Along with Turgenev, Diaghilev and Ezra Pound, Stravinsky was one of many émigrés enchanted by the magic of Venice.

Hotel Excelsior
When it was built in 1907, the Hotel Excelsior (see p231) *was the world's largest hotel.*

THE LIDO

From the turn of the century, grand hotel developments along the sandy Adriatic shore turned the Lido into Europe's most stylish seaside resort. The island has since given its name to bathing establishments the world over.

TIMELINE

1870 | 1880 | 1890 | 1900 | 1910

1881 Venice becomes second largest port in Italy after Genoa

1883 Wagner dies in Palazzo Vendramin-Calergi

Richard Wagner (1813–83)

1889 Poet Robert Browning dies in Ca' Rezzonico

1895 First Biennale art exhibition

1902 Collapse of campanile in Piazza San Marco

1903 Patriarch Sarto of Venice becomes Pope Pius X

1912 Opening of rebuilt campanile; Thomas Mann writes *Death in Venice*

The International Exhibition of Modern Art
Venice became a showcase for all that was new in world art and architecture when the Biennale was launched. The first exhibition, in 1895, showed work by Renoir and Monet.

The manicured beaches of the Lido became a catwalk for style-conscious holidaymakers.

The Campanile
After the appearance of ominous warning cracks, the 1,000-year-old bell tower crashed to the ground in 1902. It was rebuilt within a decade (see p76).

Where to See Turn-of-the-Century Venice

Regular *vaporetto* services link Venice to the Lido *(p156)*, with its deluxe hotels, sports facilities and beaches. The pavilions of the Biennale *(p121)* are usually only open during the exhibition. A lift carries visitors to the top of the rebuilt Campanile *(p76)* for panoramic views of Venice.

***San Michele**, the cemetery isle* (p151), *is the last resting place of eminent foreigners, such as Serge Diaghilev, Igor Stravinsky and Ezra Pound.*

***The exclusive** Grand Hôtel des Bains* (p231) *on the Lido has retained its Art Deco style and private section of beach.*

1917 Work starts on constructing the port of Marghera

1918 Fierce fighting in mountain passes of the Veneto in the last weeks of World War I

1920

1926 Mestre is formally granted town status

1930

1931 Venice is linked to the mainland by a road causeway

1932 First Venice Film Festival

German travel poster from 1936

1940

1943–5 Mussolini rules a puppet state, the Salò Republic

1950

1951 Stravinsky's *The Rake's Progress* premièred in Venice

1954 Britten's *Turn of the Screw* premièred in Venice

1956 Cortina d'Ampezzo hosts Winter Olympics

1959 Patriarch Roncalli elected Pope John XXIII

1960

1960 Venice airport opens

Venice Preserved

IN NOVEMBER 1966 Venice was hit by the worst floods in its history, sparking worldwide concern for the future of the city's delicate and decaying fabric. Major steps have since been taken to protect Venice and its unique heritage, though some difficult issues remain, including the erosion and wave damage caused by public and private waterborne craft, and pollution from the mainland. However, the allure of Venice, set in its watery lagoon, is as compelling as ever.

Pink Floyd in Venice
Pink Floyd's 1989 rock concert threatened the city's equilibrium.

Venice as Film Set
Venice has served as the backdrop to countless films, including Fellini's Casanova *(1976) and* Indiana Jones and the Last Crusade *(1989).*

The Regata Storica, held in September, is an annual trial of strength and skill for gondoliers.

After the Flood
During the 1966 floods, the waters rose nearly 2 m (6 ft). Great damage was done by fuel oil, washed out of broken tanks. It is now banned from the city in favour of gas.

TOURISM

Venetian regattas are part of a rich tradition that enhances the city's attraction to tourists, providing employment for many on the mainland as well as in Venice itself. Even so, some complain that tourism has turned Venice from a living city into one vast museum.

TIMELINE

1966 Floods cause devastation in Venice. UNESCO launches its Save Venice appeal

Visconti and Dirk Bogarde on the set of Death in Venice

1978 Patriarch Luciani of Venice elected Pope John Paul I, but dies 33 days later

1983 Venice officially stops sinking after extraction of underground water prohibited

1960 | 1970 | 1980

1968 Protestors prevent part of the lagoon being drained to extend Marghera's industrial zone

1970 Luchino Visconti's film, *Death in Venice*

1973 Laws passed to reduce pollution, subsidence and flooding.

1979 Venetian Carnival is revived

Carnival reveller

Benetton
The famous clothing firm, originating in Treviso, represents the modern face of Veneto industry.

Venice plays host to over 12 million visitors every year.

Glass Blowing
This age-old tradition still contributes to the economy.

Subsidence, caused by water extraction for use in Marghera, is being remedied by piping water into Venice.

The Acqua Alta
High tides can cause floods and paralyze the city. Plans for a flood barrier across the lagoon are subject to controversy.

Restoration in Venice

One positive result of the 1966 floods was a major international appeal for funds to pay for the cleaning of historic buildings, statues and paintings. Funds raised are coordinated under the auspices of UNESCO, with offices in Venice.

Restorers *learn how to repair and conserve fragile works of art at a European centre for conservation on San Servolo* (p154).

Madonna dell'Orto (p140) *was restored by the Italian Art and Archives Rescue Fund (later renamed Venice in Peril).*

1988 First experimental stage of MOSE, the lagoon flood barrier, is completed

1992 Venice Film Festival celebrates 60 years

1992 Venice rocked by corruption scandals. Metro network beneath lagoon proposed

1990

1932–1992 Venice Film Festival poster

1994 Voters decide against a divorce between Venice and Mestre, which share a mayor and city council

1995 Centenary of Biennale Exhibition

2000

2002 State government approves construction of the lagoon flood barrier

2002 Construction begins on the fourth bridge over the Grand Canal

2010

Venice Area by Area

Venice at a Glance

VENICE IS SMALL and most of the sights can be comfortably visited on foot. The heart of the city is the Piazza San Marco, which is overlooked by the great Basilica and the Doge's Palace. For many, these are attractions enough, but there are delights worth exploring beyond the Piazza, such as the galleries of the Accademia, Ca' Rezzonico and the imposing Frari church. Unique to Venice are the naval Arsenale to the east and the Ghetto in the north.

Ghetto
Established in the early 16th century, this fascinating quarter was the world's first ghetto (see p145).

Santa Maria Gloriosa dei Frari
This soaring Gothic edifice, founded by the Franciscans in 1340, is a rich repository of Venetian painting and sculpture (see pp102–3).

CANNAREGIO
Pages 136–45

SAN POLO AND SANTA CROCE
Pages 96–107

DORSODURO
Pages 122–35

SAN MARC[O]
Pages 72–

0 metres 500

0 yards 500

Ca' Rezzonico
The splendid rooms of this palace, overlooking the Grand Canal, are decorated with 18th-century furniture and paintings (see p126).

Accademia
Carpaccio's St Ursula *cycle (1490–5) is one of the treasures of the Accademia, which has a comprehensive collection of Venetian art* (see pp130–3).

Ca' d'Oro
This ornate palace is the finest example of Venetian Gothic style (see p142).

Rialto Bridge
The bustling Rialto Bridge (see p100) *was named after the ancient commercial seat of Venice, where the first inhabitants settled.*

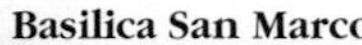

Basilica San Marco
Magnificent mosaics sheathe the domes, walls and floor of the Byzantine Basilica (see pp78–83).

Arsenale
The great dockyard, first of its kind in Europe, was the naval nerve centre of the Venetian Empire (see p119).

CASTELLO
Pages 108–21

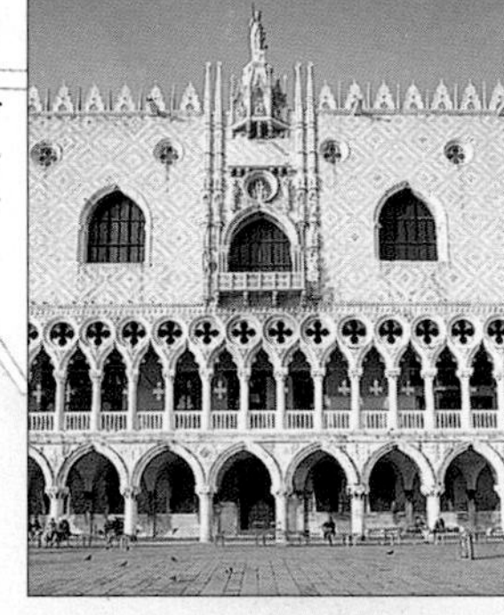

Doge's Palace
The colonnaded Gothic palace was the seat of government as well as home to the doge and his family (see pp84–89).

Santa Maria della Salute
Marking the southern end of the Grand Canal, this great Baroque church is one of the city's landmarks (see p135).

202

A VIEW OF THE GRAND CANAL

KNOWN to the Venetians as the *Canalazzo*, the Grand Canal sweeps through the heart of Venice, following the course of an ancient river bed. Since the founding days of the empire it has served as the city's main thoroughfare. Once used by great galleys or trading vessels making their stately way to the Rialto, it is nowadays teeming with *vaporetti*, launches, barges and gondolas. Glimpses of its glorious past, however, are never far away. The annual re-enactment of historic pageants, preserving the traditions of the Venetian Republic, brings a blaze of colour to the canal. The most spectacular is the Regata Storica held in September *(see p35)*, a huge procession of historic craft packed with crews in traditional costumes, followed by boat and gondola races down the Grand Canal.

Venetian gondolier

The parade of palaces bordering the winding waterway, built over a span of around 500 years, presents some of the finest architecture of the Republic. Historically it is like a roll-call of the old Venetian aristocracy, with almost every *palazzo* bearing the name of a once-grand family. Bright frescoes may have faded, precious marbles worn, and foundations frayed with the tides, but the Grand Canal is still, to quote Charles VIII of France's ambassador in 1495, "the most beautiful street in the world".

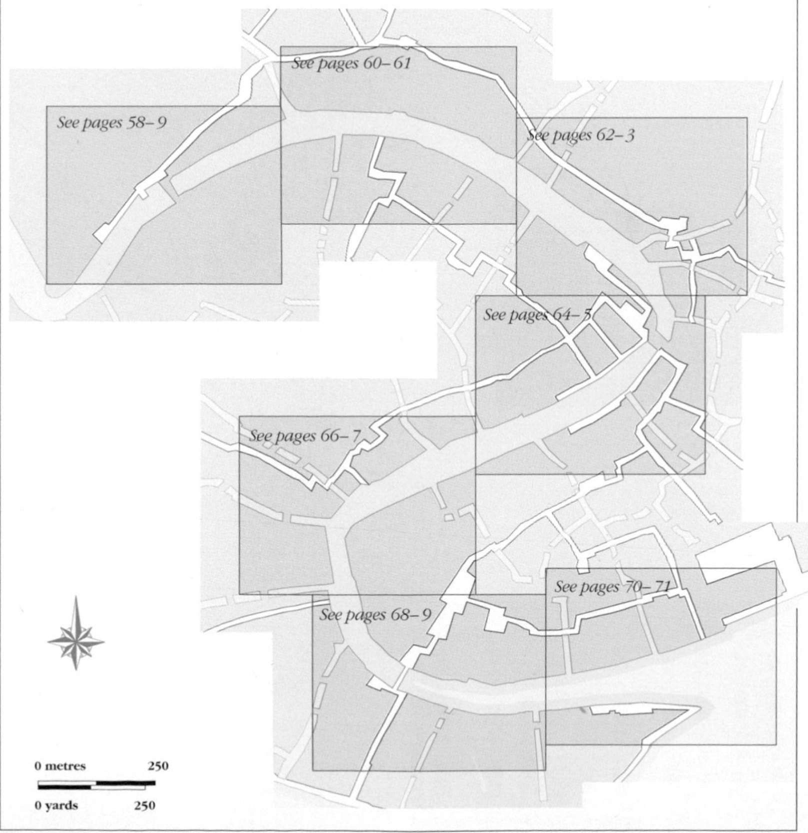

◁ **The Grand Canal at its most colourful, during the Regata Storica**

Santa Lucia to Palazzo Flangini

Vaporetto ticket office, Grand Canal

Locator Map

THE GRAND CANAL is best admired from a gondola or, more cheaply, from a *vaporetto*. Several lines travel the length of the canal *(see p275)* but only the No. 1 goes sufficiently slowly for you to take in any of the individual palaces. The journey from the station to San Zaccaria takes about 40 minutes. Ideally you should take a return trip, absorbing one bank at a time. Nearly 4 km (2½ miles) long, the canal varies in width from 30 to 70 m (98 to 230 ft) and is spanned by three bridges, the Scalzi, the Rialto and the Accademia.

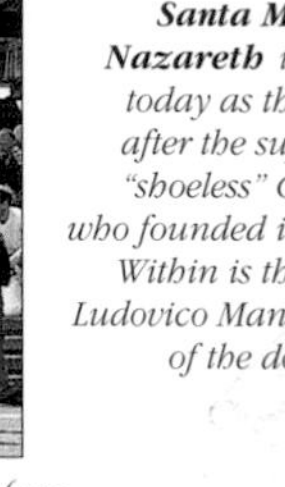

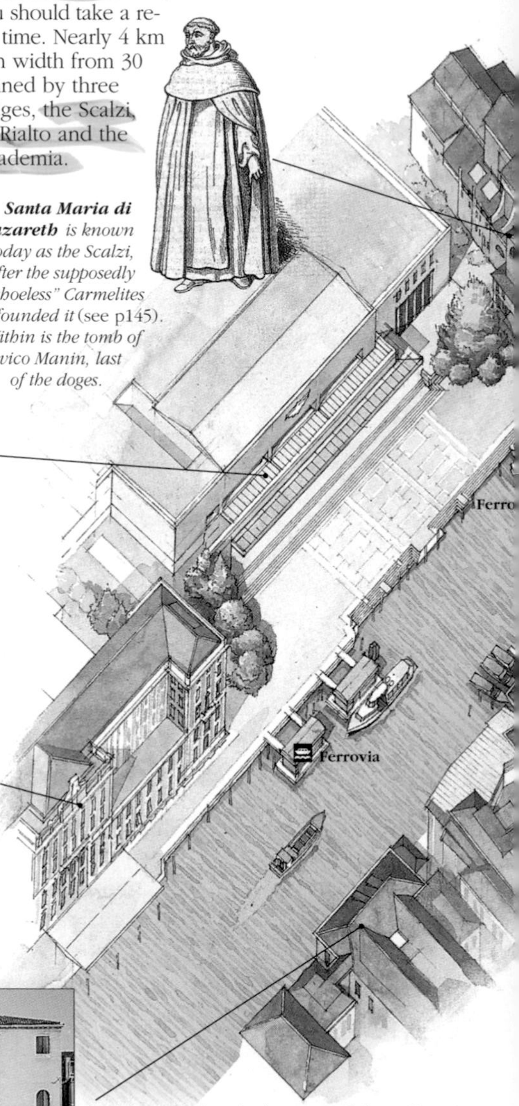

Santa Maria di Nazareth *is known today as the Scalzi, after the supposedly "shoeless" Carmelites who founded it* (see p145). *Within is the tomb of Ludovico Manin, last of the doges.*

Santa Lucia railway station (see p272), *built in the mid-19th century and remodelled in the 1950s, links the city with the mainland.*

La Direzione Compartimentale*, the administration offices for the railway, was built at the same time as the station, on the site of the church of Santa Lucia and other ancient buildings.*

Ferro

Ferrovia

Palazzo Diedo*, also known as Palazzo Emo, is a Neo-Classical palace of the late 18th century. It is believed to be the birthplace of Angelo Emo (1731–92), the last admiral of the Venetian fleet. The palace was built by Andrea Tirali, an engineer who worked on the restoration of San Marco.*

Palazzo Calbo Crotta *is now the 4-star Hotel Principe. Fine antiques and fabrics which once decorated the palace are now in Ca' Rezzonico* (see p126).

Palazzo Flangini *was designed by Giuseppe Sardi, a leading 17th-century architect.*

Palazzo Gritti *was built in the 16th century. The Grittis were a wealthy family who produced one of the most intelligent doges, Andrea Gritti (reigned 1523–38).*

The Scalzi Bridge was built in 1934, replacing the original wrought-iron bridge.

Campo San Simeone Grande*, named after the nearby church (otherwise called San Simeone Profeta), is one of the few* campi *overlooking the canal.*

Casa Adoldo and Palazzo Foscari-Contarini *were both rebuilt in the 16th century. According to local tradition, the great Doge Francesco Foscari (ruled 1423–57) was born in the original Foscari-Contarini palace.*

San Simeone Piccolo *is a large church, in spite of its name (*piccolo *means small). Built in 1738, its design was based partly on the Pantheon in Rome. It is closed to the public.*

San Geremia to San Stae

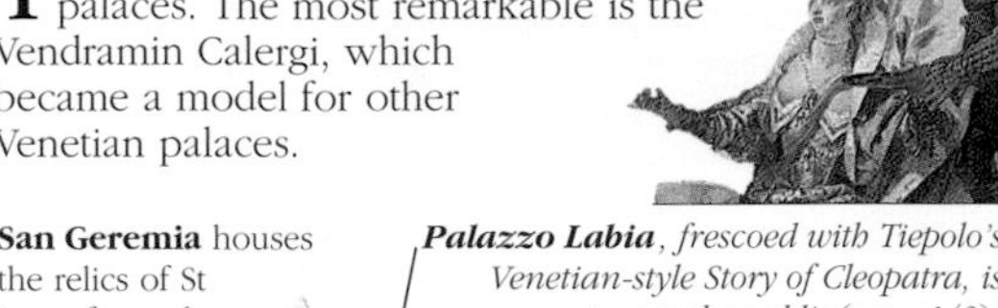

THIS STRETCH sees the start of the great palaces. The most remarkable is the Vendramin Calergi, which became a model for other Venetian palaces.

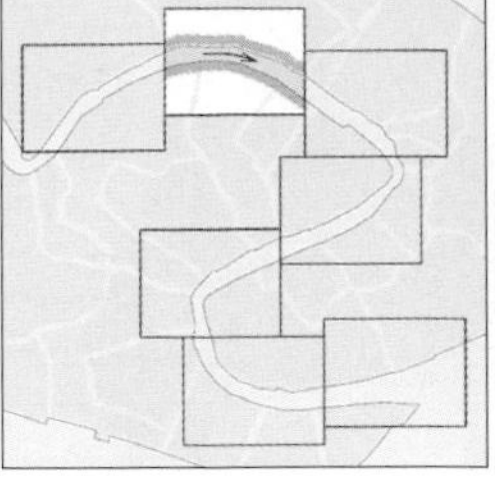

LOCATOR MAP

San Geremia houses the relics of St Lucy, formerly preserved in Santa Lucia where the station now stands.

Palazzo Labia, *frescoed with Tiepolo's Venetian-style Story of Cleopatra, is open to the public* (see p143).

Palazzo Querini has the family coat of arms on the façade.

Ca' dei Cuori (House of Hearts) was named after the hearts in the family coat of arms.

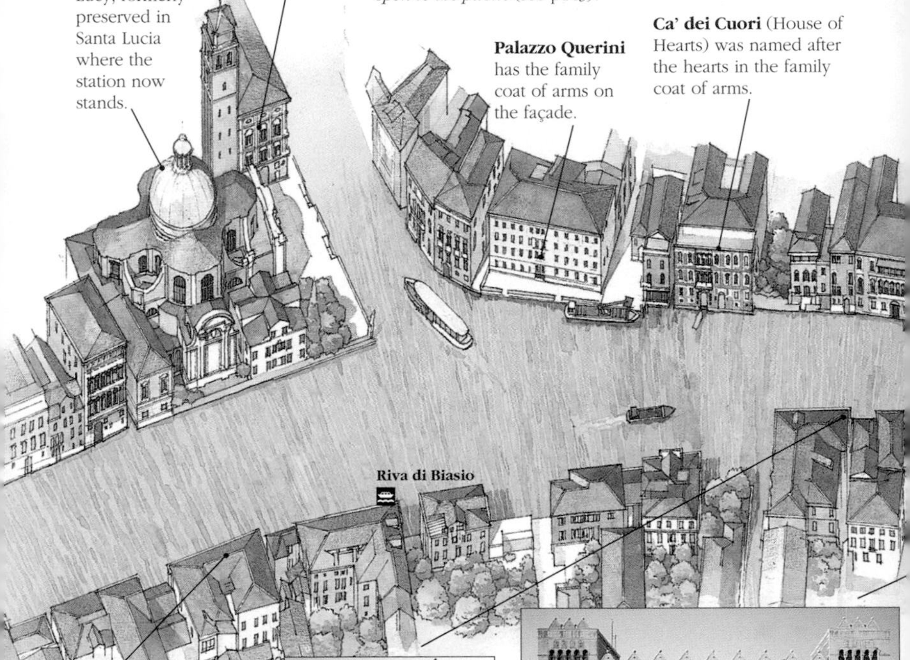

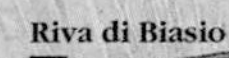

Riva di Biasio

Palazzo Giovanelli, *a restored Gothic palace, was acquired by the Giovanellis in 1755. This titled non-Venetian family had been admitted into the Great Council in 1668 for a fee of 100,000 ducats.*

Fondaco dei Turchi *was a splendid Veneto-Byzantine building before last century's brutal restoration. Today it houses the Natural History Museum* (see p105).

Palazzo Donà Balbi, *built in the 17th century, is named after two great Venetian families who intermarried. The Donà family produced four doges.*

Deposito del Megio, *a crenellated building with a reconstructed Lion of St Mark, was a granary in the 15th century.*

San Marcuola, dedicated to St Ermagora and St Fortunatus, was built in 1728–36 by Giorgio Massari, but the façade was never completed.

***Palazzo Vendramin Calergi**, an early Renaissance palace, was designed by Mauro Coducci. The composer Richard Wagner died here in 1883. Today, Venice's casino is housed in the palace.*

Palazzo Marcello, rebuilt in the early 18th century, was the birthplace of composer Benedetto Marcello in 1686.

Palazzo Erizzo has two huge paintings depicting the feats of Paolo Erizzo, who died heroically fighting the Turks in 1469.

Palazzo Emo belonged to the family of a famous Venetian admiral *(see p58)*.

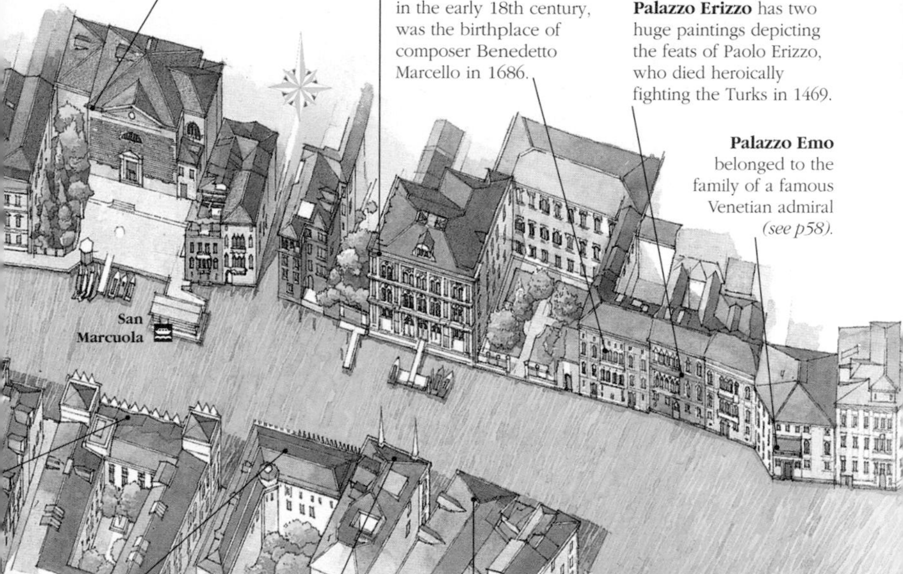

San Marcuola

San Stae

***Palazzo Tron**, built in the late 16th century, hosted a famous ball in 1775 in honour of Emperor Joseph II of Austria.*

***Palazzo Belloni Battagia**, with its distinctive pinnacles, was built by Longhena in the mid-17th century for the Belloni family, who had bought their way into Venetian aristocracy.*

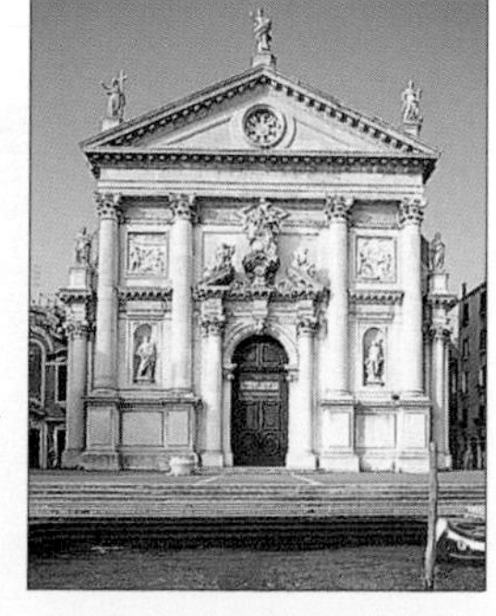

***San Stae** is striking for its Baroque façade, graced by marble statues. It was funded by a legacy left by Doge Alvise Mocenigo in 1709* (see p105).

Palazzo Barbarigo to the Markets

HERE THE CANAL is flanked by stately palaces, built over a period of five centuries. The most spectacular is the Gothic Ca' d'Oro, whose façade once glittered with gold.

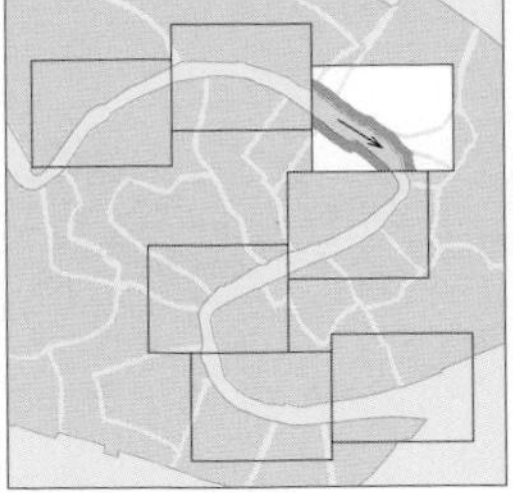

LOCATOR MAP

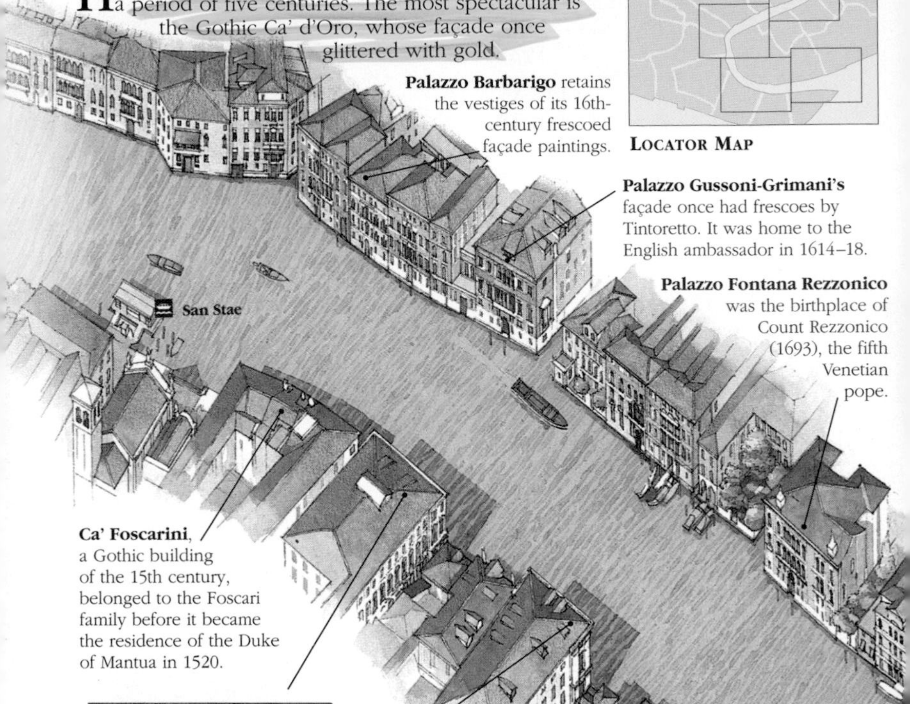

San Stae

Palazzo Barbarigo retains the vestiges of its 16th-century frescoed façade paintings.

Palazzo Gussoni-Grimani's façade once had frescoes by Tintoretto. It was home to the English ambassador in 1614–18.

Palazzo Fontana Rezzonico was the birthplace of Count Rezzonico (1693), the fifth Venetian pope.

Ca' Foscarini, a Gothic building of the 15th century, belonged to the Foscari family before it became the residence of the Duke of Mantua in 1520.

***Ca' Pesaro**, a huge and stately Baroque palace designed by Longhena* (see p23)*, today houses the Gallery of Modern Art and the Oriental Museum* (see p105)*. It was built for Leonardo Pesaro, a Procurator of San Marco.*

Casa Favretto (Hotel San Cassiano) was the home of the painter Giacomo Favretto (1849–87).

***Palazzo Morosini Brandolin** belonged to the Morosini family, one of the* Case Vecchie *families, deemed to be noble before the 9th century.*

***Ca' Corner della Regina** is named after Caterina Cornaro, Queen of Cyprus, who was born here in 1454. The present building (1724–7) was designed by Domenico Rossi.*

***The Pescheria** has been the site of a busy fish market for six centuries. Today it takes place in the striking mock-Gothic market hall, built in 1907.*

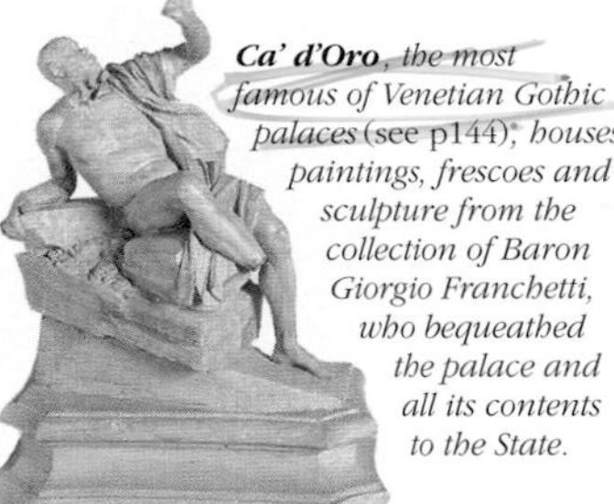

***Ca' d'Oro**, the most famous of Venetian Gothic palaces* (see p144)*, houses paintings, frescoes and sculpture from the collection of Baron Giorgio Franchetti, who bequeathed the palace and all its contents to the State.*

CANALETTO

Antonio Canale (Canaletto) (1697–1768) is best known for his *vedute* or views of Venice. He studied in Rome, but lived here for most of his life. One of his patrons was Joseph Smith *(see below)*. Sadly there are very few of his paintings left on view in the city.

***Palazzo Sagredo** passed from the Morosini to the Sagredo family in the early 18th century. The façade shows characteristics of both Veneto-Byzantine and Gothic styles.*

***Palazzo Foscarini** was the home of Marco Foscarini, a diplomat, orator and scholar who rose to the position of doge in 1762.*

***Palazzo Mangili Valmarana** was designed by Antonio Visentini (above) in Classical style for Joseph Smith, who became the English consul in Venice. Smith (1682–1770) was a patron of both Visentini and Canaletto.*

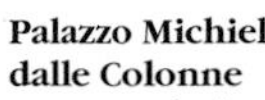

Palazzo Michiel dalle Colonne was named after its distinctive colonnade.

Palazzo Michiel del Brusà was rebuilt and named after the great fire *(brusà)* that swept the city in 1774.

Ca' D'Oro

***Ca' da Mosto** is a good example of 13th-century Veneto-Byzantine style. Alvise da Mosto, the 15th-century navigator, was born here in 1432.*

Tribunale Fabbriche Nuove, Sansovino's market building (1555), is now the seat of the Assize Court.

The Rialto Quarter

THE AREA AROUND THE RIALTO BRIDGE is the oldest and busiest quarter of the city. Traditionally a centre of trade, crowded quaysides and colourful food markets still border the canal south of the bridge.

LOCATOR MAP

***Palazzo Papadopoli**, formerly known as Coccina-Tiepolo, was built in 1560. Its splendid hall of mirrors has been preserved.*

***Riva del Vin** is one of the few spots where you can sit and relax on the banks of the Grand Canal* (see p98).

***Ca' Corner-Martinengo-Ravà** became the Leon Bianco Hotel in the 19th century. The American writer, James Fenimore Cooper, stayed here in 1838.*

Palazzo Barzizza, rebuilt in the 17th century, still preserves its early 13th-century façade.

San Silvestro

***Palazzo Grimani**, a fine, if somewhat austere looking, Renaissance palace* (see p23)*, was built in 1556 by Michele Sanmicheli for the Procurator, Girolamo Grimani. The State purchased the palace in 1807 and it is now occupied by the city's Court of Appeal.*

***Palazzo Farsetti and Palazzo Loredan**, both occupied by the City Council, were built around 1200 and finally merged in 1868. Palazzo Farsetti became an academy for young artists, one of whom was Canova.*

Fondaco dei Tedeschi, *originally used as a warehouse and lodgings for German traders, is now the main post office.*

Palazzo Camerlenghi, built in 1528, was once the offices of the city treasurers *(camerlenghi)*. The ground floor was the State prison.

Rialto

Riva del Ferro is the quayside where German trading barges offloaded iron *(ferro)*.

The Rialto Bridge (see p100) *was built to span the Grand Canal in what was, and still is, the most commercial quarter of the city.*

Casetta Dandolo's predecessor is said to have been the birthplace of Doge Enrico Dandolo (ruled 1192–1205).

Palazzo Manin-Dolfin *was built by Sansovino in 1538–40 but only his Classical stone façade survives. The interior was completely transformed for Ludovico Manin, last doge of Venice (died 1797). He intended to turn the house into a magnificent palace extending as far as Campo San Salvatore.*

Palazzo Bembo, *a 15th-century Gothic palace, was the birthplace of the Renaissance cardinal and scholar, Pietro Bembo, who wrote one of the earliest Italian grammars.*

The Dandolo Family

Doge Enrico Dandolo

The illustrious Dandolo family produced four doges, 12 procurators of San Marco, a patriarch of Grado and a queen of Serbia. The first of the doges was Enrico who, despite being old and blind, was the principal driving force in the Crusaders' plan to take Constantinople in 1204 *(see p42)*. The other remarkable doge in the family was the humanist and historian, Andrea Dandolo (died 1354).

La Volta del Canal

THE POINT WHERE THE CANAL doubles back sharply on itself is known as La Volta – the bend. This splendid curve was long ago established as the finishing stretch for the annual Regata Storica *(see p35)*.

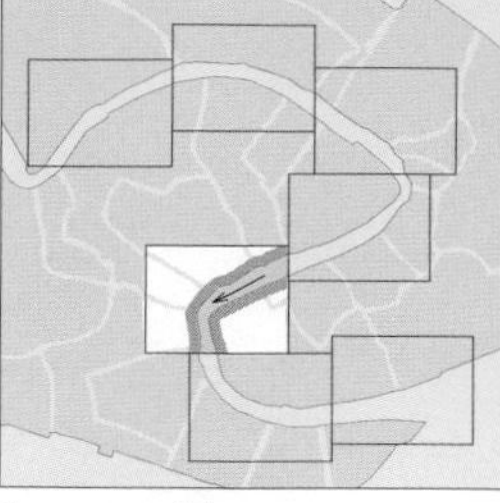

LOCATOR MAP

***Palazzo Marcello**, which belonged to an old Venetian family, is also called "dei Leoni" because of the lions either side of the doorway.*

Palazzo Persico, on the corner of Rio San Polo, is a 16th-century house in Lombardesque style.

Palazzo Civran-Grimani is a Classical building of the early 17th century.

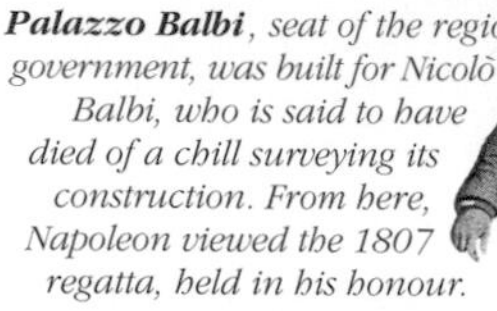

***Palazzo Balbi**, seat of the regional government, was built for Nicolò Balbi, who is said to have died of a chill surveying its construction. From here, Napoleon viewed the 1807 regatta, held in his honour.*

***Ca' Foscari** was built for Doge Francesco Foscari in 1437* (see p22). *It is now part of the University of Venice.*

Palazzo Giustinian was the residence of Wagner in 1858–9, when he was composing the second act of *Tristan and Isolde*.

***Ca' Rezzonico**, now the museum of 18th-century Venice* (see p126), *became the home of the poet Robert Browning and his son, Pen, in 1888.*

San Tomà

San Samuele

Ca' Rezzonico

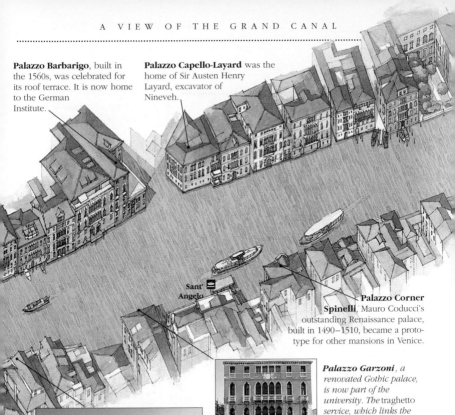

Palazzo Barbarigo, built in the 1560s, was celebrated for its roof terrace. It is now home to the German Institute.

Palazzo Capello-Layard was the home of Sir Austen Henry Layard, excavator of Nineveh.

Sant' Angelo

Palazzo Corner Spinelli, Mauro Coducci's outstanding Renaissance palace, built in 1490–1510, became a prototype for other mansions in Venice.

Palazzo Garzoni, *a renovated Gothic palace, is now part of the university. The* traghetto *service, which links the neighbouring Calle Garzoni to San Tomà on the other side of the canal, is one of the oldest in Venice.*

Palazzo Mocenigo, *formed by four palaces linked together, has a plaque to the poet Byron who stayed here in 1818.*

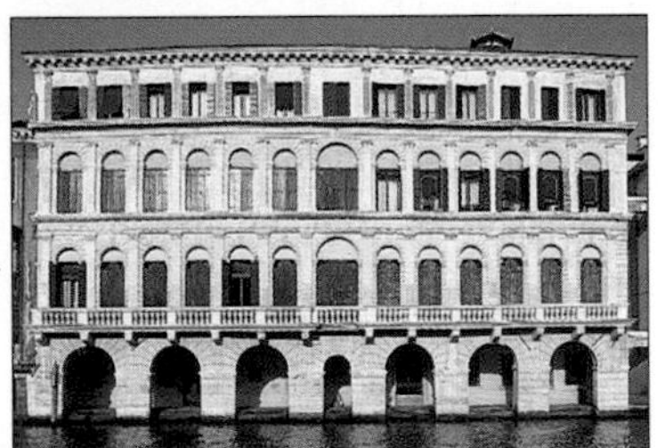

Palazzo Moro Lin, *also known as the "palace of the 13 windows", was created in the 17th century for the painter Pietro Liberi by merging two Gothic houses.*

Palazzo Grassi, *built in the 1730s, was bought by Fiat in 1984 and turned into a venue for art exhibitions.*

Palazzo Capello Malipiero, *a Gothic palace, was reconstructed in 1622. Beside it, in Campo di San Samuele, stands the church of San Samuele which has a 12th-century Veneto-Byzantine campanile.*

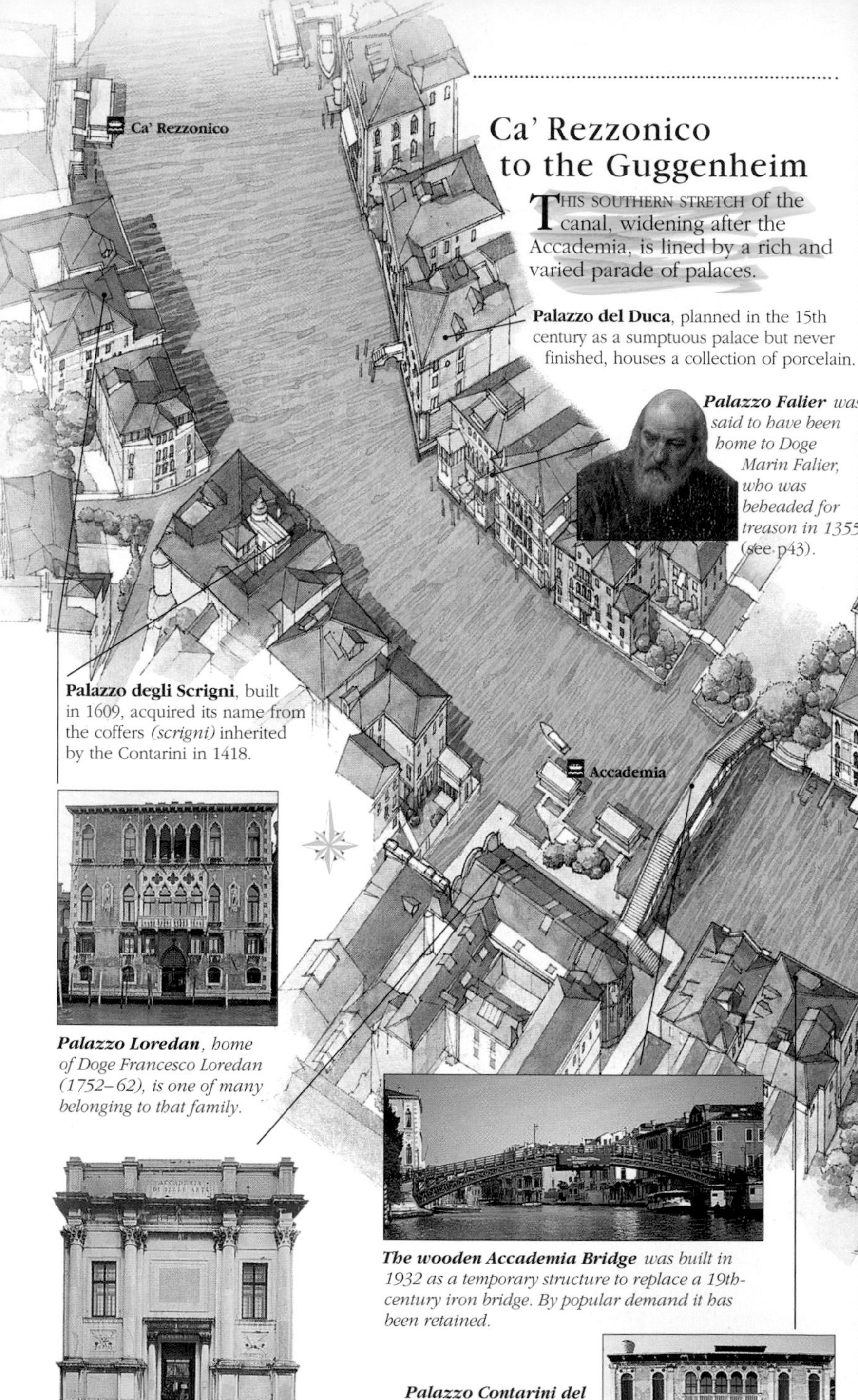

Ca' Rezzonico to the Guggenheim

THIS SOUTHERN STRETCH of the canal, widening after the Accademia, is lined by a rich and varied parade of palaces.

Palazzo del Duca, planned in the 15th century as a sumptuous palace but never finished, houses a collection of porcelain.

Palazzo Falier *was said to have been home to Doge Marin Falier, who was beheaded for treason in 1355* (see p43).

Palazzo degli Scrigni, built in 1609, acquired its name from the coffers *(scrigni)* inherited by the Contarini in 1418.

Palazzo Loredan*, home of Doge Francesco Loredan (1752–62), is one of many belonging to that family.*

The Accademia *galleries, within the former church, monastery and Scuola della Carità, house the world's greatest collection of Venetian paintings* (see pp130–33).

The wooden Accademia Bridge *was built in 1932 as a temporary structure to replace a 19th-century iron bridge. By popular demand it has been retained.*

Palazzo Contarini del Zaffo*, a magnificent Renaissance palace of the late 1400s, was built for a branch of the ubiquitous Contarini family. Early this century it was acquired by the Polignac family.*

LOCATOR MAP

__Ca' Grande__, a huge Classical palace, was designed in 1545 by Sansovino for Giacomo Cornaro, nephew of the Queen of Cyprus. The family was one of the richest in Venice and spared no expense in the palace's decoration. This family tree illustrates the extent of the Cornaro's wealth and influence in Venice.

Palazzo Franchetti Cavalli belonged to Archduke Frederick of Austria, who died here in 1836.

__Palazzo Barbaro__ comprises two palaces, one of which was bought by the Curtis family in 1885. Monet and Whistler painted here and Henry James (right) wrote The Aspern Papers.

__Casetta delle Rose__, one of the smallest houses on the canal, was the home of Italian poet Gabriele d'Annunzio during World War I. Canova (above) had his studio here in 1770.

***Palazzo Barbarigo**, beside the Campo San Vio, stands out for the harsh mosaics, added in 1887.*

__Peggy Guggenheim__ established her collection of modern art in Venice in 1951 (see p134). *She chose as her venue the Palazzo Venier dei Leoni, which had been built in 1749 and never finished.*

__Palazzo Dario__, built in 1487, is a charming but strangely ill-fated palace (see p135).

To La Salute and San Marco

The view along the final stretch of the canal is one of the finest – and most familiar – in Venice. Near the mouth rises the magnificent church of La Salute with busy St Mark's Basin beyond.

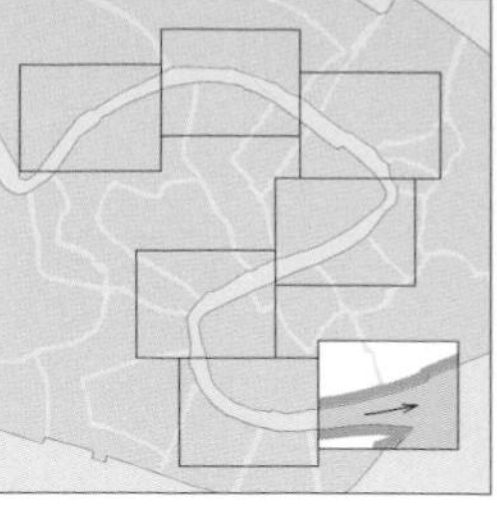

Locator Map

***The Palazzo Gritti-Pisani**, where Ruskin stayed in 1851, is better known today as the luxurious 5-star Hotel Gritti Palace* (see p229).

***Palazzo Contarini Fasan**, a tiny 15th-century palace with an elegant façade, is popularly known as the House of Desdemona from Shakespeare's* Othello.

Salute

***Palazzo Salviati** was the headquarters of the Salviati glass-producing company, hence the glass mosaics on the façade.*

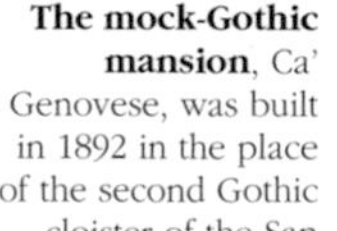

The mock-Gothic mansion, Ca' Genovese, was built in 1892 in the place of the second Gothic cloister of the San Gregorio monastery.

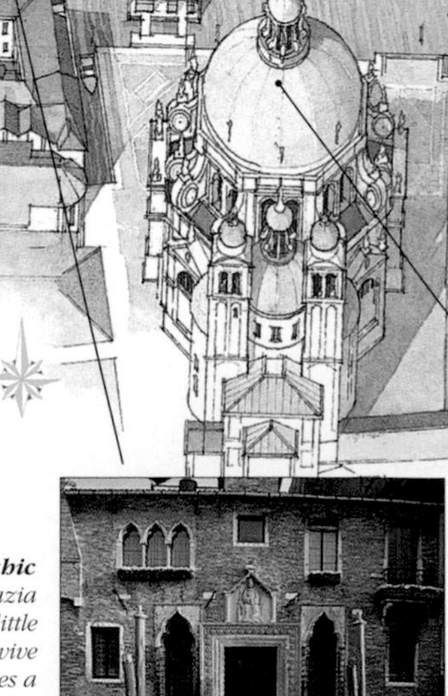

***The deconsecrated Gothic brick church** of Abbazia San Gregorio and a little cloister are all that survive of what was for centuries a powerful monastic centre. The church is now used as a laboratory for the renovation of large-scale paintings.*

Palazzo Tiepolo, *the Hotel Europa and Regina, was formerly owned by the Tiepolo family, associated with an unsuccessful uprising in 1310.*

Harry's Bar (see p92) *was popular with Hemingway and other writers. This was the very first Harry's Bar in the world.*

Palazzo Giustinian, head-quarters of the Biennale, used to be a hotel, where Turner, Verdi and Proust stayed.

San Marco Vallaressa

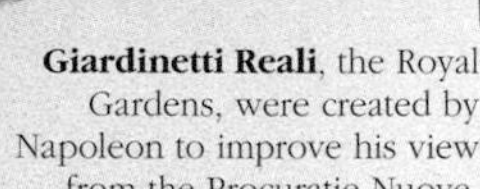

Giardinetti Reali, the Royal Gardens, were created by Napoleon to improve his view from the Procuratie Nuove.

Palazzo Treves Bonfili, a Classical building of the 17th century, is decorated with Neo-Classical frescoes, paintings and statuary.

The view from the Dogana, *taking in the Doge's Palace, the Campanile of San Marco and the Zecca, is one of the most memorable in Venice.*

Santa Maria della Salute, *a Baroque church of monumental proportions, is supported by over a million timber piles. Built to commemorate the end of the 1630 plague, it was the work of Baldassare Longhena* (see p135).

Dogana di Mare, *the customs house, is topped by a weathervane figure of Fortune* (see p135).

San Marco

Home of the political and judicial nerve centres of Venice, the *sestiere* of San Marco has been the heart of Venetian life since the early days of the Republic. The great showpiece of the Serenissima was the Piazza San Marco, conceived as a vista for the Doge's Palace and the Basilica. The square, described by Napoleon as "the most elegant drawing room in Europe", was the only one deemed fit to be called a piazza – the others were merely *campi*, or fields.

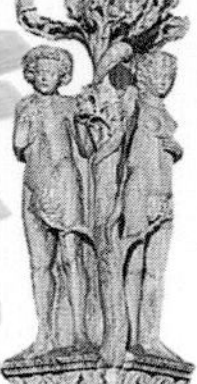

Adam and Eve on the corner of the Doge's Palace

The San Marco area has the bulk of luxury hotels, restaurants and shops. It is also home to several imposing churches, three theatres, including the famous Fenice, and a wealth of handsome *palazzi*. Many of these line the sweeping southern curve of the Grand Canal which borders the *sestiere*.

Sights at a Glance

Churches

Basilica San Marco pp78–83 3
Santa Maria Zobenigo 13
San Moisè 11
San Salvatore 18
Santo Stefano 16
San Zulian 21

Museums and Galleries

Libreria Sansoviniana 5
Museo Archeologico 6
Museo Correr 8
Museo Fortuny 17

Palaces

Doge's Palace pp84–9 4
Palazzo Contarini del Bovolo 12

Historic Buildings and Monuments

Campanile 1
Columns of San Marco and San Teodoro 7
San Giorgio Maggiore 22
Torre dell'Orologio 2

Streets and Squares

Campo San Bartolomeo 19
Campo Santo Stefano 15
Mercerie 20

Bars

Harry's Bar 9

Theatres

La Fenice 14
Ridotto 10

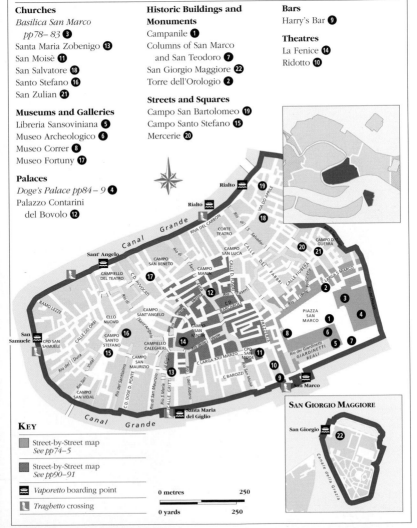

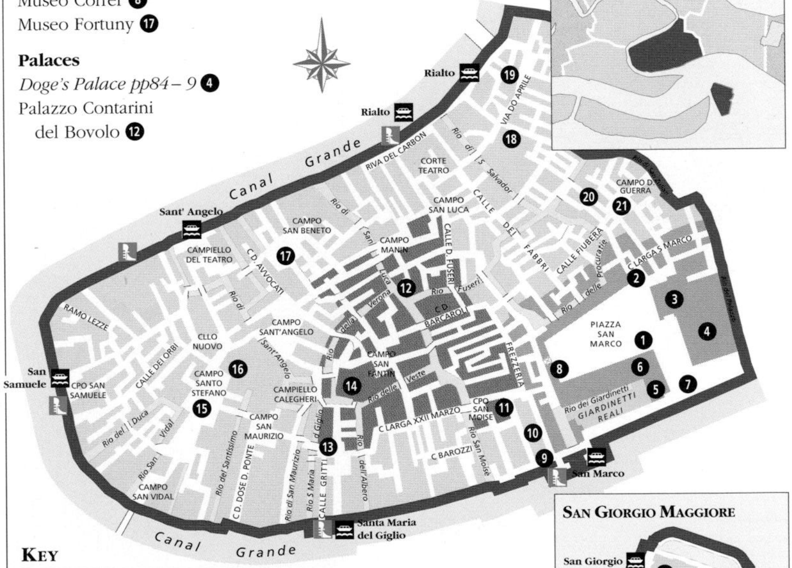

San Giorgio Maggiore

Key

Street-by-Street map *See pp74–5*

Street-by-Street map *See pp90–91*

Vaporetto boarding point

Traghetto crossing

0 metres 250

0 yards 250

◁ **Central dome of the Basilica San Marco**

Street-by-Street: Piazza San Marco

Lion of St Mark

Throughout its long history the Piazza San Marco has witnessed pageants, processions, political activities and countless Carnival festivities. Tourists flock here in their thousands, for the Piazza's eastern end is dominated by two of the city's most important historical sights – the Basilica and the Doge's Palace. In addition to these magnificent buildings there is plenty to entertain, with elegant cafés, open-air orchestras and smart boutiques beneath the arcades of the Procuratie.

So close to the waters of the lagoon, the Piazza is one of the first points in the city to suffer at *acqua alta* (high tide). Tourists and Venetians alike can then be seen picking their way across the duckboards which are set up to crisscross the flooded square.

Gondolas customarily moor in the Bacino Orseolo, named after Doge Pietro Orseolo who established a hospice for pilgrims here in 977.

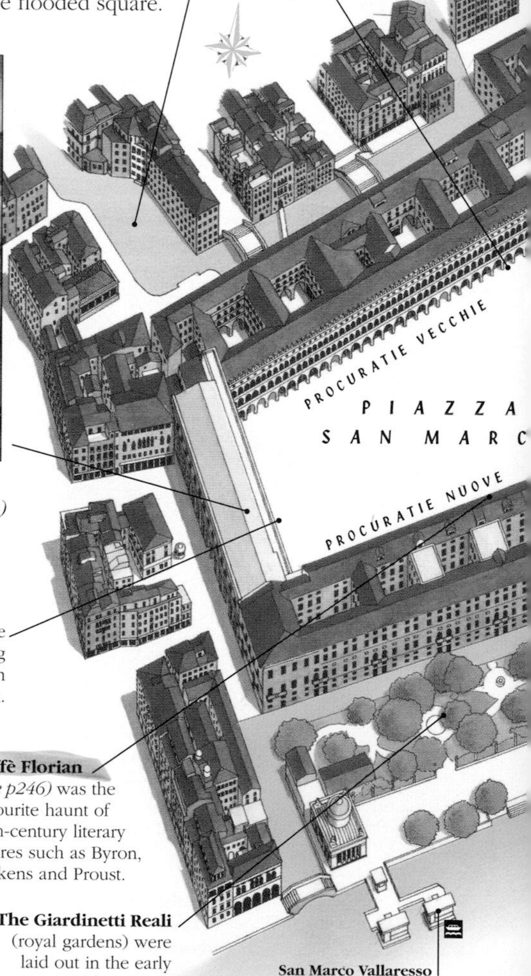

Quadri's café was the favourite haunt of Austrian troops during the Occupation *(see p48)*.

Museo Correr
Giovanni Bellini's Pietà *(1455–60) is one of many Renaissance masterpieces hanging in the picture galleries of the Correr* ❽

PROCURATIE VECCHIE

PIAZZA SAN MARC

PROCURATIE NUOVE

The Ala Napoleonica is the most recent wing enclosing the square, built by Napoleon to create a new ballroom.

0 metres 75

0 yards 75

Star Sights

- ★ **Basilica San Marco**
- ★ **Doge's Palace**
- ★ **Campanile**

Caffè Florian *(see p246)* was the favourite haunt of 19th-century literary figures such as Byron, Dickens and Proust.

The Giardinetti Reali (royal gardens) were laid out in the early 19th century.

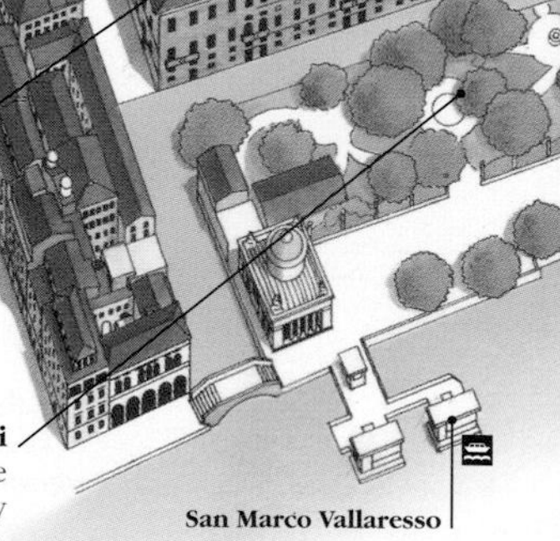

San Marco Vallaresso

Torre dell'Orologio
The Madonna on the clock tower is greeted each Epiphany and Ascension by clockwork figures of the Magi ❷

LOCATOR MAP
See Street Finder, map 7

Piazzetta dei Leoncini was named after the pair of porphyry lions which stand in the square.

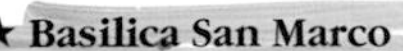

★ Basilica San Marco
The remarkable Basilica of St Mark is a glorious reflection of the city's Byzantine connection ❸

★ Doge's Palace
Once the Republic's seat of power and home to its rulers, the Doge's Palace, beside the Basilica, is a triumph of Gothic architecture ❹

★ Campanile
Today's tower replaced the one that collapsed in 1902. The top provides spectacular views of the city ❶

Museo Archeologico
The museum sculptures had a marked influence on Venetian Renaissance artists ❻

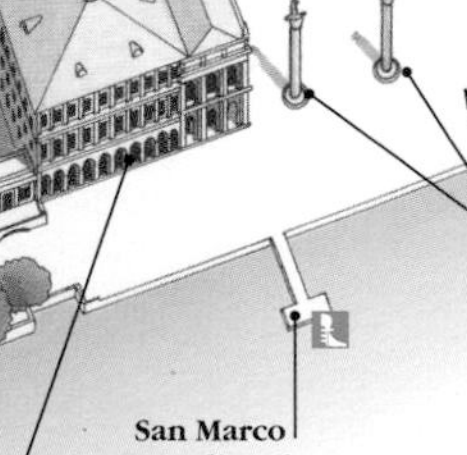

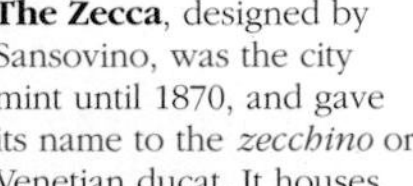

Columns of San Marco and San Teodoro
The columns marked the main entrance to Venice when the city could be reached only by sea ❼

San Marco Giardinetti

The Zecca, designed by Sansovino, was the city mint until 1870, and gave its name to the *zecchino* or Venetian ducat. It houses the Biblioteca Marciana.

Libreria Sansoviniana
The ornate vaulting of the magnificent library stairway is decorated with frescoes and gilded stucco ❺

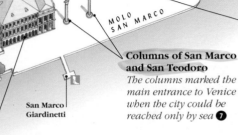

Campanile ❶

Piazza San Marco. **Map** 7 B2. *041 522 40 64. San Marco. Oct–Easter: 9:30am–3:45pm daily; Easter–Sep: 9am–7pm daily (Jun–mid-Sep: to 9pm). Jan.*

FROM THE TOP of St Mark's campanile, high above the Piazza, visitors can enjoy sublime views of the city, the lagoon and, visibility permitting, the peaks of the Alps. It was from this viewpoint that Galileo demonstrated his telescope to Doge Leonardo Donà in 1609. To do so he would have climbed the internal ramp. Access today is gained via a lift that can carry 14 people. Nevertheless there is almost always a queue. If you are at the top of the tower on the hour, beware the resonant ringing of the five bells.

The first tower, completed in 1173, was built as a lighthouse to assist navigators in the lagoon. It took on a less benevolent role in the Middle Ages as the support for a torture cage where offenders were imprisoned and in some cases left to die. The tower's present appearance dates from the early 16th century, when it was restored by Bartolomeo Bon after an earthquake.

The tower survived the vicissitudes of time until 14 July 1902 when, with little warning, its foundations gave way and it suddenly collapsed. The only casualties were the Loggetta at the foot of the tower and the custodian's cat. Donations for reconstruction came flooding in and the following year the foundation stone was laid for a campanile *"dov'era e com'era"* ("where it was and how it was"). The new tower was finally opened on 25 April (St Mark's Day) 1912.

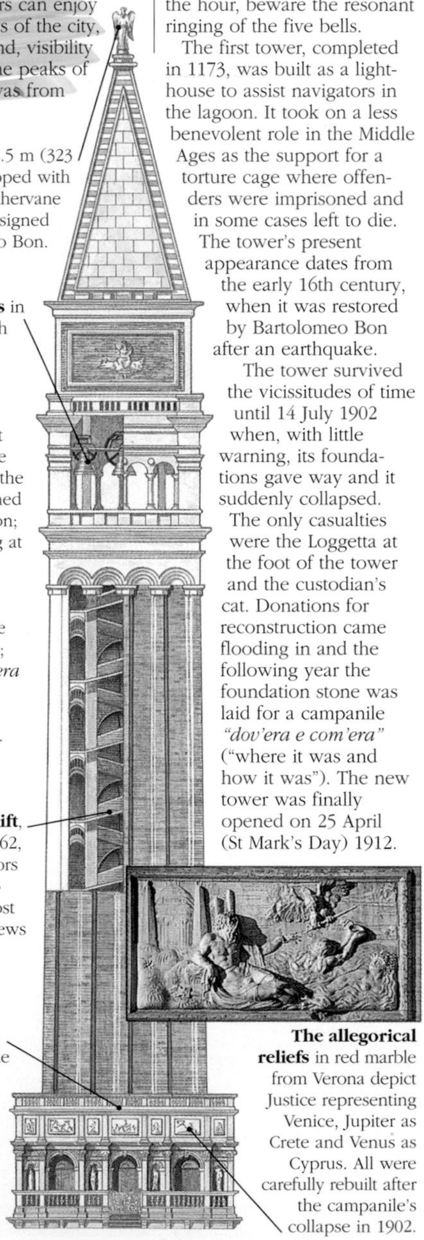

The spire, 98.5 m (323 ft) high, is topped with a golden weathervane which was designed by Bartolomeo Bon.

The five bells in the tower each had their role during the Republic. The *marangona* tolled the start and end of the working day; the *malefico* warned of an execution; the *nona* rang at noon; the *mezza terza* summoned senators to the Doge's Palace; and the *trottiera* announced a session of the Great Council.

An internal lift, installed in 1962, provides visitors with access to one of the most spectacular views across Venice.

The Loggetta was built in the 16th century by Jacopo Sansovino. Its Classical sculptures celebrate the glory of the Republic.

The allegorical reliefs in red marble from Verona depict Justice representing Venice, Jupiter as Crete and Venus as Cyprus. All were carefully rebuilt after the campanile's collapse in 1902.

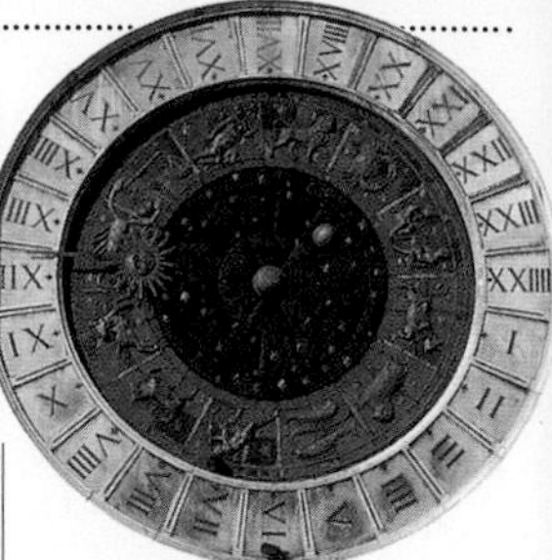

The highly ornamented clock face of the Torre dell'Orologio

Torre dell'Orologio ❷

Piazza San Marco. **Map** 7 B2. *San Marco. for restoration. Due to re-open in late 2004.*

THE RICHLY decorated Renaissance clock tower stands on the north side of the Piazza, over the archway leading to the Mercerie *(see p95)*. It was built in the late 15th century, and the central section is thought to have been designed by Mauro Coducci. Displaying the phases of the moon and the zodiac, the gilt and blue enamel clock was originally designed with seafarers in mind. A story was spread by scandalmongers that once the clock was complete, the two inventors of the complex clock mechanism had their eyes gouged out to prevent them creating a replica.

The clock mechanism is currently on display in the Doge's Palace, awaiting the completion of restoration work at the tower. During Ascension Week, when working, the clock draws large crowds who watch the figures of the Magi emerge from side doors to pay their respects to the Virgin and Child, whose figures are set above the clock. At the very top two huge bronze figures, known as the *Mori*, or Moors, strike the bell on the hour.

Basilica San Marco ❸

See pp78–83.

Doge's Palace ❹

See pp84–9.

Libreria Sansoviniana ❺

Piazzetta. **Map** 7 B3. *041 520 87 88.* *San Marco.* *9am–7pm daily.* *public hols.*

PRAISED BY Andrea Palladio as the finest building since antiquity, the library was designed in the Classical style by the Tuscan architect Jacopo Sansovino. A graceful building, it is surmounted by a procession of statues of mythological gods. During construction (1537–88) the vaulting collapsed: Sansovino was blamed and imprisoned. He was freed after appeals from eminent acquaintances, but had to reconstruct the building at his own expense.

At the top of the monumental stairway *(see p75)*, behind a booth, is a rare example of Jacopo de' Barbari's bird's-eye map of Venice dating to 1500.

The salon is sumptuously decorated, and two fine ceiling paintings by Paolo Veronese, *Arithmetic and Geometry* and *Music*, won for the artist the prize of a golden necklace.

Museo Archeologico ❻

Piazzetta (entrance Ala Napoleonica). **Map** 7 B3. *041 522 59 78.* *San Marco.* *9am–8pm daily.* *1 Jan, 25 Dec.*

HOUSED IN ROOMS in both the Libreria Sansoviniana and the Procuratie Nuove, the museum provides a quiet retreat from the bustle of San Marco. The collection owes its existence to the generosity of Domenico Grimani, son of Doge Antonio Grimani, who bequeathed all of his Greek, Roman and earlier sculpture, together with his library, to the State in 1523.

Columns of San Marco and San Teodoro ❼

Piazzetta. **Map** 7 C3. *San Marco.*

ALONG WITH ALL the bounty from Constantinople came the two huge granite columns which now tower above the Piazzetta. These were said to have been erected in 1172 by the engineer Nicolò Barattieri, architect of the very first Rialto Bridge. For his efforts he was granted the right to set up gambling tables between the columns. A more gruesome spectacle on the same spot was the execution of criminals, which took place here until the mid-18th century. Even today, superstitious Venetians will not be seen walking between the columns.

Columns of San Marco and San Teodoro

The western column is crowned by a marble statue of St Theodore, who was the patron saint of Venice before St Mark's relics were smuggled from Alexandria in AD 828. The statue is a modern copy – the original is kept for safety in the Doge's Palace *(see p88)*.

The second column is surmounted by a huge bronze of the Lion of St Mark. Its origin remains a mystery, though it is thought to be a Chinese chimera with wings added to make it look like a Venetian lion. In September 1990 the 3,000-kg (3-ton) beast went to the British Museum in London for extensive restoration, and was returned with great ceremony and skill to the top of the column.

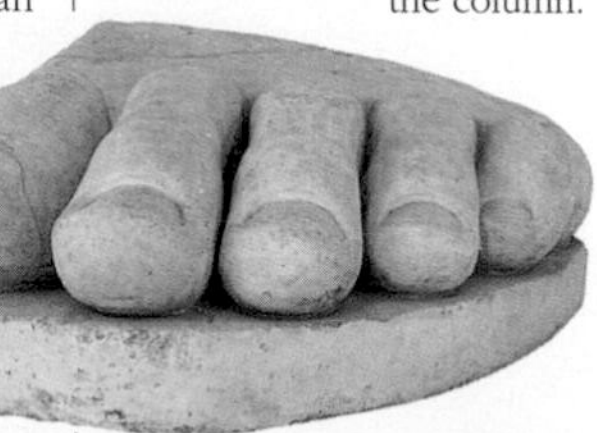

Fragment from a monumental statue, in the Museo Archeologico

***A Portrait of a Young Man in a Red Hat* by Carpaccio (c.1490)**

Museo Correr ❽

Procuratie Nuove. Entrance in Ala Napoleonica. **Map** 7 B2. *041 522 56 25.* *San Marco.* *9am–7pm daily (to 5pm Nov–Mar).* *1 Jan, 25 Dec.* *allows access to Libreria Sansoviniana & Museo Archeologico.*

THE WEALTHY Abbot Teodoro Correr's extensive collection of works of art and documents forms the nucleus of the civic museum.

The first rooms form a suitably Neo-Classical backdrop for early statues by Antonio Canova (1757–1822). The rest of the floor covers the history of the Venetian Republic, with maps, coins, armour and a host of doge-related exhibits.

On the second floor, the Museo del Risorgimento is devoted to the history of the city, until Venice became part of unified Italy in 1866. Also here is the Quadreria, or picture gallery. The paintings are hung chronologically and the rooms have the bonus of explanations in English. The collection enables you to trace the evolution of Venetian painting, and to see the influence that Ferrarese, Paduan and Flemish artists had on the Venetian school. The most famous works in the gallery are the Carpaccios: *A Portrait of a Young Man in a Red Hat* (c.1490), and *Two Venetian Ladies* (c.1507). The latter is traditionally, but probably incorrectly, known as *The Courtesans* because of the ladies' décolleté dresses.

Basilica San Marco ❸

THIS AWESOME BASILICA, built on a Greek cross plan and crowned with five huge domes, is the third church to stand on this site. The first, built to enshrine the body of St Mark in the 9th century, was destroyed by fire. The second was pulled down in the 11th century in order to make way for a more spectacular edifice designed by an unknown architect (1063–94), reflecting the escalating power of the Republic. The basilica continued to be remodelled over the following centuries, and in 1807 it succeeded San Pietro in the *sestiere* of Castello *(see p120)* as the cathedral of Venice; it had until then served as the doge's private chapel for State ceremonies.

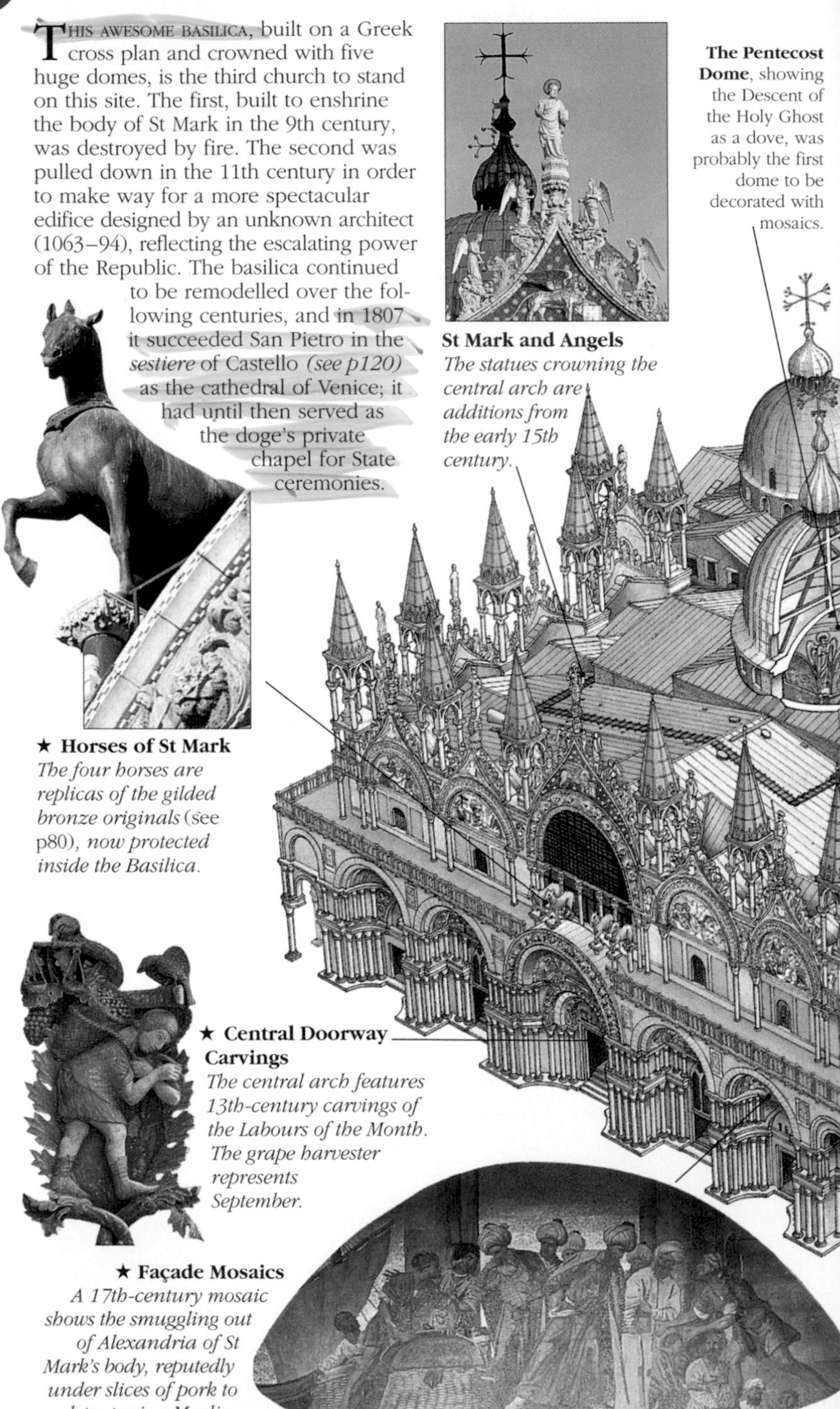

The Pentecost Dome, showing the Descent of the Holy Ghost as a dove, was probably the first dome to be decorated with mosaics.

St Mark and Angels
The statues crowning the central arch are additions from the early 15th century.

★ Horses of St Mark
The four horses are replicas of the gilded bronze originals (see p80), *now protected inside the Basilica.*

★ Central Doorway Carvings
The central arch features 13th-century carvings of the Labours of the Month. The grape harvester represents September.

★ Façade Mosaics
A 17th-century mosaic shows the smuggling out of Alexandria of St Mark's body, reputedly under slices of pork to deter prying Muslims.

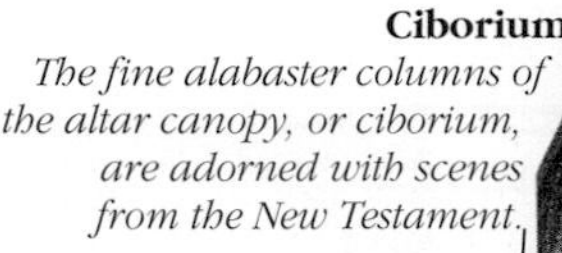

Ciborium
The fine alabaster columns of the altar canopy, or ciborium, are adorned with scenes from the New Testament.

The Ascension Dome features a magnificent 13th-century mosaic of Christ surrounded by angels, the 12 Apostles and the Virgin Mary.

St Mark's body, believed lost in the fire of AD 976, supposedly reappeared when the new church was consecrated in 1094. The remains are housed in the altar.

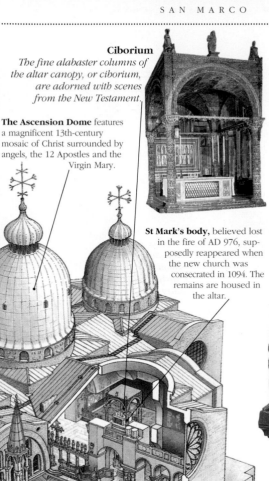

VISITORS' CHECKLIST

Piazza San Marco. **Map** 7 B2. 041 522 52 05. *San Marco.* **Basilica, Treasury and Pala d'Oro** *Apr–Sep: 9:30am–5pm Mon–Sat, 2–4pm Sun; Oct–Mar: 10am–4pm Mon–Sat, 2–4pm Sun.* *for Treasury only.* **Museum** *10am–4pm daily.* *Museum, Treasury and Pala d'Oro only.* *9 times a day. Sightseeing is limited during services.* *in English twice a week in season.*

★ The Tetrarchs
This charming sculptured group in porphyry (4th-century Egyptian) is thought to represent Diocletian, Maximian, Valerian and Constance. Collectively they were the tetrarchs, appointed by Diocletian to help rule the Roman Empire.

Allegorical mosaics

St Mark's Treasury

The so-called Pilasters of Acre in fact came from a 6th-century church in Constantinople.

Baptistry

Baptistry Mosaics
Herod's Banquet *(1343–54) is one of the mosaics in a cycle of scenes from the life of St John the Baptist.*

STAR FEATURES

- ★ **Façade Mosaics**
- ★ **Horses of St Mark**
- ★ **The Tetrarchs**
- ★ **Central Doorway Carvings**

Inside the Basilica

Dark, mysterious and enriched with the spoils of conquest, the Basilica is a unique blend of Eastern and Western influences. This oriental extravaganza, embellished over a period of six centuries with fabulous mosaics, marble and carvings, made a fitting location for the ceremonies of the Serene Republic. It was here that the doge was presented to the city following his election, that heads of State, popes, princes and ambassadors were received, and where sea captains came to pray for protection before embarking on epic voyages.

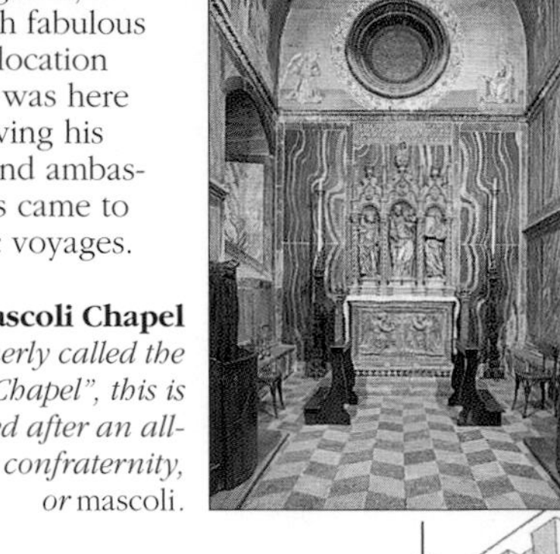

Mascoli Chapel
Formerly called the "New Chapel", this is named after an all-male confraternity, or mascoli.

North Aisle
The gallery leading off the museum affords visitors a splendid overall view of the mosaics.

The Porta dei Fiori or Gate of Flowers is decorated with 13th-century reliefs.

★ Pentecost Dome
Showing the Apostles touched by tongues of flame, the Pentecost Dome was decorated in the 12th century.

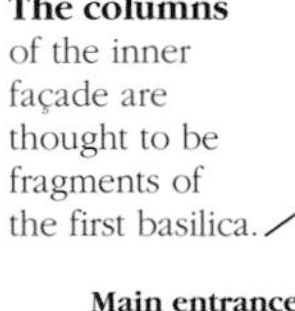

The columns of the inner façade are thought to be fragments of the first basilica.

Main entrance

★ Atrium Mosaics
In the glittering Genesis Cupola the Creation of the World is described in concentric circles. Here, God creates the fish and birds.

The baptistry is also called Chiesa dei Putti (church of the cherubs).

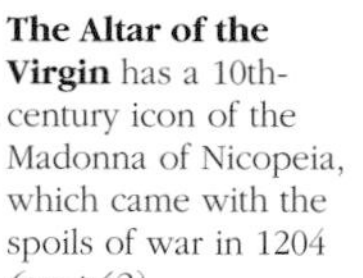

The Altar of the Virgin has a 10th-century icon of the Madonna of Nicopeia, which came with the spoils of war in 1204 *(see p42).*

The Chapel of St Peter has a 14th-century altar screen relief of St Peter worshipped by two Procurators.

★ Pala d'Oro
The magnificent altarpiece, created in the 10th century by medieval goldsmiths, is made up of 250 panels such as this one, each adorned with enamels and precious stones.

The sacristy door (always locked) has fine bronze panels by Sansovino, including portraits of himself with Titian and Aretino.

★ Ascension Dome
A mosaic of Christ in Glory decorates the enormous central dome. This masterpiece was created by 13th-century Venetian craftsmen, who were strongly influenced by the art and architecture of Byzantium.

The Altar of the Sacrament is surrounded by mosaics of the parables and miracles of Christ dating from the late 12th or early 13th century.

South aisle

★ Treasury
A repository for precious booty from Constantinople, the Treasury also houses ancient Italian works of art, such as this 12th- or 13th-century incense burner.

Star Features

- **★ Pala d'Oro**
- **★ Atrium Mosaics**
- **★ Treasury**
- **★ Ascension and Pentecost Domes**

Exploring the Basilica

THE BASILICA cannot comfortably be covered in one visit. The mosaics, the rich store of eastern bounty, the mysterious lighting and the sheer size of the place create a feeling of confusion for first-time visitors. Make several visits, ideally at different times of the day. The mosaics look especially splendid when the church is fully illuminated (11:30am–12:30pm Mon–Fri, 11:30am–4pm Sat, 2–4pm Sun). Visitors with organized tours are often led towards the Pala d'Oro and Treasury and miss out on other sections of the church. Avoid the crowds by visiting early in the morning or in the evening. If a mass is in progress you will be expected to be silent and will only be able to visit certain areas.

The Genesis Cupola of the atrium

Mosaics

CLOTHING THE DOMES, walls and floor of the basilica are over 4,000 sq m (40,000 sq ft) of gleaming golden mosaics. The earliest, dating from the 12th century, were the work of mosaicists from the east. Their techniques were adopted by Venetian craftsmen who gradually took over the decoration, combining Byzantine inspiration with western influences. During the 16th century, sketches and cartoons by Tintoretto, Titian, Veronese, and other leading artists were reproduced in mosaic. The original iconographical scheme, depicting stories from the Testaments, has more or less been preserved by careful restoration.

Among the finest mosaics in the basilica are those decorating the 13th-century central Dome of the Ascension and the 12th-century Dome of the Pentecost over the nave.

The *pavimento*, or basilica floor, spreads out like an undulating Turkish carpet. Mosaics, made of marble, porphyry and glass are used to create complex and colourful geometric patterns and beautiful scenes of beasts and birds. Some of these scenes are allegorical. The one in the left transept of two cocks carrying a fox on a stick was designed to symbolize cunning vanquished by vigilance.

Atrium (Vestibule)

THE 13TH-CENTURY mosaics decorating the cupolas, vaults and lunettes of the atrium are among the finest in the basilica. The scenes depict Old Testament stories, starting at the southern end with the Genesis Cupola (showing 26 detailed episodes of the Creation), to the Stories of Joseph and of Moses in the domes at the north end. The figures of saints on either side of the main doorway date from the 11th century and are among the earliest mosaics in the church. Just in front of the central doorway there is a lozenge of porphyry to mark the spot where the Emperor Frederick Barbarossa was obliged to make peace with Pope Alexander III in 1177 *(see p41)*.

Museo Marciano

A PRECARIOUS STAIRWAY from the atrium, marked *Loggia dei Cavalli*, takes you up to the church museum. The gallery gives a splendid view into the basilica, while from the exterior loggia you can survey the Piazza San Marco and take a close look at the replica horses on the church façade. It was from this panoramic balcony that doges and dignitaries once looked down on ceremonies taking place in the square. The original gilded bronze horses, housed in a room at the far end of the museum, were stolen from the top of the Hippodrome (ancient racecourse) in Constantinople in 1204 but their origin, either Roman or Hellenistic, remains a mystery. In the same room is Paolo Veneziano's 14th-century *pala feriale*, painted with stories of St Mark, which once covered the Pala d'Oro. Also on show are medieval

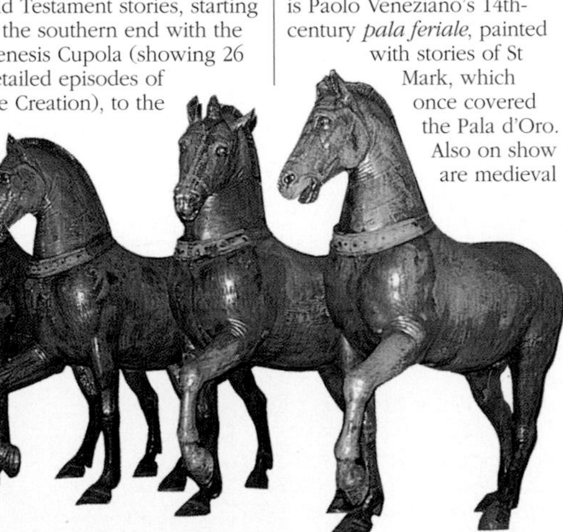

The Quadriga, the original gilded bronze horses in the museum

Noah and the Flood – atrium mosaics from the 13th century

illuminated manuscripts, fragments of ancient mosaics and antique tapestries.

SANCTUARY AND PALA D'ORO

BEYOND THE CHAPEL of St Clement, tickets are sold to view the most valuable treasure of San Marco: the Pala d'Oro. This jewel-spangled altarpiece situated behind the high altar consists of 250 enamel paintings on gold foil, enclosed within a gilded silver Gothic frame. Originally commissioned in Byzantium in AD 976, the altarpiece was embellished over the centuries. Following the fall of the Republic, Napoleon helped himself to some of the precious stones, but the screen still gleams with pearls, rubies, sapphires and amethysts.

The iconostasis, the screen dividing nave from chancel, is adorned with marble Gothic statues of the Virgin and Apostles, and was carved in 1394 by the Dalle Masegne brothers. Above the high altar the imposing green marble baldacchino is supported by finely carved alabaster columns featuring scenes from the New Testament.

Statue of St Mark on the iconostasis

The archangel Michael, a Byzantine icon from the 11th century in the Treasury

BAPTISTRY AND CHAPELS

THE BAPTISTRY (closed to the public) was added in the 14th century by Doge Andrea Dandolo (1343–54) who is buried here. Under his direction the baptistry was decorated with outstanding mosaics depicting scenes from the lives of Christ and John the Baptist. Sansovino, who designed the font, is buried by the altar.

The adjoining Zen Chapel (currently closed to the public) originally formed part of the atrium. It became a funeral chapel for Cardinal Zen in 1504 in return for his bequest to the State.

In the left transept of the basilica the Chapel of St Isidore, normally accessible only for worship, was also built by Dandolo. Mosaics in the barrel vault ceiling tell the tale of the saint, whose body was stolen from the island of Chios and transported to Venice in 1125. To its left the Mascoli Chapel, used in the early 17th century by the confraternity of Mascoli (men), is decorated with scenes from the life of the Virgin Mary. The altarpiece has statues depicting the Virgin and Child between St Mark and St John.

The third chapel in the left transept is home to the icon of the Madonna of Nicopeia. Looted in 1204, she was formerly carried into battle at the head of the Byzantine army.

The revered icon of the Nicopeia Madonna, once a war insignia

TREASURY

ALTHOUGH PLUNDERED after the fall of the Republic and much depleted by the fund-raising sale of jewels in the early 19th century, the treasury nevertheless has a precious collection of Byzantine silver, gold and glasswork. Today, most of the treasures are housed in a room whose remarkably thick walls are believed to have been a 9th-century tower of the Doge's Palace. Exhibits include chalices, goblets, reliquaries, two intricate icons of the archangel Michael and an 11th-century silver-gilt reliquary made in the form of a five-domed basilica *(see p81)*. The sanctuary, with over 100 reliquaries, is normally open to the public.

Doge's Palace ❹

THE PALAZZO DUCALE started life in the 9th century as a fortified castle, but this and several subsequent buildings were destroyed by a series of fires. The existing palace owes its external appearance to the building work of the 14th and early 15th centuries. The designers broke with tradition by perching the bulk of the pink Verona marble palace on lace-like Istrian stone arcades, with a portico supported by columns below. The result is a light and airy masterpiece of Gothic architecture.

Arco Foscari
The Adam and Eve figures on this triumphal arch in the courtyard are copies of the 15th-century originals by Antonio Rizzo.

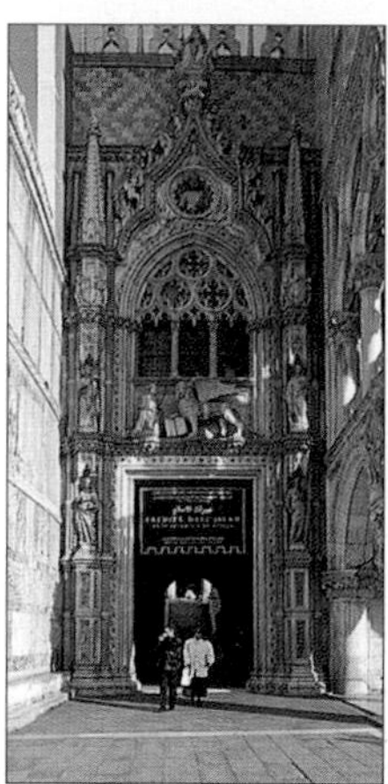

★ Porta della Carta
This 15th-century Gothic gate was the principal entrance to the palace. From it, a vaulted passageway leads to the Arco Foscari and the internal courtyard.

Exit

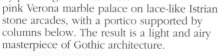

STAR FEATURES

- **★ Giants' Staircase**
- **★ Porta della Carta**

The balcony on the west façade was added in 1536 to mirror the early 15th-century balcony looking on to the quay.

★ Giants' Staircase
This late 15th-century staircase by Antonio Rizzo was used for ceremonial purposes. It was on the landing at the top that the doges were crowned with the glittering zogia.

Torture Chamber
"The court of the room of the Cord" recalls the practice of interrogating suspects as they hung by their wrists.

Bridge of Sighs
The famous bridge once crossed by offenders on their way to the State interrogators.

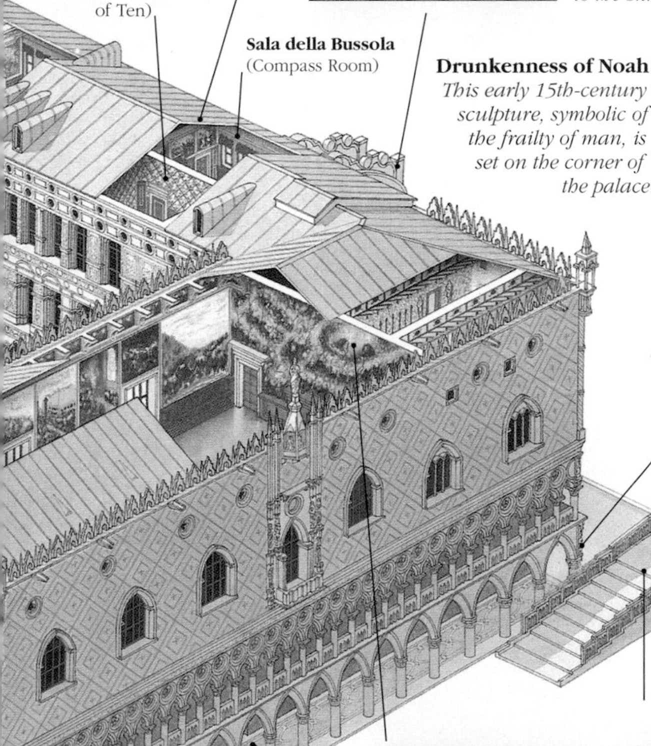

VISITORS' CHECKLIST

Piazzetta. **Map** 7 C2. *041 522 49 51.* *San Marco.* *9am–7pm daily (Nov–Mar: to 5pm).* ***Last adm****: 90 mins before closing.* ***Secret Itineraries*** *(in English, 10am & 11:30am daily): book in advance at palace or phone* *041 522 49 51. To book more than two days ahead:* *041 520 90 70.* *1 Jan, 25 Dec.* *partial.*

Sala dei Tre Capi
(Chamber of the Three Heads of the Council of Ten)

Sala della Bussola
(Compass Room)

Drunkenness of Noah
This early 15th-century sculpture, symbolic of the frailty of man, is set on the corner of the palace.

Ponte della Paglia
(see p113)

Main entrance

Adam and Eve
with the serpent are depicted in stone on the corner of the Piazzetta.

Sala del Maggior Consiglio
An entire wall of the Great Council Hall is taken up by Domenico and Jacopo Tintoretto's Paradise *(1588–92).*

Inside the Doge's Palace

Intricate carved Gothic capital

From the early days of the Republic, the Doge's Palace was the seat of the government, the Palace of Justice and the home of the doge. For centuries this was the only building in Venice entitled to the name palazzo (the others were merely called Ca', short for Casa). The power of the Serenissima is ever present in the large and allegorical historical paintings which embellish the walls and ceilings of the splendid halls and chambers. These ornate rooms are testament to the glory of the Venetian Republic, and were designed to impress and overawe visiting ambassadors and dignitaries.

Colonnade
Sunlight streams through the arches of the Loggia on the first floor of the palace.

Star Features

- ★ **Sala del Maggior Consiglio**
- ★ **Collegiate Rooms**
- ★ **Prisons**

Mars
The Giants' Staircase is named after Sansovino's monumental figures, statues of Mars and Neptune, sculpted in 1567.

Scala d'Oro
Sansovino's lavish staircase was built between 1554 and 1558. The arched ceiling is embellished with gilded stucco by Alessandro Vittoria.

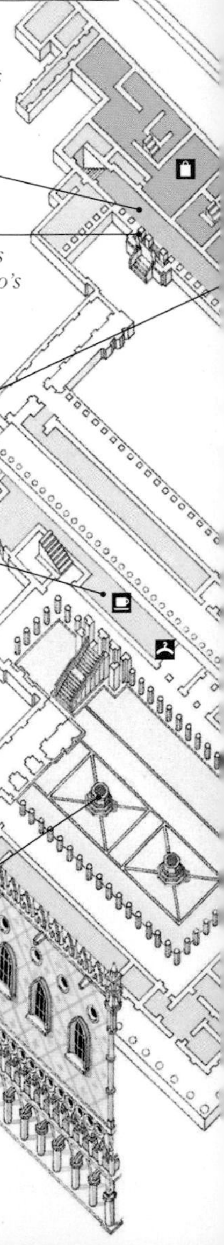

Ground floor

Exit through Porta della Carta

Key to Floorplan

- State Apartments
- Collegium and Senate Rooms
- Council of Ten and Armoury
- Great Council Rooms
- Prisons
- Non-exhibition space

Wellhead
The two 16th-century bronze wellheads in the courtyard are considered to be the finest in Venice.

★ Collegiate Rooms
Bacchus and Ariadne Crowned by Venus *is the finest of four mythological scenes by Tintoretto in the Anticollegio.*

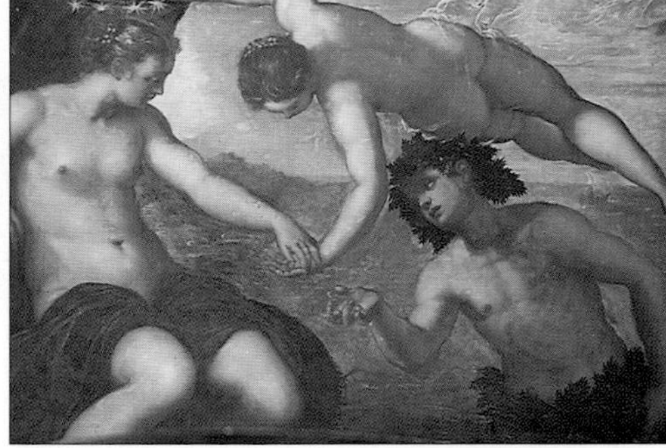

Third floor

The Sala del Consiglio dei Dieci has a ceiling decorated with paintings by Veronese (1553–4).

Sala dello Scudo
The walls of this room are covered with maps of the world. In the centre are two huge 18th-century globes.

First floor

Second floor

★ Sala del Maggior Consiglio
The first 76 doges, with the exception of the traitor Marin Falier, are portrayed on a frieze round the upper walls of the room.

★ Prisons
These 16th-century cells were mainly used for petty offenders. Serious criminals were lodged in the dank pozzi *(wells).*

The Secret Itinerary

The fascinating, though poorly publicized, Secret Itinerary (Itinerari Segreti) tour (*see* Visitors' Checklist *p85*) takes you behind the scenes in the palace to the offices and Hall of the Chancellery, the State Inquisitors' room, the Torture Chamber and the prisons.
It was from these cells that Casanova made his spectacular escape in 1755. Tours are available in Italian, English and French. Each is limited to 25 people and lasts for 75 minutes.

Casanova's cell door

Exploring the Doge's Palace

A TOUR OF THE PALACE takes you through a succession of richly decorated chambers and halls. The rooms are on four levels, and they all have name boards carrying an explanation of their function in Italian and English. The latest equipment available is an up-to-date infrared audioguide, which you can hire for a commentary on the whole palace or just the areas that interest you.

Allow plenty of time for the visit, and take a break at the coffee shop. Located at water level, it affords evocative views of gondolas gliding past in the canal.

St Theodore in the palace courtyard

COURTYARD

THE COURTYARD is reached via a vaulted passage from the Porta del Frumento. At the top of the Giants' Staircase, on the opposite side of the courtyard, new doges were crowned with the *zogia* or dogal cap.

SCALA D'ORO AND STATE APARTMENTS

THE SUMPTUOUS Scala d'Oro (golden staircase), built between 1538 and 1559, was designed by Jacopo Sansovino. It takes its name, however, from the elaborate gilt stucco vault, which was added by Alessandro Vittoria (1554–8). The doge's private apartments on the second floor were built after the fire of 1483 and later looted on the orders of Napoleon. They are bare of furnishings, but the lavish ceilings and colossal carved chimneypieces in some of the rooms give you an idea of the doges' lifestyle. The most ornate is the Sala degli Scarlatti, with a richly carved gilt ceiling, a fireplace (c.1501) designed by Antonio and Tullio Lombardo and a relief (1501–21) by Pietro Lombardo of Doge Leonardo Loredan at the feet of the Virgin.

The Sala dello Scudo, or map room, contains maps and charts. The picture gallery further on features works by Vittore Carpaccio and Giovanni Bellini, and some incongruous wooden demoniac panels by Hieronymous Bosch.

A *bocca di leone* used for denouncing tax evaders

Veronese's *Dialectic* (c.1577), Sala del Collegio

SALA DELLE QUATTRO PORTE TO SALA DEL SENATO

THE SECOND FLIGHT of the Scala d'Oro leads to the third floor and its council chambers. The first room, the Sala delle Quattro Porte, was completely rebuilt after the 1574 fire, its ceiling designed by Andrea Palladio and frescoed by Tintoretto.

The next room, the Anticollegio, was the waiting room. The end walls are decorated with mythological scenes by Tintoretto: *Vulcan's Forge*; *Mercury and the Graces*; *Bacchus and Ariadne* and *Minerva Dismissing Mars*, all painted in 1578. Veronese's masterly *Rape of Europa* (1580), opposite the window, is one of the most eyecatching works in the palace.

Off the Anticollegio, the Sala del Collegio was the hall where the doge and his counsellors met to receive ambassadors and discuss matters of State. Embellishing the magnificent ceiling are 11 paintings by Veronese (c.1577), of which the most notable – in the centre, far end – is *Justice and Peace Offering Sword, Scales and Olive Branch to Venice*.

It was in the next room, the Sala del Senato, that the doge would sit with some 200 senators to discuss matters such as foreign affairs or nominations of ambassadors. The wall and ceiling paintings, by pupils of Tintoretto or the master himself, are further propaganda for the Republic.

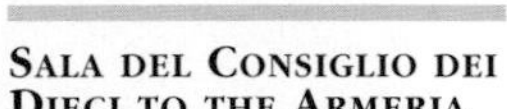

SALA DEL CONSIGLIO DEI DIECI TO THE ARMERIA

THE ROUTE RETURNS through the Sala delle Quattro Porte to the Sala del Consiglio dei Dieci. This was the meeting room of the awesomely powerful Council of Ten, founded in 1310 to investigate and prosecute crimes concerning the security of the State. Napoleon pilfered some of the Veroneses from the ceiling but two of the finest found their way back here in 1920: *Age and Youth* and *Juno Offering the Ducal Crown to Venice* (both 1553–54).

In the next room, the Sala della Bussola, offenders awaited their fate in front of the Council of Ten. The room's *bocca di leone* (lion's mouth), used to post secret denunciations, was just one of several within the palace. The wooden door here leads to the rooms of the Heads of the Ten, the State Inquisitors' Room and thence to the torture chamber and prisons. This is the route taken by those on the Secret Itinerary.

Age and Youth (1553–54) by Veronese

Others follow the flow to the Armoury – one of the finest collections in Europe, thanks in part to bequests by European monarchs.

Sala del Maggior Consiglio

Another staircase, the Scala dei Censori, takes you down again to the second floor, along the hallway and past the Sala del Guariento with fresco fragments of *The Coronation of the Virgin* by Guariento (1365–67). From the *liagò*, or veranda, where Antonio Rizzo's marble statues of Adam and Eve (1480s) are displayed, you pass into the magnificent Sala del Maggior Consiglio or Hall of the Great Council. A chamber of monumental proportions, it was here that the Great Council convened to vote on constitutional questions, to pass laws and elect the top officials of the Serene Republic. The hall was also used for State banquets. When Henry III of France paid a royal visit, 3,000 guests were entertained in this spectacular room.

By the mid-16th century the Great Council had around 2,000 members. Any Venetian of high birth over 25 was entitled to a seat – with the exception of those married to a commoner. From 1646, by which time the Turkish wars had depleted state coffers, nobility from the *terra firma* or those from merchant or professional classes with 100,000 ducats to spare could purchase their way in.

Tintoretto's huge, highly restored work called *Paradise* (1587–90) occupies the eastern wall. Measuring 7.45 by 24.65 m (25 by 81 ft) it is one of the largest paintings in the world. For a man in his late seventies, albeit assisted by his son, it is a remarkably vigorous composition.

The ceiling of the hall is decorated with panels glorifying the Republic. One of the finest is Veronese's *Apotheosis of Venice* (1583). A frieze along the walls illustrates 76 doges by Tintoretto's pupils. The portrait covered by a curtain is Marin Falier, beheaded for treason in 1355. The other 42 doges are portrayed in the Sala dello Scrutinio, where new doges were nominated.

Prisons

View of the lagoon through a grille on the Bridge of Sighs

From the Sala del Maggior Consiglio a series of passageways and stairways leads to the Bridge of Sighs *(see p113)* which links the palace to what were known as the New Prisons, built between 1556 and 1595.

Situated at the top of the palace, just below the leaded roof, are the *piombi* cells (*piombo* means lead). These cells are hardly inviting but prisoners here were far more comfortable than the criminals who were left to fester in the *pozzi* – the dark dank dungeons at ground level. The windowless cells of these ancient prisons are still covered with the graffiti of the convicts. Visitors on the Secret Itinerary tour are shown Casanova's cell in the *piombi* and told of how he made his daring escape from the palace through a hole in the roof.

Visits end with the offices of the Avogaria, where the state prosecutors *(avogadori)* prepared the trials.

The splendid Sala del Maggior Consiglio, the hall of the Great Council

Street-by-Street: Around La Fenice

West of the huge expanse of the ever-crowded Piazza San Marco there is a labyrinth of alleys to explore. At the centre of this part of the *sestiere* is Campo San Fantin, flanked by the Renaissance church of San Fantin. Nearby is the Ateneo Veneto, formerly a *scuola* whose members had the unenviable role of escorting prisoners to the scaffold. The narrow streets around these sights have some wonderfully exotic little shops, while the more recent Calle Larga XXII Marzo further south boasts big names in Italian fashion. The quarter in general has some excellent restaurants but, being San Marco, you will find that prices in the majority of establishments are steep.

Campo San Fantin has a late Renaissance church, San Fantin, with a particularly beautiful apse designed by Jacopo Sansovino.

★ La Fenice
The opera house gained its name (the phoenix) after a fire in 1836. Sadly, it was again destroyed by fire in 1996 ⓮

The Rio delle Veste leads past the rear of the theatre. This is the route taken by those fortunate enough to arrive for their night out by gondola.

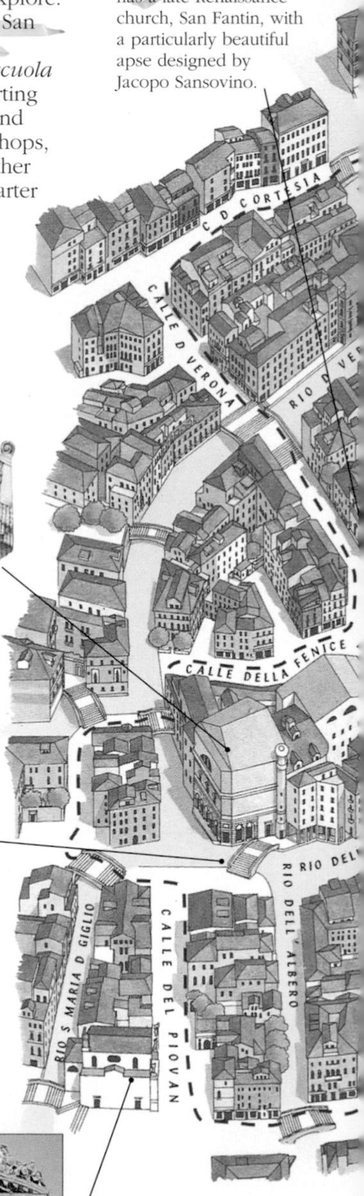

Key

— — — Suggested route

0 metres 75

0 yards 75

Star Sights

- ★ La Fenice
- ★ San Moisè

Santa Maria Zobenigo
The carvings feature the Barbaro family who paid for the church façade. Ground-level reliefs show towns where the family held high ranking posts ⓭

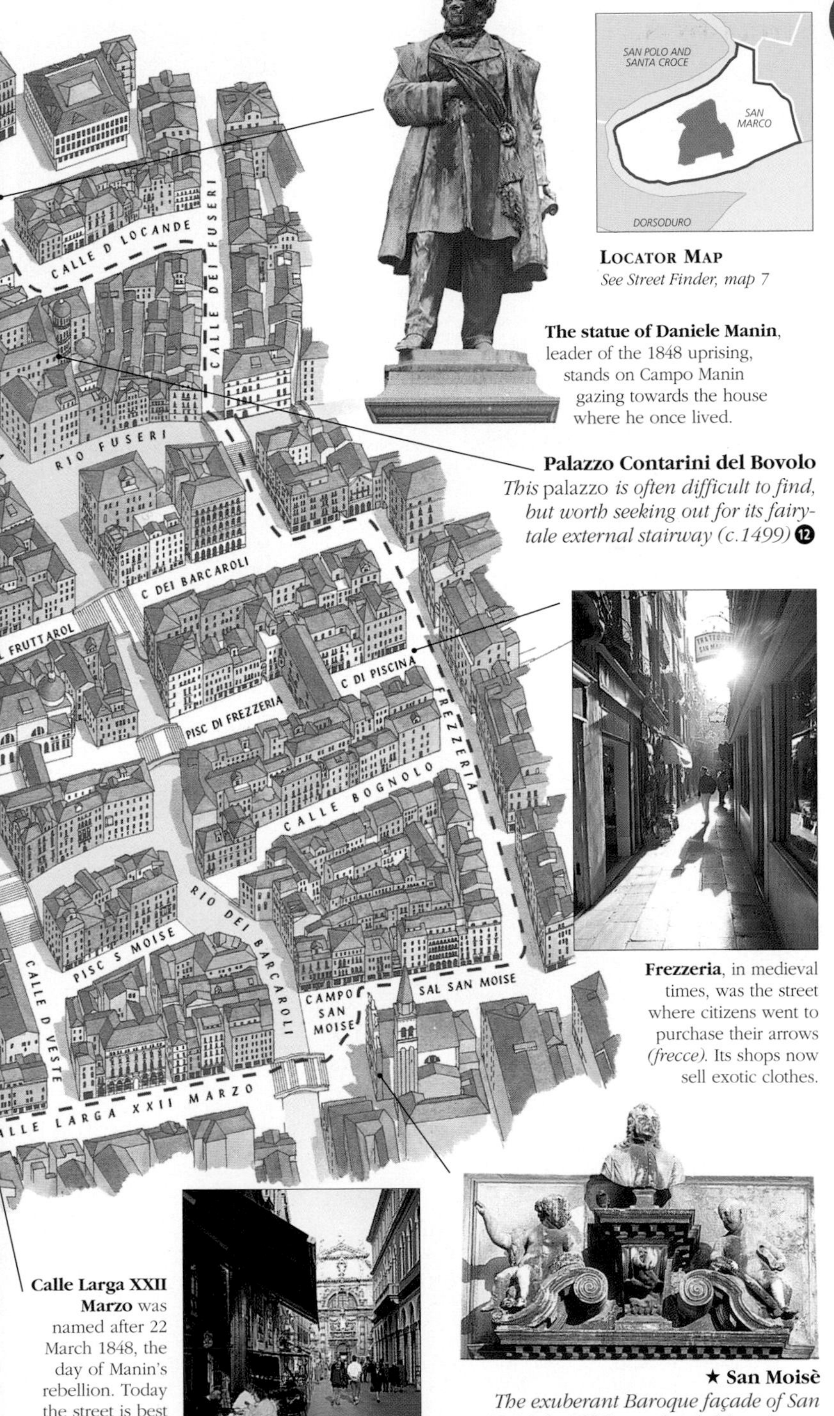

Locator Map
See Street Finder, map 7

The statue of Daniele Manin, leader of the 1848 uprising, stands on Campo Manin gazing towards the house where he once lived.

Palazzo Contarini del Bovolo
This palazzo *is often difficult to find, but worth seeking out for its fairy-tale external stairway (c.1499)* ⓬

Frezzeria, in medieval times, was the street where citizens went to purchase their arrows *(frecce)*. Its shops now sell exotic clothes.

Calle Larga XXII Marzo was named after 22 March 1848, the day of Manin's rebellion. Today the street is best known for its trendy designer boutiques.

★ San Moisè
The exuberant Baroque façade of San Moisè (c.1668) was funded by a legacy from the patrician Vincenzo Fini, whose bust features above a side door ⓫

Harry's Bar ❾

Calle Vallaresso 1323. **Map** 7 B3. *San Marco. See also* **Restaurants, Cafés and Bars** *pp246–7.*

Celebrated for cocktails, *carpaccio* and American clientèle, Harry's Bar is famous throughout Venice. Founded in 1931 by the late Giuseppe Cipriani, it was financed by a Bostonian called Harry who thought Venice had a dearth of decent bars. They chose a storeroom at the Grand Canal end of the Calle Vallaresso as their location, conveniently close to the Piazza San Marco. Since then, the bar has seen a steady stream of American visitors, among them Ernest Hemingway who used to come here after shooting in the lagoon. The bar became the most popular venue in Venice, patronized by royalty, film stars and heads of state.

These days there are far more American tourists than famous figures, often there to sample the Bellini cocktail that Cipriani invented *(see p239)*. Aesthetically, the place is unremarkable and there is no terrace for meals alfresco.

Ernest Hemingway, a regular at Harry's Bar

Ridotto ❿

Calle del Ridotto, 1332 San Marco. **Map** 7 B3. *San Marco.* *to hotel guests.*

In an effort to control the gambling mania that swept Venice in the 1600s, the State allowed Marco Dandolo to use his palace as the first public gaming house in Europe. In 1638 the Ridotto was opened, with the proviso that players came disguised in a mask. In 1774 the Great Council closed the casino's doors on account of the number of Venetians ruined at its tables.

In 1947 the old Palazzo Dandolo was converted into a theatre that staged Italian plays. Now beautifully restored, it is part of the Hotel Monaco and Grand Canal *(see p229)*.

San Moisè ⓫

Campo San Moisè. **Map** 7 A3. *041 528 58 40.* *San Marco.* *3:30–7pm daily.*

One of the churches in Venice that people love to hate, San Moisè displays a ponderous Baroque façade. Completed in 1668, it is covered in grimy statues, swags and busts. John Ruskin, in a characteristic anti-Baroque outrage, described it as the clumsiest church in Venice. The interior has a mixed collection of paintings and sculpture from the 17th and 18th centuries. In the nave is the tombstone of John Law, a financier from Scotland who founded the Compagnie d'Occident to develop the Mississippi Valley. His shares collapsed in 1770 in the notorious South Sea Bubble, and he fled to Venice, surviving on his winnings at the Ridotto.

Façade of San Moisè, encrusted with Baroque ornamentation

Palazzo Contarini del Bovolo ⓬

Corte Contarini del Bovolo, 4299 San Marco. **Map** 7 A2. *041 270 24 64.* *Rialto or Sant'Angelo.* *Apr–Oct: 10am–6pm daily; Nov–Dec: 10am–4pm Sat & Sun.*

Tucked away in a maze of alleys (follow signs from Campo Manin), this *palazzo* is best known for its graceful external stairway. In Venetian dialect *bovolo* means snail shell, appropriate to the spiral shape of the Lombardesque stairway. The Contarini, a learned family who had the 15th-century palace built, were known as "the philosophers". The collection of well-heads within the enclosure dates from the Byzantine era.

The external stairway of the Palazzo Contarini del Bovolo

Santa Maria Zobenigo ⓭

Campo Santa Maria del Giglio. **Map** 6 F3. *041 275 04 62.* *Santa Maria del Giglio.* *10am–5pm daily (from 1pm Sun & public hols).* *Sun (Jul & Aug); 1 Jan, 25 Dec.*

Named after the Jubanico family who are said to have founded it in the 9th century, this church is also referred to as "del Giglio" ("of the lily"). The exuberant Baroque façade was financed by the affluent Barbaro family and was used to glorify their naval and diplomatic achievements.

Inside is a tiny museum of church ornaments and paintings including *The Sacred Family* attributed to Rubens and two works by Tintoretto.

La Fenice ⓮

Campo San Fantin. **Map** 7 A3.
San Marco. *041 520 40 10 (PalaFenice booking office).*
Theatre *until further notice.*

THEATRE HOUSES were enormously popular in the 18th century and La Fenice, the city's oldest theatre, was no exception. Built in 1792 in Classical style, it was one of several privately owned theatres showing plays and operas to audiences from all strata of society. In December 1836 a fire destroyed the interior but a year later it was resurrected, just like the mythical bird, the phoenix *(fenice)* which is said to have arisen from its ashes.

Another fire in early 1996 again destroyed the theatre, except for its façade. While it is being rebuilt, La Fenice's season is being held at the Malibran Theatre near Rialto and at Palafenice, a temporary structure just outside the city.

Throughout the 19th century the name of La Fenice was linked with great Italian composers. The many operatic premières that took place here include Verdi's *La Traviata* (1853) and Rossini's *Tancredi* (1813) and *Semiramide* (1823). During the Austrian Occupation *(see p48)* red, white and green flowers, symbolizing the Italian flag, were thrown on stage, to shouts of "Viva Verdi" – the letters of the composer's name standing for Vittorio Emanuele Re d'Italia. More recently, the theatre saw premières of Stravinsky's *The Rake's Progress* (1951) and Britten's *Turn of the Screw* (1954).

Shop in Campo Santo Stefano selling antiques and masks

Campo Santo Stefano ⓯

Map 6 F3. *Accademia or Sant'Angelo.*

ALSO KNOWN as Campo Francesco Morosini after the 17th-century doge who once lived here, this *campo* is one of the most spacious in the city. Bullfights were staged until 1802, when a stand fell and killed some of the spectators. It was also a venue for balls and Carnival festivities. Today it is a pleasantly informal square where children play and visitors drink coffee in open-air cafés.

The central statue is Nicolò Tommaseo (1802–74), a Dalmatian scholar who was a central figure in the 1848 rebellion against the Austrians.

At the southern end of the square the austere-looking Palazzo Pisani, overlooking the Campiello Pisani, has been the Conservatory of Music since the end of the 19th century. Music wafts from its open windows all through the year. On the opposite side of the square No. 2945, Palazzo Loredan, is the home of the Venetian Institute of Sciences, Letters and Arts.

The ceiling of Santo Stefano, in the form of a ship's keel

Santo Stefano ⓰

Campo Santo Stefano. **Map** 6 F2.
041 275 04 62. *Accademia or Sant'Angelo.* *10am–5pm daily (from 1pm Sun & public hols).*
Sun (Jul & Aug); 1 Jan, 25 Dec.
Sacristy only.

DECONSECRATED six times on account of the violence that took place within its walls, Santo Stefano today is remarkably serene. Built in the 14th century and radically altered in the 15th, the church has a notable carved portal by Bartolomeo Bon and a campanile with a typical Venetian tilt. The interior has a splendid ship's keel ceiling, carved tie-beams and tall pillars of Veronese marble. The most notable works of art, including some paintings by Tintoretto, are housed in the damp sacristy.

La Fenice, destroyed by fire in 1996

Courtyard of the Palazzo Pesaro, where Fortuny lived

Museo Fortuny ⓱

Palazzo Pesaro degli Orfei, Campo San Beneto, San Marco 3780.
Map 6 F2. *041 520 09 95.*
Sant'Angelo. *for special exhibitions only, during restoration work.*

KNOWN PRINCIPALLY for his fantastic pleated silk dresses, Fortuny was also a painter, sculptor, set designer, photographer, and scientist. One of his inventions was the Fortuny Dome which is used in theatre performances to create the illusion of sky.

Mariano Fortuny y Madrazo, or Don Mariano as he liked to be called, was born in 1871 in Granada and moved to Venice in 1889. In the early 20th century he purchased the Palazzo Pesaro, a late Gothic *palazzo* which had originally been owned by the fabulously rich and influential Pesaro family. Fortuny spent the remainder of his life here and the house and its contents were bequeathed to the city by his wife in 1956.

The large rooms and *portego* make a splendid and appropriate setting for the precious Fortuny fabrics. Woven with gold and silver threads, these were created by Fortuny's reintroduction of Renaissance techniques and use of ancient dyes. The collection also includes paintings by Fortuny (less impressive than the fabrics), decorative panels and a few of the finely pleated, clinging silk dresses regarded as a milestone in early 20th-century women's fashion.

San Salvatore ⓲

Campo San Salvatore.
Map 7 B1. *041 270 24 64.*
Rialto.
9am–noon, 3–6pm, Mon–Fri.

THE INTERIOR of this church is a fine example of Venetian Renaissance architecture. If the main door is closed you can enter by the side entrance, which is squeezed between shops along the Mercerie. The present church was designed by Giorgio Spavento in the early 16th century, and continued by Tullio Lombardo and Jacopo Sansovino. The pictorial highlight is Titian's *Annunciation* (1566) over the third altar on the right. Nearby, Sansovino's monument to Doge Francesco Venier (1556–61) is one of several Mannerist tombs in the church.

On the high altar is Titian's *Transfiguration of Christ* (1560). The end of the right transept is dominated by a vast monument to Caterina Cornaro, Queen of Cyprus *(see p43)*. Executed by the sculptor Bernardino Contino in 1580–84, the tomb shows the queen handing over her kingdom to the doge.

Campo San Bartolomeo ⓳

Map 7 B1. *Rialto.*

CLOSE TO the Rialto, the square of San Bartolomeo bustles with life, particularly in the early evening when young Venetians rendezvous here. They meet at cafés, bars or by the statue of Carlo Goldoni (1707–93), Venice's prolific and most celebrated playwright. His statue, in a fitting spot for a writer who drew his inspiration from daily social intercourse, is by Antonio del Zotto (1883).

The beautiful Renaissance interior of the church of San Salvatore

St George and Dragon bas-relief on a corner of the Mercerie

Mercerie ⓴

Map 7 B2. *San Marco or Rialto.*

DIVIDED INTO the Merceria dell'Orologio, Merceria di San Zulian and Merceria di San Salvatore, this is, and always has been, a principal shopping thoroughfare. Linking Piazza San Marco with the Rialto, it is made from a string of narrow, bustling alleys, lined by small shops and boutiques. The 17th-century English author John Evelyn described it as "the most delicious streete in the World for the sweetnesse of it . . . tapisstry'd as it were, with Cloth of Gold, rich Damasks & other silk." He wrote of perfumers, apothecary shops and nightingales in cages. Today all this has been replaced with fashions, footwear and glass.

At the southern end, the relief over the first archway on the left portrays the woman who in 1310 accidentally stopped a revolt. She dropped her pestle out of the window, killing the standard-bearer of a rebel army. They retreated, and the woman was given a guarantee that her rent would never be raised.

Bronze statue of Tommaso Rangone

San Zulian ㉑

Campo San Zulian. **Map** 7 B2. *San Marco.* *041 523 53 83.* *9am–noon, 3–6pm daily (closes earlier in winter).* *in English: 9:30am Sun (May–Sep).*

ON THE BUSY Mercerie, the church of San Zulian (or Giuliano) provides a refuge from the crowded alleys. Its interior features gilded woodwork, 16th- and 17th-century paintings, and sculpture.

The central panel of the frescoed ceiling portrays *The Apotheosis of St Julian*, painted in 1585 by Palma il Giovane.

The 16th-century church façade was designed by Sansovino and financed by the rich and immodest physician Tommaso Rangone. His bronze statue, surrounded by books, stands out against the white Istrian stone walls.

San Giorgio Maggiore ㉒

Map 8 D4. *041 522 78 27.* *San Giorgio.* *9:30am–12:30pm, 2:30–5pm (later in summer).* ***Campanile*** *9:30am–12:30pm, 2:30– 5pm (later in summer).* ***Foundation*** *041 528 99 00.* *Mon–Fri by appointment.*

APPEARING LIKE a stage set across the water from the Piazzetta, the little island of San Giorgio Maggiore has been captured on canvas countless times.

The church and monastery, built between 1559–80, are among Andrea Palladio's greatest architectural achievements. The church's temple front and the spacious, serene interior with its perfect proportions and cool beauty are typically Palladian in that they are modelled on the Classical style of ancient Rome. Within the church, the major works of art are the two late Tintorettos on the chancel walls: *The Last Supper* and *Gathering of the Manna* (both 1594). In the Chapel of the Dead is his last work, *The Deposition* (1592–4), finished by his son Domenico.

The top of the tall campanile, reached by a lift, affords a superb panorama of the city and lagoon.

Centuries ago Benedictine monks occupied the original monastery, which was rebuilt in the 13th century following an earthquake. It later became a centre of learning and a residence for eminent foreign visitors. Following the Fall of the Republic in 1797 (*see p48*) the monastery was suppressed and its treasures plundered.

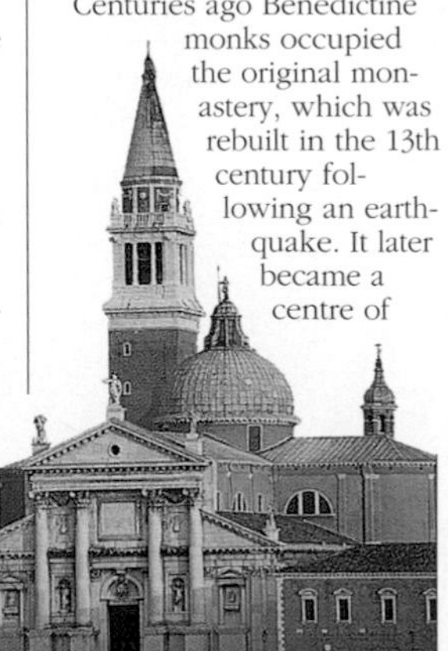

Palladio's church of San Giorgio Maggiore on the island of the same name

Cloisters designed by Palladio in the monastery of San Giorgio Maggiore

In 1829 the island became a free port, and in 1851 the headquarters of the artillery. By this time it had changed out of recognition. The complex regained its role as an active cultural centre when the monastery, embracing Palladio's cloisters, refectory and library, was purchased in 1951 by Count Vittorio Cini *(see p134)*. Today it is a thriving centre of Venetian culture, with international events and exhibitions. There is also an evocative open-air theatre.

SAN POLO AND SANTA CROCE

THE SESTIERI of San Polo and Santa Croce, bordered by the upper sweep of the Grand Canal, were both named after churches which stood within their boundaries. The first inhabitants are said to have settled on the cluster of small islands called *Rivus Altus* (high bank) or Rialto. When markets were established in the 11th century, the quarter became the commercial hub of Venice. San Polo is still one of the liveliest *sestieri* of the city, with its market stalls, small shops and local bars. The bustle of the market gives way to a maze of narrow alleys opening on to squares. Focal points are the spacious Campo San Polo, the Frari church and the neighbouring Scuola di San Rocco. Santa Croce for the most part is a *sestiere* of very narrow, tightly packed streets and squares where you will see the humbler side of Venetian life. Its grandest *palazzi* line the Grand Canal. Less alluring is the Piazzale Roma, the city's giant car park, lying to the west.

Shuttered window in Campo Sant'Aponal

SIGHTS AT A GLANCE

Churches

San Cassiano 4
San Giacomo dell'Orio 14
San Giacomo di Rialto 2
San Giovanni Evangelista 13
Santa Maria Gloriosa dei Frari pp102–3 8
San Nicolò da Tolentino 12
San Pantalon 11
San Polo 6
San Rocco 10
San Stae 16

Museums and Galleries

Ca' Mocenigo 17
Ca' Pesaro 18
Casa di Goldoni 7
Fondaco dei Turchi (Natural History Museum) 15
Scuola Grande di San Rocco pp106–7 9

Streets and Squares

Campo San Polo 5

Bridges

Rialto Bridge 1

Markets

Rialto Markets 3

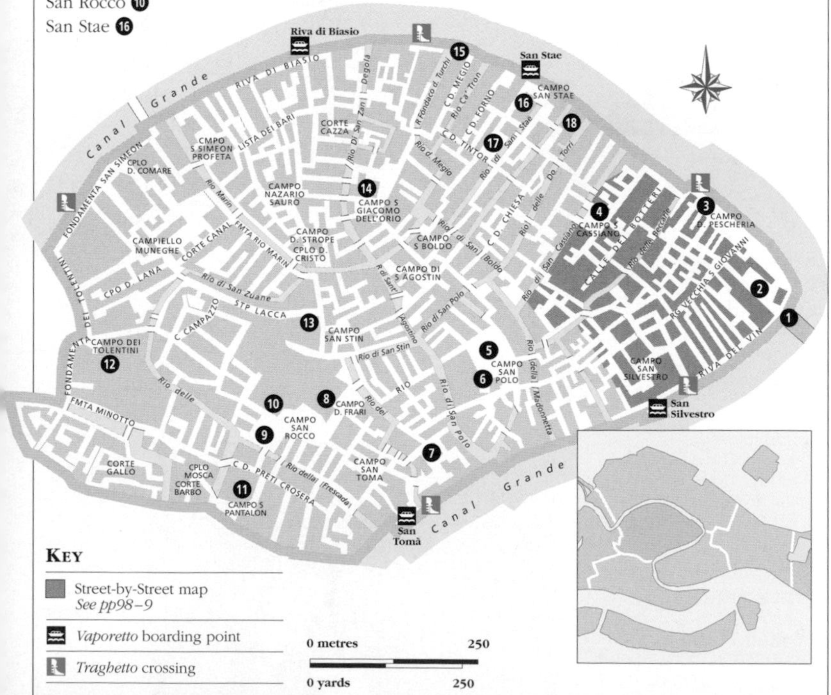

KEY

Street-by-Street map *See pp98–9*

Vaporetto boarding point

Traghetto crossing

0 metres 250
0 yards 250

◁ **Ponte del Megio, in a quiet corner of Santa Croce**

Street-by-Street: San Polo

THE RIALTO BRIDGE and markets make this a magnet for tourists. Traditionally the city's commercial quarter, it was here that bankers, brokers and merchants conducted their affairs. Streets are no longer lined with stalls selling spices and fine fabrics, but the food markets and pasta shops are a colourful sight. The old-fashioned standing-only bars called *bacari* are packed with locals. In contrast, Riva del Vin to the south, by the Grand Canal, is strictly tourist territory.

San Cassiano
Inside this church is a carved altar (1696) and a Crucifixion *by Tintoretto (1568)* ❹

SAN CASSIANO
CALLE DEL CAMPANIL
CAMPO SAN CASSIANO
C D CRISTI
CALLE DEI BOTTERI
RIO DI
R T D CARAMPANE
CAMPIELLO ALBRIZZI
C SALVIATI
RIO DELLE
BECCARIE
CAMPO SANT' APONAL
C DELL' OLIO
RUGA RA
C DEI LUGANEGHER
CAMPO SAN SILVESTRO

Ponte Storto is crooked, like many bridges in the city. It leads under a portico to Calle Stretta, a narrow alley that is only 1 m (3 ft) wide in places.

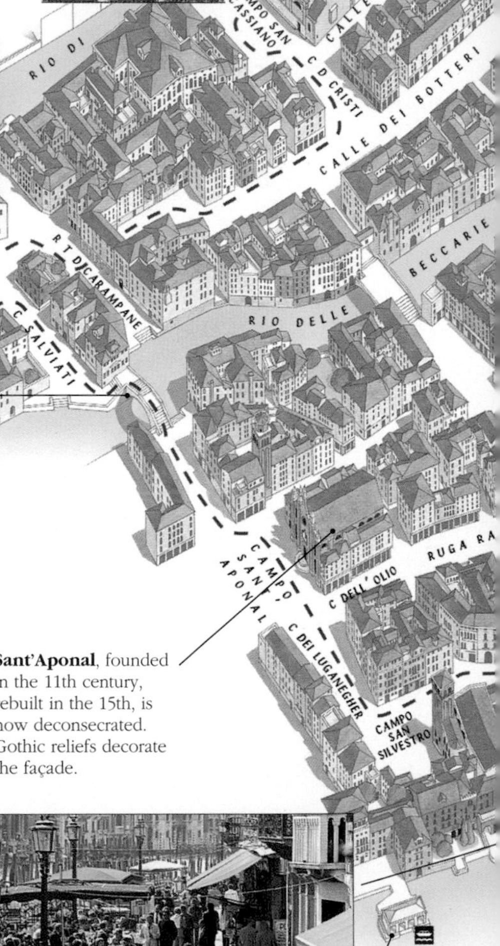

Sant'Aponal, founded in the 11th century, rebuilt in the 15th, is now deconsecrated. Gothic reliefs decorate the façade.

Riva del Vin, where wine was offloaded from boats, is one of the few accessible quaysides along the Grand Canal.

San Silvestro

STAR SIGHTS

★ **Rialto Bridge**

★ **Rialto Markets**

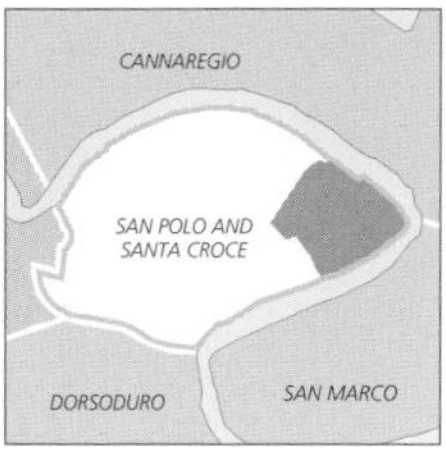

Locator Map
See Street Finder, maps 2, 3, 7

★ Rialto Markets
The Rialto markets have been in operation for centuries. The Pescheria (above) sells fresh fish and seafood, and the Erberia sells fruit and vegetables ❸

The statue of Gobbo of the Rialto, the hunchback, was sculpted in 1541 *(see p100).*

San Giacomo di Rialto
Since its installation in 1410, the clock on this church has been a notoriously poor time-keeper ❷

Key

— — — Suggested route

0 metres 75

0 yards 75

Calle della Madonna looks distinctly medieval with its overhanging first floors.

★ Rialto Bridge
A beloved landmark of the Grand Canal, the bridge marks the geographical centre of the city. The balustrades afford fine views of the canal ❶

Rialto Bridge ❶

Ponte di Rialto. **Map** 7 A1. *Rialto.*

THE RIALTO BRIDGE has been a busy part of the city for centuries. At any time of day you will find swarms of crowds jostling on the bridge, browsing among the souvenirs or taking a break to watch the constant swirl of activity on the Grand Canal from the bridge's balustrades.

Stone bridges were built in Venice as early as the 12th century, but it was not until 1588, after the collapse, decay or sabotage of earlier wooden structures, that a solid stone bridge was designed for the Rialto. One of the early wood crossings collapsed in 1444 under the weight of spectators at the wedding ceremony of the Marchese di Ferrara.

Vittore Carpaccio's painting *The Healing of the Madman* (1496, *see p133*) in the Accademia shows the fourth bridge – a rickety-looking structure with a drawbridge for the tall-masted galleys. By the 16th century this was in a sad state of decay and a competition was held for the design of a new bridge to be built in stone. Michelangelo, Andrea Palladio and Jacopo Sansovino were among the eminent contenders, but after months of deliberation it was the aptly named Antonio da Ponte who won the commission. The bridge was built between 1588 and 1591 and, until 1854, when the Accademia Bridge was constructed, this remained the only means of crossing the Grand Canal on foot.

Busy canalside restaurant near the Rialto Bridge

San Giacomo di Rialto ❷

Campo San Giacomo, San Polo. **Map** 3 A5. *041 522 47 45. Rialto, San Silvestro. 9am–noon, 4–5pm Mon–Sat, 9am–noon Sun. public hols.*

THE FIRST CHURCH to stand on this site was allegedly founded in the 5th century, making it the oldest church in Venice. The present building dates from the 11th–12th centuries, with major restoration in 1601. The original Gothic portico and huge 24-hour clock are the most striking features.

The crouching stone figure on the far side of the square is the so-called Gobbo (hunchback) of the Rialto. In the 16th century this was a welcome sight for minor offenders who were forced to run the gauntlet from Piazza San Marco to this square at the Rialto.

***Traghetto* ferrying passengers across to the Erberia**

Rialto Markets ❸

San Polo. **Map** 3 A5. *Rialto.* **Erberia** *(fruit and vegetable market) until noon Mon–Sat,* **Pescheria** *(fish market) until noon Tue–Sat.*

VENETIANS HAVE come to the Erberia to buy fresh produce for hundreds of years. Heavily laden barges arrive at dawn and offload their crates on to the quayside by the Grand Canal. Local produce includes red radicchio from Treviso, and succulent asparagus and baby artichokes from the islands of Sant'Erasmo and Vignole *(see p149)*. In the adjoining fish market are sole, sardines, skate, squid, crabs, clams and other species of seafood and fish. To see it all in full swing you must arrive early in the morning – by noon the vendors are packing up.

RIALTO BRIDGE

Until the 19th century this was the only link between the two sides of the Grand Canal.

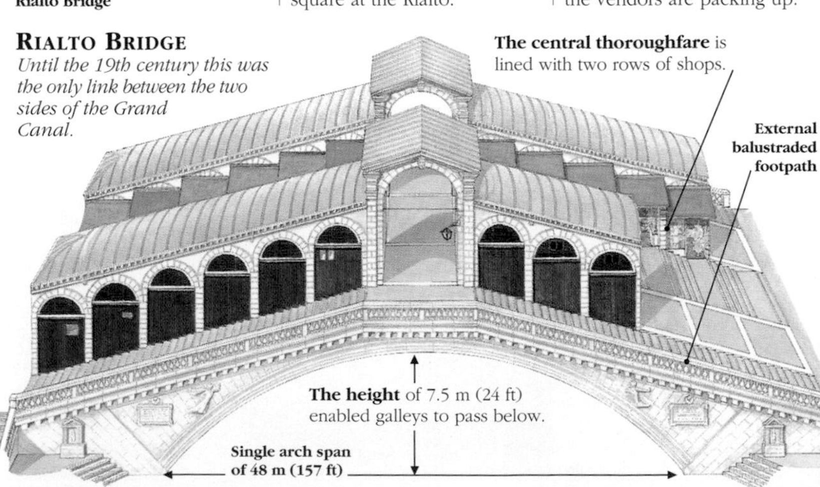
The central thoroughfare is lined with two rows of shops.
External balustraded footpath
The height of 7.5 m (24 ft) enabled galleys to pass below.
Single arch span of 48 m (157 ft)

San Cassiano ❹

Campo San Cassiano, San Polo. **Map** 2 F5. *041 721 408.* *San Stae.* *9am–noon Tue–Sat.*

THE MEDIEVAL CHURCH of San Cassiano is a bizarre mix of architectural styles. Of the original church, which was restored in the 19th century, only the campanile survives. The highlight of the interior is Jacopo Tintoretto's immensely powerful *Crucifixion* (1568), which is in the sacristy.

The campo in which the church stands was notorious for prostitutes in the 1500s.

Campo San Polo ❺

Map 6 F1. *San Silvestro.*

THE SPACIOUS SQUARE of San Polo has traditionally been host to spectacular events. As far back as the 15th century it was the venue for festivities, masquerades, ceremonies, balls and bullbaiting.

The most dramatic event was the assassination of Lorenzino de' Medici in 1548. He had taken refuge in Venice after brutally killing his cousin Alessandro, Duke of Florence. Lorenzino was stabbed in the square by two assassins who were in the service of Cosimo de' Medici, and both were handsomely rewarded by the Florentine duke.

On the eastern side of the square is the beautiful Gothic Palazzo Soranzo. This was originally two palaces – the one on the left is the older. The building is still owned by the Soranzo family.

Palazzo Corner Mocenigo, which is situated in the northwest corner (No. 2128), was once the residence of the eccentric English writer Frederick Rolfe (1860–1913), alias Baron Corvo. He was thrown out of his lodgings when his English hostess read his manuscript of *The Desire and Pursuit of the Whole* – a cruel satirization of English society in Venice.

A detail of the Gothic façade of Palazzo Soranzo, Campo San Polo

Since 1979 the square has enjoyed a revival of Carnival festivities. This wide open space is also a haven for local youngsters, who ride bikes, rollerskate or play football. Such activities would not have gone down well in the 17th century – a plaque on the apse of the church, dated 1611, forbids all games (or selling merchandise) on pain of prison, galley service or exile.

San Polo ❻

Campo San Polo. **Map** 6 F1. *041 275 04 62.* *San Silvestro.* *10am–5pm daily (from 1pm Sun & public hols).* *Sun (Jul & Aug); 1 Jan, 25 Dec.*

FOUNDED IN THE 9th century, rebuilt in the 15th and revamped in the early 19th in Neo-Classical style, the church of San Polo lacks any sense of homogeneity. Yet it is worth visiting for individual features such as the lovely Gothic portal and the Romanesque lions at the foot of the 14th-century campanile – one holds a serpent between its paws, the other a human head.

Inside, follow the signs for the *Via Crucis del Tiepolo* – fourteen canvases of the Stations of the Cross by Giandomenico Tiepolo. The church also has paintings by Veronese, Palma il Giovane (the Younger) and a dark and dramatic *Last Supper* by Tintoretto.

A lion at the foot of the campanile, Church of San Polo

Carlo Goldoni 1707–93

Casa di Goldoni ❼

Palazzo Centani, Calle dei Nomboli, San Polo 2794. **Map** 6 E1. *041 244 03 17.* *San Tomà.* *10am–4pm Mon–Sat (5pm Apr–Oct).* *Sun & public hols.*

CARLO GOLDONI, one of the city's favourite sons, wrote over 250 comedies, many based on Commedia dell'Arte figures. Goldoni was born in the beautiful Gothic Palazzo Centani (or Zantani) in 1707. The house, which has recently been restored, was left to the city in 1931 and is now a centre for theatrical studies and has a collection of theatrical memorabilia. The enchanting courtyard has a 15th-century open stairway and a magnificent wellhead, which features carved lions and a coat of arms bearing a hedgehog.

Santa Maria Gloriosa dei Frari 8

KNOWN BY ALL simply as the Frari (a corruption of *Frati*, meaning brothers), this huge, plain Gothic church dwarfs the eastern section of San Polo. The first church was built by Franciscan friars in 1250–1338, but was replaced by a larger building which was completed by the mid-15th century. The interior is striking for its sheer size and for the quality of its works of art. These include masterpieces by Titian and Giovanni Bellini *(see pp26–7)*, a statue by Donatello and a number of imposing monuments to famous Venetians.

Foscari Monument
Doge Foscari set a record by reigning for 34 years (1423–57).

★ Assumption of the Virgin
Titian's glowing and spectacular work (1518) inevitably draws the eye through the monk's choir towards the altar.

The campanile is 80 m (262 ft) high, the tallest in the city after that of San Marco.

★ Monks' Choir
This consists of three-tiered stalls (1468), carved with bas-reliefs of saints and Venetian city scenes.

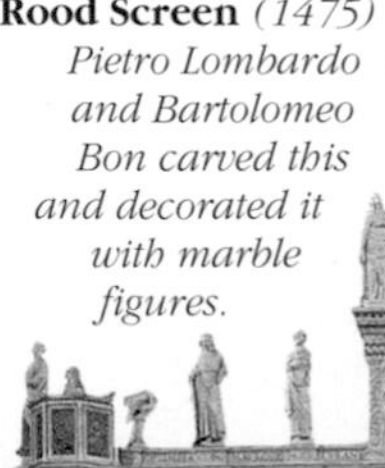

Rood Screen *(1475)*
Pietro Lombardo and Bartolomeo Bon carved this and decorated it with marble figures.

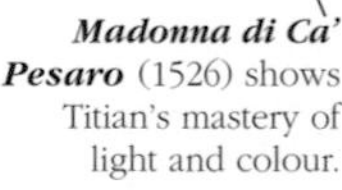

Madonna di Ca' Pesaro (1526) shows Titian's mastery of light and colour.

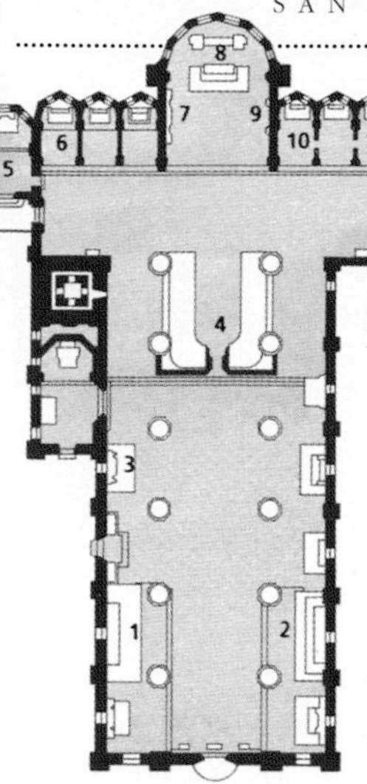

Floorplan

Exploration of the huge interior can be daunting. The floorplan pinpoints 12 highlights that should not be missed.

Key To Floorplan

1 Canova's tomb
2 Monument to Titian
3 Titian's *Madonna di Ca' Pesaro*
4 Choir stalls
5 Corner Chapel
6 Tomb of Monteverdi
7 Tomb of Doge Nicolò Tron
8 High altar with Titian's *Assumption of the Virgin*
9 Tomb of Doge Francesco Foscari
10 Donatello's *John the Baptist* (c.1450)
11 B Vivarini's altar painting (1474), Bernardo Chapel
12 Giovanni Bellini's *Madonna Enthroned with Saints* (1488)

Visitors' Checklist

Campo dei Frari. **Map** 6 D1.
041 275 04 62. San Tomà. 10am–6pm Mon–Sat, 1–6pm Sun & religious hols. 1 Jan, 25 Dec. except for those attending mass. frequent.

Monument to Titian *(1853)*
Canova's pupils, Luigi and Pietro Zandomeneghi, built this monument to Titian in place of the one conceived by Canova himself.

The former monastery, which houses the State Archives, has two cloisters, one in the style of Sansovino, another designed by Palladio.

Entrance

Canova's Tomb
Canova designed, but never actually made, a Neo-Classical marble pyramid like this as a monument for Titian. After Canova's death in 1822, his pupils used a similar design for their master's tomb.

Star Features

★ **Assumption of the Virgin by Titian**

★ **Monks' Choir**

Scuola Grande di San Rocco ❾

See pp106–7.

San Rocco ❿

Campo San Rocco, San Polo. **Map** 6 D1. *041 523 48 64.* *San Tomà.* *Apr–Oct: 8am–12:30pm, 3–5pm daily; Nov–Mar: 8am–12:30pm Mon–Fri, 2–4pm Sat, Sun & public hols.*

SHARING THE LITTLE square with the celebrated Scuola Grande di San Rocco is the church of the same name. Designed by Bartolomeo Bon in 1489 and largely rebuilt in 1725, the exterior is a mix of architectural styles. The façade, similar in concept to the Scuola, was added in 1765–71.

Inside, the main interest lies in Tintoretto's paintings in the chancel, which depict scenes from the life of St Roch, patron saint of contagious diseases. Of these the most notable is *St Roch Curing the Plague Victims* (1549).

San Pantalon ⓫

Campo San Pantalon, Dorsoduro. **Map** 6 D2. *041 270 24 64.* *San Tomà, P. Roma.* *4–6pm Mon–Sat.*

Fumiani's ceiling painting (1680–1704), San Pantalon

THE OVERWHELMING feature of this late 17th-century church is the painted ceiling, dark, awe-inspiring and remarkable for its illusionistic effects. The ceiling comprises a total of 40 scenes (admirers claim this makes it the world's largest work of art on canvas), depicting the martyrdom and apotheosis of the physician St Pantalon. The artist, Gian Antonio Fumiani, took 24 years (1680–1704) to achieve this masterpiece, but then he allegedly fell to his death from the scaffolding.

Paolo Veronese's emotive painting *St Pantalon Healing a Boy* (second chapel on the right) was his final work of art (1587). If you would like to see Antonio Vivarini and Giovanni d'Alemagna's *Coronation of the Virgin* (1444) and *The Annunciation* (1350) attributed to Paolo Veneziano, ask the custodian for access to the Chapel of the Holy Nail *(Cappella del Sacro Chiodo).*

San Nicolò da Tolentino ⓬

Campo dei Tolentini, Santa Croce. **Map** 5 C1. *041 522 21 60.* *Piazzale Roma.* *9:30am–noon, 5–6:30pm Mon–Sat, 5:30–6:30pm Sun.*

CLOSE TO Piazzale Roma *(see p271)*, San Nicolò da Tolentino is an imposing 17th-century church with a Classical portico. The interior, decorated with 17th-century paintings, is the resting place of Francesco Morosini (d.1678), the Venetian patriarch.

A cannonball embedded in the façade is a memento of an Austrian bombardment during the siege of 1849.

San Giovanni Evangelista ⓭

Campiello de la Scuola, San Polo. **Map** 6 D1. *041 71 82 34.* *San Tomà.* *phone for an appointment.*

A CONFRATERNITY of flagellants founded the Scuola of St John the Evangelist in 1261. The complex, just north of the Frari *(see pp102–3)*, has a church, *scuola* and courtyard. Separating the square from the street is Pietro Lombardo's elegant white and grey screen and portal (1480), and in the arch crowning the portal

Lombardo's marble screen and portal, San Giovanni Evangelista

there is carved eagle, which is the symbol representing St John the Evangelist.

The main hall of the Scuola is reached via a splendid 15th-century double stairway by Mauro Coducci (1498). Large, dark canvases decorate the ceiling and walls of the 18th-century hall. The Scuola's greatest art treasure, the cycle of paintings depicting *The Stories of the Cross*, is now on display in the Accademia gallery *(see p133)*. It formerly embellished the oratory (off the main hall) where the Reliquary of the True Cross is still carefully preserved.

San Giacomo dell'Orio ⓮

Campo San Giacomo dell'Orio, Santa Croce. **Map** 2 E5. *041 275 04 62.* *Riva di Biasio or San Stae.* *10am–5pm daily (from 1pm Sun & public hols).* *Sun (Jul & Aug); 1 Jan, 25 Dec.*

THIS CHURCH is a focal point of a quiet quarter of Santa Croce. The name "dell'Orio" (locally dall'Orio) may derive from a laurel tree *(alloro)* that once stood near the church.

Founded in the 9th century, rebuilt in 1225 and repeatedly modified, the church is a mix of architectural styles. The campanile, basilica ground plan and Byzantine columns survive from the 13th century. The ship's keel roof and the columns are from the Gothic period, and the apses are Renaissance. The sacristy ceiling was decorated by Veronese and there are some interesting altar paintings.

Fondaco dei Turchi ⓯

Canal Grande, Santa Croce 1730. **Map** 2 E4. *041 275 02 06.* *San Stae.* *for renovation.*

THE BUILDING that now contains Venice's natural history museum has a chequered history. In the 13th century it was one of the largest *palazzi* on the Grand Canal. In 1381 it was bought by the state for the Dukes of Ferrara and its lavishly decorated rooms were used for banquets and state functions. In 1621 the Turks set up a warehouse *(fondaco)*, and the spacious portico was used for loading merchandise. As commerce with the Orient declined further, the structure fell into disrepair until, roused by Ruskin's passionate interest, the Austrians began restoration work in the 1850s.

Since 1924 the Fondaco has housed the natural history museum (Museo di Storia Naturale). There is a collection of stuffed animals, crustacea and dinosaur fossils and a section on lagoon life. Prize exhibits include a skeleton of an *Ouranosaurus nigeriensis*, 7 m (23 ft) long and 3.6 m (12 ft) tall, and a fossil of an *Sarcosuchus imperator* – an ancestor of the crocodile.

Ouranosaurus skeleton in the Fondaco dei Turchi

San Stae ⓰

Campo San Stae, Santa Croce. **Map** 2 F4. *041 275 04 62.* *San Stae.* *10am–5pm (from 1pm Sun).* *Sun (Jul & Aug); 1 Jan, 25 Dec.*

RESTORED IN 1977–8 by the Pro Venezia Foundation, San Stae (or Sant'Eustachio) has a spick-and-span sculpted façade. It was built in 1709 by Domenico Rossi. Works by Piazzetta, Tiepolo and other 18th-century artists decorate the chancel. Near the second altar on the left is the bust of Antonio Foscarini, executed for treason in 1622 but pardoned the following year.

One of the finely furnished rooms of Ca' Mocenigo

Ca' Mocenigo ⓱

Salizzada San Stae, Santa Croce 1992. **Map** 2 F5. *041 72 17 98.* *San Stae.* *10am–5pm Tue–Sun (to 4pm Nov–Mar).* *1 Jan, 1 May, 25 Dec.*

ONE OF the oldest and greatest of all Venetian families, the Mocenigos produced seven doges. There were various branches of the family, one of which resided in this handsome 17th-century mansion. Count Alvise Nicolò Mocenigo, the last of this particular branch, died in 1954, bequeathing the palace to the Comune di Venezia (city authorities).

The entrance façade is unremarkable, but the interior is elegantly furnished and gives you a rare opportunity of seeing inside a *palazzo* preserved more or less as it was in the 18th century. The frescoed ceilings and other works of art are celebrations of the family's achievements. The illustrious Mocenigos are portrayed in a frieze around the portego on the first floor.

The Museo del Tessuto e del Costume inside the house contains antique fabrics and exquisitely made costumes.

Ca' Pesaro ⓲

Canal Grande, Santa Croce 2076. **Map** 2 F5. *San Stae.* **Galleria d'Arte Moderna** *041 524 06 95.* **Museo Orientale** *041 524 11 73.* *10am–6pm Tue–Sun (Nov–Mar: to 5pm).* *1 Jan, 1 May, 25 Dec.* *combined ticket.*

IT TOOK 58 YEARS to complete this magnificent Baroque palace. Built for the Pesaro family, it was the masterpiece of Baldassare Longhena, who worked on it until his death in 1682. Antonio Gaspari then took over Longhena's design, eventually completing the structure in 1710.

In the 19th century the Duchess of Bevilacqua La Masa bequeathed the palace to the city for exhibiting the works of unestablished Venetian artists. The Galleria d'Arte Moderna was founded in 1897. Today this features a permanent exhibition of work by artists such as Bonnard, Matisse, Miró, Klee, Klimt and Kandinsky, in addition to works by Italian artists of the 19th and 20th centuries.

The Museo Orientale has an idiosyncratic collection of Chinese and Japanese artifacts collected by the Count of Bardi during his 19th-century travels in the Far East.

Gustav Klimt's *Salome*, Gallery of Modern Art, Ca' Pesaro

Scuola Grande di San Rocco ❾

Pianta's caricature of Tintoretto

FOUNDED IN HONOUR of St Roch (San Rocco), the Scuola was set up as a charitable institution for the sick. Construction began in 1515 under Bartolomeo Bon and was completed in 1549 by Scarpagnino, financed largely by donations from Venetians who believed that St Roch, the patron saint of contagious diseases, would save them from the plague. In 1564 Tintoretto *(see p140)* was commissioned to decorate the walls and ceilings of the Scuola. His remarkable cycle of paintings starts in the Sala dell'Albergo *(see* Gallery Guide*)*.

Restored main entrance to the Scuola di San Rocco

Sala dell'Albergo

The Crucifixion

In this panorama of Calvary, Tintoretto reached a pitch of religious feeling never hitherto achieved in Venetian art.

A self-portrait was often a feature of Tintoretto's paintings.

The subsidiary figures are full of life but do not lessen the central drama.

Figure of Christ
The crucified figure of the Redeemer is raised and leaning, accentuating His divinity and saving grace.

A COMPETITION was held in 1564 to select an artist to paint the central ceiling panel of the Sala dell'Albergo in the Scuola. To the fury of his rivals, Tintoretto pre-empted his fellow competitors by installing his painting *in situ* prior to judging. He won the commission and was later made a member of the Scuola. Over the next 23 years, Tintoretto decorated the entire building.

The series of paintings, completed in 1587, reveals Tintoretto's revolutionary use of light, mastery of foreshortening and visionary use of colour. The winning painting, *St Roch in Glory* ①, can be seen on the ceiling of the Sala dell'Albergo. The most moving work in the cycle is the *Crucifixion* (1565) ②. Henry James wrote: "Surely no single picture contains more of human life; there is everything in it, including the most exquisite beauty." Of the paintings on the entrance wall, portraying the Passion of Christ, the most notable is *Christ Before Pilate* (1566–7) ③.

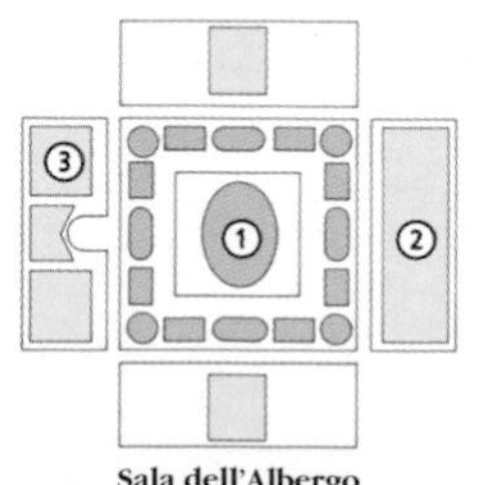

Sala dell'Albergo

UPPER HALL

SCARPAGNINO's great staircase (1544–6), decorated with two vast paintings commemorating the plague of 1630, leads to the Upper Hall. The biblical subjects on the walls and ceiling were painted in 1575–81. The ceiling paintings (viewed most comfortably with a hired mirror) portray scenes from the Old Testament. The three large central square paintings represent: *Moses Striking Water from the Rock* ④, *The Miracle of the Bronze Serpent* ⑤ and *The Gathering of the Manna* ⑥, all alluding to the Scuola's charitable aims in alleviating thirst, sickness and hunger respectively. All three paintings are crowded compositions with much violent movement. The vast wall paintings in the hall feature episodes from the New Testament. The most striking paintings are *The Temptation of Christ* ⑦, which shows a handsome young Satan offering Christ two loaves of bread, and *Adoration of the Shepherds* ⑧. Like *The Temptation of Christ*, the *Adoration* is composed in two halves, with a female figure, shepherds and ox below, and the Holy Family and onlookers above.

The beautiful carvings below the paintings were added in the 17th century by Francesco Pianta. The allegorical figures include (near the altar) a caricature of Tintoretto with his palette and brushes, which is meant to represent Painting. Near the entrance to the Sala dell'Albergo you can see Titian's *Annunciation*. The easel painting *Christ Carrying the Cross* is attributed to Giorgione, though many believe it to be a Titian.

The Temptation of Christ, 1578–81 (detail)

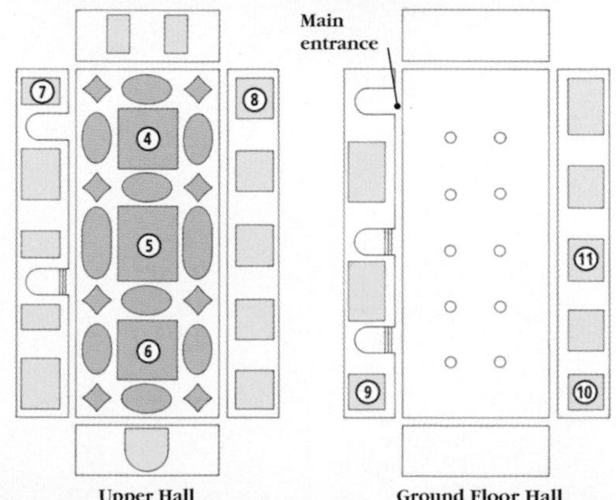

VISITORS' CHECKLIST

Campo San Rocco. **Map** 6 D1.
041 523 48 64.
San Tomà. Apr–Oct: 9am–5:30pm daily; Nov–Mar: 10am– 4pm daily. 1 Jan, Easter, 25 Dec.

GROUND FLOOR HALL

***The Flight into Egypt* (1582–7) (detail)**

THIS FINAL CYCLE, executed in 1583–7, consists of eight paintings illustrating the life of Mary. The series starts with an *Annunciation*, and ends with an *Assumption*, which was restored some years ago. The tranquil scenes of *St Mary of Egypt* ⑨, *St Mary Magdalene* ⑩ and *The Flight into Egypt* ⑪, painted when Tintoretto was in his late sixties, are remarkable for their serenity. This is portrayed most lucidly by the Virgin's isolated spiritual contemplation in the *St Mary of Egypt*. In all three paintings, the landscapes, rendered with rapid strokes, play a major role.

GALLERY GUIDE

The paintings, which unfortunately are not well lit, have no labels, but a useful plan of the Scuola is available (in several languages) free of charge at the entrance.

To see the paintings in chronological order, start in the Sala dell'Albergo (off the Upper Hall), followed by the Upper Hall and finally the Ground Floor Hall.

KEY

- Wall paintings
- Ceiling paintings

CASTELLO

THE LARGEST *sestiere* of the city, Castello stretches from San Marco and Cannaregio in the west to the modern blocks of Sant'Elena in the east. The area takes its name from the 8th-century fortress that once stood on what is now San Pietro, the island which for centuries was the religious focus of the city. The church here was the episcopal see from the 9th century and the city's cathedral from 1451 to 1807. The industrial hub of Castello was the Arsenale, where the great shipyards produced Venice's indomitable fleet of warships. Castello's most popular and solidly commercial area is the Riva degli Schiavoni promenade. Behind the waterfront it is comparatively quiet, characterized by narrow alleys, elegantly faded *palazzi* and fine churches, including the great Santi Giovanni e Paolo *(see pp116–17)*.

Water stoup, Santa Maria Formosa

SIGHTS AT A GLANCE

Churches
La Pietà 3
San Francesco della Vigna 14
San Giorgio dei Greci 2
San Giovanni in Bragora 17
Santi Giovanni e Paolo pp116–17 12
San Lorenzo 15
San Zaccaria 1

Historic Buildings and Monuments
Arsenale 19
Hotel Danieli 4
Ospedaletto 13
Statue of Colleoni 10

Streets, Bridges and Squares
Campo Santa Maria Formosa 9
Ponte della Paglia and Bridge of Sighs 6
Riva degli Schiavoni 5

Walk
Exploring Eastern Castello 20

Museums, Galleries and Scuole
Fondazione Querini Stampalia 8
Museo Diocesano d'Arte Sacra 7
Museo Storico Navale 18
Scuola di San Giorgio degli Schiavoni 16
Scuola Grande di San Marco 11

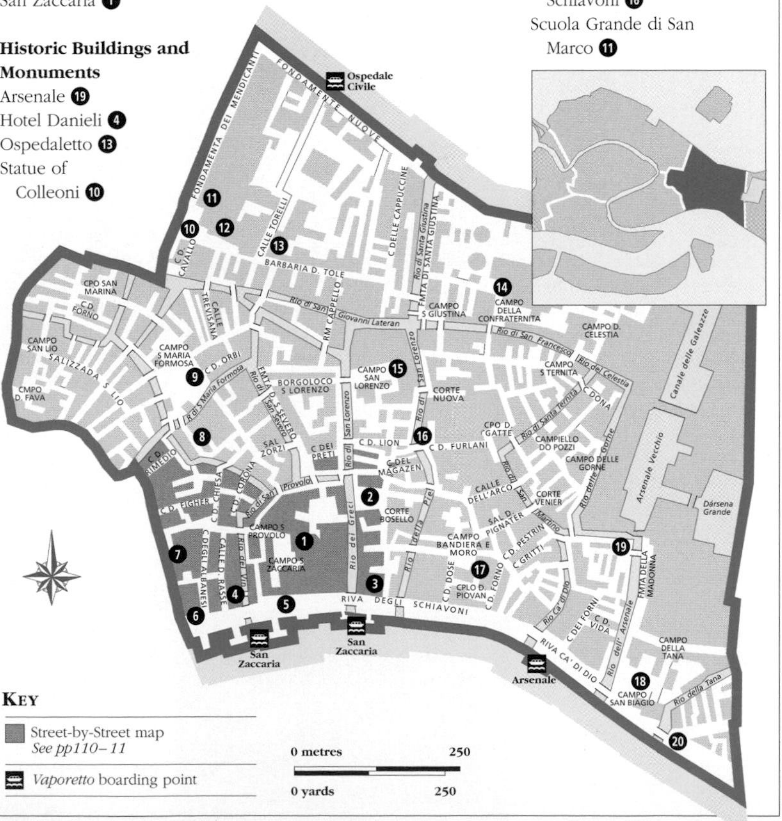

KEY

Street-by-Street map *See pp110–11*

Vaporetto boarding point

0 metres 250

0 yards 250

◁ **Bas relief on Rio Terrà Garibaldi, eastern Castello**

Street-by-Street: Castello

13th-century Madonna in the Museo Diocesano

A STROLL ALONG the Riva degli Schiavoni is an integral part of a visit to Venice. Glorious views of San Giorgio Maggiore compensate for the commercialized aspects of the quayside: souvenir stalls, excursion touts and an overabundance of tourists. Associations with literary figures are legion. Petrarch lived at No. 4145, Henry James was offered "dirty" lodgings at No. 4161, and Ruskin stayed at the Hotel Danieli. Inland, the quiet, unassuming streets and squares of Castello provide a contrast to the bustling waterfront.

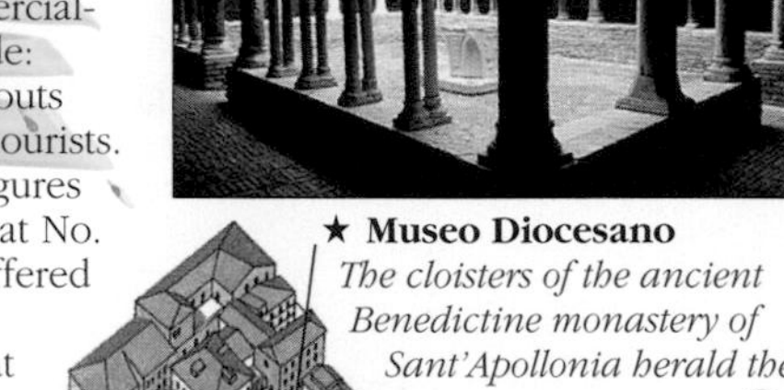

★ Museo Diocesano
The cloisters of the ancient Benedictine monastery of Sant'Apollonia herald the museum ❼

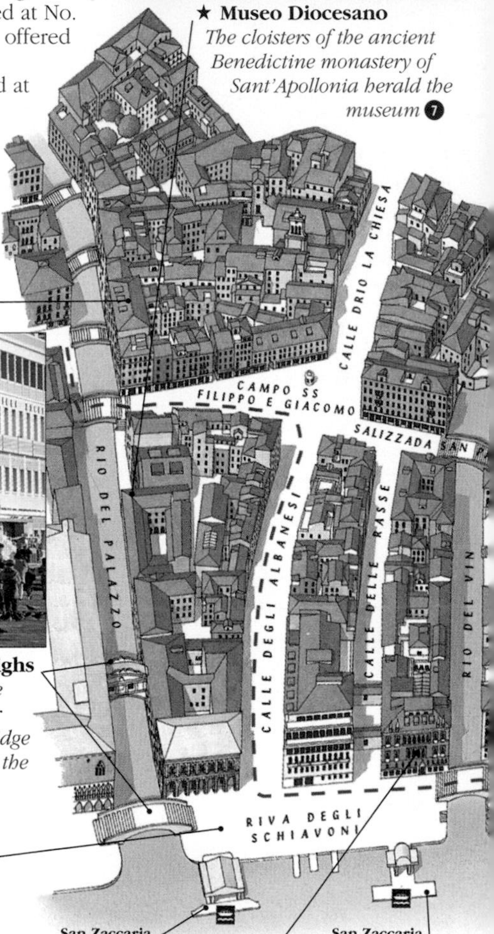

Palazzo Trevisan-Cappello, used as a showroom for Murano glass, was the home of Bianca Cappello, wife of Francesco de' Medici.

CALLE DRIO LA CHIESA
CAMPO SS FILIPPO E GIACOMO
SALIZZADA SAN P
RIO DEL PALAZZO
CALLE DEGLI ALBANESI
CALLE DELLE RASSE
RIO DEL VIN
RIVA DEGLI SCHIAVONI

Ponte della Paglia and Bridge of Sighs
Crowds throng the Istrian stone Ponte della Paglia – the "straw bridge" – for the best views of the neighbouring Bridge of Sighs, the covered bridge that links the Doge's Palace to the old prisons ❻

Riva degli Schiavoni
This paved quayside was established over 600 years ago, and widened in 1782 ❺

San Zaccaria Paglia

San Zaccaria Danieli

STAR SIGHTS

- ★ **La Pietà**
- ★ **San Zaccaria**
- ★ **Museo Diocesano**

Hotel Danieli
Joseph da Niel, after whom this hotel was named, turned the Palazzo Dandolo into a haunt for 19th-century writers and artists ❹

Palazzo Priuli, overlooking the quiet Fondamenta Osmarin, is a fine Venetian Gothic palace. The corner window is particularly beautiful, but the early 16th-century façade frescoes have long since disappeared.

Locator Map
See Street Finder, maps 7, 8

San Giorgio dei Greci
Subsidence is the cause of the city's tilting bell-towers: San Giorgio dei Greci's looks particularly perilous ❷

★ San Zaccaria
Codussi added Renaissance details such as this panel to the Gothic façade ❶

Key

— — — Suggested route

0 metres 75

0 yards 75

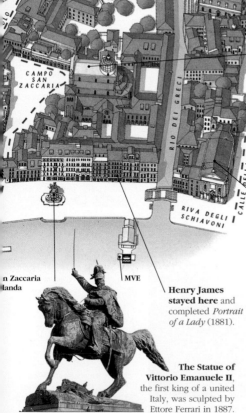

n Zaccaria
landa

MVE

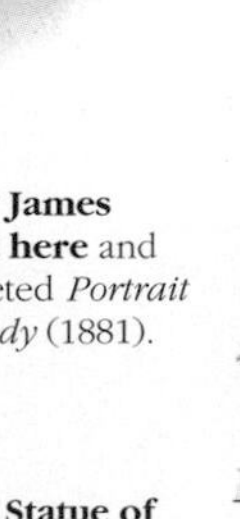

Henry James stayed here and completed *Portrait of a Lady* (1881).

The Statue of Vittorio Emanuele II, the first king of a united Italy, was sculpted by Ettore Ferrari in 1887.

★ La Pietà
In Vivaldi's day, the church became famous for the superb quality of its musical performances ❸

San Zaccaria ❶

Campo San Zaccaria. **Map** 8 D2. *041 522 12 57. San Zaccaria. 10am–noon, 4–6pm Mon–Sat; 4–6pm Sun & public hols. Chapels & Crypt.*

SET IN A QUIET square just a stone's throw from the Riva degli Schiavoni, the church of San Zaccaria is a successful blend of Flamboyant Gothic and Classical Renaissance styles. Founded in the 9th century, it was completely rebuilt between 1444 and 1515. Antonio Gambello began the façade in Gothic style and, when Gambello died in 1481, Mauro Coducci completed the upper section, adding all the Classical detail.

The adjoining Benedictine convent, which had close links with the church, became quite notorious for the riotous behaviour of its nuns. The majority were from families of Venetian nobility, many of them sent to the convent to avoid the expense of a dowry.

Every Easter the doge came with his entourage to San Zaccaria – a custom which originated as an expression of gratitude to the nuns, who had relinquished part of their garden so that Piazza San Marco could be enlarged.

The artistic highlight of the interior (illuminate with coins in the meter) is Giovanni Bellini's sumptuously coloured and superbly serene *Madonna and Child with Saints* (1505) in the north aisle.

On the right of the church is a door to the Chapel of St Athanasius which leads to the Chapel of San Tarasio. The chapel is decorated with vault frescoes (1442) by Andrea del Castagno of Florence, and Gothic polyptychs painted in 1443–4 by Antonio Vivarini and Giovanni d'Alemagna. The relics of eight doges lie buried in the waterlogged crypt.

Distant view of San Giorgio dei Greci's tilting campanile

San Giorgio dei Greci ❷

Map 8 D2. *San Zaccaria. 041 523 95 69. Wed–Mon. Hours vary.*
Museo dell' Icone
041 522 65 81. 9am–4:30pm Mon–Sat, 10am–5pm Sun.

THE MOST remarkable feature of this 16th-century Greek church is the listing campanile, which looks as if it is about to topple into the Rio dei Greci. Inside is the *matroneo* – the gallery where, in keeping with Greek Orthodox custom, the women sat apart from the men. Note also the iconostasis separating the sanctuary from the nave. The nearby Scuola di San Nicolò dei Greci, redesigned in 1678, is now the museum of icons of the Hellenic Institute.

Detail from *The Nun's Parlour at San Zaccaria* by Francesco Guardi

La Pietà ❸

Riva degli Schiavoni. **Map** 8 D2. *041 523 73 95. San Zaccaria. Jun–Oct: 10am–noon, 3:30–6:30pm daily. Sun pm.*

THE CHURCH of La Pietà (or Santa Maria della Visitazione) dates from the 15th century. It was rebuilt in 1745–1760 by Giorgio Massari, and the Classical façade was added in 1906. The church has a cool, elegant interior, with an oval plan. The resplendent ceiling fresco, *Triumph of Faith* (1755), was painted by Giambattista Tiepolo.

The Pietà started its life as a foundling home for orphans. It proved so popular that a warning plaque was set up (still to be seen on the side wall), threatening damnation to parents who tried to pass off their children as orphans.

From 1703 until 1740 Antonio Vivaldi directed the musical groups and wrote numerous oratorios, cantatas and vocal pieces for the Pietà choir, and the church became famous for its performances.

Today the church is a popular venue for concerts – with a strong emphasis on Vivaldi. These are held throughout the year, usually on Mondays and Thursdays.

Bas relief on La Pietà's early 20th-century façade

Hotel Danieli ❹

Riva degli Schiavoni 4196. **Map** 7 C2. *San Zaccaria.* *See also* ***Where to Stay*** *p230.*

ONE OF THE MOST celebrated hotels in Europe, the Danieli's deep pink façade is a landmark on the Riva degli Schiavoni. Built in the 14th century, it became famous as the venue for the first opera performed in Venice, Monteverdi's *Proserpina Rapita*

(1630). The palace became a hotel in 1822 and soon gained popularity with the literary and artistic set. Its famous guests included Balzac, Proust, Dickens, Cocteau, Ruskin, Debussy and Wagner. In the 1830s Room 10 witnessed an episode in the love affair between the French poet and dramatist Alfred de Musset, and novelist George Sand: when de Musset fell ill after a surfeit of orgies, Sand ran off with her Venetian doctor.

Riva degli Schiavoni – the city's most famous promenade

Riva degli Schiavoni ❺

Map 8 D2. *San Zaccaria.*

The sweeping promenade that forms the southern quayside of Castello was named after the traders from Dalmatia (Schiavonia) who used to moor their boats and barges here. For those who arrive in Venice by water, this long curving quayside is a spectacular introduction to the charms of the city.

At its western end, close to Piazza San Marco, the broad promenade teems during the day with tourists thronging around the souvenir stalls and people hurrying to and from the *vaporetto* stops. Nothing can detract, however, from the glorious views across the lagoon to the island of San Giorgio Maggiore *(see p95).*

The Riva degli Schiavoni has always been busy with boats. Canaletto's drawings in the 1740s and 1750s show the Riva bustling with gondolas, sailing boats and barges. The gondolas are still here, but it is also chock-a-block with water taxis, *vaporetti*, excursion boats and tugs. Naval ships and ocean liners can also often be seen.

The modern annexe of the Hotel Danieli caused a great furore when it was built in 1948. Intruding on a waterfront graced by fine Venetian palaces and mansions, its stark outline is still something of an eyesore. The annexe marks the spot where Doge Vitale Michiel II was stabbed to death in 1172. Three centuries earlier, in 864, Doge Pietro Tradonico had suffered the same fate in nearby Campo San Zaccaria.

Ponte della Paglia and Bridge of Sighs ❻

Map 7 C2. *San Zaccaria.*

The name of the Ponte della Paglia may derive from the boats that once moored here to off-load their cargoes of straw *(paglia).* Originally built in 1360, the existing structure dates from 1847.

According to legend the Bridge of Sighs, built in 1600 to link the Doge's Palace with the new prisons, takes its name from the lamentations of the prisoners as they made their way over to the offices of the feared State Inquisitors. Access to the bridge is available to the public via the Doge's Palace *(see p87).*

Ponte della Paglia behind the Bridge of Sighs

Museo Diocesano d'Arte Sacra ❼

Sant'Apollonia, Ponte della Canonica. **Map** 7 C2. *041 522 91 66.* *San Zaccaria.* *10:30am–12:30pm Mon–Sat.* *public hols.* ***Donations** appreciated.*

One of the architectural gems of Venice, the cloister of Sant'Apollonia is the only Romanesque building in the city. Only a few steps from St Mark's, the cloister provides a quiet retreat from the hubbub of the Piazza.

The monastery was once the home of Benedictine monks, but its non-ecclesiastical uses have been manifold. In 1976 its cloisters became the home of the diocesan museum of sacred art, founded in order to provide a haven for works of art from closed or deconsecrated churches. The collection includes paintings, statues, crucifixes and many pieces of valuable silver. The museum has two workshops, staffed by volunteers who restore the paintings and statues. The collection is ever-changing, but among the major permanent exhibits are works by Luca Giordano (1634–1705), which came from the Church of Sant'Aponal, and a 16th-century wood and crystal tabernacle.

Fondazione Querini Stampalia ❽

Campo Santa Maria Formosa, 5252 Castello. **Map** 7 C1. *041 271 14 11.* *San Zaccaria.* **Palace** *10am–6pm Tue–Sun (to 10pm Fri & Sat).* *Mon.* **Library** *4pm–midnight Mon–Fri, 2:30pm–midnight Sat, 3–7pm Sun.*

THE LARGE PALAZZO Querini Stampalia was commissioned in the 16th century by the descendants of the old Venetian Querini family. Great art lovers, they filled the palace with fine paintings.

In 1868 the last member of the dynasty bequeathed the palace and the family collection of art to the foundation that bears his name. The paintings include works by Giovanni Bellini, Giambattista Tiepolo, and some vignettes by Pietro and Alessandro Longhi. The library on the first floor, which is open to the public, contains over 200,000 books.

Campo Santa Maria Formosa ❾

Campo Santa Maria Formosa. **Map** 7 C1. *Rialto, Fondamente Nuove.* **Church** *041 275 04 62.* *10am–5pm daily (from 1pm Sun).* *Sun (Jul & Aug); 1 Jan, 25 Dec.*

LARGE, RAMBLING, and flanked by handsome palaces, this market square is one of the most characteristic *campi* of Venice. On the southern side is the church of Santa Maria Formosa, distinctive for its swelling apses. Built on ancient foundations, the church was designed by Mauro Coducci in 1492 but took over a century to assume its current form. Unusually, it has two main façades – one overlooking the *campo*, the other the canal. The campanile was added in 1688. Its most notable feature is the truly grotesque stone face that decorates its foot.

Inside, Palma il Vecchio's polyptych *St Barbara and Saints* (c.1523) ranks among the great Venetian masterpieces and looks particularly splendid since its restoration by the American Save Venice organization. Palma's portrayal of the handsome and dignified figure of St Barbara glorifies Venice's ideal female beauty. She is surrounded by saints, with a central lunette of the *pietà* above. St Barbara was the patron saint of soldiers: in wartime they prayed to her for protection, in victory they came for thanksgiving.

Palma il Vecchio's *St Barbara* in Santa Maria Formosa

Statue of Colleoni ❿

Campo Santi Giovanni e Paolo. **Map** 3 C5. *Ospedale Civile.*

BARTOLOMEO COLLEONI, the famous *condottiere* or commander of mercenaries, left his fortune to the Republic on condition that his statue was placed in front of San Marco. A prominent statue in the Piazza would have broken with precedent, so the Senate cunningly had Colleoni raised before the Scuola di San Marco instead of the basilica. A touchstone of early Renaissance sculpture, the equestrian statue of the proud warrior (1481–8) is by the Florentine Andrea Verrocchio and, after his death, was cast in bronze by Alessandro Leopardi. The statue has a strong sense of power and movement which arguably ranks it alongside works of Donatello.

Statue of Bartolomeo Colleoni

Scuola Grande di San Marco ⓫

Campo Santi Giovanni e Paolo. **Map** 3 C5. *Ospedale Civile.* **Library** *041 529 43 23.* *8:30am–2pm Mon–Fri (ring bell).* *public hols, one week in mid-Aug, 24 Dec–1 Jan.* **Church** *041 522 56 62.* *8am–noon Mon–Sat, 9–10am Sun.*

FEW HOSPITALS can boast as rich and unusual a façade as that of Venice's Ospedale Civile. It was built originally as one of the six great confraternities of the city *(see p127)*. Their first headquarters were destroyed by fire in 1485, but the Scuola was rebuilt at the end of the 15th century.

The delightful asymmetrical façade, with its arcades, marble panels and *trompe l'oeil* effects, was the work of Pietro Lombardo working in conjunction with Giovanni Buora. The upper order was finished by Mauro Coducci in 1495. The interior was revamped in the 19th century and, since then, most of the artistic masterpieces have been dispersed.

The library has a fine carved 16th-century ceiling, and the hospital chapel, the Church of San Lazzaro dei Mendicanti, contains an early Tintoretto and a work by Veronese.

Santi Giovanni e Paolo ⓬

See pp116–17.

Ospedaletto ⓭

Calle Barbaria delle Tole, 6691 Castello. **Map** 4 D5. *041 270 24 64.* *Ospedale Civile.* *3:30–6:30pm Thu–Sat.*

BEYOND THE SOUTH flank of Santi Giovanni e Paolo *(see pp116–17)* is the façade of the Ospedaletto or, more correctly, Santa Maria dei Derelitti. The Ospedaletto was set up by the Republic in 1527 as a charitable institution to care for the sick and aged, and to educate orphans and abandoned girls. Such an education consisted largely of the study of music. The girls became leading figures in choirs and orchestras, with concerts bringing in funds for the construction in 1776 of a *sala della musica,* which became the main performance venue. This elegant room features frescoes by Jacopo Guarana.

The church, which formed part of the Ospedaletto, was built by Andrea Palladio in 1575. Its façade was added in 1674 by Baldassare Longhena. The huge, hideous heads on the façade have been described as anti-Classical abominations, likened to diseased figures and swollen fruit. The interior of the church is decorated with less provocative works of art and notable paintings from the 18th century, including *The Sacrifice of Isaac* (1720) by Giambattista Tiepolo.

Fresco by Guarana in the *sala della musica* of the Ospedaletto

The decorative façade of the Scuola Grande di San Marco

San Francesco della Vigna ⓮

Ramo San Francesco. **Map** 8 E1. *041 520 61 02.* *Celestia.* *8am–12:30pm, 3–7pm daily.*

THE NAME "della Vigna" derives from a vineyard that was bequeathed to the Franciscans in 1253. The church which the order built here in the 13th century was rebuilt under Jacopo Sansovino in 1534, with a façade added in 1562–72 by Palladio.

The interior has a rich collection of works of art, including sculpture by Alessandro Vittoria, Paolo Veronese's *The Holy Family with Saints* (1562) and Antonio da Negroponte's *Virgin and Child* (c.1450). The *Madonna and Child with Saints* (1507) by Giovanni Bellini hangs near the cloister.

San Lorenzo ⓯

Campo San Lorenzo. **Map** 8 D1. *San Zaccaria.* *for restoration.*

DECONSECRATED and closed for restoration, the church of San Lorenzo's only claim to fame is as the alleged burial place of Marco Polo *(see p143).* Unfortunately there is nothing to show for it because his sarcophagus disappeared during rebuilding in 1592. A collection of paintings was dispersed, and for many years the church was abandoned.

In 1987 restorers discovered the foundations of two earlier churches, dating from AD 850 and the late 12th century. The foundations of the present medieval structure, as well as substantial remains of the marble floor, have been damaged by water seeping in from the adjacent canal. Restoration work funded by the British Venice in Peril Fund has long been at a standstill.

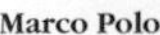

Marco Polo

Santi Giovanni e Paolo ⓬

Figure in left transept

MORE FAMILIARLY known as San Zanipolo, Santi Giovanni e Paolo vies with the Frari *(see pp102–3)* as the city's greatest Gothic church. It was built in the late 13th to early 14th centuries by the Dominican friars, and is striking for its huge dimensions and architectural austerity. Known as the Pantheon of Venice, it houses monuments to no less than 25 doges. Many of these are outstanding works, executed by the Lombardi family and other leading sculptors of the day.

★ Cappella del Rosario
The Adoration of the Shepherds *is one of many works by Paolo Veronese which decorate the Rosary Chapel.*

★ Tomb of Nicolò Marcello
This magnificent Renaissance monument to Doge Nicolò Marcello (d.1474) was sculpted by Pietro Lombardo.

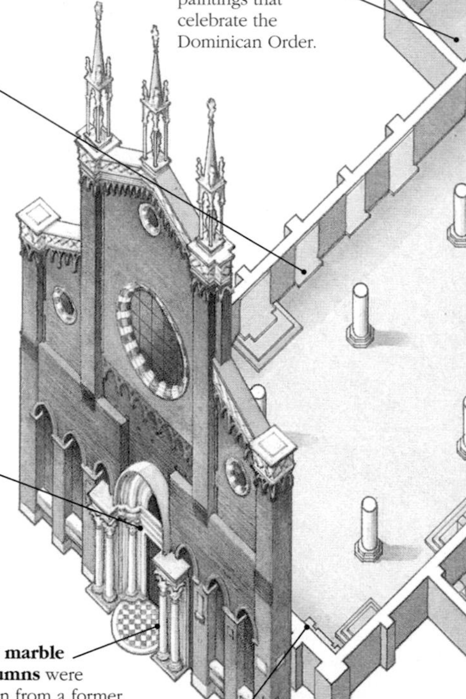

The sacristy has paintings that celebrate the Dominican Order.

The doorway, which is decorated with Byzantine reliefs, is one of the earliest Renaissance architectural features in Venice. The portico carvings are attributed to Bartolomeo Bon.

The marble columns were taken from a former church on the island of Torcello.

★ Tomb of Pietro Mocenigo
Pietro Lombardo's great masterpiece (1481) commemorates the doge's military pursuits when he was Grand Captain of the Venetian forces. This west side wall is largely devoted to Mocenigo monuments.

STAR FEATURES

- **★ Doges' Tombs**
- **★ Cappella del Rosario**
- **★ Cappella di San Domenico**

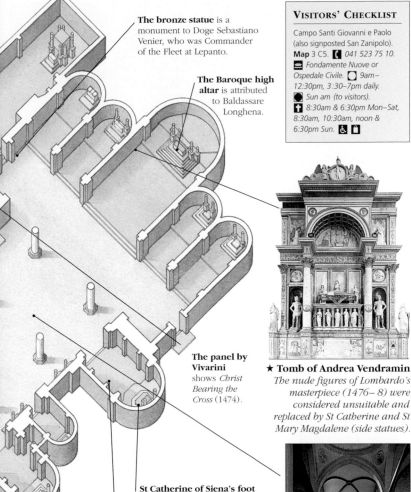

The bronze statue is a monument to Doge Sebastiano Venier, who was Commander of the Fleet at Lepanto.

The Baroque high altar is attributed to Baldassare Longhena.

Visitors' Checklist

Campo Santi Giovanni e Paolo (also signposted San Zanipolo). **Map** 3 C5. *041 523 75 10.* *Fondamente Nuove or Ospedale Civile.* *9am–12:30pm, 3:30–7pm daily.* *Sun am (to visitors).* *8:30am & 6:30pm Mon–Sat, 8:30am, 10:30am, noon & 6:30pm Sun.*

★ Tomb of Andrea Vendramin
The nude figures of Lombardo's masterpiece (1476–8) were considered unsuitable and replaced by St Catherine and St Mary Magdalene (side statues).

The panel by Vivarini shows *Christ Bearing the Cross* (1474).

St Catherine of Siena's foot is buried here in a precious reliquary; her relics are scattered in churches throughout Italy.

The Nave
The vast interior is cross-vaulted, held by wooden tie-beams and supported by ten huge columns of Istrian stone blocks.

★ Cappella di San Domenico
Piazzetta's Glory of St Dominic *for this chapel – his only ceiling painting – displays a mastery of colour, perspective and foreshortening. The artist had a profound influence on the young Tiepolo.*

***St George slaying the Dragon* by Carpaccio, in the Scuola di San Giorgio degli Schiavoni**

Scuola di San Giorgio degli Schiavoni ⓰

Calle Furlani. **Map** 8 E1. *041 522 88 28. San Zaccaria. Apr–Oct: 9:30am–12:30pm, 3:30–6:30pm Tue–Sun; Nov–Mar: 10am–12:30pm, 3–6pm Tue–Sun. Sun pm, 1 Jan, public hols & special events.*

WITHIN THIS surprisingly simple Scuola are some of the finest paintings of Vittore Carpaccio, commissioned by the Schiavoni community in Venice.

From the earliest days of the Republic, Venice forged trade links with the coastal region of Schiavonia (Dalmatia) across the Adriatic. By 1420 permanent Venetian rule was established there, and many of the Schiavoni came to live in Venice. By the mid-15th century the Slav colony in the city had grown considerably and the State gave permission for them to found their own confraternity *(see p127)*.

The Scuola was established in 1451. It is a delightful spot to admire Carpaccio's really exceptional works of art, and has changed very little since the rebuilding of the Scuola in 1551. The exquisite frieze, executed between 1502 and 1508, shows scenes from the lives of favourite saints: St George, St Tryphon and St Jerome. Each episode of the narrative cycle is remarkable for its vivid colouring, minutely observed detail and historic record of Venetian life. Outstanding among them are *St George Slaying the Dragon, St Jerome Leading the Tamed Lion to the Monastery*, and *The Vision of St Jerome.*

San Giovanni in Bragora ⓱

Campo Bandiera e Moro. **Map** 8 E2. *041 270 24 64. Arsenale. 3:30–5:30pm Mon–Sat.*

THE FOUNDATIONS of this simple church date back to ancient times but the existing building is essentially Gothic (1475–9). The intimate interior has major works of art which demonstrate the transition from Gothic to early Renaissance. Bartolomeo Vivarini's altarpiece, *Madonna and Child with Saints* (1478) is unmistakably Gothic. Contrasting with this is Cima da Conegliano's *Baptism of Christ* (1492–5) on the main altar. This large-scale narrative scene, in a realistic landscape, set a precedent for later Renaissance painters.

Museo Storico Navale ⓲

Campo San Biagio, Arsenale. **Map** 8 F3. *041 520 02 76. Arsenale. 8:45am–1:30pm Mon–Fri, 8:45am–1pm Sat. public hols.*

IT WAS THE Austrians who, in 1815, first had the idea of assembling the remnants of the Venetian navy and creating a historical naval museum. They began with a series of models of vessels that had been produced in the 17th century by the Arsenale, and to these added all the naval paraphernalia they could obtain. The exhibits include friezes preserved from famous galleys of the past, a variety of maritime firearms and a replica of the Doge's ceremonial barge, the *Bucintoro.*

The collection has been housed in an ex-warehouse on the waterfront since 1958, and now traces Venetian and Italian naval history to the present day.

The first exhibits you see on entering are the World War II human torpedoes or "pigs". Torpedoes such as these helped sink HMS *Valiant* and HMS *Queen Elizabeth*: they were guided to their target by naval divers who jumped off just before impact.

The rest of the museum is divided into the Venetian navy, the Italian navy from 1860 to today, Adriatic vessels and the Swedish room. The museum is well laid out and there are very informative explanations in English.

Model of the *Bucintoro* in the Museo Storico Navale

Arsenale ⓳

Map 8 F1. Arsenale.
Limited public access.

HEART OF the city's maritime power, the Arsenale was founded in the 12th century and enlarged in the 14th to 16th centuries to become the greatest naval shipyard in the world. The word "arsenal" derives from the Arabic *darsina'a*, house of industry – which indeed it was.

At its height in the 16th century, a workforce of 16,000, the *arsenalotti*, was employed to construct, equip and repair the great Venetian galleys *(see pp44–5)*. One of the first production lines in Europe, it was like a city within a city, with its own workshops, warehouses, factories, foundries and docks.

THE ASSEMBLY-LINE SYSTEM

The *arsenalotti*, master shipbuilders of the 16th century

During the Arsenale's heyday, a Venetian galley could be constructed and fully equipped with remarkable speed and efficiency. From the early 16th century the hulls, which were built in the New Arsenal, were towed past a series of buildings in the Old Arsenal to be equipped in turn with rigging, ammunition and food supplies. By 1570, when Venice was faced with the Turkish threat to take Cyprus, the Arsenale proved capable of turning out an entire galley in 24 hours. Henry III of France witnessed the system's efficiency in 1574 when the *arsenalotti* completed a galley in the time it took for him to partake in a state feast.

Entrance to the Arsenale, guarded by 16th-century towers

Surrounded by crenellated walls, the site today is largely abandoned. The huge gateway and vast site are the only evidence of its former splendour. The gateway, in the form of a triumphal arch, was built in 1460 by Antonio Gambello and is often cited as Venice's first Renaissance construction.

The two lions guarding the entrance were pillaged from Piraeus (near Athens) by Admiral Francesco Morosini in 1687. A third lion, bald and sitting upright, bears runic inscriptions on his haunches, thought to have been carved by Scandinavian mercenaries who in 1040 fought for the Byzantine emperor against some Greek rebels.

By the 17th century, when the seeds of Venetian decline were well and truly sown, the number of *arsenalotti* plummeted to 1,000. Following the Fall of the Republic in 1797, Napoleon destroyed the docks and stripped the *Bucintoro* (the Doge's ceremonial ship) of its precious ornament. Cannons and bronzes were melted down to contribute to victory monuments celebrating the French Revolution.

Today the area is under military administration and for the most part closed to the public. The bridge by the arched gateway affords partial views of the shipyard, else you can take a trip on a *vaporetto* (route 41 or 42), which follows the perimeter of the Arsenale.

Some parts of the Arsenale, such as the Corderie, the old rope factory, are now being used as performance spaces or exhibition centres, mostly for the Biennale *(see p256)*. A research consortium developing marine and coastal technologies also operates from the Arsenale.

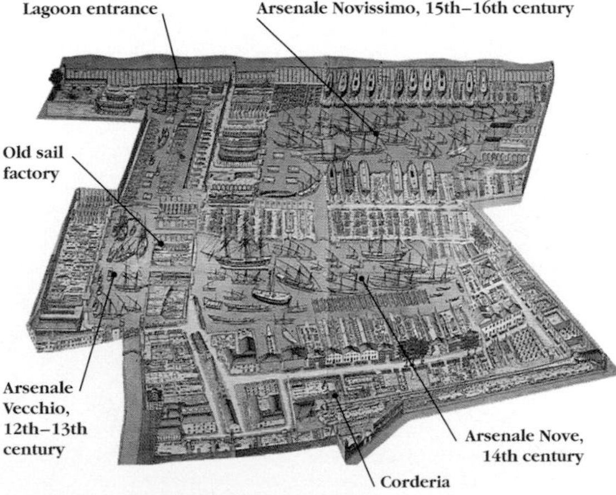

Late 18th-century engraving of the Arsenale

Exploring Eastern Castello ⓴

THIS PEACEFUL STROLL takes you from the animated Castello quayside to the quieter eastern limits of the city. The focal point of the tour is the solitary island of San Pietro di Castello, site of the former cathedral of Venice. From here you head south to the island of Sant'Elena with its historic church and Venice's football stadium, and return via the public gardens along the scenic waterfront.

The calm and leafy Giardini Pubblici ⑯

A tribute to the women fallen in World War II ⑱

Via Garibaldi

This broad, busy street ① was created by Napoleon in 1808 by filling in a canal. The first house on the right ② was the home of John Cabot and his son Sebastian, the Italian navigators who in 1497 found what they thought to be the coast of China (but in reality was the Labrador coast of Newfoundland). Near the end of the street, through a gate on the right, a bronze monument of Garibaldi ③ by Augusto Benvenuti (1885) marks the northern end of the Viale Garibaldi, which leads to the public gardens.

Returning to Via Garibaldi, take the left-hand embankment at the end of the street, pausing on the bridge ④ for distant views of the Arsenale *(see p119)*. Then take the first on the left, marked Calle San Gioachin, cross a small bridge and turn left at the "crossroads". Once you are past Campo Ruga ⑤, take the second turning on the right and cross the bridge over the broad Canale di San Pietro.

The island of San Pietro di Castello

The old church of San Pietro di Castello ⑥ and its free-standing, tilting campanile ⑦ overlook a grassy square. The island, once occupied by a fortress *(castello)*, was one of Venice's earliest settlements. The church, which was probably founded in the 7th century, became the cathedral of Venice and remained so until 1807 when San Marco took its place *(see p80)*. The existing church, built to a Palladian design in the mid-16th century, has several notable features. These include the Lando Chapel, the Vendramin Chapel and the marble throne from an Arabic tombstone, originally said to have been the Seat of St Peter.

In the south of the square, Mauro Coducci's elegant stone campanile was built in 1482–8, and the cupola was added in 1670. Beside the church, the Palazzo Patriarcale (Bishop's

The busy Via Garibaldi, with John Cabot's house on the far right ②

KEY

••• Walk route

View point

 *Vaporetto* boarding point

Palace) ⑧ was turned into barracks by Napoleon. The old cloisters are overgrown and strung with washing and fishing nets.

From the Bishop's Palace take the Calle drio il Campanile south from the square and turn left when you come to the canal. The first turning right takes you across the Ponte di Quintavalle ⑨, a wooden bridge with good views of brightly coloured boats anchored on either side of the waterway.

ampanile
an Pietro

The island of San Pietro, with its curious leaning campanile ⑦

San Pietro to Sant'Elena

The large and semi-derelict building at the foot of the bridge is the ex-church and monastery of Sant'Anna ⑩. Take the first left off the *fondamenta*, cross Campiello Correr and then take Calle GB Tiepolo and cross the Secco Marina. Continue straight ahead and over the bridge for the Church of San Giuseppe ⑪. On the rare occasions it is open you can see Vincenzo Scamozzi's monument to Doge Marino Grimani (1595–1605). Cross the square beyond the church and zigzag left, right and left again for Paludo San Antonio, an uninspiring modern street that has been reclaimed from marshland *(palude)*. At the far end cross the bridge over the Rio dei Giardini ⑫ and take the street ahead. A right turn along Viale 4 Novembre brings you down to the spacious gardens of Parco delle Rimembranze ⑬. At the southern end of the park, cut left at Calle Buccari ⑭, then right for the bridge over Rio di Sant'Elena. In front, the Church of Sant'Elena ⑮ is a pretty Gothic church founded in the 13th century. Retrace your steps over the bridge and turn left, following the waterfront back through the park.

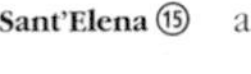

Detail from Gothic façade of Sant'Elena ⑮

Giardini Pubblici and the Biennale Pavilions

At the far side of the park, the bridge across the Rio dei Giardini brings you to the public gardens and to the Biennale gate entrance ⑯. If it happens to be summer in an odd-numbered year, the gardens will be open with the Biennale pavilions ⑰ at which 40 to 50 nations exhibit many examples of contemporary art *(see p256)*.

Riva dei Partigiani

Outside the public gardens on Riva dei Partigiani is a large bronze statue. Lying on the steps of the embankment, the monument can only be seen at low tide. Known as La Donna Partigiana, this is a memorial to all the women who were killed fighting in World War II ⑱.

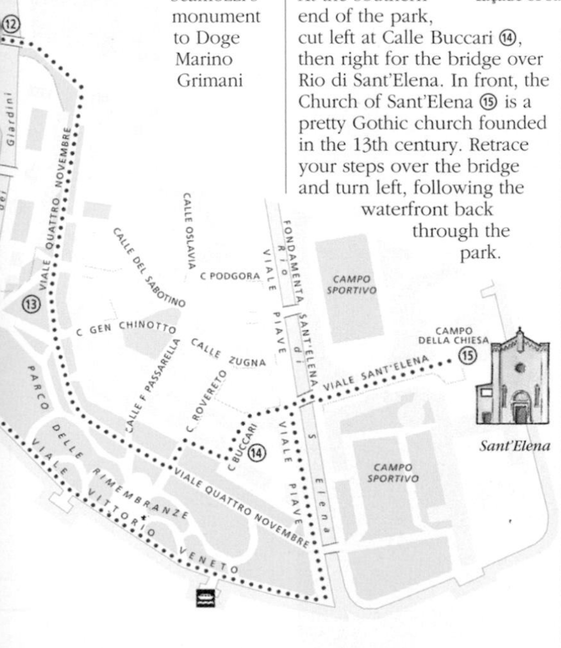

> **Tips for Walkers**
>
> ***Starting point:*** *The western end of Via Garibaldi.*
>
> ***Length:*** *Just under 5 km (3 miles).*
>
> ***Getting there:*** *Vaporetto No. 1, 41 or 42 to Arsenale.*
>
> ***Stopping-off points:*** *There are a handful of simple cafés and trattorias along the route, most of them on Via Garibaldi. The waterside Caffè Paradiso at the entrance to the Giardini Pubblici has excellent views. For good seafood, try the Hostaria Da Franz (see p241) along Fondamenta San Giuseppe (No. 754). The green shady parks are a welcome retreat from the bustle of the city.*

Sights at a Glance

Churches

Angelo Raffaele 8
Gesuati 14
Santa Maria dei Carmini 6
Santa Maria della Salute 19
Santa Maria della Visitazione 13
San Nicolò dei Mendicoli 7
San Sebastiano 9
San Trovaso 12

Museums and Galleries

Accademia see pp130–33 15
Ca' Rezzonico 3
Cini Collection 16
Peggy Guggenheim Collection 17

Historic Buildings

Dogana di Mare 20
Scuola Grande dei Carmini 5
Squero di San Trovaso 11

Streets, Bridges and Squares

Campiello Barbaro 18
Campo San Barnaba 1
Campo Santa Margherita 4
Ponte dei Pugni 2
Zattere 10

Key

Street-by-Street map *See pp124–5*

Vaporetto boarding point

Traghetto crossing

◁ **View across the Grand Canal to Santa Maria della Salute**

DORSODURO

DORSODURO IS NAMED after the solid subsoil on which this area has been built up (the name means "hard backbone"). The western part, the island of Mendigola, was colonized centuries before the Rialto was established in AD 828 as the permanent seat of Venice. The settlement then spread eastwards, covering another six islands.

East of the Accademia, the Dorsoduro is a quiet and pretty neighbourhood with shaded squares, quiet canals and picturesque residences belonging to wealthy Venetians and foreigners. In the early 1900s the area was favoured by British expatriates who used to attend the Anglican church of St George in Campo San Vio. Among the area's attractions are the wide-embracing lagoon views, both from the eastern tip near the Salute and from the Zattere across to the island of Giudecca. West of the Accademia, the *sestiere* is more vibrant, with the busy Campo Santa Margherita as its attractive focal point. Further west, the shabbier area around the beautiful church of San Nicolò dei Mendicoli was originally the home of fishermen and sailors. The Dorsoduro plays host to several major collections of art, notably the Accademia Gallery and the Peggy Guggenheim Collection of 20th-century art. The churches are also rich repositories of paintings and sculpture: San Sebastiano has fine paintings by Paolo Veronese; the Scuola Grande dei Carmini and the church of the Gesuati have ceilings painted by Giambattista Tiepolo.

Squero di San Trovaso, the gondola boatyard

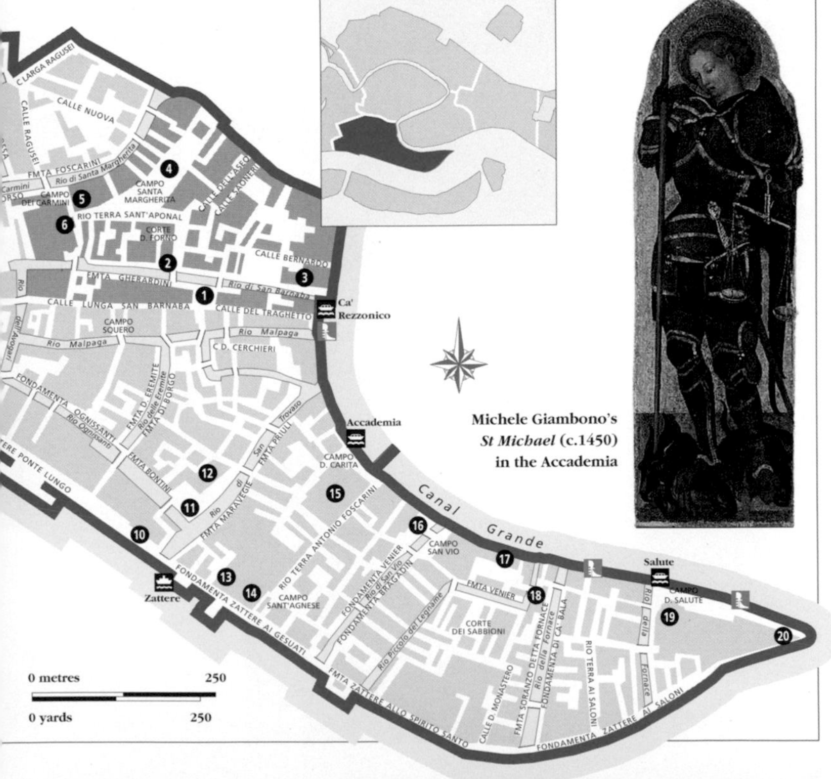

Michele Giambono's *St Michael* (c.1450) in the Accademia

Street-by-Street: Dorsoduro

Reliefs on a house at Ponte Trovaso

BETWEEN THE IMPOSING palaces on the Grand Canal and the Campo Santa Margherita lies an almost silent neighbourhood of small squares and narrow alleys. The delightful Rio San Barnaba is best appreciated from the Ponte dei Pugni, near the barge selling fruit and vegetables. The Rio Terrà, though architecturally uninspiring, has a fascinating mask shop and some cafés that are lively at night-time. All roads seem to lead to Campo Santa Margherita, the heart of Dorsoduro. The square bustles with activity, particularly in the morning when the market stalls are functioning.

★ Scuola Grande dei Carmini
Tiepolo painted nine ceiling panels for the Scuola in 1739–44. The central panel features the Virgin and St Simeon Stock ❺

Palazzo Zenobio has been an Armenian college since 1850. Occasionally visitors can see the sumptuous 18th-century ballrooom.

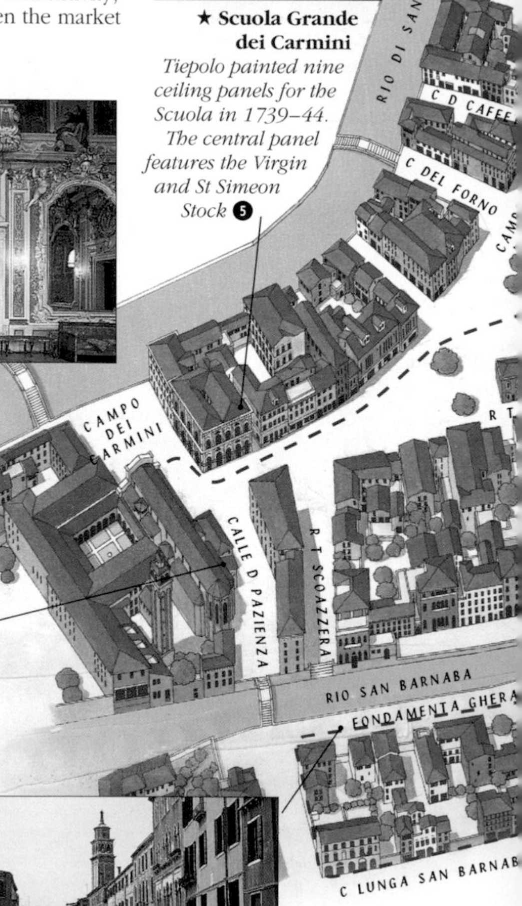

RIO DI SANTA MARGHERITA
C DEL
C D CAFFE
C DEL FORNO
CAMPO DEI CARMINI
CALLE D PAZIENZA
R T SCOAZZERA
RIO SAN BARNABA
FONDAMENTA GHERA
C LUNGA SAN BARNAB

Santa Maria dei Carmini
The church's oldest feature is the Gothic side porch with fragments of decorative Byzantine reliefs ❻

KEY

— — — Suggested route

0 metres 50

0 yards 50

STAR SIGHTS

- **★ Scuola Grande dei Carmini**
- **★ Ca' Rezzonico**
- **★ San Barnaba**

Fondamenta Gherardini runs beside the Rio San Barnaba, one of the prettiest canals in the *sestiere*.

Campo Santa Margherita
Open-air cafés are an integral part of the square. Causin sells particularly delicious Italian ice cream ❹

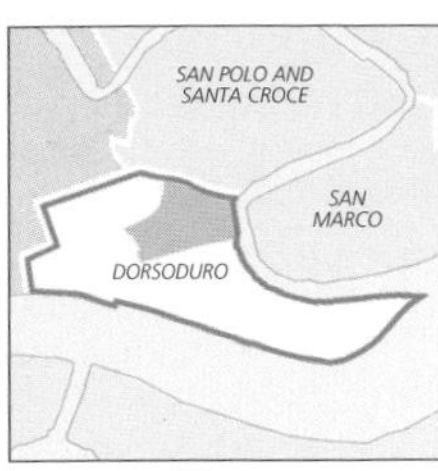

LOCATOR MAP
See Street Finder, map 6

Palazzo Giustinian is the 15th-century palace where Richard Wagner stayed while he was writing the second act of *Tristan and Isolde* in 1858.

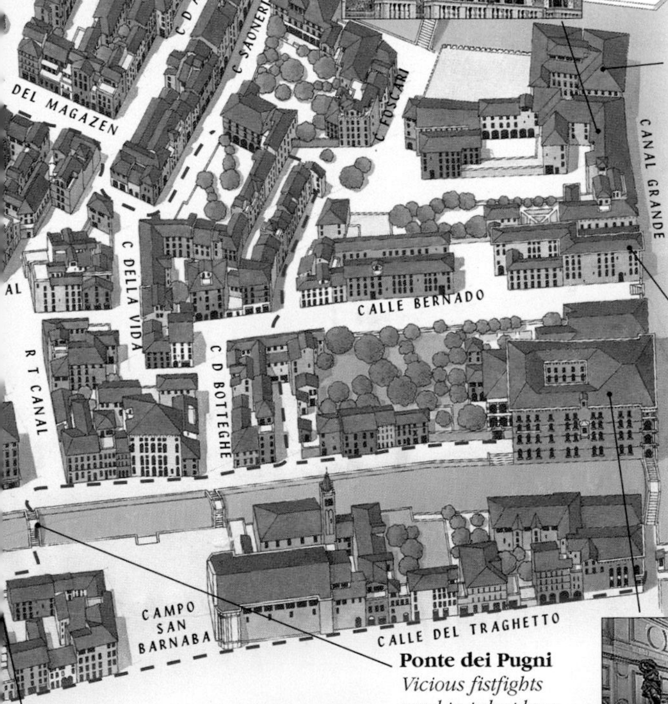

Ca' Foscari, with its splendid setting, was chosen as the lodging place for Henry III of France in 1574.

Palazzo Nani is one of the fine palaces that lie on the great curve called the Volta del Canal.

Ca' Rezzonico

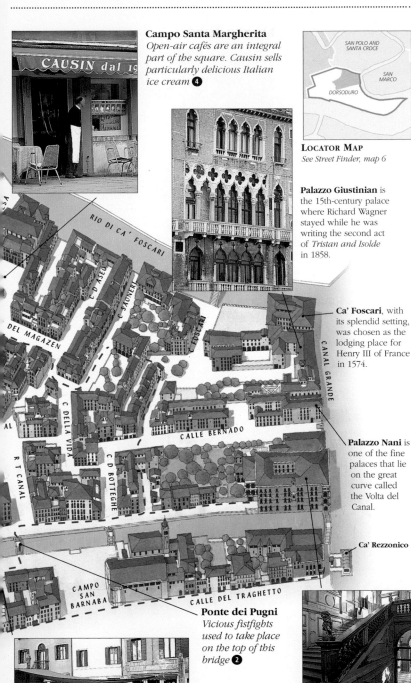

Ponte dei Pugni
Vicious fistfights used to take place on the top of this bridge ❷

★ San Barnaba
A floating barge crammed with crates of fruit and vegetables lends a colourful note to the area ❶

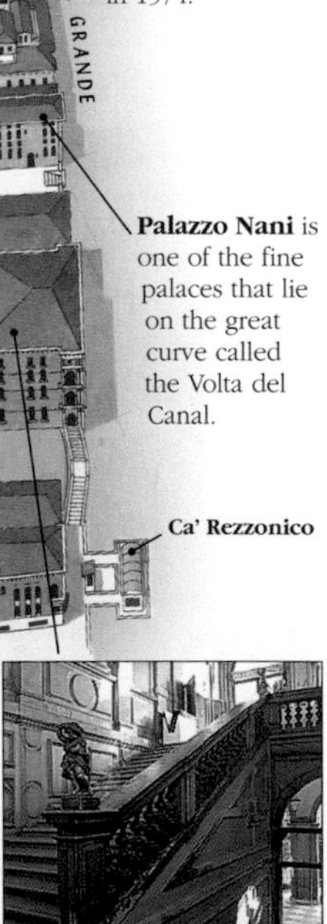

★ Ca' Rezzonico
The grand stairway has two putti, symbolizing winter and autumn ❸

Campo San Barnaba ❶

Map 6 D3. *Ca' Rezzonico.*

THE PARISH OF San Barnaba, with its canalside square at the centre, was known in the 18th century as the home of impoverished Venetian patricians. These *barnabotti* were attracted by the cheap rents, and while some relied on state support or begging, others worked as bankers in the State gambling house.

Today the square and canal, with its laden vegetable barge, are quietly appealing. The church is fairly unremarkable, apart from a Tiepolesque ceiling and a *Holy Family* attributed to Paolo Veronese.

Ponte dei Pugni ❷

Fondamenta Gherardini. **Map** 6 D3. *Ca' Rezzonico.*

VENICE HAS SEVERAL Ponti dei Pugni ("bridges of fists"), but this is the most famous. Spanning the peaceful Rio San Barnaba, the small bridge is distinguished by two pairs of footprints set in white stone on top of the bridge. These mark the starting positions for the fights which traditionally took place between rival factions. Formerly there were no balustrades and contenders hurled each other straight into the water. The battles became so bloodthirsty that they were banned in 1705.

Boats and barges moored along the Rio San Barnaba

Tiepolo's *New World* fresco, part of a series in Ca' Rezzonico

Ca' Rezzonico ❸

Fondamenta Rezzonico 3136. **Map** 6 E3. *041 241 01 00.* *Ca' Rezzonico.* *Nov–Mar: 10am–5pm Wed–Mon; Apr–Oct: 10am–6pm Wed–Mon.* *1 Jan, 1 May, 25 Dec.*

THIS RICHLY furnished Baroque palace is one of the most splendid in Venice. It is also one of the few palaces in the city, which opens its doors to the public. Since 1934 it has housed the museum of 18th-century Venice, its rooms furnished with frescoes, paintings and period pieces taken from other local palaces or museums.

The building was begun by Baldassare Longhena (architect of La Salute, *see p135*) in 1667, but the funds of the Bon family, who commissioned it, ran dry before the second floor was started. In 1712, long after Longhena's death, the unfinished palace was bought by the Rezzonicos, a family of merchants-turned-bankers from Genoa. A large portion of the Rezzonico fortune was spent on the purchase, construction and decoration of the palace. By 1758 it was in a fit state for the Rezzonicos to throw the first of the huge banquets and celebratory parties for which they later became renowned.

In 1888 the palace was bought by the poet Robert Browning and his son, Pen, who was married to an American heiress. Browning spoke of the "gaiety and comfort of the enormous rooms" but had little time to enjoy them. In 1889 he died of bronchitis.

***Allegory of Strength*, Andrea Brustolon**

The outstanding attraction in the palace today is Giorgio Massari's ballroom, which occupies the entire breadth of the building. It has been beautifully restored and is embellished with gilded chandeliers, carved furniture by Andrea Brustolon and a ceiling with *trompe l'oeil* frescoes. Three rooms between the ballroom and Grand Canal side of the palace have ceilings with frescoes by Giambattista Tiepolo including, in the Sala della Allegoria Nuziale, his lively *Nuptial Allegory* (1758).

Eighteenth-century paintings occupy the *piano nobile* (second floor). A whole room is devoted to Pietro Longhi's portrayals of everyday Venetian life. Other paintings worthy of note are Francesco Guardi's *Ridotto* (1748) and *Nuns' Parlour* (1768), and one of the few Canalettos in Venice, his *View of the Rio dei Mendicanti* (1725). Giandomenico Tiepolo's fascinating series of frescoes painted for his villa at Zianigo (1770–1800) are also to be found here. On the floor above is a reconstructed 18th-century apothecary's shop and a puppet theatre.

Campo Santa Margherita ❹

Map 6 D2. *Ca' Rezzonico.*

THE SPRAWLING square of Santa Margherita, lined with houses from the 14th and 15th centuries, is the lively hub of western Dorsoduro. Market stalls, off-beat shops and cafés attract many young people. The fish stalls sell live eels and lobster, the *erborista* alternative medicine, and the bakers some of the tastiest loaves in Venice.

The former church of Santa Margherita, now an auditorium owned by the university, lies to the north of the square. Visitors can see sculptural fragments from the original 18th-century church, including gargoyles, on the truncated campanile and adjacent house. The Scuola dei Varotari (Scuola of the tanners), the isolated building in the centre of the square, has a faded relief of the Madonna della Misericordia protecting the tanners.

A 15th-century carving of Santa Margherita and the dragon

Scuola Grande dei Carmini ❺

Campo Carmini. **Map** 5 C2. *041 528 94 20. Ca' Rezzonico. Apr–Oct: 9am–6pm Mon–Sat, 9am–4pm Sun; Nov–Mar: 9am–4pm daily. 1 Jan, 25 Dec.*

THE HEADQUARTERS of the Carmelite confraternity was built beside their church in 1663. In the 1740s Giambattista Tiepolo was commissioned to decorate the ceiling of the *salone (*hall) on the upper floor. These nine ceiling paintings so impressed the Carmelites that Tiepolo was promptly made an honorary member of the brotherhood.

The ceiling used to show *St Simeon Stock Receiving the Scapular of the Carmelite Order from the Virgin* but, unfortunately, in 2000 the painting crashed to the floor, its support having been eaten by woodworm. The work is currently in Bologna, where it is being restored. The Carmelites honoured St Simeon Stock because he re-established the order in Europe after its expulsion from the Holy Land in the 13th century.

Santa Maria dei Carmini

Santa Maria dei Carmini ❻

Campo Carmini. **Map** 5 C3. *041 270 24 64. Ca' Rezzonico or San Basilio. 2:30–5:30pm Mon–Sat.*

KNOWN ALSO as Santa Maria del Carmelo, this church was built in the 14th century but has since undergone extensive alterations.

The most prominent external feature is the lofty campanile, whose perilous tilt was skilfully rectified in 1688. The impressive interior is large, sombre and richly decorated. The arches of the nave are adorned with gilded wooden statues, and a series of paintings illustrating the history of the Carmelite Order.

There are two interesting paintings in the church's side altars. Cima da Conegliano's *Adoration of the Shepherds* (c.1509) is in the second altar on the right (coins in the light meter are essential). In the second altar on the left is Lorenzo Lotto's *St Nicholas of Bari with Saints Lucy and John the Baptist* (c.1529). This painting demonstrates the artist's religious devotion, personal sensitivity and his love of nature. On the right-hand side of this highly detailed, almost Dutch-style landscape, there is a tiny depiction of St George killing the dragon.

SCUOLE

The *scuole* were peculiarly Venetian institutions. Founded mainly in the 13th century, they were lay confraternities existing for the charitable benefit of the neediest groups of society, the professions or resident ethnic minorities (such as the Scuola dei Schiavoni, *see p118*). Some became extremely rich, spending large sums on buildings and paintings, often to the disadvantage of their declared beneficiaries.

Upper Hall of the Scuola Grande dei Carmini

Nave of San Nicolò dei Mendicoli, one of the oldest churches in Venice

San Nicolò dei Mendicoli ❼

Campo San Nicolò. **Map** 5 A3. *041 275 03 82.* *San Basilio.* *10am–noon, 4–6pm Mon–Sat.*

CONTRASTING WITH the remote and rundown area that surrounds it, this church remains one of the most charming and delightful in Venice. Originally constructed in the 12th century, it has been rebuilt extensively over the centuries; the little porch on the north flank dates from the 15th century.

Thanks to the Venice in Peril Fund, in the 1970s the church underwent one of the most comprehensive restoration programmes since the floods of 1966 *(see p50)*. The floor, which was 30 cm (1 ft) below the level of the canals, was rebuilt and raised slightly to prevent further damage, the roofs and lower walls were reconstructed, and paintings and statues restored. The interior is richly embellished, particularly the nave with its 16th-century gilded wood statues. On the upper walls is a series of paintings of the life of Christ by Alvise dal Friso and other pupils of Veronese.

Angelo Raffaele ❽

Campo Angelo Raffaele. **Map** 5 B3. *041 522 85 48.* *San Basilio.* *8am–noon, 4–6pm Mon–Sat; 8am–noon Sun & public hols.*

THE MAIN ATTRACTION of this 17th-century church is the series of panel paintings on the organ balustrade. These were executed in 1749 by Antonio Guardi, brother of the more famous Francesco. They tell the tale of Tobias, the blind prophet cured by the archangel Raphael, after whom the church is named.

San Sebastiano ❾

Campo San Sebastiano. **Map** 5 C3. *041 275 04 62.* *San Basilio.* *10am–5pm daily (from 1pm Sun).* *Sun (Jul & Aug); 1 Jan, 25 Dec.*

THIS 16th-century church has one of the most colourful and homogeneous interiors of Venice. This is thanks to the artist Veronese who, from 1555 to 1560 and again in the 1570s, was commissioned to decorate the sacristy ceiling, the nave ceiling, the frieze, the east end of the choir, the high altar, the doors of the organ panels and the chancel – in that order. The paintings, which are typical of Veronese, are rich and radiant, with sumptuous costumes and colours. Among the finest of his works are the three ceiling paintings which tell the story of Esther, Queen of Xerxes I of Persia, who brought about the deliverance of the Jewish people. Appropriately, the artist is buried in San Sebastiano, alongside the organ.

Zattere ❿

Map 5 C4. *Zattere or San Basilio.*

STRETCHING ALONG the southern part of the *sestiere*, the Zattere is the long quayside looking across to the island of Giudecca. The name derives from the rafts *(zattere)* made of and carrying timber from the Republic's forests. After skilful navigation along

San Sebastiano, viewed from the bridge of the same name

Café tables laid out along the Zattere

the River Piave, the rafts were dismantled on arrival in Venice. On a sunny day it is a pleasure to sit at a water-side café here, looking across to the Church of the Redentore *(see p154)* or watching the waterbuses as they cross back and forth between the shores.

Squero di San Trovaso ⓫

Rio San Trovaso. **Map** 6 D4.
Zattere. ***No public access.***

THIS IS ONE of the few surviving gondola workshops in Venice *(see pp28–9)* and the most picturesque. Its Tyrolean look dates from the days when craftsmen came down from the Cadore area of the Dolomites *(see p215)*.

It is not open to the public, but from the far side of the Rio San Trovaso you can often watch the upturned gondolas being given their scraping and tarring treatment. You may see a new one under construction, but nowadays only around ten are made each year.

San Trovaso ⓬

Campo San Trovaso. **Map** 6 D4.
041 270 24 64. Zattere or Accademia. 3–6pm Mon–Sat.

THE CHURCH OF Santi Gervasio e Protasio, which in the eccentric Venetian dialect is slurred to San Trovaso, was built in 1590. Unusually it has two identical façades, one overlooking a canal, the other a quiet square. The church stood on neutral ground between the parishes of the rival factions of the Castellani and Nicolotti families, and tradition has it that this necessitated a separate entrance for each party.

The interior houses some late paintings by Jacopo Tintoretto, and there are two notable works of art worth seeking out. Michele Giambono's 15th-century Gothic painting, *St Chrysogonus on Horseback*, is situated in the chapel on the right of the chancel, and exquisite marble reliefs of angels with instruments decorate the altar of the Clary chapel opposite.

Santa Maria della Visitazione ⓭

Fondamenta delle Zattere. **Map** 6 E4.
041 522 40 77. Zattere.
8am–6pm daily (to 5pm in winter).

SITUATED BESIDE the Gesuati, this Renaissance church was built between 1494 and 1524 by the Order of the Gesuati. After a period of closure and renovation, mass is once again held here. Inside the church is a fine wooden ceiling painted by 16th-century Umbrian and Tuscan artists. The exterior *bocca di leone* to the right of the façade is one of several "lion's mouth" denunciation boxes surviving from the rule of the Council of Ten *(see p42)*; this one was used to complain about the state of the streets.

Gesuati ⓮

Fondamenta delle Zattere. **Map** 6 E4.
041 275 04 62. Zattere.
10am–5pm daily (from 1pm Sun).

NOT TO BE CONFUSED with the Gesuiti *(see p142)*, this church was built by the Dominicans, who took possession of the site in the 17th century, when the Gesuati Order was suppressed. Work began in 1726 and the stately façade reflects that of Palladio's Redentore church across the Giudecca. It is the most conspicuous landmark of the long Zattere quayside. The interior of the church is richly decorated. Tiepolo's frescoed ceiling, *The Life of St Dominic* (1737–39) demonstrates the artist's mastery of light and colour. Equally impressive (and far easier to see) is his *Virgin with Saints* (1740), situated in the first chapel on the right. The church also boasts two altar paintings by Sebastiano Ricci and Giambattista Piazzetta.

Gesuati façade statue

Squero di San Trovaso, where gondolas are given a facelift

Accademia ⓯

Exterior detail of the Accademia

THE LARGEST COLLECTION of Venetian art in existence, the Gallerie dell'Accademia, is housed in three former religious buildings. The basis of the collection was the Accademia di Belle Arti, founded in 1750 by the painter Giovanni Battista Piazzetta. In 1807 Napoleon moved the academy to these premises, and the collection was greatly enlarged by works of art from churches and monasteries he suppressed.

Ceiling Sketch
Tiepolo's The Translation of the Holy House to Loreto *(c.1742) was a sketch for the ceiling of the Scalzi church* (see p145).

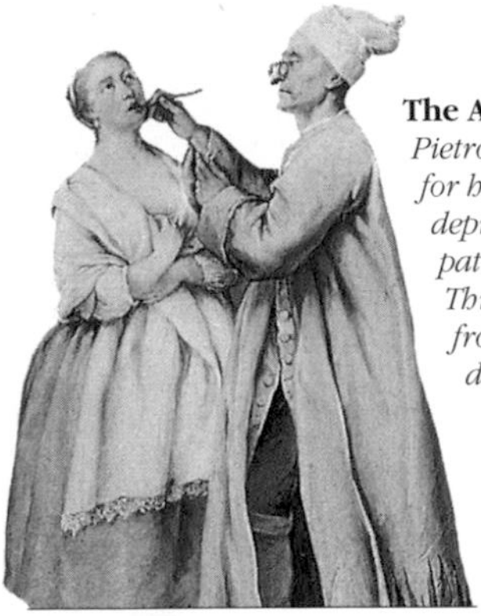

The Apothecary's Shop
Pietro Longhi is best known for his witty, gently satirical depictions of domestic patrician life in Venice. This detail comes from a painting dated c.1752.

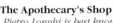

13 14 16 16a 15 17 20 18 19 21 23 22 24

KEY TO FLOORPLAN

- Byzantine and International Gothic
- Early Renaissance
- High Renaissance
- Baroque, genre and landscapes
- Ceremonial paintings
- Temporary exhibitions
- Non-exhibition space

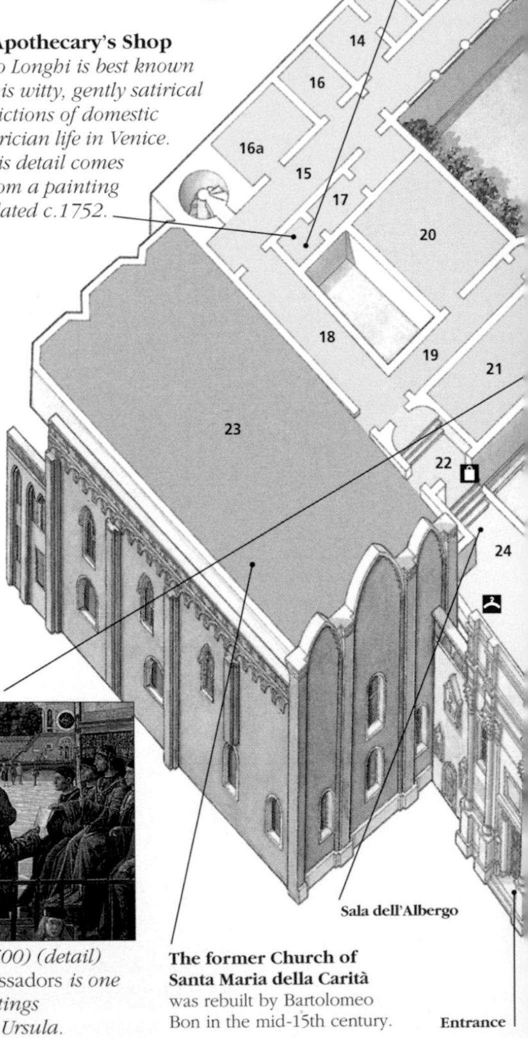

★ Cycle of St Ursula *(1495–1500) (detail)*
The Arrival of the English Ambassadors *is one of Vittore Carpaccio's eight paintings chronicling the tragic story of St Ursula.*

Sala dell'Albergo

The former Church of Santa Maria della Carità was rebuilt by Bartolomeo Bon in the mid-15th century.

Entrance

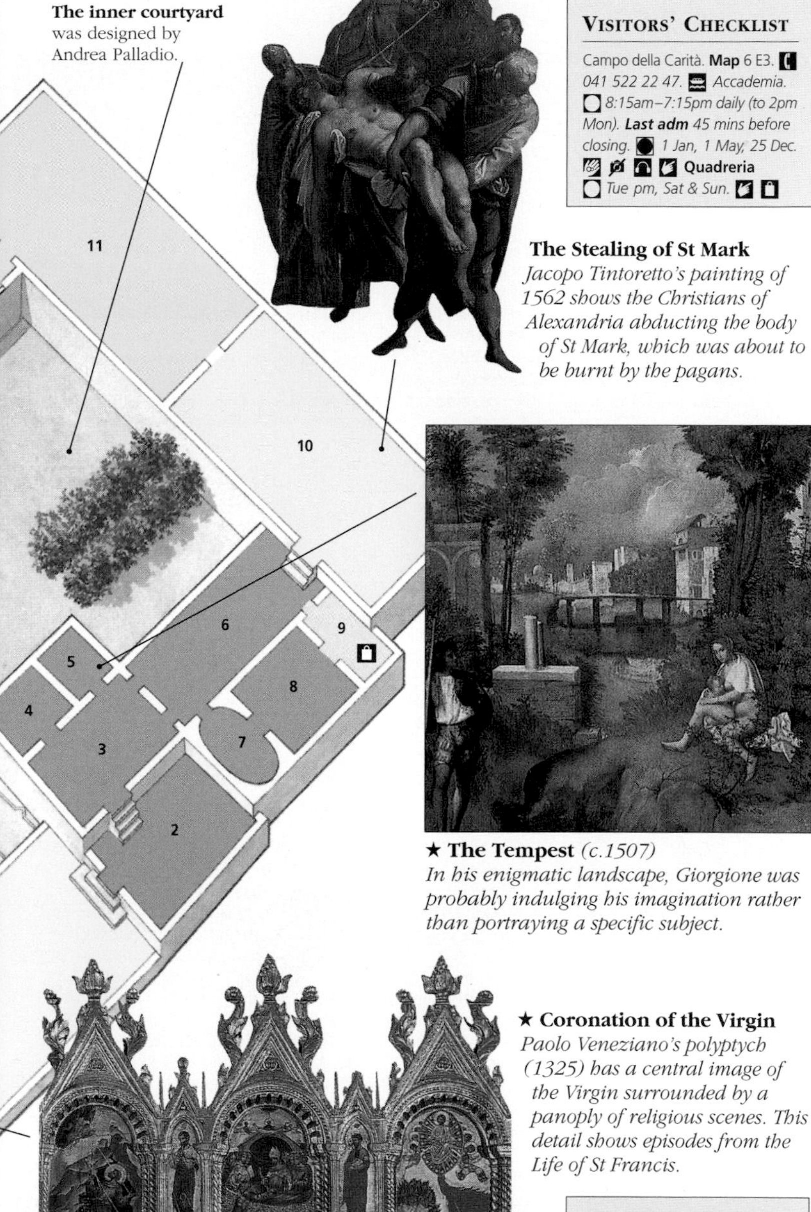

The inner courtyard was designed by Andrea Palladio.

The Stealing of St Mark
Jacopo Tintoretto's painting of 1562 shows the Christians of Alexandria abducting the body of St Mark, which was about to be burnt by the pagans.

★ The Tempest *(c.1507)*
In his enigmatic landscape, Giorgione was probably indulging his imagination rather than portraying a specific subject.

★ Coronation of the Virgin
Paolo Veneziano's polyptych (1325) has a central image of the Virgin surrounded by a panoply of religious scenes. This detail shows episodes from the Life of St Francis.

Gallery Guide

Most of the paintings are housed on one floor divided into 24 rooms. Restoration work is ongoing, so be prepared for absent paintings or whole sections closed off. The paintings are dependent on natural light, so to see them at their best try to visit on a bright morning. Upstairs, a second gallery, called Quadreria, contains works by Italian artists including Bellini, Veronese and Tintoretto. Guided visits are free of charge, but it is essential to book in advance.

Visitors' Checklist

Campo della Carità. **Map** 6 E3. 041 522 22 47. *Accademia.* *8:15am–7:15pm daily (to 2pm Mon). **Last adm** 45 mins before closing.* *1 Jan, 1 May, 25 Dec.* **Quadreria** *Tue pm, Sat & Sun.*

Star Paintings

- **★ Cycle of St Ursula by Carpaccio**
- **★ Coronation of the Virgin by Veneziano**
- **★ The Tempest by Giorgione**

Exploring the Accademia's Collection

SPANNING FIVE CENTURIES, the fascinating collection of paintings in the Accademia provides a complete spectrum of the Venetian school, from the medieval Byzantine period through the Renaissance to the Baroque and Rococo *(see pp26–7)*. The order is more or less chronological, with the exception of the final rooms, which take you back to the Renaissance.

BYZANTINE AND INTERNATIONAL GOTHIC

ROOM 1 SHOWS the influence of Byzantine art on the early Venetian painters. Paolo Veneziano, the true founder of the Venetian school, displays a blend of both western and eastern influences in his sumptuous *Coronation of the Virgin* (1325). The linear rhythms are quite unmistakably Gothic, yet the overall effect and the glowing gold background are distinctly Byzantine.

In the same room, *Coronation of the Virgin* (1448) by Michele Giambono shows the influence of International Gothic style, which was brought to Venice by Gentile da Fabriano and Pisanello. This particular style was characterized by delicate naturalistic detail, as typified by the birds and animals in the foreground of Giambono's painting.

***Coronation of the Virgin* (c.1448) by Michele Giambono**

EARLY RENAISSANCE

THE RENAISSANCE came late to Venice, but by the second quarter of the 15th century it had transformed the city into an art centre rivalling those of Florence and Rome. The Bellini family – Jacopo, the father, and his two sons Gentile and Giovanni – played a dominant role in the early Venetian Renaissance.

Central to Venetian art in the 15th century was the *Sacra Conversazione*, where the Madonna is portrayed in a unified composition with saints. Giovanni Bellini's altarpiece for San Giobbe (c.1487) in Room 2 is one of the finest examples. Giovanni, the younger Bellini, was profoundly influenced by the controlled rational style and mastery of perspective in the works of his brother-in-law, Andrea Mantegna, whose work *St George* (c.1460) is in Room 4. To Mantegna's rationality and harsh realism Giovanni added humanity. This is seen in his Madonna paintings (Rooms 4 and 5), which are masterpieces of warmth and harmony. Outstanding examples are *The Virgin and Child between St Catherine and St Mary Magdalene* (c.1490) in Room 4; *Madonna of the Little Trees* (c.1487) and *Virgin and Child with John the Baptist and a Saint* (c.1505) in Room 5. The inventive young artist

***Portrait of a Gentleman* (c.1525) by Lorenzo Lotto (detail)**

Giorgione was influenced by Bellini, but went way beyond his master in his development of the landscape to create mood. In the famous, atmospheric *Tempest* (c.1507) in Room 5, this treatment of the landscape and the use of the figures to intensify that mood was an innovation adopted in Venetian painting of the 16th century and beyond.

Out on a limb from the main 16th-century Venetian tradition was the enigmatic Lorenzo Lotto, best known for portraits conveying moods of psychological unrest. His melancholic *Portrait of a Gentleman* (c.1525) in Room 7 is a superb example. More in the Venetian tradition, Palma il Vecchio's sumptuously coloured *Sacra Conversazione* in Room 8, painted around the same time, shows the unmistakable influence of the early work of Titian.

HIGH RENAISSANCE

OCCUPYING an entire wall of Room 10, the monumental *Feast in the House of Levi* by Paolo Veronese (1573) was originally commissioned

Paolo Veronese's *Feast in the House of Levi* (detail)

as *The Last Supper.* However, the hedonistic detail in the painting, such as the drunkard and the dwarfs, was not well received and Veronese found himself before the Inquisition. Ordered to eliminate the profane content of the picture, he simply changed the title.

Jacopo Tintoretto made his reputation with *The Miracle of the Slave* (1548), which is also in Room 10. The painting shows his mastery of the dramatic effects of light and movement. This was the first of a series of works painted for the Scuola Grande di San Marco *(see p114)*. In the next room, Veronese's use of rich colour is best admired in the *Mystical Marriage of St Catherine* (c.1575).

***Healing of the Madman* (c.1496) by Vittore Carpaccio**

Baroque, Genre and Landscapes

***The Rape of Europa* (1740–50) by Francesco Zuccarelli (detail)**

Venice suffered from a lack of native Baroque painters, but a few non-Venetians kept the Venetian school alive in the 17th century. The most notable among these was the Genoese Bernardo Strozzi (1581–1644). The artist was a great admirer of the work of Veronese, as can be seen in his *Feast at the House of Simon* (1629) in Room 11. Also represented in this room is Giambattista Tiepolo, the greatest Venetian painter of the 18th century.

The long corridor (12) and the rooms which lead from it are largely devoted to light-hearted landscape and genre paintings from the 18th century. Among them are pastoral scenes by Francesco Zuccarelli, works by Marco Ricci, scenes of Venetian society by Pietro Longhi and a view of Venice by Canaletto (1763). This was the painter's entry for admission to the Accademia, and is a fine example of his sense of perspective.

Ceremonial Paintings

Rooms 20 and 21 return to the Renaissance, featuring two great cycles of paintings from the late 16th century. The detail in these large-scale anecdotal canvases provides a fascinating glimpse of the life, customs and appearance of Venice at the time. Room 20 houses *The Stories of the Cross* by Venice's leading artists, commissioned by the Scuola di San Giovanni Evangelista *(see p104)*. Each one depicts an episode of the relic of the Holy Cross, which the kingdom of Cyprus donated to the Scuola. In *The Procession in St Mark's Square* (1496) by Gentile Bellini, you can compare the square with how it looks today. Another, Vittore Carpaccio's *Healing of the Madman* (1496), shows the Rialto bridge which collapsed in 1524.

The second series, minutely detailed *Scenes from the Legend of St Ursula* (1490s) by Carpaccio in Room 21, provides a brilliant kaleidoscope of life. Mixing reality and imagination, Carpaccio relates the episodes from the life of St Ursula using settings and costumes of 15th-century Venice.

Sala dell'Albergo

When the Scuola della Carità became the site of the Academy of Art in the early 19th century, the Scuola's *albergo* (where students lodged) retained its original panelling and 15th-century ceiling. The huge *Presentation of the Virgin* (1538) is one of the surprisingly few Titians in the gallery, and was painted for this very room. The walls are also adorned with a grandiose triptych (1446) by Antonio Vivarini and Giovanni d'Alemagna.

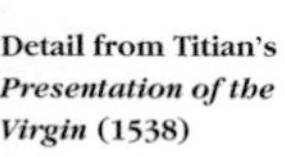

Detail from Titian's *Presentation of the Virgin* (1538)

Cini Collection 16

Palazzo Cini, San Vio 864. **Map** 6 E4. 041 521 07 55. Accademia. 10am–1pm, 2–7pm Tue–Sun. Aug, Dec–Mar.

THE PALAZZO CINI belonged to Count Vittorio Cini (1884–1977), a collector and patron of the arts. Between 1951 and 1956 he restored San Giorgio Maggiore *(see p95)* and created the Cini Foundation as a memorial to his son, who was killed in an air crash in 1949.

The collection displayed here includes china, ivories, books, illuminated manuscripts, miniatures, porcelain and furniture, but the outstanding works of art are the Tuscan Renaissance paintings that Cini collected. These include works by or attributed to Botticelli, Piero di Cosimo, Piero della Francesca, Filippo Lippi and Pontormo.

The Cini Collection has been open to the public since 1984, but unfortunately, it is only open for seven months of the year.

Madonna col Bambino (c.1437) by Filippo Lippi, the Cini Collection

Peggy Guggenheim Collection 17

Palazzo Venier dei Leoni, Dorsoduro 701. **Map** 6 F4. 041 240 54 11. Accademia. 10am–6pm Wed–Mon (Apr– Oct, to 10pm Sat). 25 Dec.

INTENDED AS A four-storey palace, the 18th-century Palazzo Venier dei Leoni in fact never rose beyond the ground floor – hence its nickname, *Il Palazzo Nonfinito* (The Unfinished Palace). In 1949 the building was bought as a home by the American millionairess Peggy Guggenheim (1898–1979), a collector, dealer and patron of the arts. A perspicacious and high-spirited woman, she befriended and furthered the careers of many innovative abstract and surrealist artists. One was her second husband, Max Ernst.

The collection consists of 200 paintings and sculptures, representing almost every modern art movement. The dining room has notable

Interno Olandese II (c.1928) by Joan Miró

Cubist works of art including *The Poet* by Pablo Picasso. An entire room is devoted to Jackson Pollock, who was a Guggenheim discovery. Other artists represented are Miró, de Chirico, Magritte, Kandinsky, Mondrian and Malevich.

Sculpture is laid out in the house and garden. One of the most elegant works is Constantin Brancusi's *Maiastra* (1912). The most provocative piece is Marino Marini's *Angelo della Città* (Angel of the City, 1948), a prominently displayed man sitting on a horse, erect in all respects. Embarrassed onlookers avert their gaze to enjoy views of the Grand Canal.

The Guggenheim is one of the most visited sights of the city. The light-filled rooms and the large modern canvases provide a striking contrast to the Renaissance paintings which are the main attraction in Venetian churches and museums. The team of interns here are usually arts graduates from English-speaking countries, which is of great help to many tourists.

***Maiastra* by Constantin Brancusi**

There are plans by the Guggenheim to acquire the splendidly located customs house at Punta della Dogana. If fulfilled, it will allow many works currently in storage to see the light of day.

Façade of the Palazzo Venier dei Leoni, the home of the Peggy Guggenheim Collection of modern art

Campiello Barbaro 18

Map 6 F4. *Salute.*

An enchanting little square, the Campiello Barbaro is shaded by trees and flanked on one side by the wisteria-clad walls of Ca' Dario. It is hard to believe the stories of murder, bankruptcy and suicide that have befallen the owners of this Grand Canal palace. The most recent was Raul Gardini, one of Italy's best-known industrialists, who shot himself in 1992.

The ill-fated Ca' Dario, which backs on to Campiello Barbaro

Santa Maria della Salute 19

Campo della Salute. **Map** 7 A4. *041 522 55 58.* *Salute.* *9am–noon, 3–5:30pm daily.* *for Sacristy.*

The great Baroque church of Santa Maria della Salute, standing at the entrance of the Grand Canal, is one of the most imposing architectural landmarks of Venice. Henry James likened the church to "some great lady on the threshold of her salon… with her domes and scrolls, her scalloped buttresses and statues forming a pompous crown and her wide steps disposed on the ground like the train of a robe". The church was built in thanksgiving for the deliverance of the city from the plague of 1630, hence the name *Salute*, meaning health and salvation. Every 21 November, in celebration, *(see p35)*, worshippers approach across a bridge of boats which span the mouth of the Grand Canal for the occasion. Baldassare Longhena started the church in 1630 and worked on it for the rest of his life. It was completed in 1687, some five years after his death.

The Baroque church of Santa Maria della Salute viewed from across the Grand Canal

The interior is comparatively sober. It consists of a large octagonal space below the cupola and six chapels radiating from the ambulatory. The large domed chancel and grandiose high altar dominate the view from the main door. The altar's sculptural group by Giusto Le Corte represents the Virgin and Child giving Venice protection from the plague. Unfortunately, some of the best works, such as Titian's ceiling paintings of *Cain and Abel*, *The Sacrifice of Abraham and Isaac* and *David and Goliath* (1540–49), are beyond the altar, where visitors are not allowed. In the sacristy, to the left of the altar, is Titian's early altarpiece of *St Mark Enthroned with Saints Cosmos, Damian, Roch and Sebastian* (1511–12), while on the wall opposite the entrance is *The Wedding at Cana* (1551), a major work by Tintoretto.

Interior of the Salute showing the octagonal core of the church

Dogana di Mare 20

Map 7 A4. *Salute.*

This eastern promontory of the Dorsoduro provides a panorama which embraces the Riva degli Schiavoni, the island of San Giorgio Maggiore and the eastern section of Giudecca. The *dogana di mare*, or sea customs post, was originally built in the 15th century to inspect the cargo of ships which were intending to enter Venice. The customs house you see today was constructed in the late 17th century and replaced a tower which originally guarded the entrance to the Grand Canal. On the corner tower of the house two bronze Atlases support a striking golden ball with a weathervane figure of Fortuna on the top.

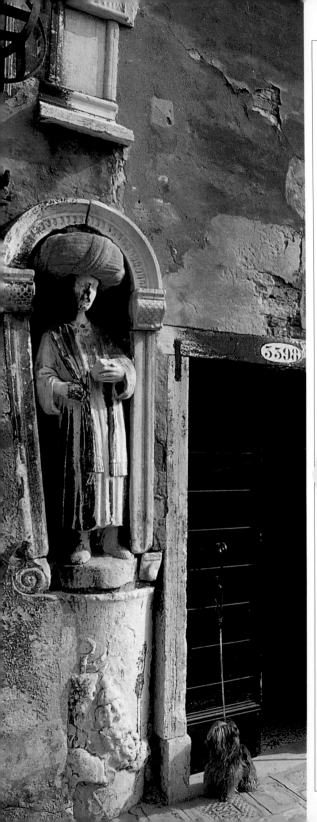

Sights at a Glance

Churches
Gesuiti 7
Madonna dell'Orto 1
Santi Apostoli 10
San Giobbe 14
San Giovanni Grisostomo 9
Santa Maria dei Miracoli 8
San Marziale 4
Scalzi 13

Streets and Squares
Campo dei Mori 2
Fondamente Nuove 5
Fondamenta della Sensa 3

Historic Buildings
Oratorio dei Crociferi 6
Palazzo Labia 12

Art Gallery
Ca' d'Oro p144 11

Historic Area
The Ghetto 15

0 metres 250

0 yards 250

◁ **The façade of Tintoretto's house in Fondamenta dei Mori**

CANNAREGIO

THE CITY'S MOST northerly *sestiere,* Cannaregio, stretches in a large arc from the 20th-century railway station in the west to one of the oldest quarters of Venice in the east. The northern quays look out towards the islands in the lagoon, while to the south the *sestiere* is bounded by the upper sweep of the Grand Canal.

The name of the quarter derives either from the Italian *canne,* meaning canes or reeds, which grew here centuries ago, or perhaps from "Canal Regio" or Royal Canal – the former name of what is now the Canale di Cannaregio. This waterway was the main entry to Venice before the advent of the rail link with the mainland. Over a third of the city's population lives in Cannaregio. For the most part it is an unspoilt area, divided by wide canals, crisscrossed by alleys and characterized by small stores, simple bars and the artisans' workshops. One of the prettiest and most remote quarters is in the north, near the church of Madonna dell'Orto and around Campo dei Mori.

Tourism is concentrated along two main thoroughfares: the Lista di Spagna and the wide Strada Nova, both on the well-worn route from the station to the Rialto. Just off this route lies the world's oldest ghetto. Though the Jewish community now lives all over the city, this is historically the most fascinating quarter of Cannaregio.

Hanukah lamp in the Ghetto

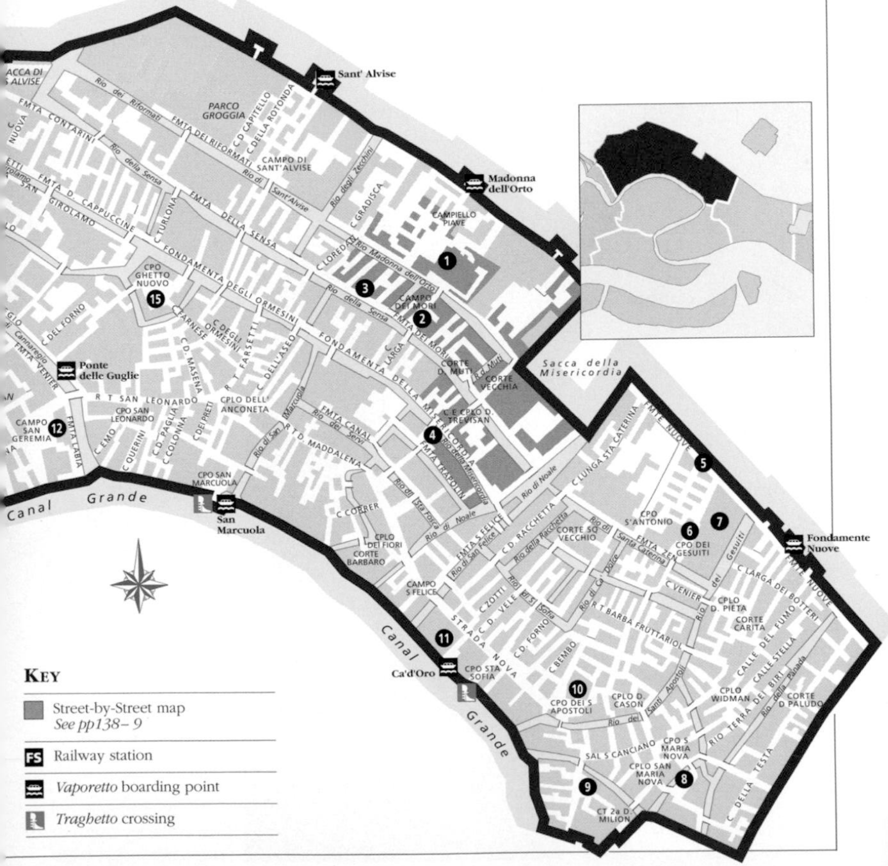

Street-by-Street: Cannaregio

Channel marker in the lagoon

Surprisingly few tourists find their way to this unspoilt quarter of northern Cannaregio. This is the more humble, peaceful side of Venice, where clean washing is strung over the waterways and the streets are flanked by the softly crumbling façades of shuttered houses. Along the wide *fondamente*, the little shops and stores stock basic groceries and the bars are always crowded with local Venetians. The quarter's cultural highlight is the lovely Gothic church of Madonna dell'Orto, Tintoretto's parish church.

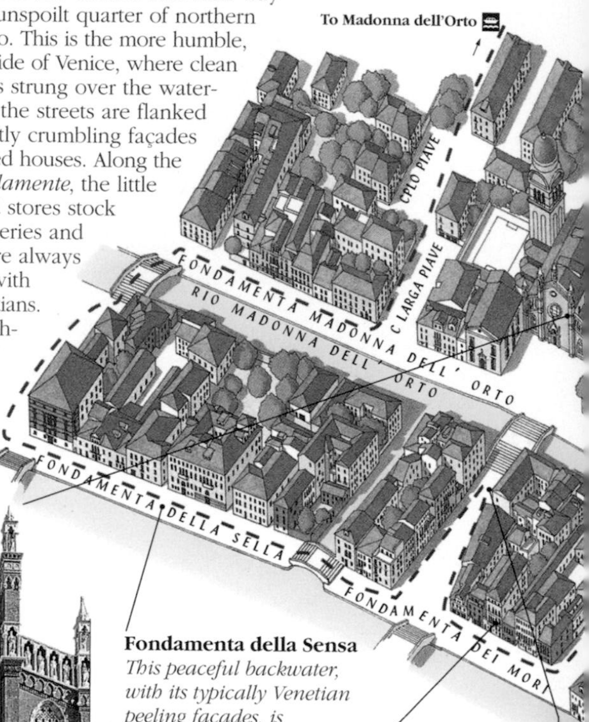

To Madonna dell'Orto

CPLO PIAVE

C LARGA PIAVE

FONDAMENTA MADONNA DELL' ORTO

RIO MADONNA DELL' ORTO

FONDAMENTA DELLA SENSA

FONDAMENTA DEI MORI

★ Madonna dell'Orto
One of the finest Gothic churches in Venice, Madonna dell'Orto has a richly decorated façade and a wealth of works by Tintoretto ❶

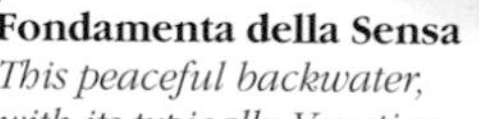

Fondamenta della Sensa
This peaceful backwater, with its typically Venetian peeling façades, is undisturbed by tourism ❸

★ Campo dei Mori
This square is named after the stone statues of three Moors (Mori) which are carved on its walls ❷

Tintoretto lived with his family in this house, No. 3399 Fondamenta dei Mori, from 1574 until his death in 1594.

To Ca' d'Oro

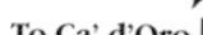

Key

— — — Suggested route

San Marziale
Ceiling paintings by Sebastiano Ricci (1700–25) and a bizarre Baroque altar adorn this Baroque church ❹

Star Sights

★ Madonna dell'Orto

★ Campo dei Mori

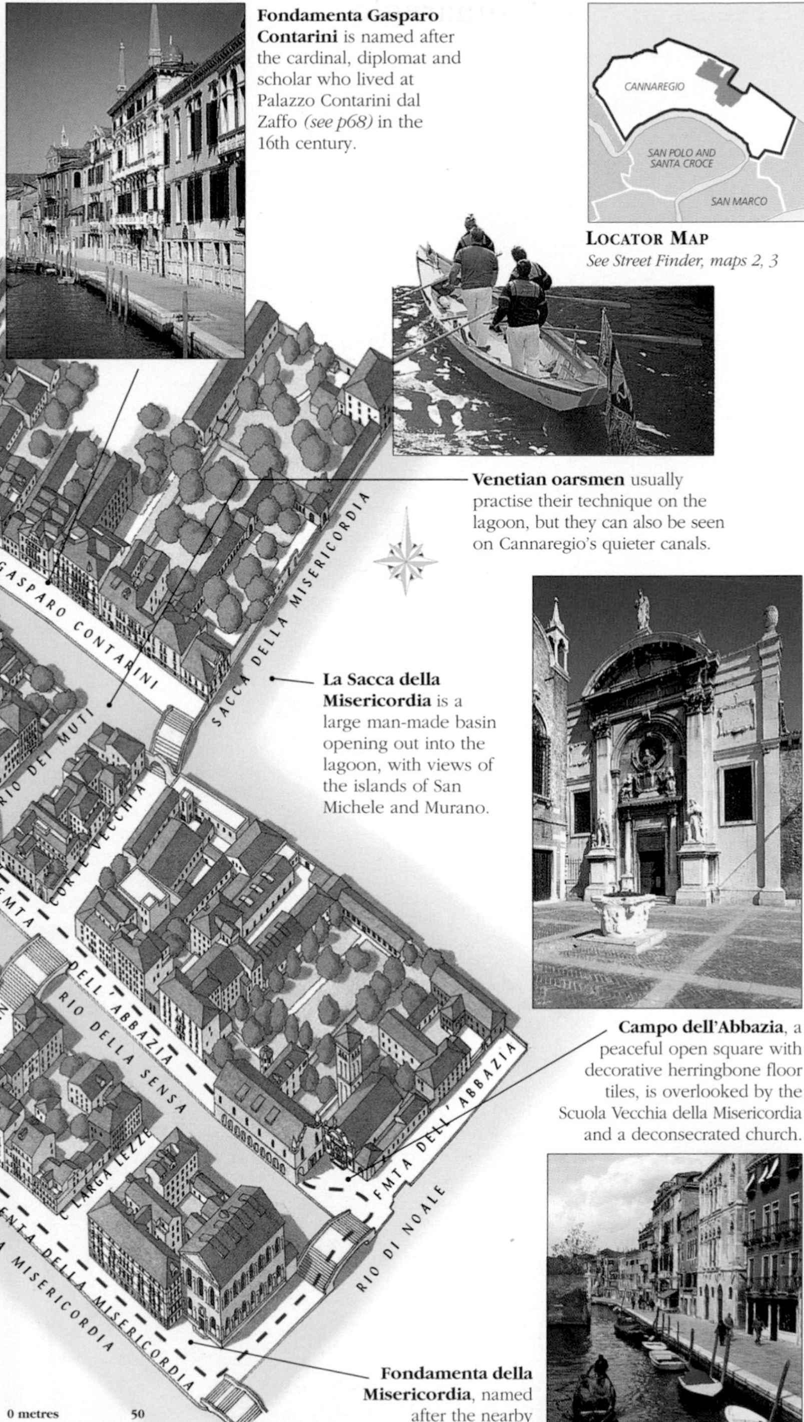

Fondamenta Gasparo Contarini is named after the cardinal, diplomat and scholar who lived at Palazzo Contarini dal Zaffo *(see p68)* in the 16th century.

Locator Map
See Street Finder, maps 2, 3

Venetian oarsmen usually practise their technique on the lagoon, but they can also be seen on Cannaregio's quieter canals.

La Sacca della Misericordia is a large man-made basin opening out into the lagoon, with views of the islands of San Michele and Murano.

Campo dell'Abbazia, a peaceful open square with decorative herringbone floor tiles, is overlooked by the Scuola Vecchia della Misericordia and a deconsecrated church.

Fondamenta della Misericordia, named after the nearby *scuola*, was built in the Middle Ages.

The campanile of Madonna dell'Orto, crowned by an onion-shaped cupola

Madonna dell'Orto ❶

Campo Madonna dell'Orto. **Map** 2 F2. ☎ *041 275 04 62.* 🚤 *Madonna dell'Orto.* ◯ *10am–5pm Mon–Sat, 1–5pm Sun.*

THIS LOVELY Gothic church is frequently referred to as the English Church in Venice for it was British funds that helped restore the building after the 1966 floods *(see p50).* The original church, founded in the mid-14th century, was dedicated to St Christopher, patron saint of travellers, to protect the boatmen who ferried passengers to the islands in the northern lagoon. The dedication was changed and the church reconstructed in the early 15th century, following the discovery, in a nearby vegetable garden *(orto),* of a statue of the Virgin Mary said to have miraculous powers. However, a 15th-century statue of St Christopher, newly restored, still stands above the portal.

The interior, faced almost entirely in brick, is large, light and uncluttered. The greatest treasures are the works of art by Tintoretto, who was a parishioner of the church. His tomb, which is marked with a plaque, lies in the chapel to the right of the chancel. The most dramatic of his works are the towering paintings in the chancel (1562–4). On the right wall is *The Last Judgment,* whose turbulent content caused John Ruskin's wife Effie to flee the church. In the painting *The Adoration of the Golden Calf* on the left wall, the figure carrying the calf, fourth from the left, is said to depict Tintoretto himself.

Inside the chapel of San Mauro you can see the radically restored statue of the Madonna which inspired the reconstruction of the church.

To the right of the entrance is Cima da Conegliano's magnificent painting, *St John the Baptist and Other Saints* (c.1493). The vacant space opposite belongs to Giovanni Bellini's *Madonna with Child* (c.1478) which was stolen for the third time in 1993.

TINTORETTO (1518–94)

Jacopo Robusti, nicknamed Tintoretto because of his father's occupation of silk dyer, was born, lived and died in Cannaregio. He left Venice only once in his life. A devout Christian, volatile and unworldly, his was a highly individual and theatrical style, conveyed by vivid exaggeration of light and movement, bold foreshortening and fiery, fluid brushstrokes. His remarkably prolific output has never been ascertained, but scores of his works survive, many still in the places for which they were painted. Examples of his canvases can be seen in the church of Madonna dell'Orto, the Accademia *(see pp130–33),* and the Doge's Palace *(see pp84–9)* His crowning achievement, however, was the great series of works for the Scuola Grande di San Rocco *(see pp106–7).*

Campo dei Mori ❷

Map 2 F3. 🚤 *Madonna dell'Orto.*

ACCORDING TO popular tradition, the "Mori" were the three Mastelli brothers who came from the Morea (the Peloponnese). The brothers, who were silk merchants by trade, took refuge in Venice in 1112 and built the Palazzo Mastelli, visible from Fondamenta Gasparo Contarini and recognizable by its camel bas relief. The brothers' stone figures are embedded in the wall of the *campo* on its eastern side. The corner figure with the makeshift rusty metal nose (added in the 19th century) is "Signor Antonio Rioba" who, like the Roman Pasquino, was the focus of malicious fun and satire. A fourth oriental merchant with a large turban faces the Rio della Sensa on the façade of Tintoretto's house *(see p138).*

One of the stone Moors which gave the Campo dei Mori its name

The peaceful and atmospheric Fondamenta della Sensa

Fondamenta della Sensa ❸

Map 2 E2. *Madonna dell'Orto.*

When the marshy lands of Cannaregio were drained in the Middle Ages, three long, straight canals were created, running parallel to each other. The middle of these is the Rio della Sensa, which stretches from the Sacca di Sant'Alvise at its western end to the Canale della Misericordia in the east. The Fondamenta cuts through a quiet quarter of Cannaregio, where daily life goes on undisturbed by tourism. With its small grocery shops, and simple local bars and *trattorias*, the neighbourhood feels far removed from San Marco.

This is one of the poorer areas of the city, though it is interspersed with fine (but neglected) palaces that once belonged to wealthy Venetians. Abbot Onorio Arrigoni lived at No. 3336 with his collection of antiques, and Palazzo Michiel (No. 3218) is an early Renaissance palace which became the French embassy.

San Marziale ❹

Campo San Marziale. **Map** 2 F3. *041 71 99 33.* *San Marcuola.* *4–6:30pm Mon–Sat.*

A baroque church on medieval foundations, San Marziale was rebuilt between 1693 and 1721. The church is mainly visited for the ceiling frescoes by Sebastiano Ricci, a painter of the decorative Rococo style. Executed between 1700 and 1705, relatively early in Ricci's career, these bold, foreshortened frescoes already combine the Venetian tradition with flamboyant Rococo flourishes. Sadly though, the vivid colours for which Ricci was known have been sullied by decades of grime. The central painting shows *The Glory of Saint Martial*, while the side paintings relate to the image of the Virgin.

Fondamente Nuove ❺

Map 3 B3. *Fondamente Nuove.*

The Fondamente Nuove or "New Quays" are actually over 400 years old. This chain of waterside streets borders the northern lagoon for one kilometre (over half a mile), from the solitary Sacca della Misericordia to the Rio di Santa Giustina in Castello on the eastern side.

Altar of San Marziale showing a carving of the Virgin and Child

Before the construction of the quays in the 1580s, this was a desirable residential area where the air was said to be healthy and the houses had gardens sloping down to the lagoon.

One of the residents was Titian, who lived from 1531 to his death in 1576 in a now demolished house at Calle Larga dei Botteri No. 5182–3 (a plaque marks the site).

Today the quaysides are aesthetically uninspiring but they do provide splendid views of the northern lagoon and, on a clear day, the peaks of the Dolomites. The island most visible from the quays is San Michele in Isola *(see p151)*, its dark, stately cypress trees rising high above the cemetery walls.

Oratorio dei Crociferi ❻

Campo dei Gesuiti, 4905 Cannaregio. **Map** 3 B3. *041 270 24 64.* *Fondamente Nuove.* *Apr–Oct: 10am–12:30pm Fri, 3:30–7:30pm Sat. Nov–Mar: phone to arrange a visit.*

Founded in the 13th century as a hospital for returning Crusaders, the Oratorio dei Crociferi (built for the order of the Bearers of the Cross) was turned into a charitable institution for old people in the 15th century.

Between 1583 and 1591 the artist Palma il Giovane, commissioned by the Crociferi, decorated the chapel with a glowing cycle of paintings, depicting the crucial events in the history of this religious order. The paintings suffered terrible damage in the floods of 1966 *(see p50)*, but were successfully restored and the chapel reopened in 1984.

The inscriptions on the walls of some of the surrounding houses in the square are those of art and craft guilds, such as silk weavers and tailors, whose works formerly occupied the buildings.

The sumptuous ceiling frescoes of the Gesuiti church

Gesuiti ❼

Campo dei Gesuiti. **Map** 3 B4. *041 528 65 79.* *Fondamente Nuove.* *10am–noon, 4–6pm daily.*

THE JESUITS' close links with the papacy provoked Venetian hostility during the 17th century, and for 50 years they were refused entry to the city. However, in 1714 they were given permission to build this church in the north of Venice, on the site of a 12th-century church which had belonged to the Order of the Crociferi. Consecrated as Santa Maria Assunta, the church is always referred to simply as the Gesuiti; thus it is often confused with the Gesuati in Dorsoduro *(see p129)*.

Domenico Rossi's imposing Baroque exterior gives only a hint of the opulence of the interior. The proliferation of green and white marble, carved in parts like great folds of fabric, gives the impression that the church is clothed in damask.

Titian's *Martyrdom of St Lawrence* (c.1555), above the first altar on the left, has been described by the art historian Hugh Honour as "the first successful nocturne in the history of art".

Santa Maria dei Miracoli ❽

Campo dei Miracoli. **Map** 3 B5. *041 275 04 62.* *Fondamente Nuove or Rialto.* *10am–5pm Mon–Sat, 1–5pm Sun & public hols.*

AN EXQUISITE masterpiece of the early Renaissance, the Miracoli is the favourite church of many Venetians and the one where they like to get married. Tucked away in a maze of alleys and waterways in eastern Cannaregio, it is small and somewhat elusive, but well worth the effort needed to find it.

Often likened to a jewel box, the façade is decorated with various shades of marble, with fine bas-reliefs and sculpture. It was built in 1481–9 by the architect Pietro Lombardo and his sons to enshrine *The Virgin and Child* (1408), a painting believed to have miraculous powers. The picture, by Nicolò di Pietro, can still be seen above the altar. The interior of the church, which ideally should be visited when pale shafts of sunlight are streaming in through the windows, is embellished by pink, white and grey marble and crowned by a barrel-vaulted ceiling (1528) which has 50 portraits of saints and prophets. The balustrade, between the nave and the chancel, is decorated by Tullio Lombardo's carved figures of St Francis, Archangel Gabriel, the Virgin and St Clare. The screen around the high altar and the medallions of the Evangelists in the cupola spandrels are also by Lombardo.

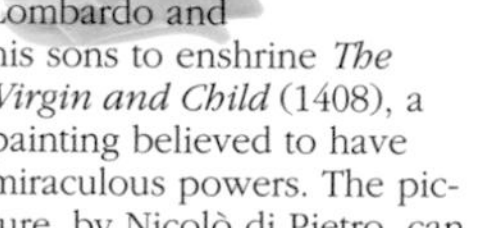

Decorative column, interior of Santa Maria dei Miracoli

Above the main door, the choir gallery was used by the nuns from the neighbouring convent, who entered the church through an overhead gallery. The Miracoli has recently undergone a major restoration programme, which was funded by the American Save Venice organization.

SANTA MARIA DEI MIRACOLI

The façade is a harmonious tapestry of decorated panels and multi-coloured polished stone.

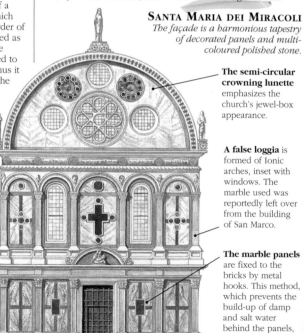

The semi-circular crowning lunette emphasizes the church's jewel-box appearance.

A false loggia is formed of Ionic arches, inset with windows. The marble used was reportedly left over from the building of San Marco.

The marble panels are fixed to the bricks by metal hooks. This method, which prevents the build-up of damp and salt water behind the panels, dates from the Renaissance.

San Giovanni Grisostomo, the last work of Mauro Coducci

San Giovanni Grisostomo ❾

Campo San Giovanni Grisostomo. **Map** 3 B5. *041 522 71 55.* *Rialto.* *10:30am–noon, 3:30–6pm daily.*

THIS PRETTY little terracotta-coloured church lies in a bustling quarter close to the Rialto. Built between 1479 and 1504, the church was the last work of Mauro Coducci.

The interior, which is built on a Greek-cross plan, is dark and intimate. Notable works of art include Giovanni Bellini's *St Jerome with Saints Christopher and Augustine* (1513), which hangs above the first altar on the right. Influenced by Giorgione, this was probably Bellini's last painting, executed when he was in his eighties.

There is also Sebastiano del Piombo's *St John Chrysostom and Six Saints* (1509–11), hung above the high altar. Also influenced by Giorgione, some believe he actually painted the figures of St John the Baptist and St Liberal himself.

Marco Polo

Born around 1254 in the quarter of Cannaregio near the Rialto, Marco Polo left Venice at the age of 18 for his four-year voyage to the court of the Emperor Kublai Khan. He impressed the Mongol emperor and stayed for some 20 years, working as a travelling diplomat.

Returning to Venice in 1295, he brought with him a fortune in jewels and a host of spellbinding stories about the Khan's court.

As a prisoner of war in Genoa in 1298 he compiled an account of his travels, with the cooperation of an inmate. Translated into French, this was to become *Le Livre des merveilles*. Despite the fact that many Italians disbelieved his wondrous tales of the east, the book was an instant success. His nickname became Marco Il Milione (of the million lies); hence the name of the two little courtyards where the Polo family lived: Corte Prima del Milion and Corte Seconda del Milion.

Marco Polo leaving on his travels, from a manuscript c.1338

Santi Apostoli ❿

Campo Santi Apostoli. **Map** 3 B5. *041 528 01 10.* *Ca' d'Oro.* *7:30–11:30am, 5–7pm daily.*

THE CAMPO Santi Apostoli is a busy crossroads for pedestrians en route to the Rialto or the railway station. Its church is unremarkable architecturally and little remains of the 16th-century building. A notable exception, however, is the enchanting late 15th-century Renaissance Corner Chapel on the right of the nave, believed to have been designed by Mauro Coducci. The chapel contains *The Communion of St Lucy* by Giambattista Tiepolo (1748), the tomb of Marco Corner, probably by Tullio Lombardo (1511), and an inscription to Corner's daughter, Caterina Cornaro, Queen of Cyprus, who was buried here before she was moved to the Church of San Salvatore *(see p94)*.

Tomb of Doge Marco Corner in Santi Apostoli (Corner Chapel)

Ca' d'Oro ⓫

See p144.

Palazzo Labia ⓬

Fondamenta Labia (entrance on Campo S Geremia). **Map** 2 D4. *041 781 277.* *Ponte Guglie.* *by appt only (visits 3–4pm Wed–Fri).* *public hols.*

THE LABIAS were a wealthy family of merchants from Catalonia who bought their way into the Venetian patriciate in 1646. Towards the end of the century they built their prestigious palace on the wide Cannaregio Canal, close to its junction with the Grand Canal. In 1745–50 the ballroom was frescoed by Giambattista Tiepolo. The wonderfully painted scenes are taken from the life of Cleopatra but the setting is Venice, and the queen's attire is that of a 16th-century noble lady.

Passed from one owner to another the palace gradually lost all trace of its former grandeur and variously served as a religious foundation, a school and a doss-house. Between 1964 and 1992 it was owned by the Italian broadcasting network, RAI, who undertook its restoration.

The frescoes can be seen free of charge, but only by making an appointment.

Ca' d'Oro ⓫

ONE OF THE GREAT showpieces of the Grand Canal, the Ca' d'Oro (or House of Gold) is the finest example of Venetian Gothic architecture in the city. The façade, with its finely carved ogee windows, oriental pinnacles and exotic marble tracery, has an unmistakable flavour of the east. But this once gloriously embellished *palazzo* suffered many changes of fortune and there is now little inside to remind you that this was once a 15th-century palace. Since 1984 it has been home to the Giorgio Franchetti Collection.

History

IN 1420 THE wealthy patrician, Marino Contarini, commissioned the building of what he was determined would be the most magnificent palace in the city. The decoration and the intricate carving were executed by a team of Venetian and Lombard craftsmen, and he had the façade adorned in ultramarine, gold leaf and vermilion.

In the course of the 16th century the house was remodelled by a succession of owners, and by the early 18th century was semi-derelict. In 1846 the Russian Prince Troubetzkoy bought it for the famous ballerina Maria Taglioni. Under her direction, the Ca' d'Oro suffered barbaric restoration. The open staircase was ripped out, the wellhead by Bartolomeo Bon (1427–8) was sold and much of the stonework removed. It was finally rescued by Baron Franchetti, a patron of the arts, who restored it to its former glory and bequeathed it to the state in 1915. A restoration programme for the façade, first put into action in the 1970s, is now finally completed, revealing the building's exotic design. The pretty paved courtyard contains Bon's beautifully carved wellhead. This was one of the pieces retrieved by Franchetti.

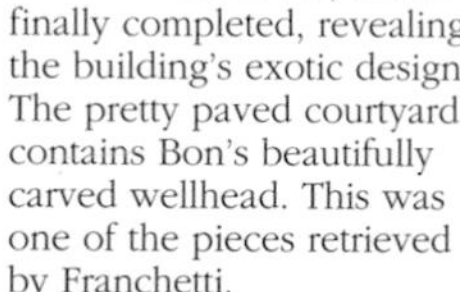

Tullio Lombardo's *Double Portrait*

First Floor

PRIDE OF PLACE is given to Andrea Mantegna's *St Sebastian* (1506), the artist's last painting and Franchetti's favourite work of art. The *portego* (gallery) opening on to the Grand Canal is a showroom of sculpture. Among the finest pieces are bronze reliefs by the Paduan sculptor, Il Riccio (1470–1532), Tullio Lombardo's marble *Double Portrait* (c.1493) and Sansovino's lunette of the Virgin and Child (c.1530). Rooms to the right of the *portego* have some fine Renaissance bronzes and, among the paintings, an *Annunciation* and *Death of the Virgin* (both c.1504) by Vittore Carpaccio and assistants. A room to the left of the *portego* is devoted to non-Venetian painting, and includes Luca Signorelli's *Flagellation* (c.1480).

Second Floor

THE UPPER FLOOR houses paintings by Venetian masters, including a *Venus* by Titian, two Venetian views by Guardi, and fresco fragments by Titian. Other exhibits include tapestries and ceramics. Explanatory cards in each room aid visitors.

Visitors' Checklist

Canal Grande (Calle Ca' d'Oro). **Map** 3 A4. *041 523 87 90.* *Ca' d'Oro.* *8:15am–7:15pm daily (to 2pm Mon).* *1 Jan, 1 May, 25 Dec.*

***The Annunciation* (1504) by Vittore Carpaccio and assistants**

Scalzi ⓭

Fondamenta Scalzi. **Map** 1 C4.
041 71 51 15. *Ferrovia.*
7am–noon, 4–7pm daily.

Beside the modern railway station *(see p58)* stands the church of Santa Maria di Nazareth, known as the Scalzi. The *scalzi* were "barefooted" Carmelite friars who came to Venice during the 1670s and commissioned their church to be built on the Grand Canal. Designed by Baldassare Longhena, the huge Baroque interior is an over-elaboration of marble, gilded woodwork and sculptures. The ceiling painting, *The Council of Ephesus* by Ettore Tito (1934), replaced Giambattista Tiepolo's fresco of *The Translation of the Holy House to Loreto* (1743–5), which was destroyed by the Austrian bombardment of 24 October 1915.

San Giobbe ⓮

Campo San Giobbe.
Map 1 C3. *041 524 18 89.*
Ponte dei 3 Archi.
10am–noon, 3:30–6pm Mon–Fri, 3:30–6pm Sat & Sun.

The church of San Giobbe stands in a remote *campo* full of cats. The early Gothic structure of the church was modified in the 1470s by Pietro Lombardo who added Renaissance elements such as the saints over the portal. The Martini chapel, second on the left, is decorated with Della Robbia-style glazed terracotta. The altarpieces by Giovanni Bellini and Vittore Carpaccio were removed when Napoleon suppressed the monastery of San Giobbe, and are now in the Accademia Gallery *(pp130–33)*.

Saint by Lombardo, San Giobbe portal

The Ghetto ⓯

Map 2 E3. *Ponte Guglie.*
Museo Ebraico Campo del Ghetto Nuovo. *041 71 53 59.* *Ponte Guglie.* *10am–7pm (Oct–May: 10am-5:30pm) Sun–Fri.* *25 Dec, 1 Jan, 1 May, Jewish hols.*

In 1516 the Council of Ten *(see p42)* decreed that all Jews in Venice be confined to an islet of Cannaregio. The quarter was cut off by wide canals and the two watergates were manned by Christian guards. The area was named the Ghetto after a foundry – *geto* in Venetian – that formerly occupied the site. The name was subsequently given to Jewish enclaves throughout the world. By day Jews were allowed out of the Ghetto, but at all times they were made to wear identifying badges and caps. The only trades they could pursue were in textiles, money-lending and medicine.

The rising number of Jews forced the Ghetto to expand.

The wrought-iron bridge leading northwards out of the Ghetto

Campo del Ghetto Nuovo, the oldest part of the Ghetto

Buildings rose vertically (the so-called skyscrapers of Venice) and spread into the Ghetto Vecchio (1541) and the neighbouring Ghetto Novissimo (1633). By the mid-17th century the Jewish population numbered over 5,000.

In 1797 Napoleon pulled down the gates, but under the Austrians the Jews were again forced into confinement. It was not until 1866 that they were granted their freedom.

Of the 500 Jews now in Venice, only 33 live in the Ghetto. However, the quarter has not lost its ethnic character. There are kosher food shops, a Jewish baker, a Jewish library, and two synagogues where religious ceremonies still take place. There are also several shops on the large, recently restored Campo del Ghetto Nuovo, which sell items such as glass rabbis and Hanukah lamps.

Flowers in front of the Holocaust Memorial

Museo Ebraico

The small Jewish Museum in the Ghetto Nuovo houses a collection of artifacts from the 17th–19th centuries. A guided tour of the quarter's synagogues leaves from the museum daily except Saturday, every hour from 10:30am to 5:30pm (3:30pm in winter). Led by English-speaking guides, the tours give a fascinating glimpse into the past life of the Ghetto. A short history of the quarter is followed by a visit to the lavishly decorated German, Spanish and Levantine synagogues.

The Lagoon Islands

Shrouded in myth and superstition, the lagoon was once the preserve of fishermen and hunters. But marauders in the 5th and 6th centuries AD drove mainland dwellers to the safety of the marshy lagoon *(see p40)*. Here, they conquered their watery environment, which was protected from the open sea by thin sandbanks *(lidi)*, created from silt washed down by the rivers of the Po delta. In the 13th century the first *murazzi* were built – sea walls of angular stone which safeguard the *lidi* from erosion. Experiments with tidal barriers continue in an effort to combat the ever-present threat of flooding *(see p51)*.

Image of the Madonna, Torcello

The thriving communities that once lived and traded here are long gone. Many of the islands, formerly used as sites for monasteries, hospitals or powder factories, are now abandoned, but a handful of them are undergoing development – one as an international university, another as an exclusive resort.

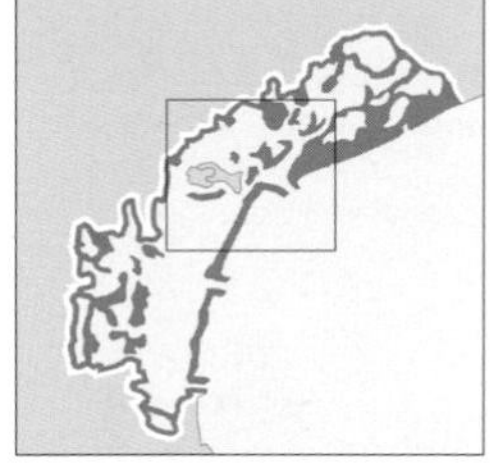

Sights at a Glance

- Burano 2
- Giudecca 6
- Lazzaretto Nuovo 12
- Lido 10
- Murano 4
- Poveglia 13
- San Clemente 11
- San Francesco del Deserto 3
- San Lazzaro degli Armeni 9
- San Michele 5
- San Servolo 7
- Santa Maria della Grazia 8
- *Torcello pp152–3* 1

Key

- Airfield
- Railway station

0 kilometres 5

0 miles 3

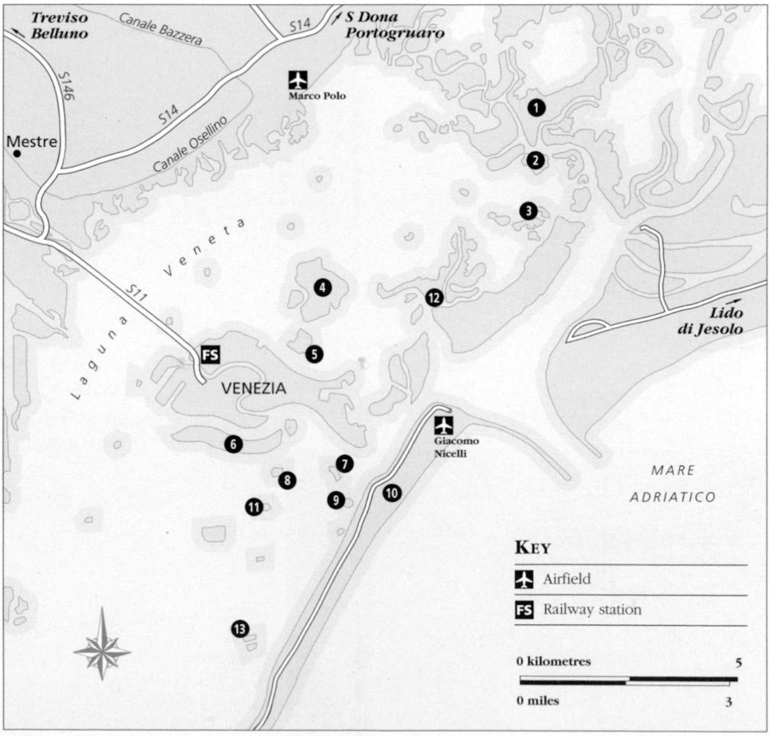

◁ **Colourful houses in Burano**

Exploring the Lagoon

A TRIP TO THE LAGOON ISLANDS makes a welcome break from the densely packed streets of the city. Murano, celebrated for its glass, can be reached in a matter of minutes. Further north, Burano, the "lace island", and ancient Torcello are well worth the longer ride. The Lido, with its sandy beaches, is an easy journey from San Marco. Some of the lesser known islands are worth exploring too, but access can sometimes be difficult.

Murano and San Michele are clearly visible from the northern quaysides of Venice.

Murano
Some of Murano's canalside porticoes survive from medieval days 4

San Michele
World-famous writers and artists are buried alongside Venetians on this island 5

Giudecca
Palladio's great church of the Redentore, on the waterfront, is the island's cultural highlight 6

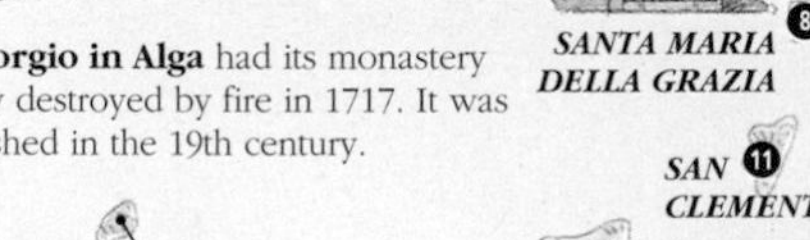

San Giorgio in Alga had its monastery partially destroyed by fire in 1717. It was demolished in the 19th century.

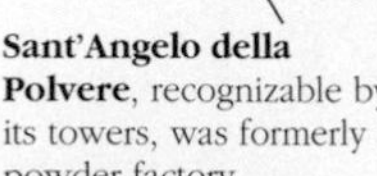

Sant'Angelo della Polvere, recognizable by its towers, was formerly a powder factory.

Sacca Sessola, an artificial island, was the site of a hospital until 1980.

Lido
Behind the crowded beaches and grand hotels, the Lido has some pleasantly peaceful waterways 10

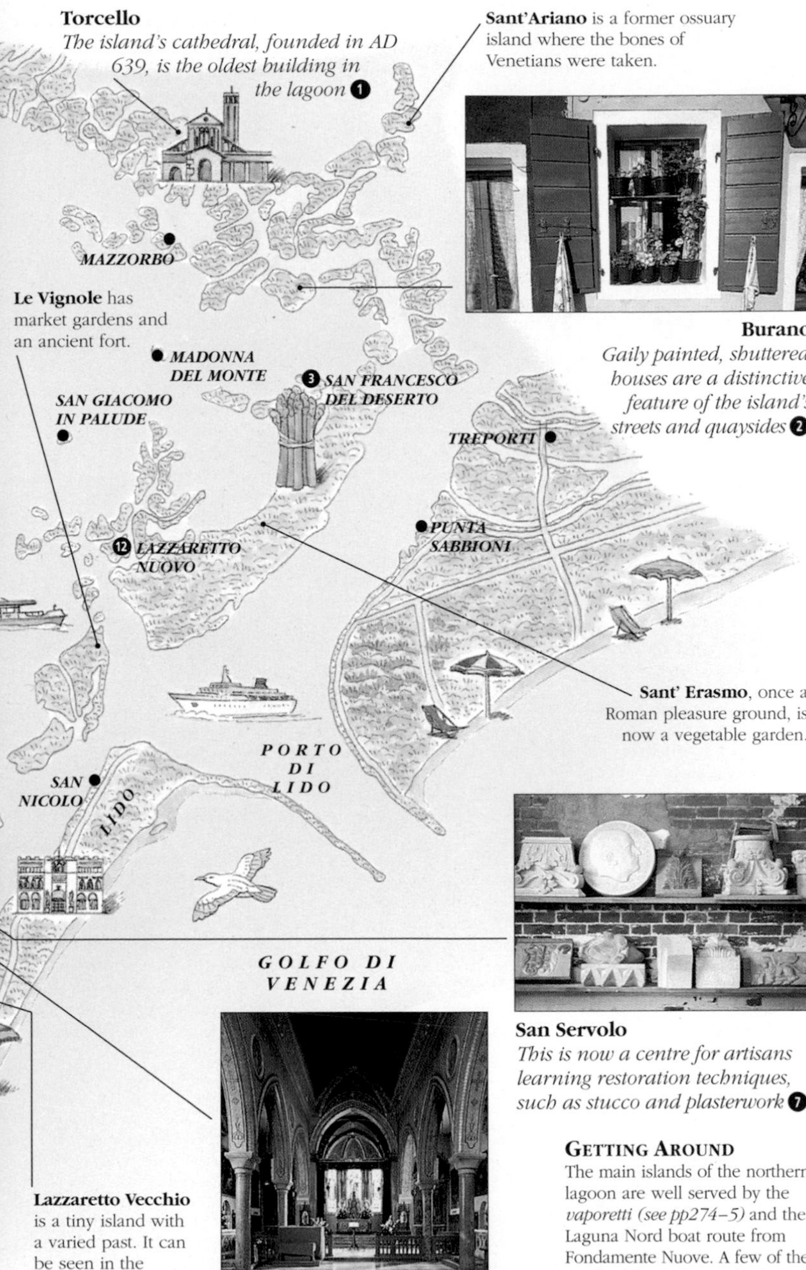

Torcello
The island's cathedral, founded in AD 639, is the oldest building in the lagoon ❶

Sant'Ariano is a former ossuary island where the bones of Venetians were taken.

Le Vignole has market gardens and an ancient fort.

Burano
Gaily painted, shuttered houses are a distinctive feature of the island's streets and quaysides ❷

Sant' Erasmo, once a Roman pleasure ground, is now a vegetable garden.

San Servolo
This is now a centre for artisans learning restoration techniques, such as stucco and plasterwork ❼

Lazzaretto Vecchio is a tiny island with a varied past. It can be seen in the distance from the boat that runs from San Marco to the Lido.

San Lazzaro degli Armeni
Visits to this green and pretty monastery island take in the church, library, museum and printing press ❾

GETTING AROUND

The main islands of the northern lagoon are well served by the *vaporetti* *(see pp274–5)* and the Laguna Nord boat route from Fondamente Nuove. A few of the smaller islands have a limited public service; others can only be reached by water taxi.

KEY

- Major road
- Minor road

0 kilometres 2

0 miles 1

Torcello ❶

See pp152–3.

A stall selling lace and linen in Burano's main street

Burano ❷

No. 12 from Fondamente Nuove, approx. 40–50 minutes (some go direct, others via Torcello). No. 14 from San Zaccaria via the Lido and Punta Sabbioni, approx. 1½ hours.

Burano is the most colourful of the lagoon islands. Lying in a lonely expanse of the northern lagoon, it is distinguished from a distance by the tall, dramatically tilted tower of its church. In contrast to the desolate Torcello, the island is densely populated, its waterways lined by brightly painted houses.

A tour of the island's sights will take an hour or so. The street from the ferry stop takes you to the main thoroughfare, Via Baldassare Galuppi, named after the Burano-born composer (1706–85). The street is lined with lace and linen stalls and open-air trattorias serving fresh fish.

Scuola dei Merletti

Piazza Baldassare Galuppi. *041 73 00 34.* *for refurbishment until spring 2005.*

The Buranese are fishermen and lacemakers by trade. You can still see the men scraping their boats or mending nets, but lacemakers are rare. In the 16th century the local lace was the most sought after in Europe. It was so delicate it became known as *punto in aria* ("points in the air"). Foreign competition, coupled with the Republic's decline, led to a slump in the 18th century in Burano's industry. However, the need for a new source of income led to a revival of the skill in 1872 and the founding of a lacemaking school, the Scuola dei Merletti.

Today, authentic Burano lace is hard to find. Genuine pieces take weeks of painstaking labour, and are expensive. At the lacemaking school, however, visitors can watch Buranese women stitching busily. Attached to the school is a museum, displaying fine antique lace.

Mazzorbo

Linked to Burano by a footbridge, Mazzorbo is an island of orchards and gardens. Ferries en route to Burano and Torcello pass through its canal. The only surviving church is the Romanesque-Gothic Santa Caterina.

Brightly painted street in Burano

San Francesco del Deserto ❸

Access via water taxi from the landing stage in Burano.
Visits to the island: 9–11am, 3–5pm Tue–Sun.
Monastery *041 528 68 63.*

This little oasis of greenery, inhabited by nine friars, lies just south of Burano. There is no *vaporetto* service and to get there you must bargain with the boatmen on Burano's quayside, who will row you across the shallow waters and await your return.

One of the multilingual friars will give you a tour of the old church and the enchanting gardens, which have a tree said to have sprouted from the staff of St Francis of Assisi.

A Buranese fisherman about to haul in the day's catch

Murano ❹

No. 12, 41 or 42 from Fondamente Nuove; DM from Piazzale Roma.

Like the city of Venice, Murano comprises a cluster of small islands, connected by bridges. It has been the centre of the glassmaking industry since 1291, when the furnaces and glass craftsmen were moved here from the city, prompted by the risk of fire to the buildings and the disagreeable effects of smoke.

Historically Murano owes its prosperity entirely to glass. From the late 13th century, when the population numbered over 30,000, Murano enjoyed self-government, minted its own coins and had its own Golden Book *(see p42)* listing members of the aristocracy. In the 15th and 16th centuries it was the principal glass-producing centre in Europe. Murano's glass artisans were granted unprecedented privileges, but for those who left the island to found businesses elsewhere there were severe penalties – even death.

Although a few of Murano's *palazzi* bear testimony to its former splendour, and its basilica still survives, most tourists visit for glass alone. Some are enticed by offers of free trips from factory touts in San Marco, others go by excursion launch or independently on the public *vaporetti*.

Some of the factories are now derelict, but glass is still produced in vast quantities. Among the plethora of kitsch (including imports from the Far East) are some wonderful pieces, and it pays to seek out the top glass factories *(see p249)*. Many furnaces, however, close at the weekend.

Museo Vetrario

Palazzo Giustinian, Fondamenta Giustinian. 041 73 95 86. 10am–5pm Thu–Tue (Nov–Mar: to 4pm). 1 Jan, 1 May, 25 Dec.

The Museo Vetrario (glass museum) in the huge Palazzo Giustinian houses a splendid collection of antique pieces. The prize exhibit of the collection is the Barovier wedding cup (1470–80), with enamelwork decoration by Angelo Barovier. There is also a section devoted to modern glass, with some splendid items on view.

Basilica dei Santi Maria e Donato

Fondamenta Giustinian. 041 73 90 56. 9am–noon, 4–7pm daily (to 6pm in winter). Sun am.

The colonnaded exterior of Murano's Basilica dei Santi Maria e Donato

The island's architectural highlight is the Basilica dei Santi Maria e Donato, whose magnificent colonnaded apse is reflected in the waters of the San Donato canal. Despite some heavy-handed restoration undertaken in the 19th century, this 12th-century church still retains much of its original beauty. Visitors should note the Veneto-Byzantine columns and Gothic ship's keel roof. An enchantingly evocative mosaic portrait of the Madonna, seen standing alone against a gold background, decorates the apse.

The church's floor, or *pavimento*, dating from 1140, is equally beautiful. With its medieval mosaics of geometric figures, exotic birds, mythical creatures and inexplicable symbols, it incorporates fragments of ancient glass from the island's foundries into its imagery.

Diaghilev's tombstone

San Michele ❺

No. 41 or 42 from Fondamente Nuove.

STUDDED WITH dark cypresses and enclosed within high terracotta walls, the cemetery island of San Michele lies just across the water from Venice's Fondamente Nuove. The bodies of Venetians were traditionally buried in church graveyards in Venice, but for reasons of hygiene and space, San Michele and its neighbour were designated cemeteries in the 19th century.

The church of San Michele in Isola stands by the landing stage. Designed by Mauro Coducci (c.1469), it was the first church in Venice to be faced in white Istrian stone. The cemetery itself rambles over most of the island. With its carved tombstones and chapels it has a curious fascination. Some graves have suffered neglect, but most are well-tended and enlivened by a riot of flowers.

The most famous graves are those of foreigners: Ezra Pound (1885–1972), in the *Evangelisti* (Protestant) section, and Sergei Diaghilev (1872–1929) and Igor Stravinsky (1882–1971) in the *Greci* or Orthodox section. These bodies have been allowed to rest in peace. Most others are dug up after about ten years to make way for new arrivals, and the bones taken to the ossuary island of Sant'Ariano. Today, however, because of increasing lack of space on San Michele, most bodies are buried on the mainland.

Glass Blowing

A main attraction of a trip to Murano is a demonstration of the glass-blowing technique. Visitors can watch while a glass blower takes a blob of molten paste on the end of an iron rod and, by twisting, turning and blowing, miraculously transforms it into a vase, bird, lion, wine goblet or similar work of art. The display is followed by a tour of the showroom and a certain amount of pressure from the salespeople. There is no obligation to buy, however.

Glass blower at work in Murano

Torcello ❶

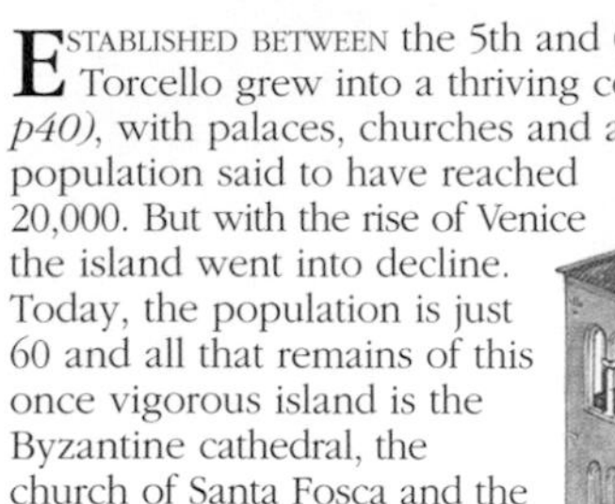

ESTABLISHED BETWEEN the 5th and 6th centuries, Torcello grew into a thriving colony *(see p40)*, with palaces, churches and a population said to have reached 20,000. But with the rise of Venice the island went into decline. Today, the population is just 60 and all that remains of this once vigorous island is the Byzantine cathedral, the church of Santa Fosca and the memory of its former glory.

★ Apse Mosaic
The 13th-century Madonna, set against a gold background, is one of the most moving mosaics in Venice.

★ Domesday Mosaics
The huge and highly decorative mosaic of the Last Judgment covers the entire west wall.

Pulpit
The present basilica dates from 1008, but includes many earlier features. The marble pulpit is made of fragments from the first, 7th-century church.

The Roman sarcophagus below the altar is said to contain the relics of St Heliodorus.

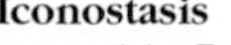

★ Iconostasis
The exquisite Byzantine marble panels of the rood screen are carved with peacocks, lions and flowers. This detailed relief shows two peacocks drinking from the fountain of life.

Nave Columns
The finely carved capitals on the marble nave columns date from the 11th century.

Torcello's Last Canals
Silted canals and malaria hastened Torcello's decline. One of the remaining waterways runs from the vaporetto *stop to the basilica.*

Visitors' Checklist

No. 12 from Fondamente Nuove. **Basilica di Santa Maria dell' Assunta** *041 270 24 64. Apr–Oct: 10:30am–5:30pm daily; Nov–Mar: 10am–5pm daily.* **Campanile** *Apr–Oct: 10:30am–5:30pm daily; Nov–Mar 10am–5pm daily.* **Santa Fosca** *mass.* **Museo** *041 73 07 61. Mar–Oct: 10:30am–5:30pm Tue–Sun; Nov–Feb: 10am–5pm Tue–Sun. public hols.*

Santa Fosca
Built in the 11th and 12th centuries on a Greek-cross plan, the church has a lovely portico and a serene Byzantine interior.

The central dome and cross sections are supported by columns of Greek marble with fine Corinthian capitals.

Attila's Throne
It was said that the 5th-century king of the Huns used this marble seat as his throne.

To ***vaporetto*** **boarding point** →

Museo dell' Estuario
Old church treasures and archaeological fragments are housed here.

Star Features

- ★ **Apse Mosaic**
- ★ **Domesday Mosaics**
- ★ **Iconostasis**

Boats moored along the Ponte Lungo on the Giudecca

Giudecca 6

No. 41, 42 or 82.

In the days of the Republic, the island of Giudecca was a pleasure ground of palaces and gardens. Today it is very much a suburb of the city, its dark, narrow alleys flanked by apartments, its squares overgrown and its *palazzi* neglected. Many of its old factories have been converted into modern housing. However, the long, wide quayside skirting the city side of the island makes a very pleasant promenade and provides stunning views of Venice across the water. The island was originally named Spinalunga (long spine) on account of its shape. The name Giudecca, once thought to have referred to the Jews, or *giudei,* who lived here in the 13th century, is more likely to have originated from the word *giudicati* meaning "the judged". This referred to troublesome aristocrats who, as early as the 9th century, were banished to the island.

The Hotel Cipriani *(see p231)*, among the most luxurious places to stay in Venice, is quietly and discreetly located at the tip of the island. In contrast, at the western end of the island looms the massive Neo-Gothic ruin of the Mulino Stucky. It was built in 1895 as a flour mill by the Swiss entrepreneur Giovanni Stucky, an unpopular employer who was murdered by one of his workers in 1910. The mill ceased functioning in 1954, and plans have recently been approved for its conversion into a hotel, apartments and a park.

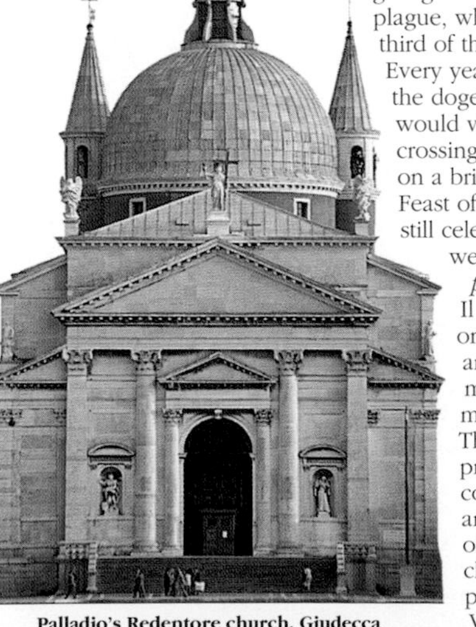

Palladio's Redentore church, Giudecca

Il Redentore

Campo Redentore. 041 275 04 62. *Redentore.* *10am–5pm daily (from 1pm Sun & public hols).* *Sun (Jul & Aug); 1 Jan, 25 Dec.*

Giudecca's principal monument is Palladio's church of Il Redentore (the Redeemer). It was built in 1577–92 in thanksgiving for the end of the 1576 plague, which wiped out a third of the city's population. Every year since its creation, the doge and his entourage would visit the church, crossing from the Zattere on a bridge of boats. The Feast of the Redeemer is still celebrated on the third weekend in July *(see p34)*. The church of Il Redentore, styled on the architecture of ancient Rome, is a masterpiece of harmony and proportion. The Classical interior presents a marked contrast to the ornate and elaborate style of most Venetian churches. The main paintings, by Paolo Veronese and Alvise Vivarini, are in the sacristy to the right of the choir. The most rewarding views of the Redentore are from Venice across the water. For special festivities the church is often floodlit after dark, which makes a spectacular sight.

Le Zitelle

Fondamenta delle Zitelle. *041 270 24 64.* *Zitelle.* *for restoration; call for information.*

Palladio's church is now the site of Venice's most up-to-date congress centre. The building adjoining the church used to be a hostel for spinsters *(zitelle)*, who occupied themselves by making fine lace.

An artisan at work at the San Servolo training centre

San Servolo 7

No. 20 from San Zaccaria.
Venice International University
041 271 95 11.

Half-way between San Marco and the Lido is the island of San Servolo. Now a centre for teaching crafts and home to the Venice International University, it started life as one of the original monastery islands of Venice. Benedictine monks established a monastery here in the 8th century, and later added a hospital.

In 1725 the island became a lunatic asylum and a new hospital was built to house the patients. The Council of Ten *(see p42)* declared that this was to be strictly a shelter for "maniacs of noble family or comfortable circumstances". Poor maniacs were imprisoned or left to their own devices. In 1797 Napoleon scrubbed this discriminatory decree and the asylum became free to all.

In 1980 this spartan island

was taken over by The Venice European Centre for the Trades and Professions of Conservation. Later, in 1996, Venice International University opened its doors here. Extensive renovation work on the historic buildings, and the large park in which they are set, is ongoing.

Santa Maria della Grazia ❽

No public access.

ORIGINALLY CALLED La Cavana or Cavanell, the island lies just a short distance away from San Giorgio Maggiore *(see p95)*. Formerly a shelter for pilgrims on their journey to the Holy Land, it became a monastery island in the 15th century. Its name was changed when a church was constructed to enshrine a miraculous image of the Virgin, brought from Constantinople. The religious buildings, including a Gothic church with some fine paintings, were secularized under Napoleon. The island became a military zone under his rule, but the buildings were subsequently destroyed during the 1848 revolutionary uprising *(see p48)*.

More recently occupied by a hospital for infectious diseases, this has now been transferred to the main hospital in Venice and the island sold.

San Lazzaro degli Armeni ❾

No. 20 from Riva degli Schiavoni. *041 526 01 04.* *3–5pm daily.* *at 3:10pm.*

LYING JUST OFF the Lido *(see p156)*, San Lazzaro degli Armeni is a small, very green monastery island, recognizable by the onion-shaped cupola of its white campanile. The buildings are surrounded by well-groomed gardens and dark groves of cypress trees. Since the 18th century it has been an Armenian monastery and centre of learning.

Early history

This small island served as an asylum in the 12th century and later became a hospital island for lepers, named after their patron saint, Lazarus. The lepers were then transferred to the Ospedale di San Lazzaro dei Mendicanti at Santi Giovanni e Paolo *(see pp116–17)*. In 1717 an Armenian monk, Manug di Pietro, known as Mechitar ("the consoler"), was forced to flee his homeland, the Morea, when the Turks invaded. Venetian rulers gave him the island of San Lazzaro in the southern lagoon as a place of shelter. Here, he established a religious order. The Armenians rebuilt the island, setting up a monastery, church, library, study rooms, gardens and orchards. The island became a place of study where monks taught (and still teach) young Armenians their culture.

Illuminated manuscript, San Lazzaro degli Armeni

Prince Nehmekhet's sarcophagus (c.1000 BC), San Lazzaro

The island today

Today, multilingual monks give visitors guided tours of the church, the art collection, the library and the museum, which houses Armenian, Greek, Indian and Egyptian artifacts. One of the most famous is an Egyptian sarcophagus complete with mummy, which is one of the best-preserved in the world. The most impressive exhibit is the printing hall where, over 200 years ago, a press produced works in 36 languages. A polyglot press is still in use, producing postcards, maps and prints for visitors.

Lord Byron

In 1816 the poet Byron would often row from Venice to absorb Armenian culture. Full of admiration for the monks, he wrote that the monastery "appears to unite all the advantages of the monastic institution without any of its vices . . . the virtues of the brethren . . . are well fitted to strike a man of the world with the conviction that 'there is another and a better', even in this life." The room where he studied, with mementoes, has been carefully preserved.

The garden and cloisters of San Lazzaro degli Armeni

The Lido, away from the crowds and glare of the beaches

Lido ⑩

No's 1, 6, 14, 51, 52, 61, 62 and 82 (summer) to Santa Maria Elisabetta; No. 17 from Tronchetto to San Nicolò.

THE LIDO is a slender sandbank 12 km (8 miles) long, which forms a natural barrier between Venice and the open sea. It is both a residential suburb of the city and – more importantly for tourists – the city's seaside resort. The only island in the lagoon with roads, it is linked to the Tronchetto island car park by car ferry. From Venice, the Lido is served by regular *vaporetti.* The fastest of these (Motonave No. 6) takes little more than ten minutes to reach its destination.

The Lido's main season runs from June to September, the most crowded months being July and August. In winter most hotels are closed.

The elegant bar of the Hôtel des Bains on the Lido

The world's first lido

In the 19th century, before the Lido was developed, the island was a favourite haunt of Shelley, Byron and other literary figures. Byron swam from the Lido to Santa Chiara via the Grand Canal in under four hours.

Bathing establishments were gradually opened and by the turn of the century the Lido had become one of Europe's most fashionable seaside resorts, frequented by royalty, film stars and leading lights of the literati. They stayed in the grand hotels, swam in the sea or sat in deckchairs on the sands by the striped *cabanas.* Life in the Lido's heyday was brilliantly evoked in Thomas Mann's book *Death in Venice* (1912). The Hôtel des Bains, where the melancholic Von Aschenbach stays, features in the novel and in Visconti's 1970 film. It is still a prominent landmark and an elegant place to stay *(see p231).*

The Lido is no longer the prestigious resort it was in the 1930s. Beaches are crowded, the streets busy and the ferries packed with daytrippers. Nevertheless the sands, sea and sporting facilities provide a welcome break from city culture. The backwaters provide a green respite from the heat of Venice.

Exploring the island

The Lido can be covered by bus but a popular form of transport is the bicycle. You can hire one from the shop almost opposite the *vaporetto* stop at Santa Maria Elisabetta.

The east side of the island is fringed by sandy beaches. For passengers arriving by ferry at the main landing stage, these beaches are reached by bus, taxi or on foot along the Gran Viale Santa Maria Elisabetta. This is the main shopping street of the Lido. At the end of the Gran Viale you can turn left for the beaches of San Nicolò or right along the Lungomare G Marconi, which boasts the grandest hotels and the best beaches. The former control the latter in this area, and levy exorbitant charges (except to hotel residents) for the use of beach facilities.

The long straight road parallel to the beach leads southwest to the village of

Cabanas **on the Lido beaches, hired out to holidaying Venetians**

Malamocco. There are some pleasant fish restaurants, but there is little evidence that this was once the 8th-century seat of the lagoon's government.

Alberoni, at the southern end of the Lido, is the site of a golf course, a public beach and the landing stage for the ferry across to Pellestrina.

San Nicolò

The Lido's only quarter of cultural interest is San Nicolò in the north.

Across the Porto di Lido, you can see the fortress of Sant'Andrea on the island of Le Vignole, built by Michele Sanmicheli between 1435 and 1449 to guard the main entrance of the lagoon.

It was to the Porto di Lido that the doge was rowed annually to cast a ring into the sea in symbolic marriage each spring *(see p33)*. After the ceremony he would visit the nearby church and monastery of San Nicolò, which was founded in 1044 and rebuilt in the 16th century.

The nearby Jewish cemetery, open to the public, dates from 1386.

The rest of this northern area is given over to an airfield. The aeroclub located there organizes private flying lessons.

Jewish Cemetery

041 71 53 59.
call in advance for a guided visit (excluding winter).

San Clemente ⓫

No public access.

From a refuge for pilgrims en route to the Holy Land, the island of San Clemente became a hermitage and site of a monastery. During the Republic it was the island where doges frequently met distinguished visitors, but from 1630 when the island was hit by the plague (said to have been brought by the Duke of Mantua) it served as a military depot. In the 19th century the island was turned into a lunatic asylum and most of the existing buildings date from that time.

International Film Festival

Film fans flock to the Lido every year in late summer for the International Film Festival. The event was inaugurated in 1932 under the auspices of the Biennale *(see p256)* and was so successful that the Palazzo del Cinema was built four years later. During its history the festival has attracted big names in the film world; it has also been plagued by bureaucracy and political in-fighting. There are signs however that the event is making a comeback and the famous names are now returning to the Lido.

The event takes place over two weeks in late August/early September. Films are shown day and night in numerous venues including the Palazzo del Cinema (tickets are sold outside). You can normally spot the stars (along with the paparazzi) for the price of a drink on the terrace of the Excelsior Hotel. See also page 255.

Poster advertising the first Lido International Film Festival, 1932

Lazzaretto Nuovo ⓬

041 244 40 11. *No. 13.*
Apr–Oct: 9:45am & 4pm Sat & Sun. *donation.*

A mere stone's throw from Sant'Erasmo, in the northern lagoon, Lazzaretto Nuovo is one of the few uninhabited visitable islands. Archaeologists continue to unearth medieval structures dating back to the late 1400s, when the island was used as a quarantine station for crews of ships hailing from distant lands where the plague was rife. Cargoes would be fumigated with rosemary and juniper. During the terrible pestilence that afflicted Venice in 1576, the island housed 10,000 victims.

Poveglia ⓭

No public access.

Formerly called Popilia on account of all its poplar trees, the island was once a thriving community with its own government. After the 1380 war with Genoa, it fell into decline, and over the centuries became a refuge for plague victims, an isolation hospital and a home for the aged. Today the land is used for growing crops and vines.

San Clemente in the southern lagoon, seen through the evening mist

SPORTHOTEL EUROPA

THE VENETO AREA BY AREA

The Veneto at a Glance

THE VENETO'S SHEER VARIETY makes it one of Italy's most fascinating regions to explore. The cities of Verona, Padua and Vicenza are all noted for outstanding architecture, churches and museums. Villas in the rural hinterland are gorgeously frescoed with scenes from ancient mythology. The lagoon has busy fishing ports and beach resorts, while Lake Garda, with its glorious mountain scenery, historic castles and water sports, makes a perfect holiday playground. Northwards lie the majestic Dolomites, Italy's premier region for skiing, which attract visitors in the summer, too, with their alpine beauty and excellent hiking facilities.

Monti Lessini
Scores of scenic villages, such as Giazza (see p191), *nestle in the vineyard-clad valleys of the Lessini mountains.*

Verona
An ancient Roman stronghold, famous as the home of the lovers Romeo and Juliet, Verona today is a city of opera, theatre and art (see pp192–203).

Lake Garda
Most beautiful of all the Italian lakes, Garda is surrounded by Scaligeri castles such as the magnificent Sirmione (see p204).

Vicenza
Dominated by the architecture of Palladio, Vicenza (see pp168–73) *is the model Renaissance city.*

Dolomites
Erosion has sculpted the limestone peaks of the Dolomites into bizarre columns and spires, with alpine villages hidden in steep valleys (see p216).

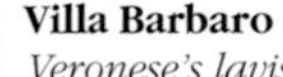

Villa Barbaro
Veronese's lavish frescoes are the perfect complement to one of Palladio's grandest rural villas, surrounded by statue-filled formal gardens, grottoes and pools (see p24).

THE DOLOMITES
Pages 210–219

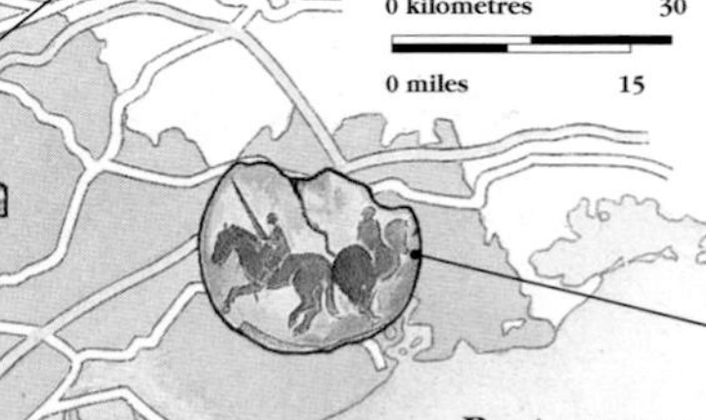

THE VENETO PLAIN
Pages 162–185

Portogruaro
Roman and early Christian finds fill the museums of this ancient town (see p175).

Padua
The domes and minaret-like spires of St Anthony's basilica (see p182) *lend an Eastern air to this historic university town.*

Chioggia
Flocks of wading birds frequent the wild marshland around Chioggia (see p185), *the Venetian lagoon's principal fishing port.*

THE VENETO PLAIN

THE GREAT ARC OF LAND *that forms the Veneto Plain is one of tremendous contrast, and has much to offer the visitor. Its ancient cities are rich in history and their magnificent architecture is world-renowned. The source of the region's wealth is manifest in the industrial landscapes around the towns, but these are never far from beautiful countryside, which includes the green Euganean Hills, calm lagoons and the undulating foothills of the Dolomites.*

The area known as the Veneto Plain sweeps round from the Po river delta in the southwest to the mountains that form the border between Italy and Slovenia. The whole region is crossed by a series of rivers, canals and waterways, all of which converge in the Adriatic sea.

The river-borne silt deposits that created the Venetian Lagoon cover the region, making the land fertile. The Romans established their frontier posts here, and these survive today as the great cities of Vicenza, Padua and Treviso. Their strategic position at the hub of the empire's road network enabled them to prosper under Roman rule, as they continued to do under the benign rule of the Venetian empire more than 1,000 years later.

Wealth from agriculture, commerce and the spoils of war paid for the beautification of these cities through the construction of Renaissance palaces and public buildings, many of them designed by the region's great architect, Andrea Palladio. His villas can be seen all over the Veneto, symbols of the idyllic and leisured existence once enjoyed by the region's aristocrats.

The symbols of modern prosperity – factories and scarred landscapes – are encountered frequently, especially around the town of Mestre. Yet there are areas of extraordinary beauty as well. Petrarch *(see p184)*, the great medieval romantic poet, so loved the area that he made his home among the gently wooded Euganean Hills.

Fishing from a breakwater in the lagoon at Chioggia

◁ **Classical figure in the nymphaeum of the Villa Barbaro near Asolo**

Exploring the Veneto Plain

THE LANDSCAPE OF THE VENETO PLAIN is as flat as a board, but it is far from dull. Villagers in the small communities dotted throughout the region used to compete to build the tallest church tower, and these seemingly needle-thin landmarks soaring skywards draw the traveller on. Great stone castles, dating from the 14th century, rise on almost every promontory, each with a backdrop on clear days of the distant Alps.

SIGHTS AT A GLANCE

Asolo 7
Bassano del Grappa 4
Caorle 12
Castelfranco 6
Chioggia 20
Cittadella 5
Conegliano 10
Este 17
Euganean Hills (Colli Euganei) 15
Maròstica 3
Mestre 13
Monsélice 18
Montagnana 16
Padua (Padova) pp176–83 14
Polésine and Rovigo 19
Portogruaro 11
Thiene 2
Treviso 9
Valdobbiadene 8
Vicenza pp168–73 1

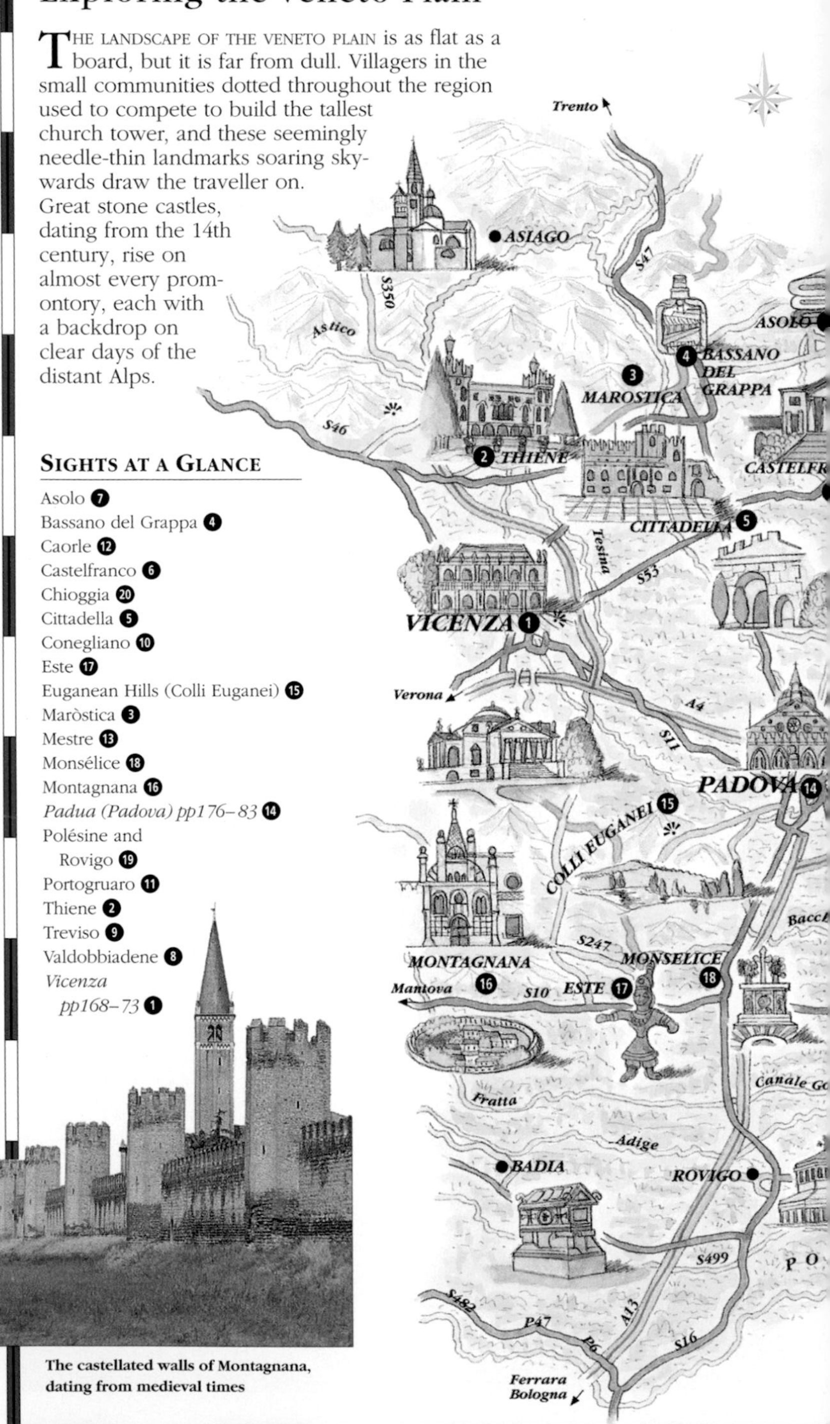

The castellated walls of Montagnana, dating from medieval times

Getting Around

An extensive rail network and good bus services make this region easy to explore by public transport. Roads are heavily used, so avoid cities and *autostrade* during rush hours.

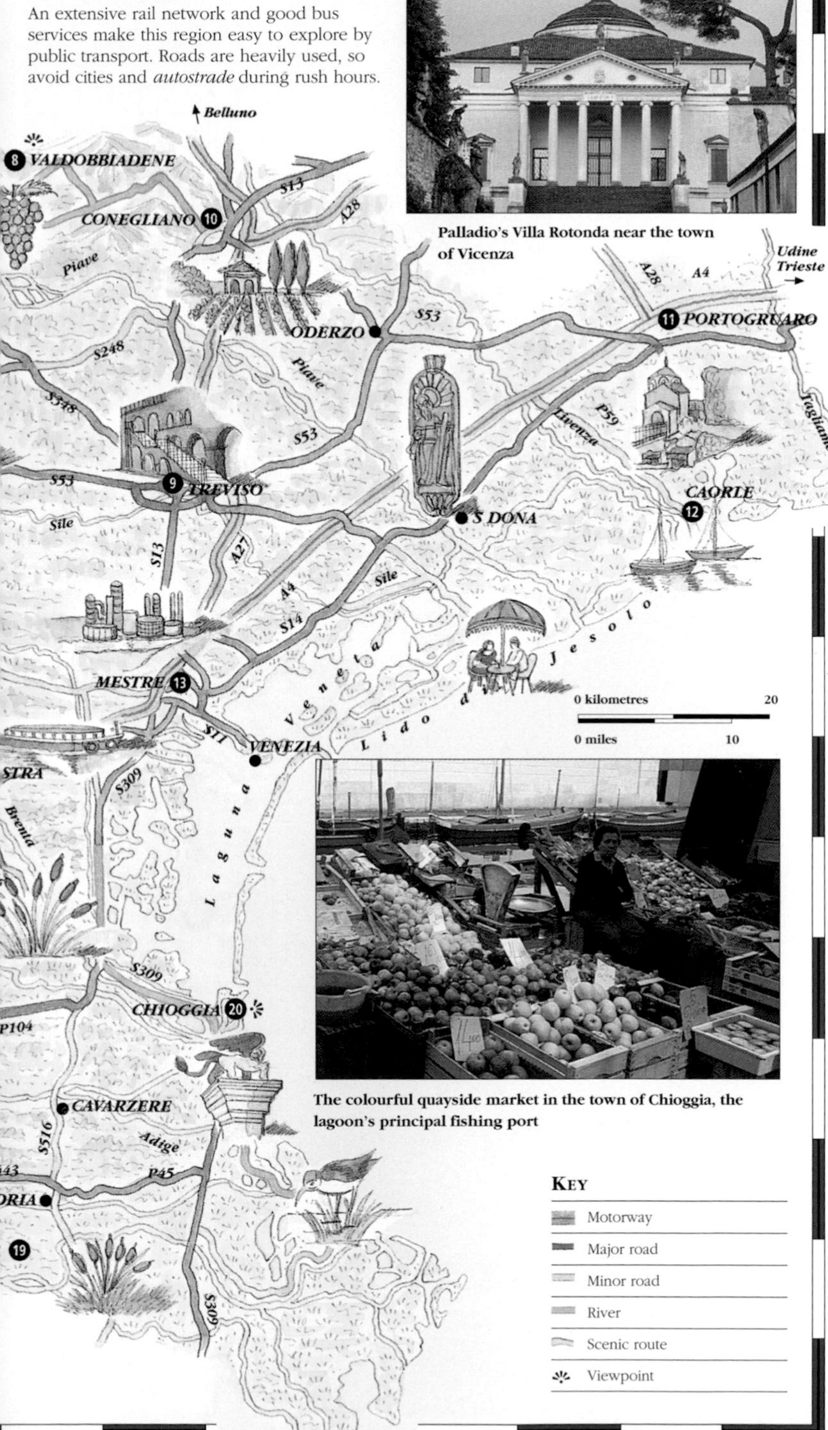

Palladio's Villa Rotonda near the town of Vicenza

The colourful quayside market in the town of Chioggia, the lagoon's principal fishing port

Vicenza ❶

See pp168–73.

Thiene ❷

Road map C3. *20,000.* *Piazza Ferrarin 20. (0445 36 95 44).* *Mon am.*

THIENE IS ONE of the area's many textile towns, manufacturing jeans and sweatshirts for sale all over Europe. Two villas nearby are worth a visit. The heavily fortified towers and battlemented walls of the **Castello Porto-Colleoni** are offset by pretty Gothic windows. At the time it was built, it stood in open countryside, and the defences were a precaution against bandits and raiders. Inside, 16th-century frescoes by Giambattista Zelotti add a lighter note and many portraits of horses remind the visitor that the villa's owners, the Colleoni family, were employed by the Venetian cavalry.

Zelotti also frescoed the **Villa Godi Malinverni**, the first villa designed by Palladio *(see pp24–5)*. The garden is charming, and the frescoes are magnificent. Inside are works by Italian Impressionists and a lovely portrait by Pietro Annigoni (1910–88) called *La Strega* (the Sorceress).

Castello Porto-Colleoni
Via Roma 62. *0445 36 60 15.*
mid-Mar–mid-Nov: Sun pm and public hols; Groups by appt.

Villa Godi Malinverni
Via Palladio 44. *0445 86 05 61.*
Mar–Nov: Tue, Sat & Sun afternoons; other times, phone ahead.

The human chess game in the town square of Maròstica

Maròstica ❸

Road map C3. *12,500.* *Piazza Castello 1. (0424 721 27).* *Tue.*

MAROSTICA is an almost perfect medieval fortified town, surrounded by walls built in 1370 by the Scaligeri *(see p207)*. The rampart walk from the **Castello Inferiore** (lower castle), now the town hall, to the **Castello Superiore** (upper castle) has fine views.

The lower castle exhibits costumes worn by participants in the town's human chess tournament, the *Partita a Scacchi*, held every other September *(see p35)*. Up to 650 people participate in this colourful re-enactment of a game first played here in 1454.

Castello Inferiore
Piazza Castello 1. *daily.*
Easter, 1 Nov, 25 Dec.

The Ponte degli Alpini at Bassano del Grappa

Bassano del Grappa ❹

Road map C3. *38,770.* FS *Largo Corona d'Italia 35. (0424 52 43 51).* *Thu & Sat am.*

THIS PEACEFUL TOWN is synonymous with Italy's favourite after-dinner drink. Although grappa is produced here, it is not named after the town, but after the Italian term for the lees (*graspa*) used to distil the liquor. Information on this and on the role played by Bassano during both world wars is given at the **Museo degli Alpini**, across the Ponte degli Alpini bridge. Designed in 1569 by Palladio, the current bridge dates from 1948: its timber allows it to flex when hit by spring meltwaters.

Bassano is also famous for the majolica wares *(see p252)* at **Palazzo Sturm**. The locally born artist Jacopo Bassano (1510–92) and sculptor Canova (1757–1822) are celebrated in the **Museo Civico**.

Museo degli Alpini
Via Anagarano 2. *0424 50 36 50.*
9am–8pm Tue–Sun.
6–16 Jan.

Palazzo Sturm
Via Ferracina. *0424 52 49 33.*
Apr–Oct: 9am–12:30pm, 3:30–6:30pm Tue–Sun (Sun pm only); Nov–Mar: Fri am, Sat & Sun pm.

Museo Civico
Piazza Garibaldi. *0424 52 33 36.*
9am–6:30pm Tue–Sat, 3:30–6:30pm Sun. *public hols.*

Cittadella 5

Road map C3. *18,000.* FS
Via Marconi 3. (049 597 06 27).
Mon am.

THIS ATTRACTIVE TOWN is the twin of Castelfranco. Each was fortified and Cittadella still preserves its 13th-century moated walls. These are interrupted by four gates and by 16 towers. The Torre di Malta near the southern gate was used as a torture chamber by Ezzelino de Romano, who ruled in the mid-13th century. Far more pleasant to contemplate is the *Supper at Emmaus* painting in the **Duomo**, a masterpiece by local Renaissance artist, Bassano.

Fresco from the Villa Emo at Fanzolo, near Castelfranco

Castelfranco 6

Road map D3. *30,000.* FS
Via Francesco Maria Preti 66. (0423 49 14 16). *Tue & Fri am.*

FORTIFIED IN 1199 by rulers of Treviso, the historic core of this town lies within the well-preserved walls. **Casa di Giorgione**, claimed to be the birthplace of artist Giorgione (1478–1511), houses a museum devoted to the life of the man who created such moody and mysterious works as *The Tempest (see p131)*. His *Virgin and Child with Saints Liberal and Francis* (1504) is displayed in the **Duomo**. This picture was commissioned by Tuzio Costanza to stand above the tomb of his son, Matteo, killed in battle in 1504.

At Fanzolo, 8 km (5 miles) northeast of Castelfranco, is the **Villa Emo**, designed in 1564 by Palladio. Here, Zelotti's sumptuous frescoes reveal the love lives of many Greek deities.

Casa di Giorgione
Piazzetta del Duomo. *0423 49 12 40.* *phone to check.*

Villa Emo
Fanzolo di Vedelago. *0423 47 64 14.* FS *Fanzolo.* *5.* *Apr–Oct: 3–7pm Mon–Sat; 10:30am–12:30pm, 3–7pm Sun and public hols; Nov–Mar: 2–6pm Sat, Sun and public hols.* *15 Dec–15 Jan.*

The pretty town of Asolo in the foothills of the Dolomites

Asolo 7

Road map D3. *2,000.*
Piazza Garibaldi 73. (0423 52 90 46). *Sat.*

ASOLO IS beautifully sited among the cypress-clad foothills of the Dolomites. Queen Caterina Cornaro (1454–1510) once ruled this tiny walled town *(see p43)*, and the poet Cardinal Pietro Bembo coined the verb *asolare* to describe the bittersweet life of enforced idleness she endured. Others who have fallen in love with these narrow streets include poet Robert Browning, who named a volume of poems *Asolando* (1889) after the town, and travel writer Freya Stark, who lived here until her death in 1993.

Just 10 km (6 miles) east of Asolo is the **Villa Barbaro** at Masèr *(see pp24–5)*, while 10 km (6 miles) north is the village of Passagno, birthplace of Antonio Canova. Canova's remains lie inside the huge temple-like church which he designed himself. Nearby is the family home, the **Casa di Canova**. The Gypsoteca here houses the plaster casts and clay models for many of Canova's sculptures.

Villa Barbaro
Masèr. *0423 92 30 04.* *Mar–Oct: 3–6pm Tue, Sat, Sun & public hols; Nov–Feb: 2:30–5pm Sat, Sun & public hols.* *24 Dec–6 Jan, Easter.*

Casa di Canova
Piazza Canova. *0423 54 43 23.* *Tue–Sun.* *1 Jan, Easter, 25 Dec.*

Valdobbiadene 8

Road map D3. *10,700.*
Piazza Marconi 1. (0423 97 69 75). *Mon.*

VALDOBBIADENE, surrounded by vine-covered hills, is a centre for the sparkling white wine called Cartizze, a type of Prosecco. To the east, the Strada del Vino Bianco (white wine route) stretches 34 km (21 miles) to the town of Conegliano *(see p175)*, passing vineyards offering wine to try and to buy.

ENVIRONS: About 10 km (8 miles) northeast of Valdobbiadene is the small town of Follina, renowned for its wonderfully well-preserved Romanesque abbey.

Vines near Valdobbiadene

Street-by-Street: Vicenza ❶

Detail on No. 21 Contrà Porti

VICENZA IS KNOWN as the city of Andrea Palladio (1508–80), arguably the most influential architect of his time. Although Palladio was born in Padua, Vicenza was his adoptive home and, walking around the city, one can see the evolution of his distinctive style. In the centre is the monumental basilica he adapted to serve as the town hall, while all around are the palaces he built for Vicenza's wealthy citizens.

Loggia del Capitaniato
This covered arcade was designed by Palladio in 1571.

Contrà Porti has some of the most elegant *palazzi* in Vicenza.

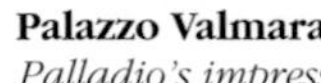

Palazzo Valmarana
Palladio's impressive building of 1566 was originally intended to be three times larger. It was not completed until 1680, 100 years after the architect's death.

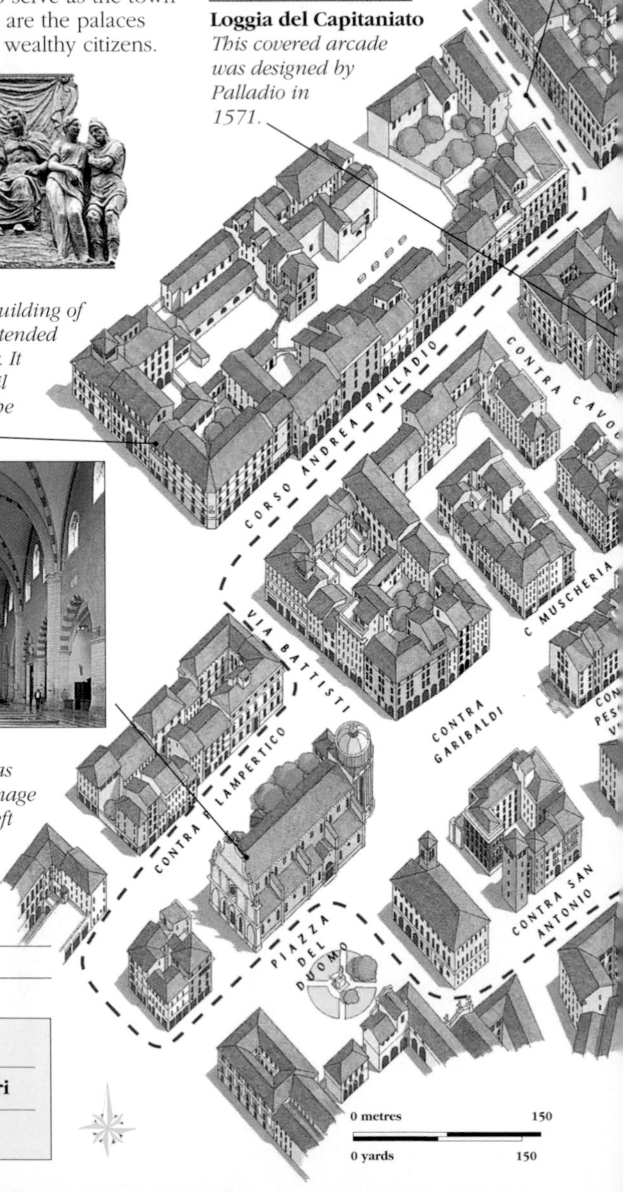

Duomo
Vicenza's cathedral was rebuilt after bomb damage during World War II left only the façade and choir intact.

CORSO ANDREA PALLADIO
CONTRA CAVOUR
VIA BATTISTI
C MUSCHERIA
CONTRA GARIBALDI
CONTRA P LAMPERTICO
PIAZZA DEL DUOMO
CONTRA SAN ANTONIO

KEY

— — — Suggested route

STAR SIGHTS
★ **Piazza dei Signori**
★ **Casa Pigafetta**

0 metres 150

0 yards 150

Visitors' Checklist

Road map C4. *116,000.*
Piazza Stazione.
Piazza Matteotti 12 (0444 32 08 54). *Tue & Thu.*
Concert season (May–Jun); Theatre season (Sep–Oct); Son et Lumière (end Jul).

★ Piazza dei Signori
Encircled by grand 15th-century buildings including the city's green-roofed basilica and slender brick tower, the piazza is a lively spot, with a colourful market and cafés.

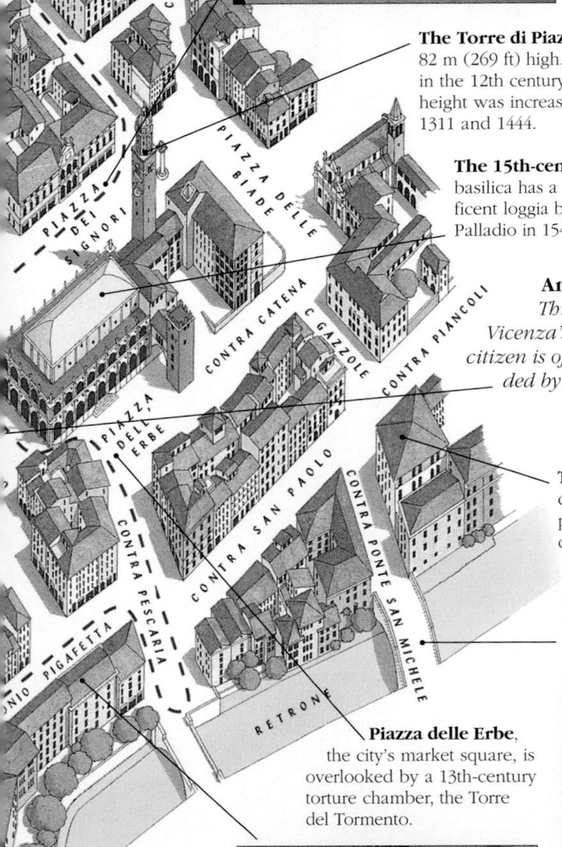

The Torre di Piazza is 82 m (269 ft) high. Begun in the 12th century, its height was increased in 1311 and 1444.

The 15th-century basilica has a magnificent loggia built by Palladio in 1549.

Andrea Palladio
This memorial to Vicenza's most famous citizen is often surrounded by market stalls.

The Quartiere delle Barche contains numerous attractive palaces built in the 14th-century Venetian Gothic style.

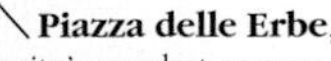

Piazza delle Erbe, the city's market square, is overlooked by a 13th-century torture chamber, the Torre del Tormento.

Ponte San Michele
This elegant stone bridge, built in 1620, provides lovely views of the surrounding town.

★ Casa Pigafetta
This striking house was the birthplace of Antonio Pigafetta, who in 1519 set sail round the world with Magellan.

Exploring Vicenza

VICENZA, THE GREAT PALLADIAN CITY, is celebrated all over the world for its architecture. It is also one of the wealthiest cities in the Veneto, with much to offer, from Roman and Renaissance art (a combined museum ticket is available) to elegant shops selling fine goods.

Statues gazing down from their pillars in the Piazza dei Signori

Piazza dei Signori

At the heart of Vicenza, this square is dominated by the startling bulk of the Palazzo della Ragione, often referred to as the "basilica". Open to the public, its green, copper-clad roof is shaped like an upturned boat with a balustrade bristling with the statues of Greek and Roman gods. The colonnades were designed by Palladio in 1549 to support the city's 15th-century town hall, which had begun to subside. This was his first public commission, and his solution ensured the survival of the building.

The astonishingly slender Torre di Piazza alongside has stood since the 12th century. Opposite is the elegant café Gran Caffè Garibaldi, which is next to Palladio's Loggia del Capitaniato (1571). The Loggia's upper rooms contain the city's council chamber.

Contrà Porti

Contrà (an abbreviation of *contrada*, or district) is the local dialect word for street. On the western side is a series of pretty Gothic buildings with painted windows and ornate balconies, including Palazzo Porto-Colleoni (No. 19). These houses reflect the architecture of Venice, a reminder that Vicenza was part of the Venetian empire.

Several fine Palladian *palazzi* stand on this street. The Palazzo Thiene (No. 12) of 1545–50, the Palazzo Porto Barbarano (No. 11) of 1570, and the Palazzo Iseppo da Porto (No. 21) of 1552 all illustrate the sheer variety of Palladio's style – Classical elements are common to all three, but each is unique. The Palazzo Thiene reveals some intriguing details of Palladio's methods: though the building appears to be of stone, close inspection reveals that it is built of cheap lightweight brick, cleverly rendered to look like masonry.

Casa Pigafetta

Contrà Pigafetta. ***No public access.***

This highly decorated Spanish Gothic building of 1481 has clover-leaf balconies, gryphon brackets and Moorish windows. The owner, Antonio Pigafetta, sailed round the world with Magellan in 1519–22, being one of only 20 men who survived the voyage.

Museo Civico

Piazza Matteotti. *0444 32 13 48.* *Tue–Sun.* *25 Dec, 1 Jan.*

The excellent Museo Civico is housed in Palladio's Palazzo Chiericati, built in 1550. Inside is a fresco by Domenico Brusazorzi of a naked charioteer, representing the Sun, who appears to fly over the ceiling of the entrance hall. In the upstairs rooms are many great pictures. Among the Gothic altarpieces from local churches is Hans Memling's *Crucifixion* (1468–70), the central panel of a triptych whose side panels are now in New York.

In the later rooms are newly cleaned works by the local artist Bartolomeo Montagna (c.1450–1523), including his remarkable *Virgin Enthroned with Child, St John the Baptist and Saints Bartholomew, Augustine and Sebastian.*

Santa Corona

This impressive Gothic church was built in 1261 to house a thorn from Christ's Crown of Thorns, donated by Louis IX of France. In the Porto Chapel is the tomb of Luigi da Porto (died 1529), author of the novel *Giulietta e Romeo*, upon which Shakespeare based his famous play. Notable paintings

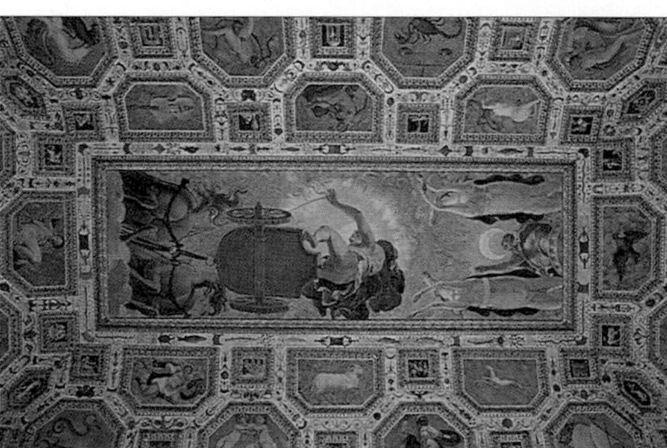

Brusazorzi's ceiling fresco in the large entrance hall of the Museo Civico

include Giovanni Bellini's *Baptism of Christ* (c.1500–5) and Paolo Veronese's *Adoration of the Magi* (1573). In the cloister the Museo Naturalistico-Archeologico exhibits natural history and archaeology.

San Lorenzo

The portal of this church is a magnificent example of Gothic stone carving, richly decorated with the figures of the Virgin and Child, and St Francis and St Clare. Sadly the frescoes inside are damaged, but there are fine tombs. The lovely cloister, north of the church, is a flower-filled haven of calm.

The beautiful cloister of the church of San Lorenzo

Palazzo Leoni Montanari

Contra' Santa Corona 25. *800 57 88 75.* *10am–6pm Fri–Sun (also Wed & Thu for temporary exhibitions).*

This Baroque building was completed around 1720, commissioned by Giovanni Leoni Montanari, who had made his fortune producing and selling cloth. Today the Palazzo houses an art gallery renowned for its collections of Venetian paintings and Russian icons.

Monte Berico

Basilica di Monte Berico. *0444 32 09 99.* *daily.*

Monte Berico is the green, cypress-clad hill to the south of the city to which wealthy Vicenzans once escaped in the heat of summer to enjoy cooler air and bucolic charms. The wide avenue linking the city to the basilica on top of the hill features shady colonnades with many shrines along the route. The Baroque basilica was built in the 15th century and is dedicated to the Virgin who appeared during the 1426–8 plague to declare that Vicenza would be spared.

Many pilgrims still travel to the lovely church, where Bartolomeo Montagna's moving *Pietà* fresco (1572) makes an impact within the ornate interior. Other attractions include a fossil collection in the cloister, and Veronese's fine painting *The Supper of St Gregory the Great* (1572) in the refectory. The large canvas was cut to ribbons by bayonet-wielding soldiers during the revolutionary outbursts of 1848 and painstakingly restored.

The elegant Villa Rotonda, most famous of all Palladio's works

Villa Valmarana

Via dei Nani 12. *0444 54 39 76.* *mid-Mar–5 Nov.* *Mon, Tue & Fri am.*

The wall alongside the Villa Valmarana (which was built in 1688 by Antonio Muttoni) is topped by the figures of dwarfs, which give this building its alternative name – *ai Nani* (at the Dwarfs). Inside the villa, the walls are covered with frescoes by Tiepolo, in which pagan gods float on clouds watching scenes from the epics of Homer and Virgil. In the separate Foresteria (guest house), the frescoes with themes of peasant life and the seasons, painted by Tiepolo's son, Giandomenico, are equally decorative but more earthily realistic.

The villa can be reached by a 10-minute walk from the basilica on Monte Berico. Head downhill along Via M d'Azeglio to the high-walled convent on the right where the road ends, then take the Via San Bastiano. There is also a bus service from town.

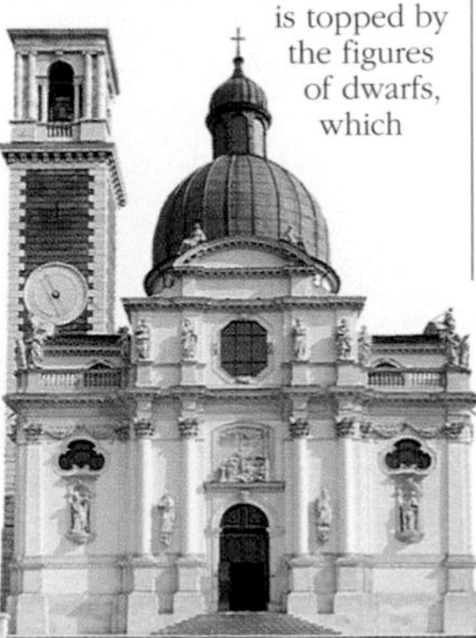

The Baroque hilltop church, the Basilica di Monte Berico

Villa Rotonda

Via della Rotonda 25. *0444 32 17 93.* **Villa** *mid-Mar–4 Nov: Wed.* **Garden** *mid-Mar–4 Nov: 10am–noon, 3–6pm Tue–Sun; 5 Nov–mid-Mar: 10am–noon, 2:30–5pm Tue–Sun.*

With its regular, symmetrical forms, this is the epitome of Palladio's architecture, and the most famous of all his villas. The design is simple yet satisfying, as is the contrast between the green lawns, white walls and terracotta roof tiles. Built between 1550 and 1552, it has inspired look-alikes in cities as far away as Delhi and St Petersburg. Fans of *Don Giovanni* will recognize locations used in Joseph Losey's 1979 film. The villa can be reached by bus from town, or on foot, following the path that passes the Villa Valmarana.

Vicenza: Teatro Olimpico

EUROPE'S OLDEST surviving indoor theatre, the Teatro Olimpico is an elegant and remarkable structure, largely made of wood and plaster and painted to look like marble. Fashionable architect Andrea Palladio *(see pp24–5)* began work on the design in 1579, but he died the following year without finishing it. His pupil, Vincenzo Scamozzi, took over the project and completed the theatre in time for its ambitious opening performance of Sophocles's tragic drama, *Oedipus Rex*, on 3 March 1585.

Bacchantes
Euripides' Greek tragedy is still performed using Scamozzi's versatile scenery.

Main ticket office

★ Odeon Frescoes
The gods of Mount Olympus, after which the theatre is named, decorate the Odeon, a room used for music recitals.

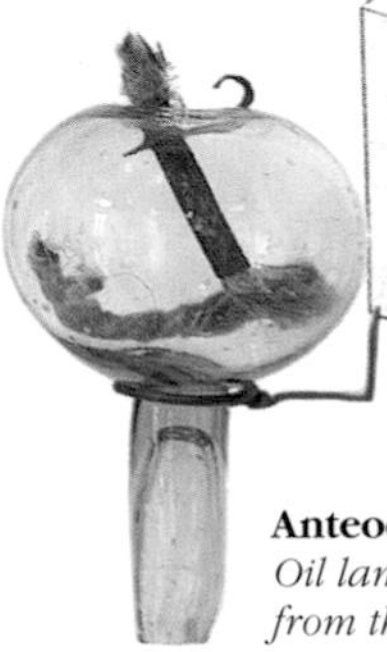

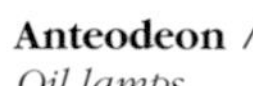

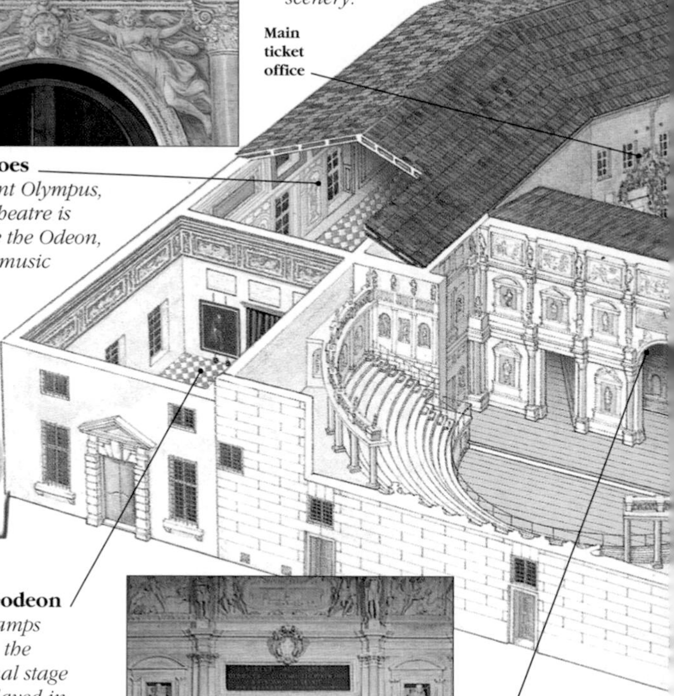

Anteodeon
Oil lamps from the original stage set are now displayed in the theatre's Anteodeon, whose frescoes (1595) depict the theatre's opening performance.

★ Stage Set
Scamozzi's scenery represents the Greek city of Thebes. The streets are cleverly painted in perspective and rise at a steep angle to give the illusion of great length.

STAR FEATURES

- ★ Stage Set by Vincenzo Scamozzi
- ★ Odeon Frescoes

Courtyard Sculptures
The courtyard of the former castle is decorated with sculpture donated by members of the Olympic Academy, the learned body that built the theatre.

VISITORS' CHECKLIST

Piazza Matteotti.
☎ *0444 22 28 00.*
🚌 *to Piazza Matteotti.*
○ *9am–5pm Tue–Sun (sometimes closes later in Jul & Aug).* ● *1 Jan, 25 Dec.*
Regular theatre performances.

Armoury Gateway
This stone gateway, with its military-style carvings, leads from Piazza Matteotti into the picturesque theatre courtyard.

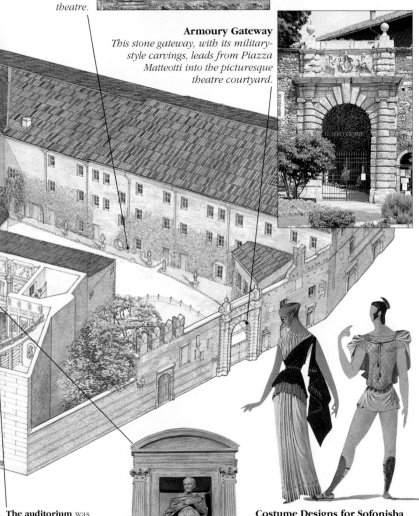

The auditorium was designed by Palladio to resemble the outdoor theatres of ancient Greece and Rome, such as the arena at Verona *(see p195)*, with a semi-circle of "stone" benches (actually made of wood) and a ceiling painted to portray the sky.

Costume Designs for Sofonisba
Ancient Greek vases inspired the costumes for this tragedy (1562) by Palladio's patron, GG Trissino.

Façade Statues
The toga-clad figures are portraits of sponsors who paid for the theatre's construction.

The medieval town of Treviso, built around ancient canals

Treviso ⑨

Road map D3. *81,700.* FS
Piazzetta Monte di Pietà 8. (0422 54 76 32). *Tue & Sat am.*

FULL OF attractive balconied houses overlooking willow-fringed canals, Treviso is a rewarding city for visitors. Comparisons are often made with Venice, but Treviso has its own distinctive character. A good place to explore the architecture is the main street, Calmaggiore, which links the cathedral with the rebuilt 13th-century town hall, the Palazzo dei Trecento. The tradition of painting the exterior of the houses dates back to the medieval period, and this form of decoration, applied to brick and timber, compensated for the lack of suitable building stone. The bustling fish market also dates back to medieval times. It is held on an island in the middle of Treviso's river Sile so that the remains of the day's trading can be flushed away instantly.

Duomo

Treviso's cathedral, founded in the 12th century, was reconstructed in the 15th, 16th and 18th centuries. Inside is Titian's *Annunciation* (1570), but it is upstaged by the striking *Adoration of the Magi* fresco (1520) of Titian's arch rival, Il Pordenone. Other memorable works are *The Adoration of the Shepherds* fresco by Paris Bordone, and the monument to Bishop Zanetti (1501) by Pietro Lombardo and his sons.

Museo Civico

Borgo Cavour 24. *0422 59 13 37.* *Tue–Sun.* *public hols.*
The Museo Civico houses an archaeology collection and a picture gallery. The best works are Lorenzo Lotto's *Portrait of a Dominican* (1526), Titian's *Portrait of Sperone Speroni* (1544) and Bassano's *Crucifixion.* Tomaso da Modena's 14th-century frescoes of the life of St Ursula have been moved to the recently restored convent of Santa Caterina dei Servi *(see map).*

San Nicolò

Nestling near the 16th-century town wall is the bulky Dominican church of San Nicolò, full of tombs and frescoes, including some by Lorenzo Lotto. There is a gigantic painting of St Christopher by Antonio da Treviso and the piers of the nave bear vivid portraits of saints by Tomaso da Modena. The latter also painted the humorous pictures of monks (1352) on the walls of the chapter house (*Sala del Capitolo*), which has a separate entrance through the Seminario Vescovile.

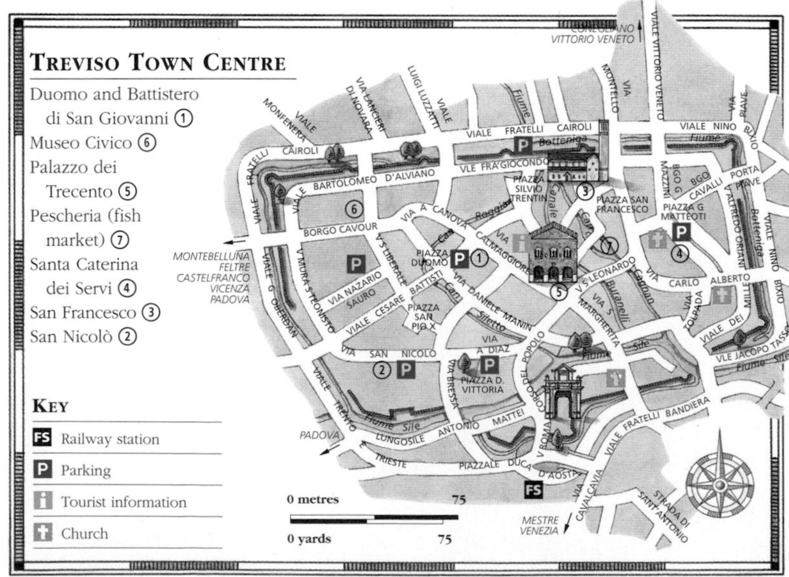

Conegliano ❿

Road map D3. 35,300. FS
Via XX Settembre 61. (0438 21 230). Fri. **Shops closed** Mon am.

CONEGLIANO lies between the Prosecco-producing vineyards and those that produce fine red wine *(see pp238–9)*. Wine makers from both areas learn their craft at Conegliano's renowned wine school. The town's winding and arcaded main street, Via XX Settembre, is lined by 15th- to 18th-century *palazzi*, some decorated with external frescoes, some in Venetian Gothic style. The **Duomo** contains a gorgeous altarpiece by Cima da Conegliano (1460–1518) showing the *Virgin and Child with Saints* (1493). This was commissioned by the religious brotherhood whose headquarters, the Scuola di Santa Maria dei Battuti (*flagellants*), stands beside the Duomo.

Reproductions of Cima's paintings are displayed in the **Casa di Cima**, the artist's birthplace. His detailed landscapes were based on the hills around the town; they can still be seen from the gardens surrounding the **Castelvecchio** (old castle). A small museum of local history is housed in the castle.

Casa di Cima
Via Cima. 0438 21 660.
phone to check.

Castelvecchio
Piazzale Castelvecchio 8. 0438 228 71. *Museum: Tue–Sun (Nov: Sun only); gardens: daily (except for two weeks in Nov).*

A mythical statue outside the theatre in Conegliano's Via XX Settembre

The foundations of Roman buildings in Concordia, near Portogruaro

Portogruaro ⓫

Road map E3. 26,000. FS
Via Martiri della Libertà 19–21. (0421 722 35). Thu am. **Shops closed** Mon.

SITUATED ON the main road linking Venice to Trieste, Portogruaro is the medieval successor to the Roman town of Concordia Sagittaria. Finds from Concordia, including statues, tomb inscriptions and mosaics, are displayed in the town's **Museo Concordiese**. These objects were unearthed in the modern village of Concordia, 2 km (1 mile) south of Portogruaro, where the footings of ruined Roman buildings can be seen all around the church and baptistry.

Museo Concordiese
Via Seminaro 26. 0421 726 74.
daily. *1 Jan, 1 May, 25 Dec.*

Caorle ⓬

Road map E3. 11,700.
Calle delle Liburniche 11. (0421 810 85). Sat am.

LIKE VENICE, Caorle was built among the swamps of the Venetian lagoon by refugees fleeing the Goths in the 5th century. Today it is a fishing village and a busy beach resort perched on the edge of a huge expanse of purpose-built lagoons, carefully managed to encourage fish to enter and spawn. The young are then fed and farmed.

The area is also of great interest to naturalists for the abundant bird life of the reed-fringed waters. The town's 11th-century **Duomo** is worth a visit for its Pala d'Oro, a gilded altarpiece made up of 12th- and 13th-century Byzantine panel reliefs.

Local fishermen at work in the village of Caorle

Mestre ⓭

Road map D4. 179,000.
Wed & Fri am.

MESTRE, the industrial offspring of Venice, is often favoured by visitors as a relatively less expensive base for exploring the region than Venice or other towns. Flying into Venice's Marco Polo airport *(see pp270–71)*, you cannot miss the factories and oil terminals that surround Mestre and its neighbour, Marghera, vital to the region's economy.

Street-by-Street: Padua ⓮

THE CITY CENTRE of Padua (Padova) is one of the liveliest in northern Italy, thanks to a large student population and to the two street markets, one specializing in fruit and the other in vegetables. These take place every day except Sunday around the vast Palazzo della Ragione, the town's medieval law court and council chamber. The colonnades round the exterior of the *palazzo* shelter numerous bars, restaurants and shops selling meat, game, cheeses and wine.

Palazzo del Capitanio
Built between 1599 and 1605 for the head of the city's militia, the tower incorporates an astronomical clock made in 1344.

Piazza dei Signori is bordered by attractive arcades which house small speciality shops, interesting cafés and old-fashioned wine bars.

Corte Capitaniato, a 14th-century arts faculty (open for concerts), contains frescoes which include a rare portrait of Petrarch.

Loggia della Gran Guardia
Now used as a conference centre, this fine Renaissance building, dating from 1523, once housed the Council of Nobles.

The Palazzo del Monte di Pietà has 16th-century arcades and statues enclosing a medieval building.

★ Duomo and Baptistry
The 12th-century baptistry of the Duomo contains one of the most complete medieval fresco cycles to survive in Italy, painted by Giusto de' Menabuoi in 1378 and now restored.

KEY

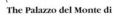

— — — Suggested route

0 metres 75

0 yards 75

★ Caffè Pedrocchi
Built like a Classical temple, the Caffè Pedrocchi has been a famous meeting place for students and intellectuals since it opened in 1831.

Visitors' Checklist

Road map D4. 220,000. FS Piazza Boschetti. Piazzale della Stazione. 049 875 20 77. Mon–Sat at Prato della Valle. **Shops closed** Mon am (clothes), Wed pm (food). concert season (Oct–Apr).

Palazzi Communali
This complex, which houses the city's council offices, has a 13th-century defensive tower.

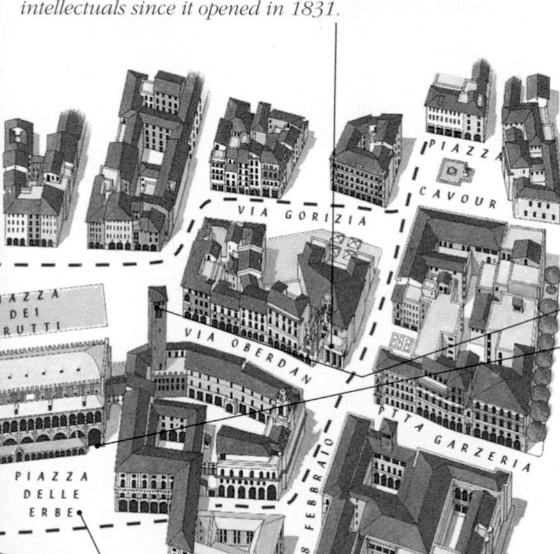

The Palazzo della Ragione, the "Palace of Reason" was, in medieval times, the city court of justice. Its interior is covered with magnificent astrological frescoes.

Padua University
Founded in 1222, this is the second oldest university in Italy. The main building dates back to the 16th century.

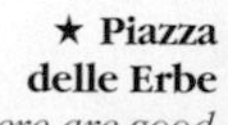

★ Piazza delle Erbe
There are good views on to the market place from Palladio's 16th-century loggia, which runs alongside the Palazzo della Ragione.

Star Sights

★ **Duomo and Baptistry**

★ **Caffè Pedrocchi**

★ **Piazza delle Erbe**

Exploring Padua

PADUA IS AN OLD UNIVERSITY TOWN with an illustrious academic history. Rich in art and architecture, it has two particularly outstanding sights. The first is the Scrovegni Chapel *(see pp180–81)*, in the north of the city, which is renowned for Giotto's lyrical frescoes. Close to the railway station, it forms part of the Eremitani museums complex. The second is the Basilica di Sant'Antonio, one of Italy's most popular pilgrim shrines, which forms the focal point for a number of sights in the south of the city *(see p182)*. A combined museum ticket is available.

Detail from the Egyptian room, upper floor of the Caffè Pedrocchi

Caffè Pedrocchi

Via VIII Febbraio 15. 049 878 12 31. *daily (Jun–Oct: Tue–Sun).*
Piano Nobile *049 820 50 07.*
Tue–Sun.

Grand cafés have long played an important role in the intellectual life of northern Italy, and many philosophical issues have been thrashed out at the Caffè Pedrocchi since it first opened in 1831. Politics superseded philosophy when it became a centre of the Risorgimento movement, dedicated to liberating Italy from Austrian rule; it was the scene of uprisings in 1848, for which several student leaders were executed. Later it became famous as the café that never closed its doors. Recently restored, these days people come to talk, read, play cards or watch the world go by as they eat and drink.

The upstairs rooms, or Piano Nobile, decorated in Moorish, Egyptian and Greek styles, are used for lectures, concerts and exhibitions.

Palazzo del Bo (University)

Via VIII Febbraio 2. 049 820 97 11.
Tue, Thu & Sat am, Mon, Wed & Fri pm (may vary, phone to check).

Named after a tavern called *Il Bo* (the ox), the historic main university building is mostly used today for graduation ceremonies. Originally it housed the medical faculty, renowned throughout Europe. Among its famous teachers and students was Gabriele Fallopio (1523–62), after whom the Fallopian tubes are named.

Elena Lucrezia Corner Piscopia became the first woman graduate in 1678 – long before women were allowed to study at many of Europe's other universities. Her statue stands on the staircase leading to the upper gallery of the 16th-century courtyard.

Visitors on the fascinating tour are shown the pulpit Galileo used when he taught here from 1592 until 1610. They also see the anatomy theatre (1594), the world's oldest surviving medical lecture theatre.

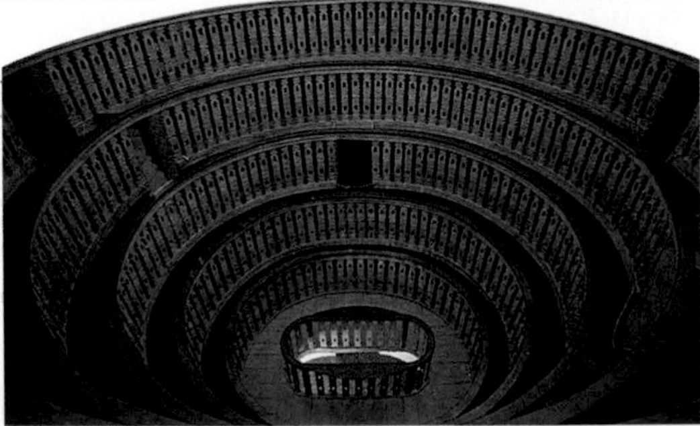

The 16th-century galleried anatomy theatre in the Palazzo del Bo

Sundial on the façade of the Palazzo della Ragione

Palazzo della Ragione

Piazza delle Erbe. *049 820 50 06.*
Tue–Sun. *1 Jan, 25 Dec.*

The "Palace of Reason", also known as the "Salone" by locals, was built to serve as Padua's law court and council chamber in 1218. The vast main hall was originally frescoed by the celebrated artist Giotto, but fire destroyed his work in 1420. The frescoes that survive today are by the relatively unknown Nicola Miretto, though their astrological theme is fascinating.

The Salone is breathtaking in its sheer size. It is Europe's biggest undivided medieval hall, 80 m (260 ft) long, 27 m (90 ft) wide and 27 m (90 ft) high. The scale is reinforced by the wooden horse displayed at one end – a massive beast, copied from Donatello's Gattamelata statue *(see p183)* in 1466 and originally made to be pulled in procession during Paduan festivities.

The walls are covered in Miretto's frescoes (1420–25), a total of 333 panels depicting the months of the year with appropriate gods, zodiacal signs and seasonal activities.

Also within the *palazzo* is the Stone of Shame, on which bankrupts were exposed to ridicule before they were sent into exile.

Eremitani Museums

THIS MAJOR MUSEUM COMPLEX occupies a group of 14th-century monastic buildings attached to the church of the Eremitani, a reclusive Augustinian order. The admission ticket includes entry to the Scrovegni Chapel *(see pp180–81)*, which stands on the same site, overlooking the city's Roman amphitheatre, and to the Archaeology Museum, the Bottacin Museum of coins and medals, and the Medieval and Modern Art Museum, all of which are housed around the cloisters.

The tomb of the Volumni family in the archaeological collection

Eremitani Church

ALONGSIDE the museum complex is the Eremitani church (1276–1306), with its magnificent roof and wall tombs. Interred here is Marco Benavides (1489–1582), a professor of law at the city university, whose mausoleum was designed by Ammannati, a Renaissance architect from Florence. Sadly missing from the church are Andrea Mantegna's celebrated frescoes of the lives of St James and St Christopher (1454–7), which were destroyed during a bombing raid in 1944. Two scenes from this magnificent work survive in the Ovetari Chapel, south of the sanctuary. *The Martyrdom of St James* was reconstructed from salvaged fragments, and *The Martyrdom of St Christopher* was removed carefully and stored elsewhere before the bombing. Otherwise only photographs on the walls remain to hint at the quality of the lost works.

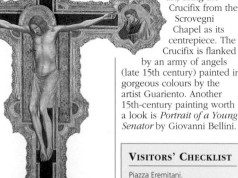

The Museums

THE HIGHLIGHT of the rich archaeological collection is the temple-like tomb of the Volumni family, dating from the 1st century AD. Among several other Roman tombstones from the Veneto region is one to the young dancer, Claudia Toreuma – sadly, a fairly dull inscribed column rather than a portrait. The collection also includes some fine mosaics, along with several impressive life-size statues depicting muscular Roman deities and toga-clad dignitaries. For most visitors the Renaissance bronzes are likely to be the most appealing feature of the museum, especially the comical *Drinking Satyr* by Il Riccio (1470–1532).

Coin collectors should make a point of visiting the Bottacin Museum. Among the exhibits there is an almost complete set of Venetian coinage and some very rare examples of Roman medallions.

The Modern Art Museum is currently closed to the public. However, the massive Medieval Museum is well worth a visit. It covers the history of Venetian art, with paintings from Giotto to the 1700s. Another museum looks at Giotto and his influence on local art, using the Crucifix from the Scrovegni Chapel as its centrepiece. The Crucifix is flanked by an army of angels (late 15th century) painted in gorgeous colours by the artist Guariento. Another 15th-century painting worth a look is *Portrait of a Young Senator* by Giovanni Bellini.

Angels in Armour **(15th century) by Guariento in the Art Museum**

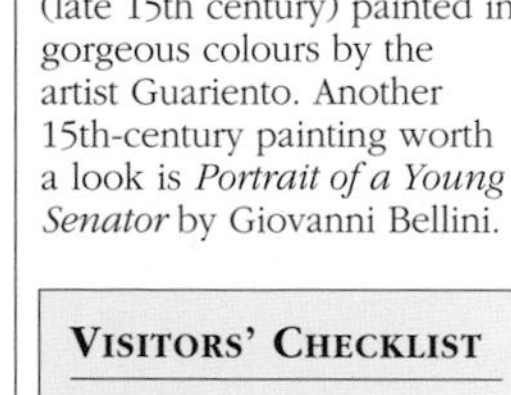

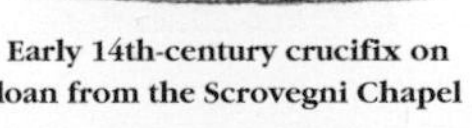

Early 14th-century crucifix on loan from the Scrovegni Chapel

Visitors' Checklist

Piazza Eremitani.
049 820 45 51.
Feb–Oct: 9am–7pm Tue–Sun; Nov–Jan: 9am–6pm Tue–Sun. **Only chapel open** *Mon.* *1 Jan, 1 May, 25 & 26 Dec.*

Padua: Scrovegni Chapel

Enrico Scrovegni built this chapel in 1303, hoping thereby to spare his dead father, a usurer, from the eternal damnation wished upon him by the poet Dante in his *Inferno*. The chapel is filled with harmonious frescoes of scenes from the life of Christ, painted by Giotto between 1303 and 1305. As works of great narrative force, they exerted a powerful influence on the development of European art.

The Nativity
The naturalism of the Virgin's pose marks a departure from Byzantine stylization, as does the use of natural blue for the sky, in place of celestial gold.

Expulsion of the Merchants
Christ's physical rage, the cowering merchant and the child hiding his face are all typical of Giotto's style.

The Coretti
Giotto painted the two panels known as the Coretti as an exercise in perspective, creating the illusion of an arch with a room beyond.

View towards altar

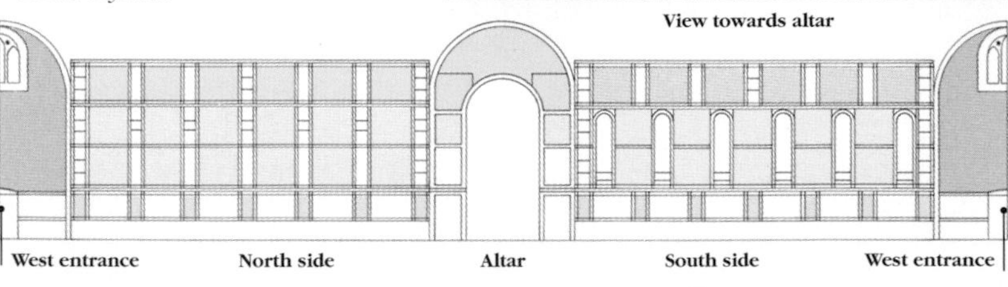

Gallery Guide

It is compulsory to book your visit to the Scrovegni Chapel in advance, since there are strict limits on the number of visitors allowed in the chapel at any one time. Prior to entry, all visitors must spend 15 minutes in a "decontamination chamber", and the duration of the visit to the chapel is also limited to 15 minutes. An explanatory film is shown while you wait in the chamber. The rest of the Eremitani complex is also worth a visit.

Key

- Episodes of Joachim and Anna
- Episodes from the Life of Mary
- Episodes from the Life and Death of Christ
- The Virtues and Vices
- The Last Judgment

The Last Judgment
This scene fills the entire west wall of the chapel. Its formal composition is closer to the Byzantine tradition than some of the other frescoes, with parts probably painted by assistants. A model of the chapel is shown, being offered to the Virgin by Scrovegni.

Visitors' Checklist

Giardini dell'Arena (entrance Piazza Eremitani). ☎ *049 201 00 20.* 🚌 *to Piazzale Boschetti.* 🕒 *9am–7pm daily (Nov–Jan: to 6pm).* ● *1 Jan, 1 May, 25 & 26 Dec.* 🎫 *see also Eremitani Museums p179.* 📷 ♿ **Booking compulsory.**
W www.cappelladegliscrovegni.it

View towards entrance

Mary is Presented at the Temple
Giotto sets many scenes against an architectural background, using the laws of perspective to give a sense of three dimensions.

Injustice
The Virtues and Vices are painted in monochrome. Here Injustice is symbolized by scenes of war, murder and robbery.

Lament over the Dead Christ
Giotto's figures express their grief in different ways, some huddled, some gesturing wildly.

Giotto

The great Florentine artist Giotto (1266–1337) is regarded as the father of Western art. His work, with its sense of pictorial space, naturalism and narrative drama, marks a decisive break with the Byzantine tradition of the preceding 1,000 years. He is the first Italian master whose name has passed into posterity, and although he was regarded in his lifetime as a great artist, few of the works attributed to him are fully documented. Some may have been painted by others, but his authorship of the frescoes in the Scrovegni Chapel need not be doubted.

The lofty interior of Padua's 16th-century duomo

Duomo and Baptistry

Baptistry 049 65 69 14. *10am–6pm daily.* *1 Jan, Easter, 25 Dec.*

Padua's duomo was commissioned from Michelangelo in 1552, but his designs were altered during the construction. Of the 4th-century cathedral which stood on the site, the domed Romanesque baptistry still survives, with its frescoes by Giusto de' Menabuoi (c.1376). The frescoes cover biblical stories, such as the Creation, Christ's Passion, Crucifixion and Resurrection and the Last Judgment.

Basilica di Sant'Antonio

This exotic church, with its minaret-like spires and Byzantine domes, is also known as Il Santo. It was begun in 1232 to house the remains of St Anthony of Padua, a preacher who modelled himself on St Francis of Assisi. Although he was a simple man who rejected worldly wealth, the citizens of Padua built one of the most lavish churches in Christendom to serve as his shrine.

The outline reflects the influence of Byzantine architecture; a cone-shaped central dome is surrounded by a further seven domes, rising above a façade that combines Gothic with Romanesque elements. The interior is more conventional, however. Visitors are kept away from the high altar, which features Donatello's magnificent reliefs (1444–5) on the miracles of St Anthony, and his statues of the Virgin, the Crucifixion and several Paduan saints. There is access to the tomb of St Anthony in the north transept, which is hung with offerings and photographs of people who have survived serious illness or car crashes with the saint's help. The walls

The Basilica di Sant'Antonio and Donatello's statue of Gattamelata

The Brenta Canal

THE RIVER BRENTA, between Padua and the Venetian Lagoon, was canalized in the 16th century. Flowing for a total of 36 km (22 miles), its potential as a transport route was quickly realized, and fine villas were built along its length. Today, these elegant buildings can still be admired. Three open their doors to the public: the Villa Foscari at Malcontenta, the Villa Widmann-Foscari at Mira, and the Villa Pisani at Stra. They can be visited either on an 8 to 9-hour guided tour from Padua to Venice (or viceversa) along the river on a motor launch, or by bus, a cheaper and faster alternative.

The picturesque town of Mira on the Brenta Canal

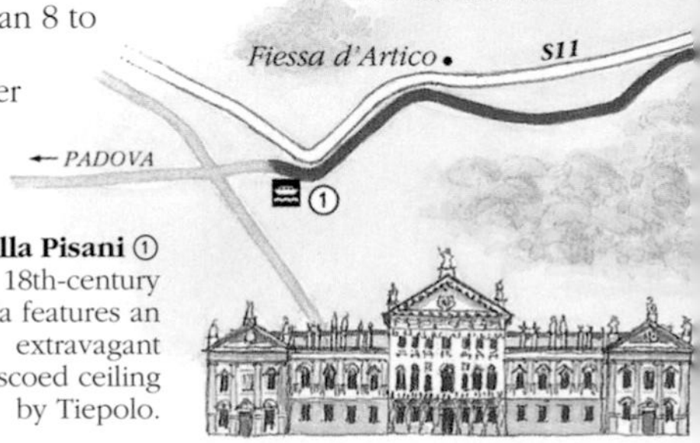

Fiessa d'Artico

S11

← PADOVA

KEY

▬	Tour route
═	Roads
⛴	Boat stops

Villa Pisani ①

This 18th-century villa features an extravagant frescoed ceiling by Tiepolo.

around the shrine are decorated with large marble reliefs depicting St Anthony's life, carved in 1505–77 by various artists, including Jacopo Sansovino and Tullio Lombardo. These are rather cold by comparison with the *Crucifixion* fresco (1380s) by Altichiero da Zevio in the opposite transept. This pageant-like painting of everyday scenes from medieval life shows depictions of people, animals and plants.

Statue of Gattamelata

Near the entrance to the basilica stands one of the great Renaissance works. This gritty portrait of the mercenary soldier Gattamelata (whose name means "Honey Cat") was created in 1443–52, honouring a man who in his life did great service to the Venetian Republic. Donatello won fame for the monument, the first equestrian statue made of this size since Roman times.

Scuola del Santo and Oratorio di San Giorgio

Piazza del Santo. 049 875 52 35. 9am–12:30pm, 2:30–7pm daily (to 5pm in winter). 1 Jan, 25 Dec. (combined ticket).

These two linked buildings contain excellent frescoes, including the earliest documented

One of four stone bridges spanning the canal around Prato della Valle

paintings by Titian. These comprise two scenes from the life of St Anthony in the Scuola del Santo, executed in 1511. The delightful saints' lives and scenes from the life of Christ in the San Giorgio oratory are the work of two artists, Altichiero da Zevio and Jacopo Avenzo, who painted them in 1378–84.

Orto Botanico

Via Orto Botanico 15. 0498 27 21 19. Apr–Oct: 9am–1pm, 3–6pm daily; Nov–Mar: 9am–1pm Mon–Sat (phone to confirm).

Founded in 1545, Padua's botanical garden is the oldest in Europe, and it retains much of its original appearance; one of the palm trees dates to 1585. Originally intended for the cultivation of medicinal plants, the pathways now spill over with exotic foliage, shaded by ancient trees. The gardens were used to cultivate the first lilacs (1565), sunflowers (1568) and potatoes (1590) grown in Italy.

Prato della Valle

The Prato (field) claims to be the largest public square in Italy, and its elliptical shape reflects the form of the Roman theatre that stood on the site.

St Anthony of Padua used to preach sermons to huge crowds here, but subsequent neglect saw the area turn into a malaria-ridden swamp. The land was drained in 1767 to create the canal that now encircles the Prato. Four stone bridges cross the picturesque channel, which is lined on both sides by statues of 78 eminent citizens of Padua.

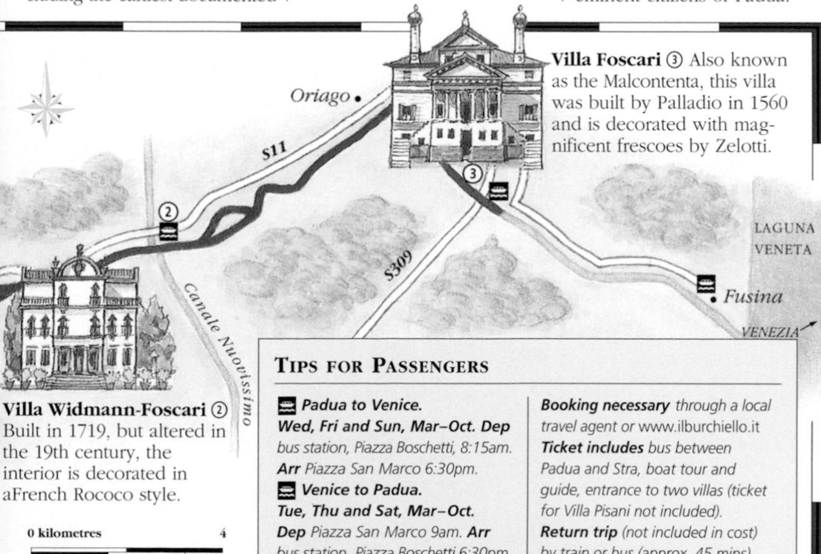

Villa Foscari ③ Also known as the Malcontenta, this villa was built by Palladio in 1560 and is decorated with magnificent frescoes by Zelotti.

Villa Widmann-Foscari ② Built in 1719, but altered in the 19th century, the interior is decorated in aFrench Rococo style.

Tips for Passengers

Padua to Venice.
Wed, Fri and Sun, Mar–Oct. Dep *bus station, Piazza Boschetti, 8:15am.* ***Arr*** *Piazza San Marco 6:30pm.*

Venice to Padua.
Tue, Thu and Sat, Mar–Oct. ***Dep*** *Piazza San Marco 9am.* ***Arr*** *bus station, Piazza Boschetti 6:30pm.*

Booking necessary *through a local travel agent or www.ilburchiello.it*
Ticket includes *bus between Padua and Stra, boat tour and guide, entrance to two villas (ticket for Villa Pisani not included).*
Return trip *(not included in cost) by train or bus (approx. 45 mins).*

The Euganean Hills, formed by ancient volcanic activity

Euganean Hills ⓯

Road map C4. *10,000.*
Viale Stazione 60, Montegrotto Terme. (049 79 33 84).

THE EUGANEAN Hills, remnants of long-extinct volcanoes, rise abruptly out of the Veneto plain and offer plenty of walking opportunities. Hot springs bubble up out of the ground at Abano Terme and Montegrotto Terme where scores of establishments offer thermal treatments, ranging from mud baths to immersion in the hot sulphurated waters. Spa cures such as these date back to Roman times, and you can see extensive remains of the Roman baths and theatre at Montegrotto.

Abbazia di Praglia

Via Abbazia di Praglia, Bresseo di Teòlo. *049 990 00 10.* *Tue–Sun pm.* *end of Jan* *Donations welcome.*
The Benedictine monastery at Praglia, 6 km (4 miles) west of Abano Terme, is a peaceful haven in the tree-clad hills. The monks have long been growing herbs commercially and there is a shop selling aromatic wares. They also lead guided tours of parts of the abbey and the Renaissance church (1490–1548), with its beautiful cloister.

Casa di Petrarca

Via Valleselle 4, Arquà Petrarca. *0429 71 82 94.* *Tue–Sun.* *most public hols.*
The picturesque town of Arquà Petrarca, on the southern edge of the Euganean hills, was once simply Arquà. Its name changed in 1868 to honour the medieval poet Francesco Petrarca, or Petrarch (1303–74), who lived here in his old age. He had often sung the praises of the well-tended landscape of olive groves and vineyards, and spent his last few years in a house frescoed with scenes from his lyrical poems. Though the house has been altered, it still contains the poet's desk and chair, his bookshelves and his mummified cat. Petrarch is buried in a simple sarcophagus located in the piazza in front of the church.

Villa Barbarigo

Valsanzibio. *049 805 56 14.* *Mar–Nov: 10am–1pm, 2pm–sunset.*
To the north of Arquà is the Villa Barbarigo at Valsanzibio, the only one of scores of villas, built by wealthy Paduans, regularly open to the public. The villa itself is of a simple design compared with the Baroque garden. Planted from 1669, it is full of variety, with fountains, statues and lakes.

The house of the poet Petrarch in the town of Arquà Petrarca

Montagnana ⓰

Road map C4. *12,000.* FS
Piazza Trieste 3. (0429 813 20).
Thu am. ***Shops closed*** *Mon am & Wed pm.*

MEDIEVAL brick walls encircle this town, extending for 2 km (1 mile), pierced by four gateways and defended by 24 towers. Just inside the castellated Padua Gate is the town's archaeological museum. The Gothic-Renaissance **Duomo** contains Paolo Veronese's *Transfiguration* (1555). Outside the city walls is Palladio's **Villa Pisani** (c.1560). Now rather neglected, its façade features the original owner's name (Francesco Pisani) in bold letters below the pediment.

Antique market in Montagnana

Este ⓱

Road map C4. *17,600.* FS
Piazza Maggiore 9A. (0429 36 35).
Wed & Sat am. ***Shops closed*** *Mon am (clothes) & Wed pm (food).*

EXCAVATIONS at Este have uncovered impressive remains of the ancient Ateste people, who flourished from the 9th century BC until they were conquered by the Romans in the 3rd century BC. The archaeological finds, including funerary urns, figurines, bronze vases and jewellery, are on display in the excellent **Museo Nazionale Atestino**, set within the walls of the town's 14th-century castle. The museum also displays examples of Roman and medieval art, and pieces of local pottery, famous since the Renaissance period, and still produced.

Museo Atestino
Palazzo Mocenigo. *0429 20 85.* *daily.* *1 Jan, 1 May, 25 Dec.*

Monsélice ⓲

Road map C4. *17,000.* FS *Piazza Mazzini 15. (0429 78 30 26).* *Mon & Fri.* ***Shops closed*** *Tue am (clothes), Wed pm (food).*

The town of Monsélice stands at the foot of two hills, one of which has been quarried extensively for rich deposits of crystalline minerals. The other is topped by ruined **Castle Rocca**, now a nature reserve. You can climb the hill up cobbled Via del Santuario as far as **San Giorgio**, to see its exquisite inlaid marble work.

Other features on the way up are the 13th-century cathedral and the statue-filled Baroque gardens of the Villa Nani that can be glimpsed through the villa gates. Nearby is **Ca' Marcello**, a 14th-century castle featuring period furnishings, suits of armour, frescoes and tapestries.

Marble inlay detail from San Giorgio

Ca' Marcello
Via del Santuario. *0429 729 31.* *Apr–Nov: Tue–Sun; Dec–Mar: groups only; book in advance.*

The sanctuary of San Giorgio on the hill top at Monsélice

Polésine and Rovigo ⓳

Road map C5. FS *Via J. Dunant 10, Rovigo. (0425 36 14 81).*

Polesine is the flat expanse of fertile agricultural land, crisscrossed by canals and subject to flooding, between the river Adige and the Po. The Po Delta is now a national park and has a wealth of fascinating birdlife, including egrets, herons, and bitterns.

The most scenic areas are around Scardovari and Porto Tolle, on the south side of the Po. Companies in Porto Tolle offer canoe and bicycle hire and half-day boat cruises.

The modern city of Rovigo has one outstanding monument, the splendid octagonal church called **La Rotonda** (1594–1602), decorated with paintings and statues in niches.

Environs: Adria, 22 km (14 miles) east of Rovigo, gave its name to the Adriatic Sea and was once a Greek and later an Etruscan port. A programme of silt deposition, undertaken to increase Adria's agricultural potential, left the city dry, apart from a 24-km (15-mile) canal. Among the exhibits on display in the **Museo Archeologico** is a complete iron chariot dating from the 4th century BC.

Museo Archeologico
Via Badini 59, Adria. *0426 216 12.* *daily.* *25 Dec, 1 Jan, 1 May.*

Chioggia ⓴

Road map D4. *56,000.* FS *Lungomare Adriatico 101. (041 40 10 68).* *Thu.*

Chioggia is the principal fishing port on the lagoon and the bustling, colourful **fish market** is a good reason to come here early in the day (open every morning except Monday). Many visitors enjoy the gritty character of the port area, with its smells, its vibrantly coloured boats and the tangle of nets and tackle. The town also has numerous inexpensive restaurants which serve fresh fish in almost every variety. Eel, crab and cuttlefish are the local specialities. There is a beach area at Sottomarina, on the western part of the island. Worth seeking out for a special visit is Carpaccio's *St Paul* (1520), the artist's last known work, which is permanently housed in the church of **San Domenico**.

Net mending in the traditional way, Chioggia

Verona and Lake Garda

Verona is one of northern Italy's *most alluring cities, its noble palaces, quiet cloisters and ancient streets every bit as romantic as you would expect of Romeo and Juliet's city. On its doorstep are the well-known vineyards of Soave, Bardolino and Valpolicella, set against the rugged slopes of the Little Dolomites. To the west lie the beautiful shores of Lake Garda, a mere 30 minutes' drive from Verona by car, but a world away in atmosphere.*

Set within the curves of the river Adige, Verona has been a prosperous and cosmopolitan city since the Romans colonized it in 89 BC. It stands astride two important trade routes – the Serenissima, connecting the great port cities of Venice and Genoa, and the Brenner Pass, used by commercial travellers crossing the Alps from northern Europe. This helps to explain the Germanic influence in Verona's magnificent San Zeno church, or the realism of the paintings in the Castelvecchio museum, owing more to Dürer than to Raphael.

Verona's passion and panache, however, are purely Italian. Stylish shops and cafés sit amid the impressive remains of Roman monuments. The massive Arena amphitheatre fills with crowds of 20,000 or more, who thrill to opera beneath the stars. All over the city, art galleries and theatres testify to a crowded calendar of cultural activities.

Italy's largest lake, Lake Garda, is renowned for its beautiful scenery. The broad southern end of the lake, with its waterfront promenades, is very popular with Italian and German visitors. Those in search of peace can escape to the heights of the Monte Baldo mountain range, rising above the eastern shore. The ridge marks the western edge of the mountainous region north of Verona. Here is the great plateau of Monti Lessini, with its little river valleys that fan out southwards to join the river Adige.

Giardino Giusti in Verona, one of Italy's finest Renaissance gardens

◁ **The pretty cobbled streets of Sirmione**

Exploring Verona and Lake Garda

Verona makes an excellent touring base, with lofty mountains, castles and vineyards all within easy reach of the city. Lake Garda, whose western shore is actually over the border in Lombardy, is a popular destination for excursions from Verona. The many resort towns have excellent hotels, harbourside fish restaurants and lakeside gardens, and the lake is perfect for watersports such as windsurfing or dinghy racing. Less exhausting are the steamer excursions, offering mid-lake views of entrancing beauty.

Sights at a Glance

Bolca 6
Bosco Chiesanuova 8
Garda 10
Gardone Riviera 15
Giazza 7
Grezzana 2
Malcésine 17
Montecchio Maggiore 4
Peschiera 11
Riva del Garda 16
Salò 14
Sant'Anna d'Alfaedo 9
Sirmione Peninsula pp206–7 13
Soave 3
Solferino 12
Valdagno 5
Verona pp192–203 1

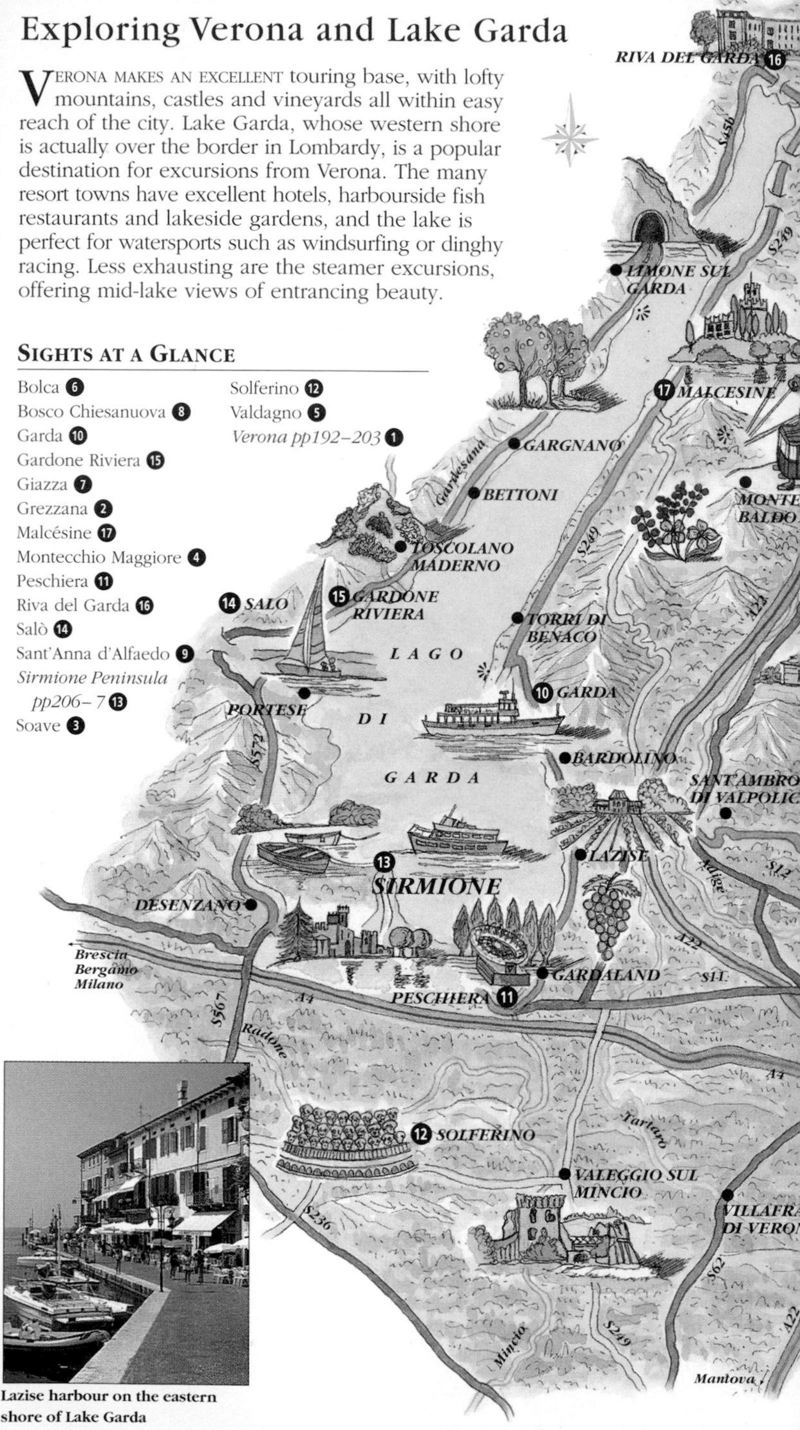

Lazise harbour on the eastern shore of Lake Garda

Getting Around

The roads around Verona are heavily used by commercial vehicles and commuter traffic, so expect delays, especially during morning and evening rush hours. Motorways are faster, even though those in this region are among the oldest in Italy. There are good rail services linking Verona with Lake Garda to the west and with Bolzano to the north. The Brenner pass also runs northwards from Verona. For information on ferries across Lake Garda, see p204.

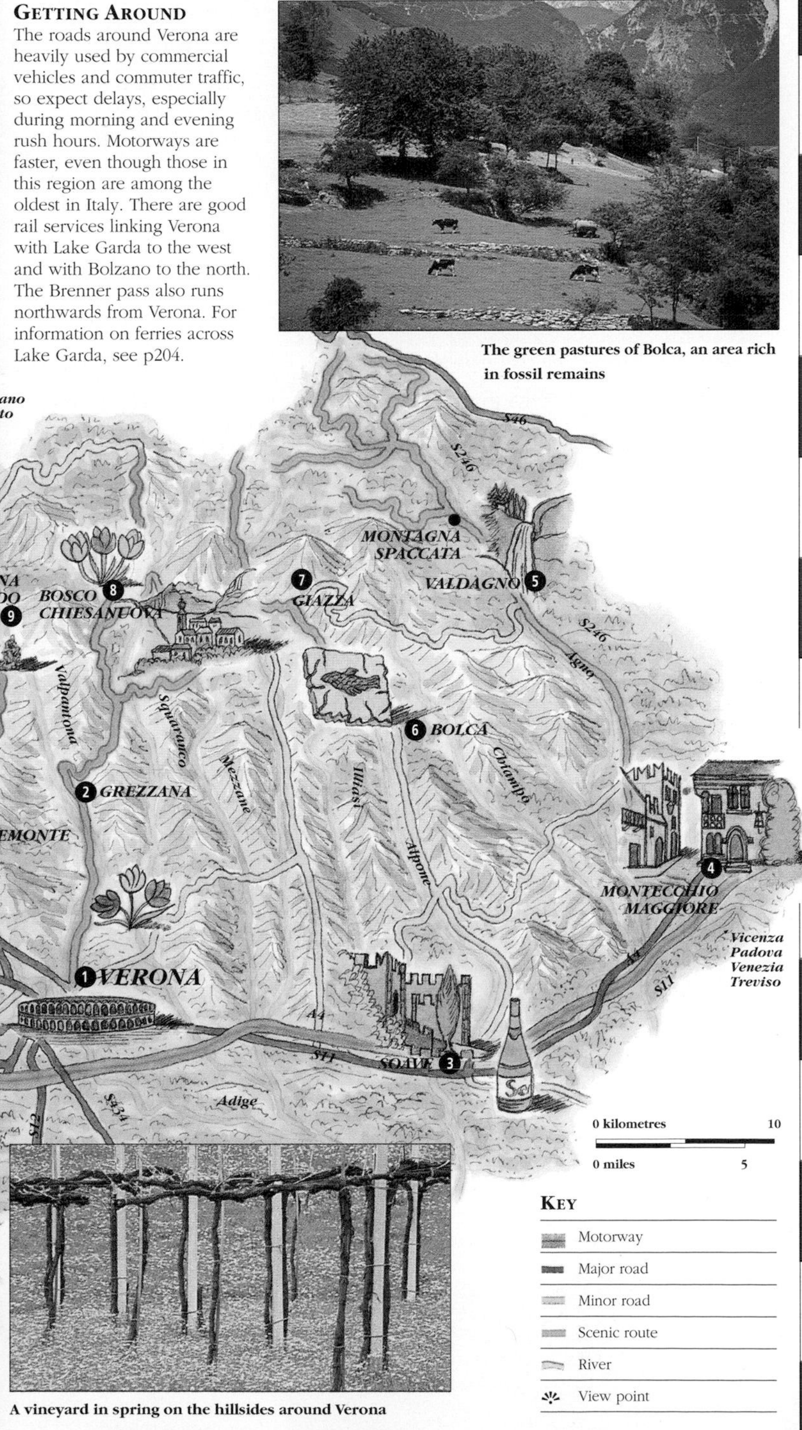

The green pastures of Bolca, an area rich in fossil remains

A vineyard in spring on the hillsides around Verona

0 kilometres 10

0 miles 5

Key

- Motorway
- Major road
- Minor road
- Scenic route
- River
- View point

The 14th-century Castello Romeo, on a hill overlooking Montecchio

Verona ❶

See pp192–203.

Grezzana ❷

Road map B4. *9,680.* *1st Wed and 3rd Fri each month.*

IN GREZZANA itself, seek out the 13th-century church of Santa Maria which, though frequently rebuilt, retains its robustly carved Romanesque font and its beautiful campanile of gold, white and pink limestone.

ENVIRONS: Grezzana is in the foothills of the scenic Piccole Dolomiti or Little Dolomites. Close to the town, at nearby Cuzzano, is the 17th-century Baroque **Villa Allegri-Arvedi**. To the south, in Santa Maria in Stelle, is a Roman nymphaeum (a shrine to the nymphs who guard the fresh-water spring) next to the church (known as the Pantheon).

Villa Allegri-Arvedi
Cuzzano di Grezzana.
045 90 70 45.
for groups only (book by phone).

Soave ❸

Road map B4. *6,200.*
Via 25 Aprile 6. (045 768 06 48).
Tue am.

SOAVE IS a heavily fortified town ringed by 14th-century walls. Its name is familiar all over Europe because of the light and dry white wine that is produced and exported from here in great quantity. Visitors will see few vineyards around the town, since they are mainly located in the hills to the north, but evidence of the industry can be seen in the gleaming factories on the outskirts, where the Garganega grapes are crushed and the fermented wine bottled. Cafés and wine cellars in the town centre provide plenty of opportunity for sampling the local wine.

The city walls rise up the hill to the dramatically sited **Rocca Scaligera**, an ancient castle enlarged in the 14th century by the Scaligeri rulers of Verona and furnished in period style.

Rocca Scaligera
Via Castello Scaligero.
045 768 00 36. *Tue–Sun.*

Rocca Scaligera, the ancient castle in Soave

Montecchio Maggiore ❹

Road map C4. *20,000.*
Via Leonardo da Vinci 50, Alta di Montecchio. (0444 69 65 46).
Fri am.

VISITORS TO industrialized Montecchio Maggiore come principally to see the two 14th-century castles on the hill above the town. Although these are known as the **Castello di Romeo** and the **Castello di Giulietta** (which includes a restaurant), there is no evidence that they belonged to Verona's rival Capulet and Montague families *(see p199)*, but they look romantic, and provide lovely views over the vineyard-clad hills to the north.

Castello di Romeo
Via Castelli 4. *Sat pm, Sun.*
Castello di Giulietta
Via Castelli 4. *0444 69 61 72.*
Thu–Mon.

The dramatic gorge of Montagna Spaccata, north of Valdagno

Valdagno ❺

Road map C3. *28,000.*
Viale Trento 4–6. (0445 40 11 90; 0445 40 60 20). *Tue am, Fri am.*

A SCENIC DRIVE of 20 km (12 miles) from Montecchio Maggiore leads to Valdagno, a town of woollen mills and 18th-century houses. Just northwest is the Montagna Spaccata, its rocky bulk split by a dramatic 100-m (330-ft) deep gorge and waterfall.

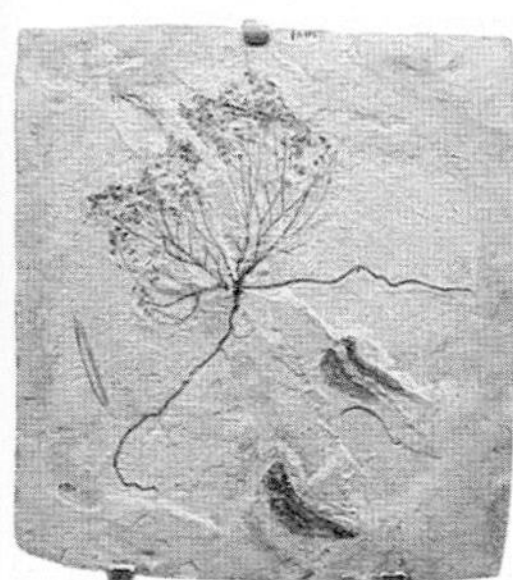

Fossilized plant remains found in the rocks near Bolca

Bolca ❻

Road map B3. 500.
Shops closed *Mon am (clothes), Wed pm (food).*

PRETTY BOLCA sits at the centre of the Monti Lessini plateau, looking down the valley of the river Alpone and surrounded by fossil-bearing hills. The most spectacular finds have been transferred to Verona's Museo Civico di Scienze Naturali *(see p203)*, but the local **Museo di Fossili** still has an impressive collection of fish, plants and reptiles preserved in the local basalt stone. A circular walk of 3 km (2 miles) from the town (details available from the museum) takes in the quarries where the fossils were found.

Museo di Fossili
Via San Giovanni Battista. *045 656 50 88.* *Tue–Sun.*

Giazza ❼

Road map B3. *150.*
Shops closed *Wed pm (food).*

THE SMALL TOWN of Giazza has an almost Alpine appearance. Its **Museo dei Cimbri** covers the history of the Tredici Comuni (the Thirteen Communes). In reality there are far more than 13 little hamlets dotted about the plateau, many of them settled by Bavarian farmers who migrated from the German side of the Alps in the 13th century. Cimbro, their German-influenced dialect, has now almost completely disappeared, but other traditions survive. For example, their huge mountain horns, *tromboni*, are still part of local festivities.

Museo dei Cimbri
Via dei Boschi, 62. *045 784 70 50.* *May–Sep: Tue–Sun; Oct–Apr: Sat & Sun.*

Bosco Chiesanuova ❽

Road map B3. *3,000.*
Piazza della Chiesa 34. (045 705 00 88). *Sat am.*

ONE OF THE principal ski resorts of the region, Bosco Chiesanuova is well supplied with hotels, ski lifts and cross-country routes. To the east, near Camposilvano, is the **Valle delle Sfingi** (valley of the sphinxes), so called because of its large and impressive rock formations.

Sant'Anna d'Alfaedo ❾

Road map B3. *2,500.* *in Bosco Chiesanuova.* *Wed am.*

DISTINCTIVELY Alpine in character, Sant'Anna d'Alfaedo is noted for the stone tiles used to roof local houses. The hamlet of Fosse, immediately to the north, is a popular base for walking excursions up the **Corno d'Aquilio** (1,546 m/5,070 ft), a mountain which boasts one of the world's deepest potholes, the **Spluga della Preta**, 850 m (2,790 ft) deep.

More accessible is another natural wonder, the **Ponte di Veia**, just south of Sant'Anna, a great stone arch bridging the valley. Prehistoric finds have been excavated from the caves at either end. This spectacular natural bridge is one of the largest of its kind in the world.

The town of Giazza, spectacularly situated on the Monti Lessini plateau

Verona ❶

Dragon carving on Duomo façade

VERONA IS A VIBRANT and self-confident city, the second biggest in the Veneto region (after Venice) and one of the most prosperous in northern Italy. Its ancient centre boasts many magnificent Roman remains, second only to those of Rome itself, and *palazzi* built of *rosso di Verona*, the local pink-tinged limestone, by the city's medieval rulers. Verona has two main focal points, the massive 1st-century AD Arena and the Piazza Erbe with its colourful market, separated by a maze of narrow lanes lined with some of Italy's most elegant boutiques.

Verona as seen from the Museo Archeologico

Verona's rulers

In 1263 the Scaligeri began their 127-year rule of Verona. They used ruthless tactics in their rise to power, earning nicknames like Mastino (Mastiff) and Cangrande (Big Dog), but once in power the Scaligeri family brought peace to a city racked by civil strife and inter-family rivalry. They proved to be relatively just and cultured rulers – the poet Dante was welcomed to their court in 1301–4 and dedicated his *Paradise*, the final part of the epic *Divine Comedy*, to Cangrande I.

Verona fell to the Visconti of Milan in 1387, and a succession of outsiders – Venice, France and Austria – followed before the Veneto was united with Italy in 1866.

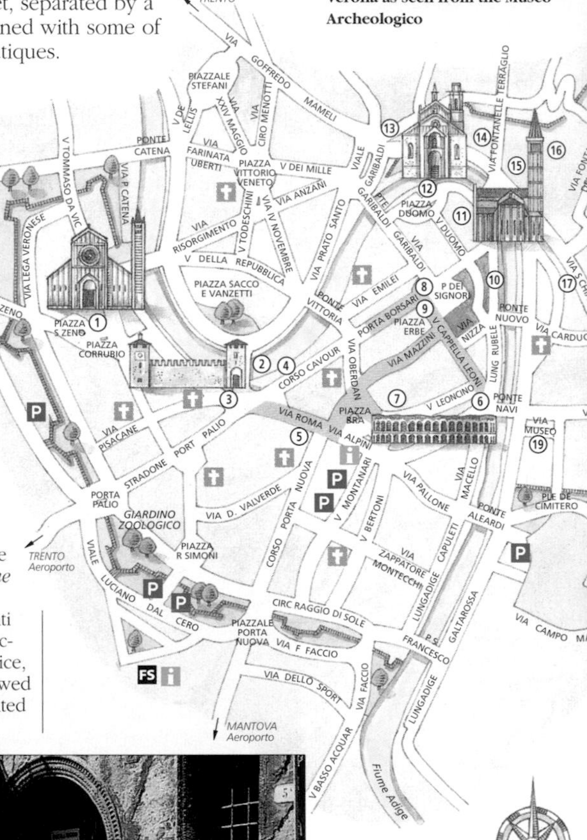

Fruit and vegetable stall in a side street of old Verona

KEY

- Street-by-Street map *See pp196–7*
- Pedestrian area
- FS Railway station
- P Parking
- Tourist information
- Church

Castelvecchio

Corso Castelvecchio 2. *045 59 47 34.* *8:30am–7:30pm daily (from 1:30pm Mon).* *1 Jan, 25–26 Dec.*

This spectacular castle, built by Cangrande II between 1355 and 1375, has been transformed into one of the Veneto's finest art galleries. Various parts of the medieval structure have been linked together using aerial walkways and corridors, designed by Carlo Scarpa to give striking views of the building itself, as well as the exhibits within, which are excellent and varied.

The first section contains a wealth of late Roman and early Christian material, including a 7th-century silver plate that shows armoured knights in combat, 5th-century brooches and glass painted with a portrait of Christ the Shepherd in gold. The martyrdom scenes depicted on the carved marble sarcophagus of Saints Sergius and Bacchus (1179) are gruesomely realistic.

The following section, which is devoted to medieval and early Renaissance art, vividly demonstrates the influence of northern art on local painters, suggesting strong links with Verona's neighbours across the Alps. Here, instead of the serene saints and virgins of Tuscan art, the emphasis is on brutal realism. This is summed up in the 14th-century *Crucifixion with Saints*, which depicts the tortured musculature of Christ and the racked faces of the mourners in painful detail. Far more lyrical is a beautiful 15th-century painting by Stefano da Verona called *The Madonna of the Rose Garden*. This contains many allusions to popular medieval fables, including the figure of Fortune with her wheel. In the painting the Virgin sits in a pretty garden alive with decorative birds and angels gathering rosebuds.

Other Madonnas from the 15th century, attributed to Giovanni Bellini, are displayed among the late Renaissance works upstairs. Jewellery, suits of armour, swords and shield bosses feature next, some dating back to the 6th and 7th centuries when Verona was under attack from Teutonic invaders from beyond the Alpine range.

After the armour room, take the walkway that leads out along the river flank of the castle, with its dizzying views of the swirling waters of the river Adige and the Ponte Scaligero *(see p194)*. Next, turning a corner, one finds Cangrande I, his equestrian statue dramatically displayed out of doors on a plinth. This 14th-century statue once graced Cangrande's tomb *(see p198)*, and is remounted here. It is possible to study every detail of the horse and rider draped in their ceremonial garb. Despite Cangrande's cherubic cheeks and inane grin, his face is compelling.

Beyond lie some of the museum's celebrated paintings, notably Paolo Veronese's *Deposition* (1565) and a portrait attributed by some to Titian, by others to Lorenzo Lotto.

Cangrande I's horse in ceremonial garb

Sights at a Glance

Arco dei Gavi ④
Arena ⑦
Castelvecchio ③
Duomo ⑫
Giardino Giusti ⑱
Museo Archeologico ⑯
Museo Civico di Scienze Naturali ⑲
Museo Lapidario Maffeiano ⑤
Piazza Erbe ⑨
Piazza dei Signori ⑧
Ponte Scaligero ②
Sant'Anastasia ⑪
San Fermo Maggiore ⑥
San Giorgio in Braida ⑬
Santa Maria Antica ⑩
Santa Maria in Organo ⑰
Santo Stefano ⑭
San Zeno Maggiore ①
Teatro Romano ⑮

Visitors' Checklist

Road map B4. *254,700.* *Villafranca 14 km (9 miles).* FS *Porta Nuova. (045 800 08 61).* *Piazza Cittadella.* *Via Degli Alpini 9. (045 806 86 80).* *daily.* ***Shops closed*** *Wed pm (food), Mon am (department & clothing stores).* *Vinitaly – Italy's largest wine fair (Apr); Festival della Lirica (opera festival) (end Jun–Aug); Estate Teatrale Veronese, including Shakespeare Festival (end Jun–Aug).*

Courtyard of Castelvecchio

Around the Arena

MOST VISITORS TO Verona first arrive at Piazza Brà, a large, irregularly shaped square with a public garden. On the north side is an archway known as the Portoni della Brà. Dominating the eastern side of the piazza is the Roman Arena, Verona's most important monument, still in use today for operatic performances. The piazza is ringed with 19th-century buildings that resemble ancient temples and historical landmarks.

Ponte Scaligero, part of the old defence system of Castelvecchio

Ponte Scaligero

This medieval bridge was built by Cangrande II between 1354 and 1376. The people of Verona love to stroll across it to ponder the river Adige in all its moods, or to admire summer sunsets and distant views of the Alps. Such is their affection for the bridge that it was rebuilt after the retreating Germans blew it up in 1945, an operation that involved dredging the river to salvage the medieval masonry. The bridge leads from Castelvecchio *(see p193)* to the Arsenal on the north bank of the Adige, built by the Austrians between 1840 and 1861 and now fronted by public gardens. Looking back from the gardens it is possible to see how the river was used as a natural moat to defend the castle, with the bridge providing the inhabitants with an escape route.

Arco dei Gavi and Corso Cavour

Dwarfed by the massive brick walls of Castelvecchio, the monumental scale of this Roman triumphal arch is now hard to appreciate. Originally the arch straddled the main Roman road into the city, today's Corso Cavour. But French troops who were occupying Castelvecchio in 1805 damaged the monument so much that a decision was made to move it to its present, less conspicuous position just off the Corso in 1933.

Continuing up Corso Cavour, there are some fine medieval and Renaissance palaces to see (especially Nos. 10, 11 and 19) before the Roman town gate, the **Porta dei Borsari**, is reached. The gate dates from the 1st century BC, but looking at the pedimented windows and niches it is easy to see what influenced the city's Renaissance architects.

The Roman Arco dei Gavi, 1st century AD

Museo Lapidario Maffeiano

Piazza Brà 8. *045 59 00 87.* *phone to check. Usually: 8:30am–7:30pm daily (from 1:30pm Mon).* *1 Jan, 25–26 Dec.*

This "museum of stone" displays all kinds of architectural fragments hinting at the last splendour of the Roman city. There are numerous carved funerary monuments, and a large part of the collection consists of Greek inscriptions collected by the museum's 18th-century founder, Scipione Maffei.

San Fermo Maggiore

San Fermo Maggiore consists of not one but two churches. This can best be appreciated from the outside, where the eastern end is a jumble of rounded Romanesque arches below with pointed Gothic arches rising above. The lower church, now rather dank because of frequent flooding, dates from 1065, but the upper church of 1313 is more impressive. It has a splendid ship's keel roof, masses of medieval fresco work and some monumental tombs. Frescoes from the 14th century, just inside the main door, are by Stefano de Zevico. They show the fate meted out to four Franciscan missionaries who journeyed to India in the mid-14th century. Nearby is the Brenzoni mausoleum (1439) by Giovanni di Bartolo with Pisanello's *Annunciation* fresco (1426) above. In the south aisle is an unusually ornate pulpit of 1396 with saints in canopied niches above, surrounded by frescoes of the Evangelists and Doctors of the Church.

The apse of the lower church of San Fermo Maggiore

The Arena

VERONA'S AMPHITHEATRE, completed around AD 30, is the third largest in the world, after Rome's Colosseum and the amphitheatre at Capua, near Naples. Originally, the Arena could hold almost the entire population of Roman Verona, and visitors came from across the Veneto to watch mock battles and gladiatorial combats. Since then, the Arena has been used for public executions, fairs, theatre performances, bullfighting and opera.

VISITORS' CHECKLIST

Piazza Brà, Verona. *045 800 32 04.* *8:30am–7:30pm daily (from 1:30pm Mon). Closes mid-afternoon on performance days Jun–Aug.* *1 Jan, 25 & 26 Dec.* *partial. Operas and classical concerts* (see pp256–7).

Interior
The interior has survived virtually intact, maintained by the Arena Conservators since 1580.

The façade of the Arena seen from Piazza Brà

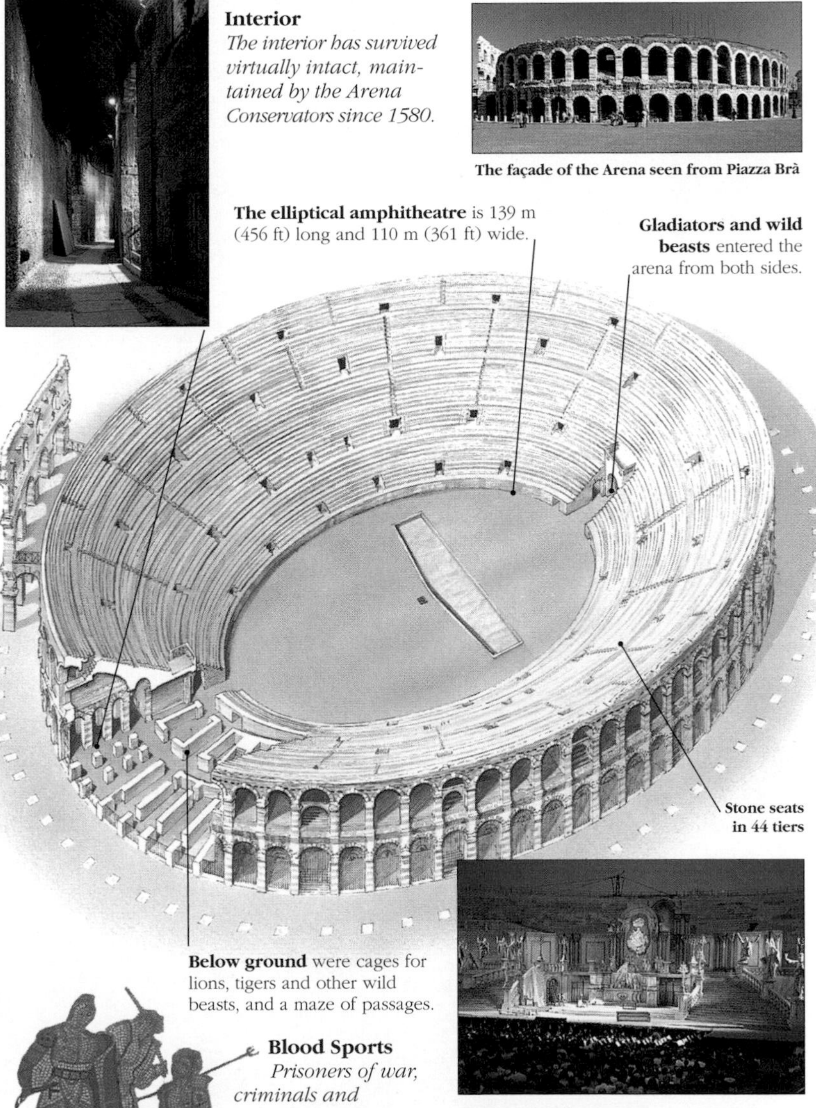

The elliptical amphitheatre is 139 m (456 ft) long and 110 m (361 ft) wide.

Gladiators and wild beasts entered the arena from both sides.

Stone seats in 44 tiers

Below ground were cages for lions, tigers and other wild beasts, and a maze of passages.

Blood Sports
Prisoners of war, criminals and Christians died in their thousands in the name of entertainment.

Opera in the Arena
Today, performances of Verdi's Aida *and other popular operas can attract a capacity crowd of 25,000.*

Street-by-Street: Verona

SINCE THE DAYS OF THE ROMAN EMPIRE, the Piazza Erbe has been the centre of Verona's commercial and administrative life. Built on the site of the ancient Roman forum, it is an enjoyably chaotic square, bustling with life. Shoppers browse in the colourful market at stalls sheltered from the sun by wide-brimmed umbrellas. The massive towers and *palazzi* of the Scaligeri rulers of Verona have retained their medieval feel, even though they have been altered and adapted many times.

★ Piazza dei Signori
This square is bordered by individual Scaligeri palazzi *linked by Renaissance arcades and carved stone archways.*

The 17th-century Palazzo Maffei is surmounted by a balustrade supporting statues of gods and goddesses.

Statue of Dante
Dante, the medieval poet, stayed in Verona as a guest of the Scaligeri during his period in exile from his native Florence. His statue (1865) looks down on Piazza dei Signori.

Colonna di San Marco (1528) is surmounted by St Mark's Lion, the symbol of Venetian rule.

Piazza Erbe
Verona's medieval herb market is now lined with art galleries, upmarket boutiques and inviting pavement cafés.

The fountain of 1368 is topped by a figure known as the Madonna of Verona; in fact, the statue is Roman and probably symbolizes Commerce.

Torre dei Lamberti, 84 m (275 ft) high

Palazzo della Ragione
The medieval Palace of Reason features an elegant Renaissance staircase. It leads from the exterior courtyard into the magistrates' rooms on the upper floor.

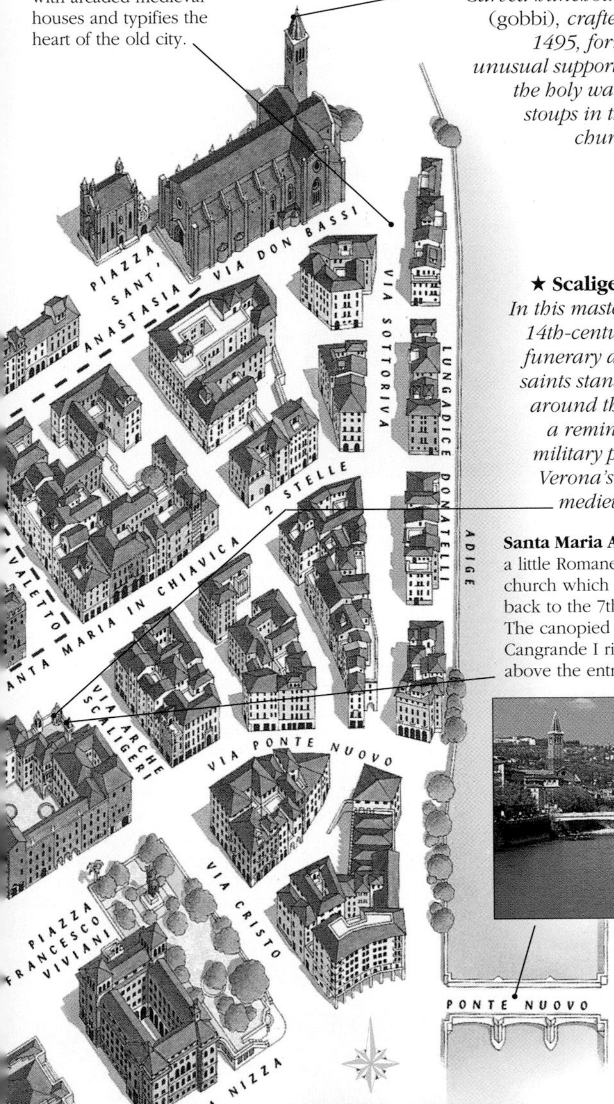

Via Sottoriva is lined with arcaded medieval houses and typifies the heart of the old city.

Sant'Anastasia
Carved hunchbacks (gobbi), crafted in 1495, form the unusual supports for the holy water stoups in this church.

★ Scaligeri Tombs
In this masterpiece of 14th-century Gothic funerary art, soldier saints stand guard around the tombs, a reminder of the military prowess of Verona's powerful medieval rulers.

Santa Maria Antica is a little Romanesque church which dates back to the 7th century. The canopied tomb of Cangrande I rises above the entrance.

Ponte Nuovo
The "new bridge" (1540) spans the river Adige, linking the hills on the east bank of the city with Verona's historic centre.

0 metres 100

0 yards 100

Key

Suggested route

Casa di Giulietta
The House of Juliet looks the part, with its marble balcony and romantic setting, although there is no evidence linking this house with the romantic legend.

Star Sights

- ★ **Piazza dei Signori**
- ★ **Scaligeri Tombs**

Central Verona

THE STREETS OF THIS ANCIENT city centre owe their grid-like layout to the order and precision of the Romans. At the heart is the lively Piazza Erbe, where crowds shop in the ancient market place. The fine *palazzi*, churches and monuments date mostly from the medieval period.

An elegant café in the spacious Piazza dei Signori

Piazza Erbe

Piazza Erbe is named after the city's old herb market. Today's stalls, shaded by huge umbrellas, sell everything from lunchtime snacks of herb-flavoured roast suckling pig in bread rolls to fresh-picked fruit or delicious wild mushrooms.

The **Venetian lion** that stands on top of a column to the north of the square marks Verona's absorption in 1405 into the Venetian empire. The statue-topped building that completes the north end of Piazza Erbe is the baroque **Palazzo Maffei** (1668), now converted to shops and luxury apartments. An assortment of boutiques and cafés lines the edge of the square.

The **fountain** that splashes away quietly in the middle of the piazza is often overlooked amid the competing attractions of the market's colourful stalls. Yet the statue at the fountain's centre dates from Roman times, a reminder that this long piazza has been in almost continuous use as a market place for 2,000 years.

Piazza dei Signori

Torre dei Lamberti *045 803 27 26. Mon pm, Tue–Sun. public hols.*

In the centre of Piazza dei Signori is a 19th-century **statue of Dante**, who surveys the surrounding buildings with an appraising eye. His gaze is fixed on the grim **Palazzo del Capitano**, home of Verona's military commander, and the equally intimidating **Palazzo della Ragione**, the palace of Reason, or law court, both built in the 14th century. The Palazzo della Ragione is not quite so grim within. The courtyard has a handsome external stone staircase, added in 1446–50. Fine views of the Alps can be had by climbing the 84-m (275-ft) **Torre dei Lamberti**, which rises from the western side of the courtyard.

Stonework detail, Piazza dei Signori

Behind the statue of Dante is the pretty Renaissance **Loggia del Consiglio**, or council chamber, with its frescoed upper façade (1493) and statues of Roman worthies born in Verona. These include Catullus the poet, Pliny the natural historian and Vitruvius the architectural theorist.

The piazza is linked to Piazza Erbe by the Arco della Costa, or the arch of the rib, whose name refers to the whale rib hung beneath it, put up here as a curiosity in the distant past.

Santa Maria Antica

This tiny Romanesque church is almost swamped by the bizarre Scaligeri tombs built up against its entrance wall. Because Santa Maria Antica was their parish church, the Scaligeri rulers of Verona chose to be buried here, and their tombs speak of their military prowess *(see p207)*.

Over the entrance to the church is the impressive tomb of Cangrande I, or Big Dog (died 1329), topped by his equestrian statue. This statue is a copy; the original is now in the Castelvecchio *(see p193)*. The other Scaligeri tombs are next to the church, surrounded by an intricate wrought-iron fence featuring the ladder motif of the family's original name (*della Scala*, meaning "of the steps"). Towering above the fence are the spire-topped tombs of Mastino II, or Mastiff (died 1351) and

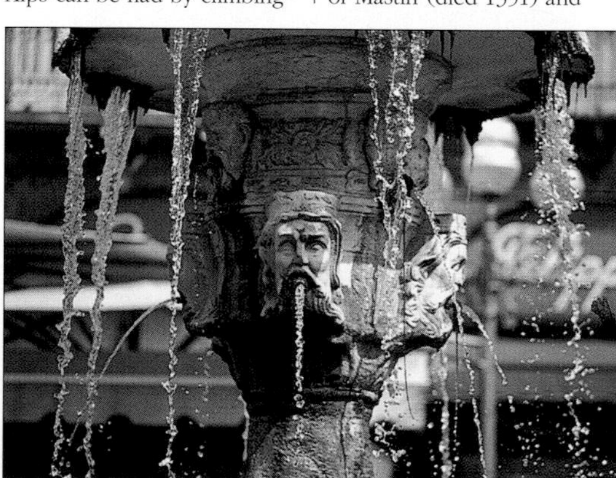

The fountain in Piazza Erbe, erected in the 14th century

Cansignorio, meaning Noble Dog (died 1375). These two tombs are splendidly decorated with Gothic pinnacles. In their craftsmanship and design there is nothing else in European funerary architecture quite like these spiky, thrusting monuments.

Plainer tombs nearer the church wall mark the resting place of other members of the Scaligeri family – Mastino (died 1277) who founded the Scaligeri dynasty, having been elected mayor of Verona in 1260, and two who did not have dog-based names: Bartolomeo (died 1304) and Giovanni (died 1359).

Sant'Anastasia

045 592 813. Sun pm, Mon–Sat. Nov–Feb: Mon.

A huge church, Sant'Anastasia was begun in 1290 and built to hold the massive congregations who came to listen to the rousing sermons preached by members of the fundamentalist Dominican order. The most interesting aspect of the church is its Gothic portal, with its faded 15th-century frescoes and carved scenes from the life of St Peter Martyr. Inside, the two holy water stoups are supported on realistic figures of beggars, known as *i gobbi*, the hunchbacks (the one on the left carved in 1495, the other a century later).

Off the north aisle is the sacristy, home to Antonio Pisanello's fresco, *St George and the Princess* (1433–38). Despite being badly damaged, the fresco still conveys something of the aristocratic grace of the Princess of Trebizond, with her noble brow and her ermine-fringed cloak, as St George prepares to mount his horse in pursuit of the dragon.

The lofty, Romanesque interior of Sant'Anastasia

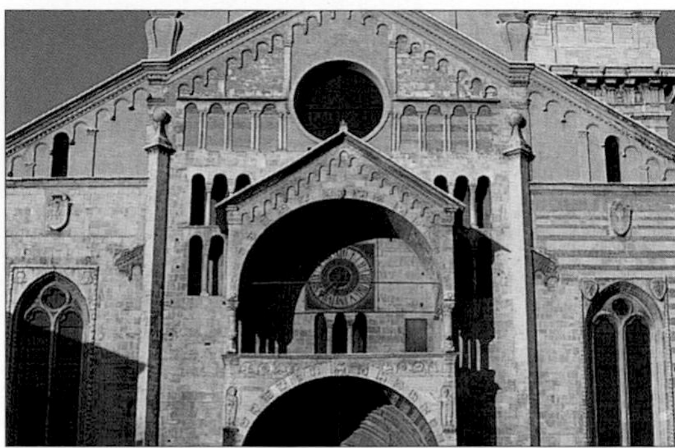

The façade of the Duomo, Santa Maria Matricolare

Duomo

045 592 813. Sun pm, Mon–Sat. Nov–Feb: Mon.

Visitors to Verona's cathedral pass through a magnificent Romanesque portal carved by Nicolò, one of the master masons who carved the façade of San Zeno *(see pp200–201)*. Here he sculpted the sword-bearing figures of Oliver and Roland, knights whose exploits in the service of Charlemagne were celebrated in medieval poetry. Nearby, stand saints and evangelists with bold staring eyes and flowing beards. To the south there is a second Romanesque portal carved with Jonah and the Whale (removed for restoration) and comically grotesque caryatids (load-bearing figures).

The highlight is Titian's *Assumption* (1535–40) in the first chapel on the left. Further down is the entrance to the Romanesque cloister containing excavated remains of earlier churches on the site. It leads to the baptistry, known as San Giovanni in Fonte (St John of the Spring). This 8th-century church, built from Roman masonry, features a huge marble font carved in 1200 with scenes from the life of Christ.

Romeo and Juliet

The tragic story of Romeo and Juliet, written by Luigi da Porto of Vicenza in the 1520s, inspired countless poems, films, ballets and dramas. At the **Casa di Giulietta** (Juliet's house), No. 27 Via Cappello (tel: 045 803 43 03), Romeo is said to have climbed to Juliet's balcony. In reality this is a restored 13th-century inn. The run-down **Casa di Romeo** is in Via delle Arche Scaligere, while the so-called **Tomba di Giulietta** (tel: 045 800 03 61) is in a crypt below the cloister of San Francesco al Corso on Via del Pontiere. The stone sarcophagus is empty and rather plain, but the setting is atmospheric. Juliet's house and tomb are open 8:30am–7:30pm daily (from 1:30pm Mon).

The lovers *Romeo and Juliet* from a 19th-century illustration

Verona: San Zeno Maggiore

Stone façade detail

BUILT BETWEEN 1120 and 1138 to house the shrine of Verona's patron saint, San Zeno is northern Italy's most ornate Romanesque church. The façade is embellished with marble reliefs of biblical scenes, matched in vitality by bronze door panels showing the miracles of San Zeno. Beneath an impressive rose window, a graceful porch canopy rests on two slim columns. A brick campanile soars to the south, while a squat tower to the north is said to cover the tomb of King Pepin of Italy (777–810).

Nave Ceiling

The nave has a magnificent example of a ship's keel ceiling, so called because it resembles the inside of an upturned boat. This ceiling was constructed in 1386 when the apse was rebuilt.

Striped brickwork is typical of Romanesque buildings in Verona. Courses of local pink brick are alternated with ivory-coloured tufa.

Altarpiece

Andrea Mantegna's three-part altarpiece (1457–59) depicts the Virgin and Child with various saints. The painting served as an inspiration to local artists.

★ Cloister

North of the church the fine, airy cloister (1293–1313) has rounded Romanesque arches on one side and pointed Gothic arches on the other.

STAR FEATURES

- ★ West Doors
- ★ Cloister
- ★ Crypt

Bronze Door Panels

The 48 bronze panels of the west doors are primitive but forceful in their depiction of biblical stories and scenes from the life of San Zeno. Those on the left date from 1030 and survive from an earlier church on the site; those on the right were made 100 years later. Huge staring eyes and Ottoman-style hats, armour and architecture feature prominently, and the meaning of some scenes is not known – the woman suckling two crocodiles, for example.

Descent into limbo **Christ in Glory** **Human head**

Visitors' Checklist

Piazza San Zeno. 045 59 28 13. *31, 32, 33 from Castelvecchio.* *Mar–Oct: 8:30am–6pm daily (from 1pm Sun); Nov–Feb: 10am–4pm Tue–Sat, 1–5pm Sun.* *times vary.* *during mass.*

Nave and Main Altar
The nave of the church is modelled on an ancient Roman basilica, the Hall of Justice. The main altar is situated in the raised sanctuary where the judge's throne would have stood.

The campanile, started in 1045, reached its present height of 72 m (236 ft) in 1173.

Rood Screen
Marble statues of Christ and the Apostles, dating from 1250, are ranged along the sanctuary rood screen.

The rose window symbolizes the Wheel of Fortune: figures around the rim show the rise and fall of human fortunes.

★ Crypt
The vaulted crypt contains the tomb of San Zeno, appointed eighth bishop of Verona in AD 362, who died in AD 380.

Marble side panels, carved in 1140, depict events from the life of Christ to the left of the doors, and scenes from the Book of Genesis to the right.

★ West Doors
Each of the wooden doors has 24 bronze plates joined by bronze masks, nailed on to the wood to look like solid metal. A bas relief above the doors depicts San Zeno vanquishing the devil.

Across the Ponte Romano

THE PONTE ROMANO, or Roman Bridge, links Verona's city centre to the eastern bank of the river Adige. This up-market residential district is dotted with fine palaces, gardens and churches, and offers good views back on to the towers and domes of the medieval city.

View from the Teatro Romano across the river Adige

Teatro Romano

Rigaste Redentore 2. *045 800 03 60.* *8:30am–7:30pm daily (from 1:30pm Mon).*

When this theatre was built, in the 1st century BC, the plays performed would have included satirical dramas by such writers as Terence and Plautus. The tradition continues with open-air performances at the annual Shakespeare festival.

The theatre is built into a bank above the river Adige. The views over the city must have been every bit as entrancing to Roman theatre-goers as the events on stage. Certainly it is for the views that the theatre is best visited today, since little survives of the original stage area, though the semi-circular seating area remains largely intact.

In the foreground of the view is one of three Roman bridges that brought traffic into the city. This is the only one to have survived, although it had to be painstakingly reconstructed after World War II. In common with all the city's bridges it was blown up in 1945 by retreating German soldiers who were attempting to delay the advance of Allied troops. Of the five arches, the two nearest to the theatre are least altered.

Museo Archeologico

Rigaste Redentore 2. *045 800 03 60.* *8:30am–7:30pm daily (from 1:30pm Mon).*

A lift carries visitors from the Teatro Romano up through the cliffs to the monastery above. This is now converted into an archaeological museum in which panoramic views over the city vie for attention with the range of exhibits. The first part of the museum displays well-restored mosaics, one of which depicts the kind of gory gladiatorial combat that once went on in Verona's amphitheatre *(see p195)*. Such barbaric performances, seen as a legitimate way of disposing of criminals and prisoners of war, finally came to an end in the early 5th century following a decree from the Christian Emperor Honorius.

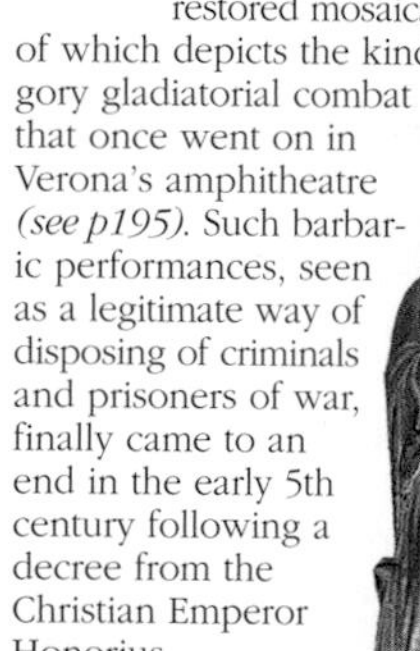

Augustus Caesar, Museo Archeologico

In the little monastic cells to the side of this room, visitors can see a bronze bust of the first Roman emperor, the young Augustus

Caesar (63 BC–AD 14), who succeeded in outmanoeuvring his opponents, including Mark Antony and Cleopatra, to become the sole ruler of the Roman world in 31 BC. The subject of the female bust in the adjoining cell is unknown. Next comes the tiny cloister, littered with mosaics and ancient masonry fragments, and an extensive warren of ancient rooms used to display pottery, glass, inscriptions and tombstones. Labelling stops after a while, leaving visitors to puzzle out the nature and age of exhibits for themselves.

Santo Stefano

This is one of the city's oldest churches; the original, long-demolished building was constructed in the 6th century. It served as Verona's cathedral until the 12th century when the new Duomo was built *(see p199)* on the opposite bank of the Adige. Visitors to Santo Stefano are afforded a striking view of the Duomo across the river, taking in the Romanesque apse and the bishop's palace alongside. Santo Stefano itself was rebuilt at the same time by Lombard architects and given its octagonal red brick campanile, but the original apse survives.

Inside the church there is a Byzantine-influenced arrangement of a stone bishop's seat and bench, and a gallery with 8th-century carved capitals. The apse (which is often locked) is even older, dating back to the original 6th-century building. In the crypt there are fragments of 13th-century frescoes and a 14th-century statue of St Peter.

Towering above the church to the east is Castel San Pietro, strikingly fronted by flame-shaped cypress trees. The present castle was built in 1854 under Austrian rule, but it stands on the ruins of an earlier castle which was built by the Visconti of Milan when the Milanese captured Verona in 1387.

Figure of St Peter, Santo Stefano

San Giorgio in Braida

San Giorgio is a rare example in Verona of a domed Renaissance church. It was begun in 1477 by Michele Sanmicheli, an architect best known for his military works. Sanmicheli also designed the classically inspired altar, which is topped by Paolo Veronese's *Martyrdom of St George* (1566). This celebrated painting is outshone by the calm and serene *Virgin Enthroned between St Zeno and St Lawrence* (1526) by Girolamo dai Libri. This work has a beautifully detailed background landscape and a lemon tree growing behind the Virgin's throne.

Marquetry cockerel in Santa Maria in Organo

Santa Maria in Organo

Some of the finest inlaid woodwork to be seen in Italy is in this church. The artist was Fra Giovanni da Verona, an architect and craftsman who worked for nearly 25 years, from 1477 to 1501, on these stunning examples of illusionistic marquetry. The seat backs in the choir and cupboard fronts in the sacristy are full of entertaining detail. By clever interpretation of perspective, Fra Giovanni gave depth to flat landscapes, depicted city views glimpsed through an open window, and created "cupboard interiors" stacked with books, musical instruments or bowls of fruit. Most charming of all are the little animal pictures – look out for the rabbit on the lectern and the owl and the cockerel in the sacristy.

Fossilized fish from Verona's natural history museum

Museo Civico di Scienze Naturali

Lungadige Porta Vittoria 9. 045 807 94 00. 9am–7pm Mon–Thu & Sat, 2–7pm Sun and public hols. 1 Jan, Easter, 1 May, 25 Dec.

Verona's natural history museum contains an outstanding collection of fossils, which can be enjoyed by experts and newcomers alike. Whole fish, trees, fern leaves and dragonflies are captured in extraordinary detail. The fossils were found in rock in the foothills of the Little Dolomites north of the city during quarrying for building stone (*see* Bolca, *p191*).

Human prehistory is represented by finds from ancient settlements round Lake Garda, and there are reconstructions of original lake villages. On the upper floor, cases full of stuffed birds, animals and fish provide an extensive account of today's living world, making this a good museum for visiting with children or on rainy days.

Giardino Giusti

Via Giardino Giusti 2. 045 803 40 29. daily. 25 Dec.

Hidden among the dusty façades of the Via Giardino Giusti is the entrance to one of Italy's finest Renaissance gardens. They were laid out in 1580 and, as with other gardens of the period, artifice and nature are deliberately juxtaposed. The formal lower garden of clipped box hedges, gravel walks and potted plants is contrasted with an upper area of wilder natural woodland, the two parts linked by stone terracing.

Past visitors have included the English traveller Thomas Coryate who, writing in 1611, called this garden "a second paradise". The diarist John Evelyn, visiting 50 years later, thought it the finest garden in Europe. Today the garden makes an excellent, picturesque spot for a quiet picnic.

Italianate topiary and statuary in the Giardino Giusti

Around Lake Garda

GARDA, THE LARGEST AND EASTERNMOST of the Italian Lakes, is a favourite summer playground for sports lovers. Strong winds make ideal conditions for windsurfing and sailing, there are numerous yacht harbours and artificial beaches, and luxury hotels offer tennis and horse-riding facilities. The less energetic can explore the lake and shore by steamer, while the magnificent scenery of snow-capped peaks and spectacular sunsets will appeal to every visitor.

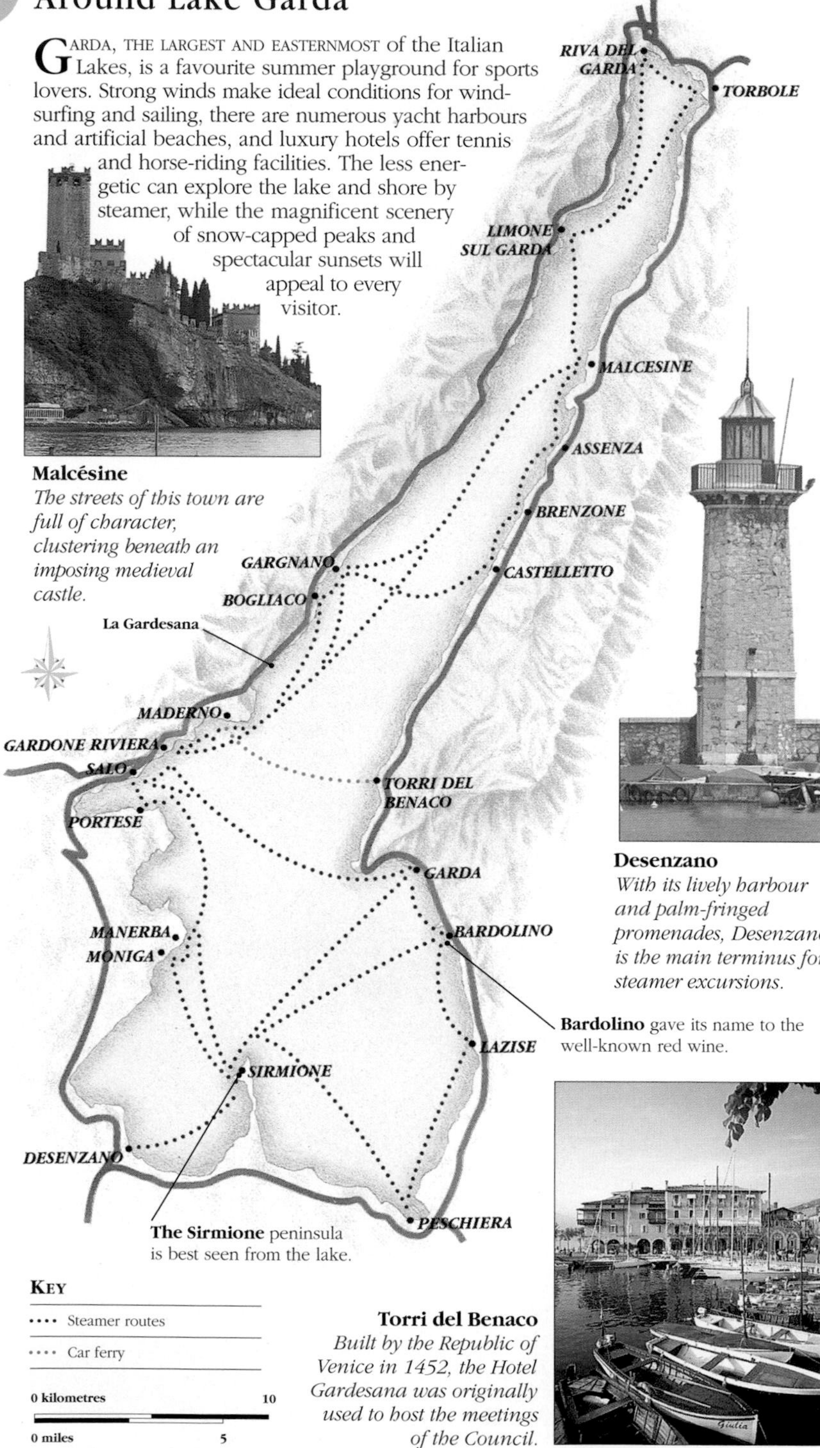

Malcésine
The streets of this town are full of character, clustering beneath an imposing medieval castle.

Desenzano
With its lively harbour and palm-fringed promenades, Desenzano is the main terminus for steamer excursions.

Bardolino gave its name to the well-known red wine.

The Sirmione peninsula is best seen from the lake.

Torri del Benaco
Built by the Republic of Venice in 1452, the Hotel Gardesana was originally used to host the meetings of the Council.

LA GARDESANA

This is the name given to the 143-km (89-mile) perimeter road that hugs the lake shore. For much of its route the road is cut through solid rock, sometimes following a narrow ledge in the cliff face, sometimes passing through tunnels (around 80 in total). The switchback route offers spectacular views at every turn, particularly at Gargnano, and there are numerous viewing points. Places of interest along La Gardesana include the splendid 18th-century gardens of Palazzo Bettoni at Bogliaco and the castle at Riva del Garda.

The scenic road to Limone

LAKE TRIPS

Lake Garda's ferries are still called steamers, even though they are diesel-powered today. The major towns around the southern rim of the lake all have jetties where you can buy a ticket and board the boat for a leisurely cruise. From the water you can see gardens and villas that are otherwise hidden from view. A trip from one end of the lake to the other takes approximately two hours 20 minutes by hydrofoil, and four hours by steamer. Catamarans also operate around the southern end of the lake.

The hydrofoil operating out of Desenzano harbour

Lake Garda steamer at dusk near Peschiera

Garda ⑩

Road map A3. *3,400.* *Lungolago Regina Adelaide 13. (045 627 03 84).* *Fri am.* ***Shops closed*** *Wed pm (food).*

NUMEROUS PAVEMENT cafés brighten the streets around the central Palazzo dei Capitani, which was built in the 15th century for the use of the Venetian militia. In a different vein, a series of prehistoric rock engravings features along the Strada dei Castei, an old route above the town.

Peschiera ⑪

Road map A4. *8,900.* FS *Piazzale Bettelone 15. (045 755 16 73).* *Mon am.* ***Shops closed*** *Wed in winter.*

AT PESCHIERA the River Mincio flows out of Lake Garda to join the River Po. The fortress at the entrance was built by Austrians in the 19th century. Named Fortezza del Quadrilatero because of its square shape, it replaced a 15th-century stronghold.

ENVIRONS: Just outside the town are **Gardaland**, a theme park with a replica of the ancient Egyptian Valley of the Kings (free bus from Peschiera station), and **Parco Natura Viva**, a zoo with a safari park and models of dinosaurs.

Gardaland
Loc. Ronchi, 37014 Castelnuovo del Garda. *045 644 97 77.* *end Mar–Sep: daily; Oct: Sat & Sun.*

Parco Natura Viva
Nr. Bussolengo. *045 717 01 13.* *mid-Mar–Oct: 9:30am–5pm daily; Nov & Feb public hols.*

Solferino ⑫

Road map A4. *2,118.* *Piazza Torelli 1. (0376 85 43 60).* *Sat pm.* ***Shops closed*** *Mon pm.*

THE BATTLE of Solferino (1859) left 40,000 Italian and Austrian troops dead and injured, abandoned without medical care or burial. Shocked by such neglect, a Swiss man named Henri Dunant began a campaign for better treatment. The result was the first Geneva Convention, signed in 1863, and the establishment of the International Red Cross. In the town of Solferino there is a war museum and an ossuary chapel, lined with bones from the battlefield. There is also a memorial to Dunant built by the Red Cross with donations from member nations.

The ossuary chapel at Solferino, lined with skulls

Sirmione Peninsula ⓭

CHARMING SIRMIONE is a finger of land extending into the southern end of Lake Garda, connected to the mainland by a bridge. The Roman poet Catullus (born in 84 BC) owned a villa here: the ruins of the Grotte di Catullo lie among ancient olive trees at the northern tip. The Rocca Scaligera castle stands guard at the base of the peninsula, and beyond, the narrow streets of the village give way to peaceful lakeside walks and elegant spa hotels.

View Towards the Grotto
The high central tower commands views over the castle and the whole of the Sirmione peninsula.

★ Rocca Scaligera
The castle was built in the 13th century by the Scaligeri of Verona. It is cleverly designed to trap shipborne invaders, leaving them vulnerable to missiles dropped from the castle walls.

The main keep tower was used for bombarding attackers trapped below.

The moat, originally a complex defence system, is today home to carp.

Piazza Castello

Sirmione Old Town
Narrow stone-paved streets are packed with shops selling crafts and souvenirs.

Visiting the Peninsula
Cars must be parked before entering Sirmione, leaving the medieval streets for pedestrians.

STAR FEATURES

- ★ Rocca Scaligera
- ★ Grotte di Catullo

Lakeside Walk
Following the eastern shores of the peninsula, this pretty walk links the village to the Grotte di Catullo.

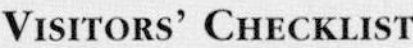

Visitors' Checklist

Road map A4. *Viale Marconi 2. (030 91 61 14).* **Rocca Scaligera** *030 91 64 68.* *8:30am–7:30pm Tue–Sun (to 5pm Nov–Mar).* *1 Jan, 1 May, 25 Dec.* **Grotte di Catullo** *030 91 61 57.* *8:30am–7pm Tue–Sun (mid-Oct–Mar: to 4:30pm).* *1 Jan, 1 May, 25 Dec.* *Sat & Sun.*

San Pietro
Founded in AD 765, on Sirmione's highest point, this church contains a 12th-century fresco of Christ in Majesty.

★ Grotte di Catullo
This complex of villas, baths and shops, built as a resort for wealthy Romans from the 1st century BC, lies ruined here. Finds are displayed in the Antiquarium building.

The inner harbour provided a haven for fishermen during lake storms and an anchorage for the castle fleet.

The drawbridge is heavily fortified, linking the castle to the mainland and offering an escape route to its inhabitants.

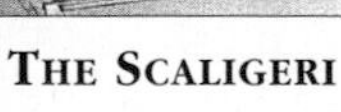

The Scaligeri

The Rocca Scaligera is one of many castles built throughout the Verona and Lake Garda region by the Scaligeri family *(see p192)*. During the turbulent 13th and 14th centuries, powerful military rulers fought each other incessantly in pursuit of riches and power. Despite the autocratic nature of their rule, the Scaligeri brought a period of peace and prosperity to the region, fending off attacks by the predatory Visconti family who ruled neighbouring Lombardy.

The Scaligeri ruler, Cangrande I

Salò ⓮

Road map A3. 10,000. *Lungolago Zanardelli. (0365 214 23).* *Sat am.*

LOCALS PREFER to associate this elegant town with Gaspare da Salò (1540–1609), the inventor of the violin, rather than with Mussolini, the World War II dictator. Mussolini set up the so-called Salò Republic in 1943 and ruled northern Italy from here until 1945, when he was shot by the Italian resistance.

Happier memories are evoked by Salò's buildings, including the cathedral with its unusual wooden altarpiece (1510) by Paolo Veneziano. The main appeal of the town derives from its pastel-coloured waterfront buildings, and the lake views. Salò marks the start of the Riviera Bresciana, where the shore is lined with villas and grand hotels set in semi-tropical gardens.

Gardone Riviera ⓯

Road map A3. 2,500. *Via Repubblica 8. (0365 203 47).*

GARDONE'S MOST appealing feature is the terraced public park that cascades down the hillside, planted with noble and exotic trees. Equally exotic are the Mediterranean and African plants in the **Hruska Botanical Gardens**, founded in 1910, which benefit from the town's mild winters. Gardone has long been a popular resort – the magnificent 19th-century **Villa Alba** (now a congress centre) was built for the Austrian emperor to escape the bitter winters of his own country. The Art Deco **Grand Hotel** on the waterfront was built for lesser beings.

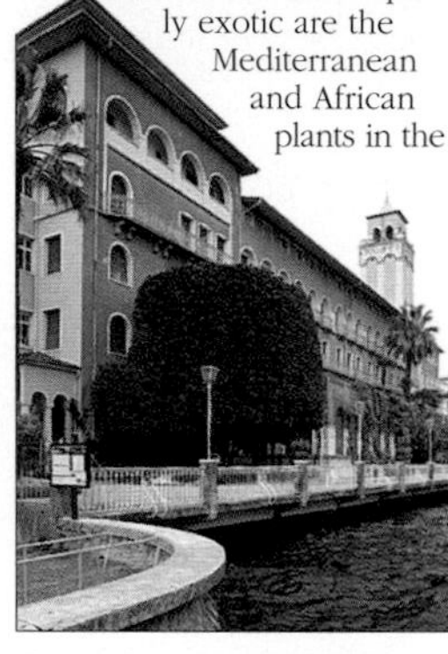

The Art Deco Grand Hotel in Gardone Riviera

High above the town is the **Villa il Vittoriale**, built for the poet Gabriele d'Annunzio. His Art Deco villa has blacked-out windows (he professed to loathe the world) and is full of curiosities, including a coffin-shaped bed. The garden has a landlocked warship, the prow raised high over Lake Garda.

Hruska Botanical Gardens
Via Roma. *336 41 08 77.* *daily mid-Mar–mid-Oct.*

Villa il Vittoriale
Via Vittoriale 12. *0365 29 65 23.* *Tue–Sun (garden daily).* *1 Jan, 24 & 25 Dec.*

Valpolicella Wine Tour

THIS CIRCULAR TOUR takes in the beautiful, remarkably varied scenery of the wine district that lies between Verona and Lake Garda. On the shores of Lake Garda itself, deep and fertile glacial soils provide sustenance for the grapes that are used to make Bardolino, a wine that is meant to be drunk young *(see pp238–9)*. Inland, the rolling foothills of the Lessini mountains shelter hamlets where lives and working rhythms are tuned to the needs of the vines. These particular vines are grown to produce the equally famed Valpolicella, a red wine that varies from light and fruity to full-bodied.

Tips for Drivers

Starting point: *Verona.*
Length: *45 km (28 miles).*
Approximate driving time: *3 hours.*
Stopping-off points: *The main village of the Valpolicella region, San Pietro in Cariano, has cafés and restaurants.*

BARDOLINO
CLASSICO SUPERIORE
1999
ZENI

Bardolino ③
Famous for its light red wine, Bardolino hosts a grape festival in September and has numerous cellars offering tastings.

Key

Tour route

Other roads

Affi ④
This wine-producing village is surrounded by vineyards planted in the sheltered basin of the Adige Valley.

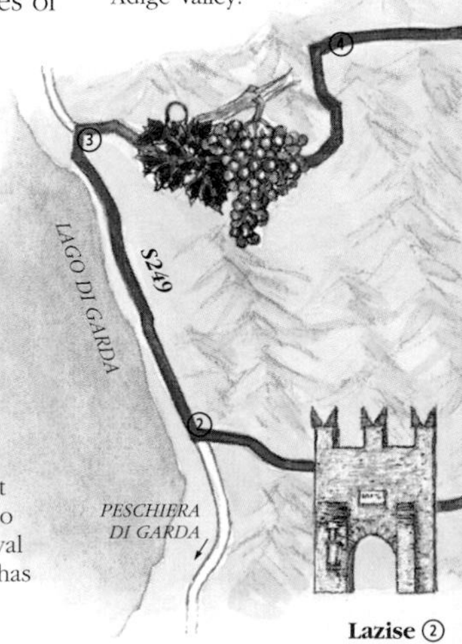

Lazise ②
Lazise has long been the chief port of Garda's eastern shore, its picturesque harbour and medieval church guarded by a 14th-century castle.

Looking across Lake Garda from Riva del Garda

Riva del Garda ⓰

Road map B3. *13,600.*
Giardini di Porta Orientale 8. (0464 55 44 44). 2nd Wed (& 4th Wed in summer). ***Shops closed*** *Mon (non-food); Mon pm (food) & Sat pm in winter.*

LIVELY RIVA'S waterfront is overlooked by the moated **Rocca di Riva**, a former Scaligeri fortress. Inside is a museum with exhibits from the region's prehistoric lake villages, built by driving huge piles far out into the lake bed to support platforms. The lake is popular with windsurfers.

Rocca di Riva

Piazza Cesare Battisti 3. *0464 57 38 69. mid-Mar–Oct: Tue–Sun (Mon also in Jul–Aug).*

Malcésine ⓱

Road map B3. *3,500.*
Via Capitanato 6–8. (045 740 05 55). Sat.

GERMAN VISITORS who come to Malcésine trace the journey taken by the poet Goethe in 1788. His travels were full of mishaps, and at Malcésine he was accused of spying and locked up.

From Malcésine, visitors can take the rotating **cable car** up to the broad ridge of Monte Baldo (1,745 m/5,725 ft). The journey takes 15 minutes, and on a clear day it is possible to see the distant peaks of the Dolomites and the Gruppo di Brenta range. Footpaths for walkers are signposted at the top. The lower slopes are designated nature reserves; a good place to see the local flora is the **Riserva Naturale Gardesana Orientale**, just to the north of Malcésine.

Sant'Ambrogio di Valpolicella ⑤
Apart from red wine, this village is a source of the pink stone used for Verona's palaces.

Gargagnago ⑥
The Alighieri wine estate is owned by a direct descendant of the medieval poet Dante, and set around a 14th-century villa built by Dante's son.

Cloisters of San Giorgio in Valpolicella

Pedemonte ⑦
The Villa Santa Sofia wine estate operates out of a theatrical villa designed by Palladio, but never completed.

Verona ①
The city has numerous old-fashioned bars, called *osterie*, where visitors can go to sample local wine.

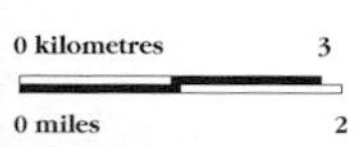

TRE CIME

The Dolomites

The name of the Dolomites *conjures up a vision of spectacular mountains, as noble and awe-inspiring as the Alps. To the south of the region lie the cities of Feltre, Belluno and Vittorio Veneto. To the north is the renowned ski resort of Cortina d'Ampezzo. In between, travellers will encounter no more cities – just ravishing views, unfolding endlessly, and pretty hamlets tucked into remarkably lush and sunny south-facing valleys.*

The Dolomites cover a substantial portion of the Veneto's land mass, and it is easy to forget, when visiting the cities of the flat Veneto plain, that behind them lies this range of mountains rising to heights of 2,000 m (6,500 ft) and more. Catering for an urban population hungry for fresh air and freedom, the towns and villages of the Dolomites have striven to balance the needs of tourism and nature.

Italian is the region's principal language, but in the northwest a German influence can sometimes be heard, reflecting the region's strong historic links with the Austrian Tyrol. Once ruled by the Hapsburgs, certain areas of the region only became part of Italy in 1918, after the break up of the Austro-Hungarian empire at the end of World War I. Some of that war's fiercest fighting took place in the Dolomites, as both sides tried to wrest control of the strategic valley passes linking Italy and Austria-Hungary. Striking war memorials in many villages and towns provide a sad reminder of that time.

Today the region is renowned for its winter sports facilities. International cross-country ski competitions were held in Cortina d'Ampezzo as early as 1902, and in 1956 the town hosted the Winter Olympics. Today, Cortina is considered to be Italy's most exclusive resort, the winter playground of film stars and royalty.

Outdoor café in the old town of Feltre

◁ **Pleasure boats on Lake Misurina, looking towards the peaks of the Sorapiss**

Exploring the Dolomites

The environment of the Dolomites is completely different from the industrialized Veneto plain. Huge areas are designated nature reserves, while others, accessible by chair lifts, allow visitors to enjoy the views and appetite-sharpening treks in the mountain meadows. Refuges, dotted along the high trails, offer dormitory accommodation and refreshments, while hamlets have comfortable hotels. Snow covers the peaks from October to May, and it is possible to ski all year round on Marmolada, at 3,343 m (10,970 ft) the highest peak in the Dolomites.

Titian's statue, Pieve di Cadore

Mountain chalet near the stadium at Cortina d'Ampezzo

Sights at a Glance

Belluno 5
Cortina d'Ampezzo 1
Dolomites (Dolomiti) *pp216–17* 4
Feltre 7
Misurina 2
Pieve di Cadore 3
Valzoldana 6
Vittorio Veneto 8

Monte Pelmo from Zoppe di Cadore

Getting Around

The S50 and S51 are kept clear of snow all year. There are steep gradients on the S48 and minor roads, so use snow chains in winter. Roadside notices warn when the high passes are closed. There is only one railway line (up the Piave valley), but the region is well served by comfortable express buses.

Piaggio Vespa truck, a common sight in the Dolomites

Key

- Motorway
- Major road
- Minor road
- Scenic route
- River
- View point

Cortina d'Ampezzo ❶

Road map D1. *6,800.* *Piazzetta San Francesco 8. (0436 3231).* *Tue am, Fri am.*

ITALY'S TOP SKI RESORT, much favoured by the smart set from Turin and Milan, is well supplied with restaurants and bars. The reason for its popularity is the dramatic scenery, which adds an extra dimension to the pleasure of speeding down the slopes. Wherever you look, crags and spires rise skyward, thrusting their weather-sculpted shapes above the trees.

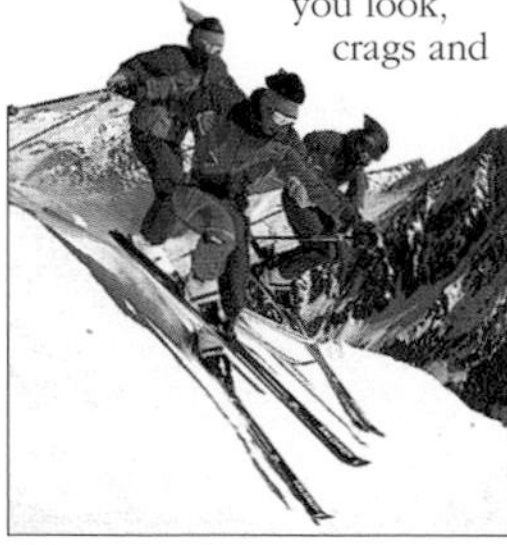

Skiers at Cortina

Strolling along the Corso Italia in Cortina d'Ampezzo

As a consequence of hosting the 1956 Winter Olympics, Cortina has better-than-normal sports facilities. There is a ski jump and a bobsleigh run, the Olympic ice stadium holds skating discotheques, and there are several swimming pools as well as tennis courts and riding facilities.

During the summer months, Cortina becomes an excellent base for walkers. Information on the many trails and guided walks is available from the tourist office or, during the summer, from the Guides' office opposite.

You can also take a ride in the cable car *Freccia nel Cielo* (Arrow in the Sky), which goes to a height of 3,243 m (10,639 ft) above sea level.

The Dolomite Road

THE STRADA DELLE DOLOMITI, or Dolomite Road, is one of the most beautiful routes anywhere in the Alps, and is a magnificent feat of highway construction. It starts in the Trentino-Alto Adige region at Bolzano and enters the Veneto region at Passo Pordoi, at 2,239 m (7,346 ft) the most scenic of all the Dolomite passes. From here the route follows the winding S48 for another 35 km (22 miles) east to the resort of Cortina d'Ampezzo.

There are plenty of stopping places along the route where you can enjoy spectacular views. In many of the ski resorts, cable cars will carry you up to alpine refuges (some with cafés attached) that are open from mid-June to mid-September. These refuges mark the start of a series of signposted walks.

Tips for Drivers

Starting point: *Passo Pordoi.*
Length (within the Veneto): *35 km (22 miles).*
Approximate driving time: *Two hours, but allow a full day to include the return journey and time to stop and enjoy the stunning scenery.*
Stopping-off points: *The small towns of Pieve di Livinallongo and Andraz have good cafés and restaurants.*

Passo Pordoi ①
To the north of Passo Pordoi, the Gruppo di Sella rises to 3,152 m (10,340 ft).

← *BOLZANO*

S48

Key

Tour route

Other roads

View point

0 kilometres 5

0 miles 2

Arabba ②
Arabba is a pleasant resort with a cable car to Porta Vescovo (2,478 m/ 8,129 ft) to the south.

Misurina ❷

Road map D1. 82.
Via Misurina. (0435 390 16).
Jul–Aug; late Dec–early Jan.

SMALLER AND QUIETER than Cortina, Misurina nestles by the exquisite Lake Misurina. The lake's mirror-like surface reflects the peaks of Monte Sorapiss and the Cadini group. Take the toll road that climbs northeast for 8 km (5 miles) to the Auronzo mountain refuge and to the base of the Tre Cime di Lavaredo peaks (2,999 m/9,840 ft).

One of the creeks flowing into Lake Misurina

Titian's house at Pieve di Cadore

Pieve di Cadore ❸

Road map D1. *4,000.*
Tai di Cadore, Piazza Venezia 20. (0435 316 44). *Wed am (at Tai).*

FOR CENTURIES the Cadore forests supplied Venice with its timber. The main town of this vast mountainous region is Pieve di Cadore, primarily known as the birthplace of Titian. The humble **Casa di Tiziano** can be visited, and the nearby **Museo Archeologico** has exhibits of finds from the pre-Roman era.

Principally, though, this is a base for touring the scenic delights of the region. North of Pieve the valley narrows to a dramatic ravine, and the road north to Comelica and Sesto is noted for its alpine scenery and its traditional balconied houses. Continuing northeast, you can follow the Piave river to its source, 8 km (5 miles) north of Sappada.

Casa di Tiziano
Via Arsenale 4. *0435 322 62.*
Jun–Sep: Tue–Sun (Aug: daily); Oct–May: by appointment.

Museo Archeologico Romano e Preromano
Palazzo della Magnifica Comunità Cadorina, Piazza Tiziano 2. *0435 322 62.* *Jun–Sep: Tue–Sun (Aug: daily); Oct–May: by appointment.*

Falzarego ⑤
War memorials record the fighting that took place here in 1914–18 on the frontier between Austria and Italy.

Cortina d'Ampezzo ⑥
Descending to Cortina, the view is dominated by the irregularly shaped Cinque Torri (Five Towers).

S51
S48
BELLUNO
Falzarego

Andraz ④
The partially restored Castello di Andraz, sitting on a rocky outcrop, was built in the 1300s to prevent banditry and to control the approach to the Passo Falzarego.

Pieve di Livinallongo ③
The chief town of the scenic Cordevole valley, Pieve offers spectacular views of dolomitic peaks and cliffs.

Visitors at Passo Falzarego, by the war memorials

The Dolomites ❹

THE DOLOMITES ARE THE MOST DISTINCTIVE and beautiful mountains in Italy. They were formed of mineralized coral which was laid down beneath the sea during the Triassic era, and uplifted when the European and African continental plates dramatically collided 60 million years ago. Unlike the glacier-eroded saddles and ridges of the main body of the Alps, the pale rocks here have been carved by the corrosive effects of ice, sun and rain, sculpting the cliffs, spires and "organ pipes" that we see today. The eastern and western ranges of the Dolomites have slightly different characteristics; the eastern section is the more awe-inspiring, especially the Catinaccio (or Rosengarten) range which is particularly beautiful, turning rose pink at sunset.

Onion dome, a common local feature

STRADA DELLE DOLOMITI

One of the most spectacular routes through the Dolomites links Bolzano *(see p166)* with Cortina d'Ampezzo *(see p155)*. It follows the lie of the land, passing some of the greatest peaks, and the most majestic landscape.

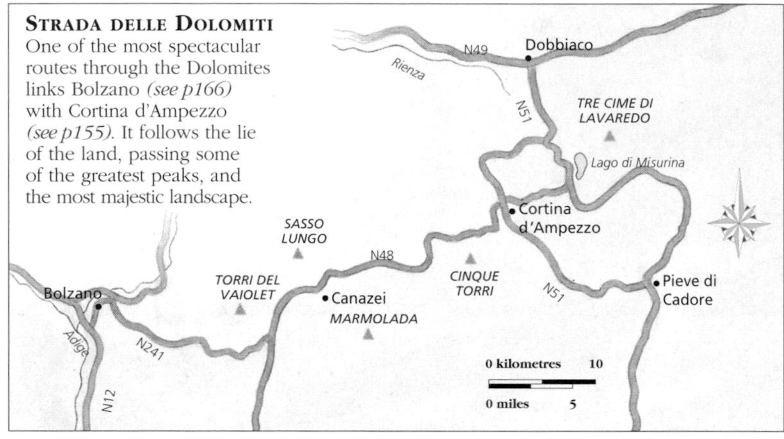

DISTINCTIVE PEAKS OF THE DOLOMITES

The peaks of the Dolomites include several with distinctive shapes and some of the highest mountains in the range. Many are easily identifiable and have been individually named.

***The Cinque Torri** or Five Towers rise from one base between Passo Falzarego and Cortina d'Ampezzo.*

***Sasso Lungo** is a tall peak easily recognized by its distinctive scar. It is joined to the Sasso Piatto.*

***Marmolada** is the highest peak in the Dolomite chain. A cable-car ascends to 3,000 m above the glacier.*

Lago di Misurina *is a large and beautiful lake lying beside the resort of Misurina. The crystal clear waters reflect the surrounding mountains, mirroring various peaks such as the distinctive and dramatic Sorapiss, in shimmering colours.*

Outdoor activities *in this area of dramatic landscapes include skiing in winter, and walking and rambling along the footpaths, and to picnic sites, in summer. Chair-lifts from the main resorts provide easy access up into the mountains themselves, transporting you into some breathtaking scenery.*

The Torri del Vaiolet *is part of the beautiful Catinaccio range, known for its colour.*

Tre Cime di Lavaredo *or Drei Zinnen dominate the valleys north of the Lago di Misurina.*

Nature in the Dolomites

Forests and meadows support a breathtaking richness of wildlife in the region. Alpine plants, which flower between June and September, have evolved their miniature form to survive the harsh winds.

The Flora

Gentian roots *are used to make a bitter local liqueur.*

The orange mountain lily *thrives on sun-baked slopes.*

The pretty *burser's saxifrage grows in clusters on rocks.*

Devil's claw *has distinctive pink flower heads.*

The Fauna

The ptarmigan *changes its plumage from mottled brown in summer to snow white in winter for effective camouflage. It feeds on mountain berries and young plant shoots.*

The chamois, *a shy mountain antelope prized for its soft skin, is protected in the national parks, where hunting is forbidden.*

Roe deer *are very common as their natural predators – wolves and lynx – have now died out. Their keen appetite for tree saplings causes problems for foresters.*

Belluno ❺

Road map D2. 35,800. FS
Piazza dei Martiri 8. (0437 94 00 83). *Sat.* ***Shops closed*** *Mon am (clothes) & Wed pm (food).*

PICTURESQUE BELLUNO, capital of Belluno province, serves as a bridge between the two very different parts of the Veneto, with the flat plains to the south and the Dolomite peaks to the north. Both are encapsulated in the picture-postcard views to be seen from the 12th-century **Porta Rugo** at the southern end of Via Mezzaterra, the main street of the old town. Even more spectacular are the views from the campanile of the 16th-century **Duomo** which was designed by Tullio Lombardo, but rebuilt twice after damage by earthquakes.

The nearby baptistry contains a font cover with the figure of John the Baptist carved by Andrea Brustolon (1662–1732), whose elaborate furnishings decorate Ca' Rezzonico in Venice *(see p126)*. Brustolon's works also grace the churches of **San Pietro** (two altarpieces) and **Santo Stefano** (crucifix and angels).

Façade and entrance to Palazzo dei Rettori in Belluno

On the same square is the 12th-century **Torre Civica**, all that survives of the Bishop's Palace, and the city's most elegant building, the Renaissance **Palazzo dei Rettori** (1491), once home to Belluno's Venetian rulers.

Exterior fresco, Zoppe di Cadore

The **Museo Civico** is worth visiting for the archaeological exhibits, and the paintings by Bartolomeo Montagna (1450–1523) and Sebastiano Ricci (1659–1734). Just to the right of the museum is the town's finest square, the **Piazza del Mercato**, which features arcaded Renaissance palaces and a fountain built in 1410.

South of the town are the ski resorts of the Alpe del Nevegal. It is worth taking the chair lift in the summer to the Rifugio Brigata Alpina Cadore (1,600 m/5,250 ft) which has superb views and a botanical garden specializing in alpine plants.

Museo Civico

Piazza Duomo 16. 0437 94 48 36. *mid-Apr–Sep: Tue–Sun; Oct–mid-Apr: Mon–Sat.*

Valzoldana ❻

Road map D1. *from Longarone.* *Via Roma 1, Forno di Zoldo (0437 78 73 49).*

THE WOODED Zoldo valley is a popular destination for walking holidays. Its main resort town is Forno di Zoldo and the surrounding villages are noted for their Tyrolean-style alpine chalets and haylofts. Examples built in wood

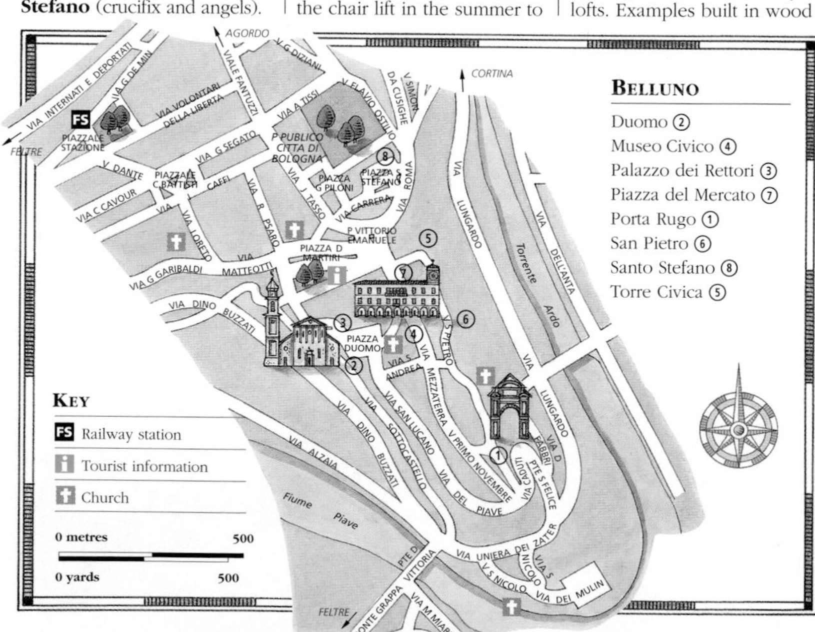

on stone foundations can be seen at Fornesighe, 2 km (1 mile) northeast of Forno di Zoldo, and on the slopes of Monte Penna at Zoppe di Cadore, 8 km (5 miles) north.

If you have the time, do a circular tour of the area. Drive north on the S251, via Zoldo Alto to Selva di Cadore, then west via Colle di Santa Lucia (a favourite viewpoint for keen photographers). From here take the S203 south through the lakeside resort of Alleghe. The route passes through wonderful scenery with woodland, flower-filled meadows and pretty mountain hamlets which complement the splendour of the rocky crags.

The southernmost town of the area is Agordo, nestling in the Cordevole Valley. From here, a spectacularly scenic route follows the S34 northeast to the Passo Duran (1,605 m/5,270 ft), descending to Dont, close to your starting point. Wayside shrines mark the route and it is worth stopping on your way down to visit village shops selling local woodcarving. Take care when driving along this narrow and winding road.

Palazzo Guarnieri, one of the Renaissance palaces in Feltre

Feltre ❼

Road map D2. 19,600. FS. Piazzetta Trento e Trieste 9. (0439 2540). Tue & Fri am. **Shops closed** Mon am (clothes), Wed pm (food).

FELTRE OWES its venerable good looks to the vengeful Holy Roman Emperor, Maximilian I. He sacked the town twice, in 1509 and in 1510, at the outbreak of the war against Venice waged by the League of Cambrai *(see p44)*. Despite the destruction of its buildings and the murder of most of its citizens, Feltre remained stoutly loyal to Venice, and Venice repaid the debt by rebuilding the town after the war. Thus the main street of the old town, Via Mezzaterra, is lined with arcaded early 16th-century houses, most with steeply pitched roofs to keep snow from settling.

Selva di Cadore from Colle di Santa Lucia, northwest of Valzoldana

Follow the steep main street to the striking Piazza Maggiore, where you can see the remains of Feltre's medieval castle, the church of **San Rocco** and a fountain by Tullio Lombardo (1520).

On the eastern side of the square, Via L Luzzo is lined with beautiful Renaissance palaces, one of which houses the **Museo Civico**. This displays a fresco by the local artist Lorenzo Luzzo, who was known as Il Morto da Feltre (The Dead Man of Feltre), a nickname given to him by his contemporaries because of the deathly pallor of his skin.

Museo Civico

Palazzo Villabruna, Via L Luzzo 23. 0439 88 52 41. Tue–Sun. public hols.

Vittorio Veneto ❽

Road map D2. 30,000. FS. Piazza del Popolo 18. (0438 572 43). **Shops closed** Tue (clothes), Wed pm (food). Mon.

TWO SEPARATE TOWNS, Ceneda and Serravalle, were merged and renamed Vittorio Veneto in 1866 to honour the unification of Italy under King Vittorio Emanuele II. The town later gave its name to the last decisive battle fought in Italy in World War I. The **Museo della Battaglia** in the Ceneda quarter, the commercial heart of the town, commemorates this. Serravalle is more picturesque, with many fine 15th-century *palazzi*, and pretty arcaded streets. Franco Zeffirelli shot scenes for his film *Romeo and Juliet* in this town that sits at the base of the rocky Meschio gorge. To the east, via Anzano, the S422 climbs up to the Bosco del Cansiglio, a wooded plateau.

Museo della Battaglia

Piazza Giovanni Paolo I. 0438 576 95. Tue–Sun.

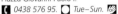

Vittorio Veneto old town and river

Travellers' Needs

Where to Stay

Venice's perennial attraction to romantics and art lovers means it has an astonishing number of hotels for its size, many of them in former *palazzi*. On the mainland, ancient cities abound with hotels and *pensioni*, often housed in magnificent old buildings and extravagantly decorated. Those in the smaller towns are often run by families who take pride in their reputation.

Sign for a small hotel

Lake Garda is a long-established resort area with many hotels to choose from, and the mountainous north of the region is an all-year-round holiday area with accommodation of all types. Here you can find self-catering in a small farmhouse at very reasonable cost, and there are also numerous idyllically situated and well-equipped campsites. Budget options in the cities include self-catering flats, hostels and dormitory accommodation, and the mountains offer simple refuges for enthusiastic walkers. For more information on hotels in Venice and the Veneto see the listings on pages 228–33.

Where to Look

Unlike most other cities, Venice has hardly any "undesirable" addresses. You will pay considerably more for a hotel in the immediate vicinity of the Piazza San Marco, but in such a compact city even apparently outlying areas such as Cannaregio or Santa Croce *(see pp14–15)* are never far from places of interest. Addresses in Venice are immensely confusing *(see p277)* but a map reference for each hotel is given in the listings. The maps referred to are to be found on pages 282–9 (Venice) and pages 12–13 (the Veneto).

Most visitors feel it is worth splashing out for a few nights' stay in Venice itself, despite the cost, though an increasing number stay in Verona or Padua and "commute" into Venice by train. Do not be tempted by the relatively low prices of the Mestre hotels, unless you are prepared to stay in a sprawling industrial town. Remember, too, that if you are travelling by car you will have to pay stiff parking charges at the Piazzale Roma car park or one of its satellites for the duration of your stay in Venice *(see pp278–279)*.

Hotel Europa e Regina *(see p229)* overlooking the Grand Canal

Outside the Hotel Marconi *(see p230)* on the busy Riva del Vin

Many of the hotels in minor inland towns of the Veneto cater primarily for business travellers, but if you plan to explore the region you will find some lovely villa hotels in the countryside. Padua and Verona have a number of hotels, but those in Verona are fully booked for months ahead in the summer opera season, so forward planning is essential. Further north there is more choice. The hotels are geared to holidaymakers, with lovely gardens, swimming pools and sports facilities. But bear in mind that Italians as well as foreign tourists flock to the lakes and mountains, so it is always advisable to plan your trip and book in advance.

Hotel Prices

Hotel charges were deregulated in 1994, so that hotels are free to charge what they feel the market will bear rather than being tied to the tariffs determined by their star rating. Venice is an expensive place to stay and nowadays can hardly be said to have a "low season" with the benefits of lower or negotiable prices. You will be unlikely to find a basic double room for less than €50. Occasionally you can find some cheaper rooms from November to February, when the weather is often superb. But remember that many hotels close out of season. Some re-open for Carnival – and raise their prices accordingly.

July and August are the most expensive months at the resorts along Lake Garda. In the Dolomites winter, when skiers flock to the area, is the high season and the hotels may close during the summer.

Single room rates are higher than individual rates for two people sharing a double room. Prices include tax.

Hidden Extras

If you are travelling on a budget, try to avoid hotels with inclusive breakfast as this is rarely good value for money. You are expected to tip at least €1 for room service and bellboys, even if service is included in the price of the room. Laundry services are usually expensive, as are drinks from the minibar and telephone calls from hotel rooms. Check all the rates when you make the booking. Some small hotels in Venice, and most in holiday areas like Lake Garda, may expect you to take full- or half-board during the high season.

Hotel Gradings and Facilities

Italian hotels are classified by a rating system from one to five stars. However, each province sets its own level for grading, so standards for each category may vary from one area to another. Some hotels may not have a restaurant, but those which do sometimes welcome non-residents who wish to eat.

Air-conditioning is rare in old buildings. Although the thick stone walls provide good insulation against the summer's heat, if you cannot tolerate high temperatures it is well worth choosing air-conditioned accommodation in Venice during the hottest months. Under Italian law, central heating remains off, whatever the temperature outside, until 1 November. This is something that is worth remembering if you plan a late-October trip.

Children are welcome everywhere but smaller hotels have limited facilities. Venice is not an ideal destination for children. If you want to take them with you, it is better to choose a hotel on the Lido where they will have access to the beach and also probably a garden.

Hotel Excelsior *(see p231)*

What to Expect

Hotels are obliged by law to register you with the police, so they will ask for your passport when you arrive. They may need to keep it for a few hours, but make sure you take it back, because you will need identification to change money or travellers' cheques. Italian hotel rooms are not "cosy": carpets are rare, the storage space is usually very limited and luxuries such as tea-making facilities are unknown, even in four- and five-star establishments. The decor may be simple and Italian taste can be rather different from what you are used to. However, hotel staff will be friendly and charming, and the standard of cleanliness is high. The bathrooms are, almost without exception, spotlessly clean, even when they are shared.

Less expensive hotels are unlikely to have bathtubs; showers are considered more hygienic and more economical on water. Rooms without a bathroom usually have a washbasin and towels are provided.

Breakfast is very light – a cup of coffee and a brioche (a plain or cream- or jam-filled pastry), though hotels generally include fruit juice, bread rolls and jam as well. It is always cheaper to have breakfast in a bar.

With the exception of Venice, where the only sounds are water-borne or human, Italian towns can be very noisy. If you are a light sleeper, ask for a room that is away from the street, or come equipped with earplugs to deaden traffic sounds and church bells.

Check-out time is usually noon in four- and five-star hotels and between ten and noon in small establishments. If you stay longer you will be asked to pay for an extra day.

Hotel Do Pozzi *(see p229)*

The elegant Villa Cortine Palace on the Sirmione peninsula *(see p232)*

Booking and Paying

Book at least two months in advance if you want to stay in a particular hotel in the high season; some people book as far as six months or a year ahead in Venice itself. The local tourist office will have listings of all the hotels in the area, and they will be able to advise you on the best hotels in each star category. Hotels above the €50 price bracket usually take credit cards, but check which cards are accepted when you make your reservation. You can generally pay the deposit by credit card, or by sending an international money order.

Under Italian law, a booking is valid as soon as the deposit is paid and confirmation is received. As in restaurants, you are required by law to keep your hotel receipts until you leave the country.

The conveniently located Hotel La Fenice *(see p229)*

Disabled Travellers

Facilities for the disabled are limited throughout Italy, and Venice poses its own particular problems. Recently several strategic bridges have been fitted with mechanized lifts for wheelchairs. The key must be requested in advance from the town hall. A list of tour operators that specialize in holidays for the disabled can be obtained from the **Italian State Tourist Office**. For further advice, see p261.

Hotels in Historic Buildings

Many of Venice's hotels are housed in buildings of historical or artistic interest, for example in Gothic *palazzi*. Some of the best are included in the listings below. In the Veneto there are also some attractive villa hotels – see the **Relais and Châteaux** guide for more details.

Self-Catering

Self-catering flats in Venice proper are fairly easy to find. **International Chapters** handle some holiday lets within the city, as do **Tailor Made Tours** and **Vacanze in Italia**. Alternatively you could try one of the Venetian agents, such as **Sant'Angelo**

Directory

Tourist Office

Italian State Tourist Office (ENIT)
1 Princes Street,
London W1R 8AY.
020 7408 1254.

Historic Hotels

Relais & Châteaux
Grosvenor Gardens House,
35–37 Grosvenor Gardens,
London SW1W 0BS.
0800 960 239.

Self-Catering Agencies

Agriturist Ufficio Regionale
Via C Monteverdi 15,
Venezia Mestre 30174.
041 98 74 00.

Centro Immobiliare NG
Rio Terra Canal,
Dorsoduro 3066.
Map 6 D2.
041 522 09 32.

International Chapters
47–51 St John's Wood
High Street,
London NW8 7NJ.
020 7722 9560.

Sant'Angelo
Campo Sant'Angelo,
San Marco 3818.
Map 6 F2.
041 522 15 05.

Tailor Made Tours
22 Church Rise,
London
SE23 2UD.
020 8291 9736.

Individual Travellers' Co
Manor Courtyard, Bignor,
West Sussex RH20 1QD.
01798 869461.

Budget Accommodation

Associazione Italiana Alberghi per la Gioventù
Via Cavour 44,
00184 Rome.
06 487 11 52.

Foresteria Valdese
Campo Santa Maria
Formosa, Castello 5170.
Map 7 C1.
041 528 67 97.

Ostello Venezia
Fondamenta delle Zitelle,
Giudecca 86. **Map** 7 B5.
041 523 82 11.

Santa Fosca
Fmta Diedo, Cannaregio
2372. **Map** 2 F3.
041 71 57 75.

Campsites and Mountain Refuges

Club Alpino Italiano
Via Petrella 19,
20124 Milan.
02 205 72 31.

Marina di Venezia
Via Montello 6,
Punta Sabbioni.
041 530 09 55.

San Nicolò
Riviera San Nicolò 65, Lido.
041 526 74 15.

Touring Club Italiano
Corso Italia 10, 20122
Milan. 02 852 61.

or **Centro Immobiliare NG**, although they may prefer to deal with longer rentals.

Under the **Agriturismo** scheme there is plenty of self-catering accommodation in the Veneto, usually on working farms. There is an Agriturist office in each region, which will give further information, although you may have to book with the owner. This type of accommodation ranges from simple conversions to luxurious and spacious villas with swimming pools. Prices reflect these variations, and they also fluctuate according to the time of year. Low-season prices for four people start at about €500 per week.

Budget Accommodation

One- or two-star budget hotels charging from €20 to €40 per person per night are generally small, family-run places. These used to be known as *pensioni*, but the term is no longer used very much officially. However, many places retain the name and the personal character that has made them so popular. They rarely offer breakfast and have very few rooms with private bathrooms. You should not expect particularly high standards of service. A variation on these *pensioni* are *affittacamere*, or rented rooms, are even smaller establishments, and they also offer excellent value for money.

Accommodation in hostels and dormitories is sometimes available at convents and religious institutions, and it is often possible to arrange it through the local tourist offices.

Detail on the Hotel Danieli

The **Associazione Italiana Alberghi per la Gioventù** (Italian Youth Hostel Association) in Rome has lists of youth hostels throughout the whole of Italy. The main youth hostel in Venice is the beautifully situated **Ostello Venezia** on the Giudecca. Book well ahead for if you want to stay in July or August.

Lists and booking forms for youth hostels are available through the Italian Tourist Board worldwide, or from local offices. The Venice office also produces a simple typed list of all kinds of hostel accommodation in Venice itself.

Campsites and Mountain Refuges

There are good campsites throughout the region, concentrated mainly on the mainland to the north of Venice, on the shores of Lake Garda and in the northern mountains. A list of campsites and mountain refuges can be obtained from **ENIT** or local tourist offices. Most huts in the mountain districts are owned by the **Club Alpino Italiano**, based in Milan, who can provide full information. The **Touring Club Italiano** publishes annually a list of campsites: *Campeggi e Villaggi Turistici in Italia*.

A suitcase boat transporting visitors' luggage to a hotel

Garden terrace of the Hôtel des Bains on the Lido ***(see p231)***

Using the Listings

Hotels on pages 229–33 are listed according to area and price category. The symbols summarize the facilities available at each hotel.

- all rooms have bath and/or shower unless otherwise indicated
- 1 single-rate rooms available
- rooms for more than two people available, or an extra bed can be put in a double room
- TV television in all rooms
- air-conditioning in all rooms
- swimming pool in the hotel
- wheelchair access
- lift
- P parking available
- restaurant
- credit cards accepted
- closed out of season *(see p223)*

Price categories for a standard double room per night, including tax and service:

- € under €100
- €€ €100–€200
- €€€ €200–€300
- €€€€ €300–€400
- €€€€€ over €400

Venice's Best Hotels

HOTELS IN VENICE range from the luxurious and renowned, which are mainly clustered along the Grand Canal, to simple, family-run places in the quieter parts of the city. Wherever you stay, you will be within easy reach of the main attractions, with restaurants and shops close at hand. All the hotels shown on this map have something special to recommend them, whether it is the waterside position, a garden or a quiet location away from the crowds. Always book well in advance, and remember that many Venetian hotels are shut at some stage in winter. The hotels shown here are the best in their particular style or price range.

Zecchini
One of the most attractive hotels on the busy Lista di Spagna, the Zecchini is good value. (See p231.)

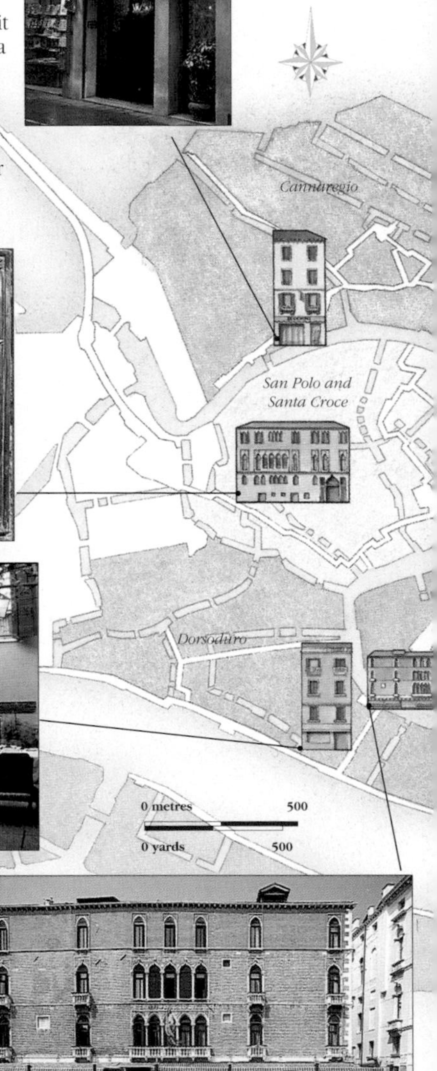

Cannaregio

San Polo and Santa Croce

Al Sole
Situated beside a tranquil canal, this Gothic palazzo *is away from the main tourist haunts, but within easy reach by foot or water of all the sights.* (See p229.)

Dorsoduro

0 metres 500
0 yards 500

Agli Alboretti
This charming hotel in a central location has attractive rooms and a garden courtyard. (See p230.)

Gritti Palace
One of Venice's most famous hotels, the Gritti offers rooms and service of impeccable standard in an historic palazzo *on the Grand Canal.* (See p229.)

Giorgione
This high-class, spacious hotel, with its excellent facilities, offers every modern comfort at lower prices than others of similar calibre. (See p231.)

Marconi
This efficiently run hotel, housed in an old palazzo*, has views of the Grand Canal and the Rialto Bridge.* (See p230.)

Castello

San Marco

La Residenza
This family-run hotel offers good value for money and is away from the crowds. It has frescoed public rooms and antiques, but the bedrooms are more simple. (See p230.)

Flora
A flower-filled garden is just one of the attractions of this delightful hotel. (See p229.)

Londra Palace
Tchaikovsky once stayed in this grand palazzo *with its views to San Giorgio Maggiore. Today's guests appreciate the welcoming bar and restaurant.* (See p230.)

Hotels in Venice

THIS CHART is a quick reference to recommended hotels in Venice and the lagoon. They are listed within each *sestiere* in price order. More details for these and for hotels in the Veneto are given on the following pages. For information on other types of accommodation, see pages 224–5.

Hotel	Price	Number of Rooms	All Rooms with Bath/Shower	Air Conditioning	Restaurant	Attractive View	Garden/Terrace	Open All Year	Easy Access
SAN MARCO *(see p229)*									
Al Gambero	€€	26			●	■		■	●
La Fenice et des Artistes	€€	68	●	■	●			■	
San Moisè	€€	16	●	■		■		■	
Santo Stefano	€€	11	●	■		■		■	
Flora	€€€	44	●	■			●	■	●
Cavalletto e Doge Orseolo	€€€€	107	●	■	●			■	●
Do Pozzi	€€€€	35	●			■	●		●
Europa e Regina	€€€€€	182	●	■	●	■	●	■	●
Gritti Palace	€€€€€	91	●	■	●	■	●	■	●
Monaco and Grand Canal	€€€€€	104	●	■	●	■	●	■	●
SAN POLO AND SANTA CROCE *(see pp229–30)*									
Alex	€	11							
Al Sole	€€	80	●	■			●	■	
Falier	€€	19	●	■				■	
Locanda Sturion	€€€	11	●	■		■		■	
Marconi	€€€€	26	●	■		■		■	●
CASTELLO *(see p230)*									
La Residenza	€€	15	●			■		■	●
Paganelli	€€€	22				■	●	■	●
Pensione Wildner	€€€	16	●	■	●	■	●	■	●
Danieli	€€€€€	233	●	■	●	■	●	■	●
Londra Palace	€€€€€	53	●	■	●	■	●	■	●
DORSODURO *(see p230)*									
Agli Alboretti	€€	23	●	■	●	■	●		●
Messner	€€	41	●	■	●		●		
Montin	€€	11			●		●	■	
Pensione Seguso	€€	36		■	●	■	●		●
Pausania	€€€	24	●	■			●	■	
Pensione Accademia Villa Maravegie	€€€	27	●	■		■	●	■	
Pensione La Calcina	€€€	29		■		■		■	●
CANNAREGIO *(see pp230–31)*									
Abbazia	€€	39	●	■			●	■	●
Giorgione	€€	71	●	■			●	■	●
Zecchini	€€	27	●					■	●
Continental	€€€	93	●	■	●	■	●	■	●
THE LAGOON ISLANDS *(see p231)*									
Villa Parco (Lido)	€€	23	●	■			●	■	
Quattro Fontane (Lido)	€€€	59	●	■	●		●		
Cipriani (Giudecca)	€€€€€	104	●	■	●	■	●	■	●
Excelsior Palace (Lido)	€€€€€	197	●	■	●	■	●		●
Hôtel des Bains (Lido)	€€€€€	191	●	■	●	■	●		●

VENICE

San Marco

Al Gambero

Calle dei Fabbri, San Marco 4687. **Map** 7 A2. *041 522 43 84.* FAX *041 520 04 31.* www.locandaalgambero.com **Rooms:** *26.* 1 €€

The Al Gambero has simple rooms, many of them singles, and several with a canal view. Situated close to the Piazza and many major shops.

La Fenice et des Artistes

Campiello Fenice, San Marco 1936. **Map** 7 A3. *041 523 23 33.* FAX *041 520 37 21.* www.fenicehotels.com **Rooms:** *68.* 1 TV €€

A pretty hotel, furnished with antiques. On fine days you can sit outside for breakfast, or later in the day enjoy a quiet drink from the bar *(see p224).*

San Moisè

Piscina San Moisè, San Marco 2058. **Map** 7 A3. *041 520 37 55.* FAX *041 521 06 70.* sanmoise@sanmoise.it **Rooms:** *16.* 1 TV €€

The San Moisè is a wonderfully quiet but centrally located hotel on a placid back canal. The rooms differ considerably in size, but are in the traditional Venetian style and furnished with antiques.

Santo Stefano

Campo Santo Stefano, San Marco 2957. **Map** 6 F3. *041 520 01 66.* FAX *041 522 44 60.* info@hotelsantostefanovenezia.com **Rooms:** *11.* 1 TV €€

The traditional Venetian rooms in this tall, narrow hotel can be rather cramped, but offer great views of this charismatic quarter of the city.

Flora

Calle Larga XXII Marzo, San Marco 2283/a. **Map** 7 A3. *041 520 58 44.* FAX *041 522 82 17.* info@hotelflora.it **Rooms:** *44.* 1 €€€

This quiet hotel is located in a secluded alley only a few minutes' walk from Piazza San Marco *(see p227).* Although some of the rooms are small, they all have their own bathroom. In summer guests can enjoy their breakfast in the pretty, flower-filled garden.

Cavalletto e Doge Orseolo

Calle Cavalletto, San Marco 1107. **Map** 7 B2. *041 520 09 55.* FAX *041 523 81 84.* cavalletto@san marcohotels.com **Rooms:** *107.* 1 TV €€€€

This excellent hotel has been welcoming visitors for more than 200 years. The rooms are bright and cheerful, with thoughtful extras ranging from minibars to window boxes.

Do Pozzi

Corte Do Pozzi, San Marco 2373. **Map** 7 A3. *041 520 78 55.* FAX *041 522 94 13.* www.dopozzi.it **Rooms:** *35.* 1 €€€€

The Do Pozzi *(see p223)* boasts a charming setting in a peaceful green courtyard. Its rooms are reasonably quiet, despite its close proximity to the busy Piazza San Marco.

Europa e Regina

Calle Larga XXII Marzo, San Marco 2159. **Map** 7 A3. *041 520 04 77.* FAX *041 523 15 33.* res075.europaeregina@westin.com **Rooms:** *182.* 1 TV *launch service, private beach.* €€€€€

The Europa e Regina *(see p222)* offers the best value of all the deluxe hotels. The rooms are large and many of them have views across the Grand Canal. The magnificent public rooms are sumptuously ornate and gilded, in typical Venetian style, and for those who like to eat and drink alfresco there is a lovely garden courtyard and canalside terrace with breathtaking views.

Gritti Palace

Santa Maria del Giglio, San Marco 2467. **Map** 7 A3. *041 79 46 11.* FAX *041 520 09 42.* www.starwood.com/grittipalace **Rooms:** *91.* 1 TV *Private launch service. Access to private beach.* €€€€€

This renowned deluxe hotel overlooking the Grand Canal is situated in the fine 15th-century *palazzo* that once belonged to the Gritti family *(see p226).* The hotel is elegant, sumptuous and old-fashioned in the best sense, with superb rooms and meticulous service. The writer Ernest Hemingway was once a guest here and described it as "the best hotel in a city of great hotels".

Monaco and Grand Canal

Calle Vallaresso, San Marco 1325. **Map** 7 B3. *041 520 02 11.* FAX *041 520 05 01.* mailbox@hotelmonaco.it **Rooms:** *104.* 1 TV €€€€€

Housed in an 18th-century *palazzo,* this elegant hotel looks across the Grand Canal to the Salute. The public rooms have an intimate feeling and the bedrooms are decorated with lovely furniture and pretty fabrics.

San Polo and Santa Croce

Alex

Rio Terrà Frari, San Polo 2606. **Map** 6 E1. & FAX *041 523 13 41.* www.hotelalexinvenice.com **Rooms:** *11.* *3.* 1 €

It is some time since the rooms of this family-run hotel were overhauled, but the excellent value and good position near the Frari compensate for any shabbiness.

Al Sole

Fondamenta Minotta, Santa Croce 136. **Map** 5 C1. *041 71 08 44.* FAX *041 71 43 98.* info@corihotels.it **Rooms:** *80.* 1 €€

This is not the most attractive part of Venice, but the Al Sole is in a pretty corner. This 14th-century building has marble-floored reception areas and pleasant rooms. There is a shady courtyard where you can have a drink.

Falier

Salizzada San Pantalon 130, Santa Croce 30135. **Map** 5 C1. *041 71 08 82.* FAX *041 520 65 54.* falier@tin.it **Rooms:** *19.* 1 TV €€

Away from the majority of the Venice hotels and on the edge of the student district, the Falier has recently been refurbished.

Locanda Sturion

Calle del Sturion, San Polo 679. **Map** 7 A1. *041 523 62 43.* FAX *041 522 83 78.* info@locandasturion.com **Rooms:** *11.* 1 TV €€€

Situated just a few yards from the Grand Canal and close to the Rialto, the Sturion's central location is part of its appeal. This friendly hotel is an attractive base offering exceptional value.

Marconi

Riva del Vin, San Polo 729. **Map** 7 A1. *041 522 20 68.* FAX *041 522 97 00.* @ info@hotelmarconi.it ***Rooms:** 26.* 1 TV €€€€

Those in search of Venetian opulence will appreciate the reception areas of the Marconi, which was once a 16th-century *palazzo (see p227).* The bedrooms are less grand but some overlook the Grand Canal and Rialto Bridge.

Castello

La Residenza

Campo Bandiera e Moro, Castello 3608. **Map** 8 E2. *041 528 53 15.* FAX *041 523 88 59.* @ info@venicelaresidenza.com ***Rooms:** 15.* 1 €€

The Residenza was once a 14th-century *palazzo (see p227).* Although the bedrooms are basic, the frescoed ceilings and antique furniture in the public areas are quite delightfully elegant.

Paganelli

Riva degli Schiavoni, Castello 4182 & 4686. **Map** 8 D2. *041 522 43 24.* FAX *041 523 92 67.* @ hotelpag@tin.it ***Rooms:** 22.* 1 TV €€€

The cosy and old-fashioned rooms in the Paganelli provide views of St Mark's Basin that would cost three times as much at other hotels along the Riva. Rooms in the *dipendenza* (annexe) on San Zaccaria do not have the view, although they are quieter.

Pensione Wildner

Riva degli Schiavoni, Castello 4161. **Map** 8 D2. *041 522 74 63.* FAX *041 526 56 15.* @ wildner@veneziahotels.com ***Rooms:** 16.* 1 TV €€€

Another family-run hotel on the Riva, the Pensione Wildner offers simple yet immaculate bedrooms with stunning views across to San Giorgio Maggiore. It has a small bar if you prefer not to sit at the tables outside, among the crowds on the busy Riva.

Danieli

Riva degli Schiavoni, Castello 4196. **Map** 7 C2. *041 522 64 80.* FAX *041 520 02 08.* @ res072.danieli@starwoodhotels.com ***Rooms:** 233.* 1 TV *Access to private beach.* €€€€€

One of Venice's top hotels, the Danieli is the epitome of luxury. It was the palace of the Dandolo family and has strong literary and musical connections *(see p113).* The reception rooms are splendid, lit by resplendent Venetian glass chandeliers, and the service is impeccable. There are two wings, one built in the 1940s, and an older section – the first choice for guests.

Londra Palace

Riva degli Schiavoni, Castello 4171. **Map** 8 D2. *041 520 05 33.* FAX *041 522 50 32.* @ info@hotellondra.it ***Rooms:** 53.* TV €€€€€

On the long Riva where hotels are cheek by jowl, the monument to King Vittorio Emanuele is a useful landmark outside this statuesque stone-faced hotel *(see p227).* It was once two palaces and has elegant public rooms, a good restaurant, a delightful bar, and an amazing view over the St Mark's basin of Palladio's San Giorgio Maggiore, on the Island of San Giorgio. The rooms are traditional in style and comfortable. It was in this hotel that Tchaikovsky composed his Fourth Symphony.

Dorsoduro

Agli Alboretti

Rio Terrà Antonio Foscarini, Dorsoduro 884. **Map** 6 E4. *041 523 00 58.* FAX *041 521 01 58.* @ alborett@gpnet.it ***Rooms:** 23.* 1 TV *Jan.* €€

Attractively situated near the Accademia, this hotel has elegant, if small, rooms. The cosy reception area is wood-panelled and there is a garden where you can relax after a hard day's sightseeing *(see p226).*

Messner

Rio Terrà dei Catecumeni, Dorsoduro 216. **Map** 6 F4. *041 522 74 43.* FAX *041 522 72 66.* @ a.nardi@flashnet.it ***Rooms:** 41.* 1 €€

The rooms in this modernized hotel are of a good size. There is a friendly bar and a peaceful courtyard. Families with children are particularly welcome.

Montin

Fondamenta Eremite, Dorsoduro 1147. **Map** 6 D3. *041 522 71 51.* FAX *041 520 02 55.* W www.locandamontin.com ***Rooms:** 11.* 1 €€

These ten rooms above one of Venice's best-known restaurants are full of charm and character, despite the lack of private bathrooms. It is essential to book.

Pensione Seguso

Zattere ai Gesuati, Dorsoduro 779. **Map** 6 E4. *041 528 68 58.* FAX *041 522 23 40.* ***Rooms:** 36.* 1 *Dec–Feb.* €€

The rooms of this pleasant *pensione* are traditionally furnished and the reception areas are crammed with antiques and books. Most rooms look out on to either the Giudecca canal or the Rio San Vio. You may find that half-board is compulsory in high season. Book in advance.

Pausania

Fondamenta Gherardini, Dorsoduro 2824. **Map** 6 D3. *041 522 20 83.* FAX *041 52 22 989.* W www.hotelpausania.it ***Rooms:** 24.* 1 TV €€€

This small, welcoming hotel offers a peaceful escape from city life. Most bedrooms are situated around a picturesque and secluded garden. With reasonable prices and friendly staff, this is a pleasant place to stay during the busy summer months.

Pensione Accademia Villa Maravegie

Fondamenta Bollani, Dorsoduro 1058–1060. **Map** 6 E3. *041 521 01 88.* FAX *041 523 91 52.* @ info@pensioneaccademia.it ***Rooms:** 27.* 1 TV €€€

This elegant 17th-century villa was once the Russian Embassy. Many rooms are furnished with antiques, and although some rooms are small, the garden makes up for these minor inconveniences.

Pensione La Calcina

Zattere ai Gesuati, Dorsoduro 780. **Map** 6 E4. *041 520 64 66.* FAX *041 522 70 45.* @ la.calcina@libero.it ***Rooms:** 29.* 1 €€€

This simply furnished and airy *pensione,* convenient for the Accademia, is very popular. All the rooms are comfortable and a few have the bonus of splendid views across the Giudecca canal.

Cannaregio

Abbazia

Calle Priuli, Cannaregio 66/68. **Map** 1 C4. *041 71 73 33.* FAX *041 71 79 49.* @ info@abbaziahotel.com ***Rooms:** 39.* 1 TV *two weeks in Jan.* €€

Situated just off the Lista di Spagna, this is probably the best hotel in the station area. The rooms are comfortable and there is a garden in which you can relax.

Giorgione

Santi Apostoli, Cannaregio 4587. **Map** 3 B5. *041 522 58 10.* FAX *041 523 90 92.* @ giorgione@hotelgiorgione.com ***Rooms:*** *71.* €€

This is a modern, recently refurbished hotel housed in a delightful colour-washed building. There is a spacious reception area and bar *(see p 227)*, and a lovely garden. It is conveniently situated for the Rialto area.

Zecchini

Lista di Spagna, Cannaregio 152. **Map** 2 D4. *041 71 50 66.* FAX *041 71 56 11.* @ info@hotelzecchini.com ***Rooms:*** *27.* €€

The Zecchini occupies two floors of an attractive building and is reached via a flight of stairs *(see p226)*. The rooms overlook one of Venice's busiest streets, so it can be a bit noisy. The rooms vary considerably.

Continental

Lista di Spagna, Cannaregio 166. **Map** 2 D4. *041 71 51 22.* FAX *041 524 24 32.* @ continental@ve.nettuno.it ***Rooms:*** *93.* €€€

The Continental is a large, well equipped hotel in the busy station area. It has modern rooms, some of which overlook the Grand Canal. Other rooms look out over the adjacent, tree-shaded *campo*.

The Lagoon Islands

Villa Parco

Via Rodi 1, Lido di Venezia. *041 526 00 15.* FAX *041 526 76 20.* W www.hotelvillaparco.com ***Rooms:*** *23.* *Dec–Jan.* €€

With the sea just a few minutes away and set in its own gardens, this family-run hotel is an ideal place to stay if you are holidaying with children. The modern rooms are pleasant and the hotel is situated in a quiet residential area.

Quattro Fontane

Via Quattro Fontane 16, Lido di Venezia. *041 526 02 27.* FAX *041 526 07 26.* W www.quattrofontane.com ***Rooms:*** *59.* *mid-Nov–Mar.* €€€

This is the nicest of the smaller hotels on the Lido. It is set in pretty gardens and has its own tennis court for the use of guests. The reception rooms and bedrooms are all furnished with antiques and the green and white gabled exterior gives the hotel a distinctive alpine look. On warm summer days you can enjoy a meal out of doors in the tranquil courtyard. The hotel is only a few minutes from the sea.

Cipriani

Giudecca 10. **Map** 7 C5. *041 520 77 44.* FAX *041 520 39 30.* @ info@ hotelcipriani.it ***Rooms:*** *104.* *Private launch service.* *Jan.* €€€€€

Set in gardens occupying the entire eastern tip of the Giudecca, the Cipriani has been one of the world's great hotels since it opened in 1963. The bedrooms and suites are furnished with tasteful opulence, and each one has been decorated in a different style. The renowned terrace restaurant is delightful.

Excelsior Palace

Lungomare Marconi 41, Lido di Venezia. *041 526 02 01.* FAX *041 526 72 76.* @ banqueting077.excelsior@westin.com ***Rooms:*** *197.* *Private launch service. Private beach.* *mid-Nov–mid-Mar.* €€€€€

When it opened in 1907, the Excelsior was the largest luxury resort hotel in the world *(see pp48– 9)*. The exterior is Moorish, with the beach *cabanas* are styled like Arabian tents. The interior, offering every service and comfort, is equally splendid. The hotel is at its liveliest during the annual Film Festival *(see p255)* – the Palazzo del Cinema and the summer home of the casino are a short walk away.

Hôtel des Bains

Lungomare Marconi 17, Lido di Venezia. *041 526 59 21.* FAX *041 526 01 13.* @ banqueting078.desbains@sheraton.com ***Rooms:*** *191.* *Private launch service. Private beach.* *mid-Nov–mid-Mar.* €€€€€

Film fans will recognize the des Bains as the location for Luchino Visconti's *Death in Venice*, set in the hotel where Thomas Mann wrote the original novel. Built in the early 1900s, its reception rooms have an Art Deco elegance, and there is a verandah for dining *(see p225)*. The bedrooms are spacious. Across the road the hotel's private beach is equipped with bathing huts with a view looking out over the Adriatic.

The Veneto Plain

Asolo

Villa Cipriani

Road map D3. Via Canova 298, 31011. *0423 52 34 11.* FAX *0423 95 20 95.* W www.sheraton.com/villacipriani ***Rooms:*** *31.* €€€€€

Situated in the gentle foothills of the mountains, Asolo is a good base for exploring the area. This superbly comfortable hotel is housed in a 16th-century villa. The standards are very high and the beautiful garden has excellent views.

Bassano Area

Victoria

Road map C3. Viale Diaz 33, 36061 Bassano del Grappa. *0424 50 36 20.* FAX *0424 50 31 30.* @ info@hotelvictoria-bassano.com ***Rooms:*** *23.* €

The Victoria is just outside the old city walls and well placed for sightseeing in Bassano. The rooms are comfortable and there is a garden, where you can enjoy a quiet drink.

Bonotto Hotel Belvedere

Road map C3. Piazzale G Giardino 14, 36061 Bassano del Grappa. *0424 52 98 45.* FAX *0424 52 98 49.* W www.bonotto.it ***Rooms:*** *87.* €€

One of Bassano's main squares, just outside the old centre, is the setting for the town's most lavishly appointed hotel. Large and busy, it can be noisy, but has comfortable rooms and a high level of service.

Chioggia

Grande Italia

Road map D4. Rione S Andrea 597, 30015. *041 40 05 15.* FAX *041 40 01 85.* W www.hotelgrandeitalia.com ***Rooms:*** *57.* *Dec–Jan.* €€

The Grande Italia stands right at the head of Chioggia's main street and is well situated for boats going to Venice. A solid, unpretentious and old-fashioned hotel, it offers comfortable rooms at low prices.

Conegliano

Canon d'Oro

Road map D3. Via XX Settembre 131, 31015. *& FAX 0438 342 49.* info@hotelcanondoro.it *Rooms: 49.* €

This three-star hotel offers comfort and a warm welcome in an old building. The location, on the main street of Conegliano, is ideal for exploring the historic town centre. There is a garden in which to relax, and you can sample a glass of Prosecco in the friendly bar.

Padua

Augustus Terme

Road map C4. Viale Stazione 150, 35036 Montegrotto Terme. *049 79 32 00.* FAX *049 79 35 18.* www.hotelaugustus.com *Rooms: 120.* 65. €

The spa town of Montegrotto Terme has several modern hotels and is a useful last-minute stopping point. The Augustus Terme is one of the best hotels here: big, comfortable and functional, with a pretty garden and tennis court. You can also sample the thermal hot springs.

Donatello

Road map D4. Via del Santo 102, 35123. *049 875 06 34.* FAX *049 875 08 29.* www.hoteldonatello.net *Rooms: 49.* *mid-Dec–mid-Jan.* €€

Named after the sculptor of the equestrian statue on the piazza outside, the Donatello is opposite the Basilica di Sant'Antonio *(see p182)*. The old shell encloses a modern comfortable hotel.

Grande Italia

Road map D4. Corso del Popolo 81, 35131. *049 876 11 11.* FAX *0498 75 08 50.* info@hotelgrandeitalia.it *Rooms: 60.* €€

Situated close to most of the city's main sights, this hotel is a very good value choice. The decor and furniture are slightly shabby, but the rooms are comfortable. Quieter rooms, located at the back of the hotel, are available.

Majestic Toscanelli

Road map D4. Via dell'Arco 2, 35122. *049 66 32 44.* FAX *049 876 00 25.* www.toscanelli.com *Rooms: 34.* €€

Situated in the heart of the city, this hotel is an ideal base for exploring Padua. The rooms have views of the Old Ghetto.

Treviso

Campeol

Road map D3. Piazza Ancillotto 4, 31100. *& FAX 0422 566 01.* info@albergocampeol.it *Rooms: 14.* €

One of Treviso's best budget hotels, Campeol is clean, comfortable and welcoming, and situated right in the middle of the historic town centre. There is an excellent local restaurant opposite.

Diana

Road map D3. Via Roma 49, 31049. *0423 97 62 22.* FAX *0423 97 22 37.* www.hoteldiana.org *Rooms: 56.* €

Lying at the northern end of the Strada del Vino Prosecco, the attractive town of Valdobbiadene stands on the slopes of the Venetian pre-Alps overlooking the Piave valley. The Diana has good facilities and comfortable rooms.

Vicenza

Casa San Raffaele

Road map C4. Viale X Giugno 10, 36100 Salita Monte Berico. *0444 54 57 67.* FAX *0444 54 22 59.* albergosanraffaele@tin.it *Rooms: 29.* €

This tranquil hotel lies on the slopes of Monte Berico, with its lovely views over the city. It takes about half an hour to walk into town, but the good rooms make it by far the best choice among the less expensive hotels.

Campo Marzio

Road map C4. Viale Roma 27, 36100. *0444 54 57 00.* FAX *0444 32 04 95.* info@hotelcampomarzio.com *Rooms: 35.* €€

This stylish, modern hotel near the city centre has good facilities. It is set in a peaceful area within walking distance of the cathedral.

VERONA AND LAKE GARDA

Lake Garda South

Peschiera

Road map A4. Via Parini 4, 37010 Peschiera del Garda. *045 755 05 26.* FAX *045 755 04 44.* hotel.peschiera@virgilio.it *Rooms: 30.* *Nov–Mar.* €

At the southern end of Lake Garda, the little town of Peschiera makes a good overnight stopping place. The Peschiera is a modern building in a traditional style set in its own grounds. The bedrooms are lofty and cool and the staff friendly.

Villa Cortine Palace

Road map A4. Via Grotte 6–12, 25019 Sirmione del Garda. *030 990 58 90.* FAX *030 91 63 90.* info@hotelvillacortine.com *Rooms: 54.* *25 Oct–10 Apr.* €€€€€ *Half-board only 20 Jun–19 Sep.*

The fabulous grounds of this tranquil hotel *(see p223)* cover a third of the Sirmione peninsula. The huge frescoed rooms of this Classical villa are furnished with antiques, and the standards of comfort, food and service are all that you would expect.

Lake Garda West

Hotel Garni Riviera

Road map A3. Via Roma 1, 25084 Gargnano. *0365 722 92.* FAX *0365 79 15 61.* www.gardalake.it/garniriviera *Rooms: 20.* *Dec–Mar.* €

Located in the centre of Gargnano, near the port, this hotel offers a warm and friendly atmosphere. It is the ideal base from which to explore the surrounding area, on foot, by bike or on horseback.

Hotel du Lac

Road map A3. Via Colletta 21, 25084 Gargnano. *0365 711 07.* FAX *0365 710 55.* *Rooms: 11.* *10 Jan–10 Mar.* €

The dining room of this pretty, stuccoed old building overhangs the water and many bedrooms have balconies facing the lake. This family-run hotel makes a good base for exploring the western shore of Lake Garda.

Capo Reamol

Road map B3. Via IV Novembre 92, 25010 Limone sul Garda. *0365 95 40 40.* FAX *0365 95 42 62.* www.gardaresort.it ***Rooms:*** *58.* *Oct–Mar.* €€

Capo Reamol has a stunning location at the lake's edge. The spacious bedrooms each have a terrace, and meals are served in the waterside dining room. The hotel's facilities are excellent for families, and include a private beach and jetty, a gym, sauna and sunbathing terraces.

LAKE GARDA EAST

Bisesti

Road map A3. Corso Italia 34, 37016 Garda. *045 725 57 66.* FAX *045 725 59 27.* www.infogarda.com/bisesti ***Rooms:*** *90.* *Nov–Mar.* €

Conveniently placed near the centre of town and only five minutes' walk from Lake Garda, the Bisesti is a well-equipped modern holiday hotel set in its own grounds and with access to a private beach. Many of the rooms have a balcony and the dining room overlooks the garden.

Kriss Internazionale

Road map A3. Lungolago Cipriani 3, 37011 Bardolino. *045 621 24 33.* FAX *045 721 02 42.* www.kriss.it ***Rooms:*** *33.* *Dec–Jan.* €€

Attractively situated on a small promontory jutting into the lake, this modern hotel caters specifically for holiday-makers. Rooms have balconies and lake views, there is a garden, and the hotel has a private beach. The hotel will provide transport from the bus station for those travellers who arrive without a car.

Sailing Center Hotel

Road map B3. Località Molini Campagnola 3, 37018 Malcésine. *045 740 00 55.* FAX *045 740 03 92.* www.sailingcenter.com ***Rooms:*** *32.* *Oct–Apr.* €€

Far from the crowds, sited on land jutting into the lake, this modern hotel just outside the main town of Malcésine makes a good base for families for a short stay. The rooms are cool and pleasant, and there is a tennis court and private beach for residents.

Locanda San Vigilio

Road map A3. San Vigilio, 37016 Garda. *045 725 66 88.* FAX *045 725 65 51.* sanvigilio@gardanews.it ***Rooms:*** *7.* *Nov–Mar.* €€€€€

One of the loveliest and most exclusive hotels on Lake Garda, the Locanda lives up to every expectation of comfort, good taste and impeccable service. There is a private beach and a walled garden.

VERONA

Il Torcolo

Road map B4. Vicolo Listone 3, 37121. *045 800 75 12.* FAX *045 800 40 58.* www.hoteltorcolo.it ***Rooms:*** *19.* *10–31 Jan.* €

An extremely popular hotel within a stone's throw of the Arena, the Torcolo has some pretty, traditional rooms, and others that are more modern, a charming interior and friendly owners. In the summer, breakfast is served alfresco.

Giulietta e Romeo

Road map B4. Vicolo Tre Marchetti 3, 37121. *045 800 35 54.* FAX *045 801 08 62.* info@giuliettaeromeo.com ***Rooms:*** *31.* €€

This hotel is situated on a quiet street near the Arena. The spacious bedrooms are comfortable, with modern furnishings. Breakfast is served in the bar and there are some good restaurants nearby.

Hotel Gabbia d'Oro

Road map B4. Corso Porta Borsari 4a, 37121. *045 800 30 60.* FAX *045 59 02 93.* ***Rooms:*** *27.* €€€

Located near the Piazza delle Erbe, this luxuriously elegant hotel offers a refined yet welcoming ambiance, splendid views of the city and impeccable service.

Due Torri Hotel Baglioni

Road map B4. Piazza Sant'Anastasia 4, 37100. *045 59 50 44.* FAX *045 800 41 30.* duetorri.verona@baglionihotels.com ***Rooms:*** *91.* €€€€€

One of the oldest and perhaps most eccentric Italian hotels, the Due Torri is right in the heart of Verona. The huge bedrooms are each decorated in the style of a different era, and the walls and ceilings are painted and frescoed.

THE DOLOMITES

BELLUNO

Astor

Road map D2. Piazza dei Martiri 26/e, 32100. *0437 94 20 94.* FAX *0437 94 24 93.* www.dolomiti.it/astor ***Rooms:*** *38.* *partial.* €

This centrally situated hotel is a good choice when visiting the region's main town. The rooms are comfortable and well designed, and offer very good value. In winter it is popular with skiers and there is a lively atmosphere in the bar.

CORTINA D'AMPEZZO

Hotel Ampezzo

Road map D1. Via 29 Maggio 15, 32043. *0436 42 41.* FAX *0436 26 98.* hampezzo@sunrise.it ***Rooms:*** *78.* €

This cosy and comfortable family hotel is situated near the town centre. The rooms in front have private balconies with breath-taking views.

Menardi

Road map D1. Via Majon 110, 32043. *0436 2400.* FAX *0436 86 21 83.* info@hotelmenardi.it ***Rooms:*** *51.* *Apr–mid-Jun, mid-Sep–mid-Dec.* €€

The Menardi family have run this hotel on the outskirts of Cortina since 1900. Originally built as a farmhouse, it is furnished with antiques and has a welcoming and homely atmosphere.

SAN VITO DI CADORE

Hotel Ladinia

Road map D1. Via Ladinia 14, 32046. *0436 89 04 50.* FAX *0436 992 11.* www.italiaabc.it/ladinia ***Rooms:*** *36 + 10 apartments.* *mid-Apr–mid-Jun, mid-Sep–mid-Dec.* €€

In the scenic Ampezzo valley, the Hotel Ladinia is in a tiny resort village 11 km (7 miles) south of Cortina. Popular in summer as well as during the skiing season, the Ladinia is geared to holiday-makers. There is a tennis court; and you can have a drink in the bar, or outside in the garden.

For key to symbols *see p225*

RESTAURANTS, CAFÉS AND BARS

RESTAURANTS IN VENICE and the Veneto serve predominantly Italian food from the region, with the emphasis in Venice very much on fish. Wherever you go, you will find the cooking simple, with dishes that make full use of the traditional local ingredients.

Most Venetians eat lunch *(pranzo)* around 12:30pm and dinner *(cena)* from 8pm, though restaurants start serving dinner earlier to cater for the many foreign visitors.

Egyptian detail, Caffè Pedrocchi

Restaurants may be closed for several weeks during the winter and also for two to three weeks during the staff summer holidays. Closing dates are included in the listings, but avoid disappointment by asking your hotel to phone first to confirm that the restaurant is open. Finding restaurants can be confusing in Venice, so use the map references provided. The restaurants listed on pages 240–45 are some of the best across all price ranges.

El Gato restaurant, Chioggia, famous for its fish *(see p242)*

TYPES OF RESTAURANTS

ITALIAN EATING PLACES have a bewildering variety of names, and the differences between them can be considerable. A *ristorante* is smarter than a *trattoria* or an *osteria*, for example, and is likely to be more expensive. Nowadays, there is also a growing number of fast-food joints and *tavola calda* establishments, which have no cover or service charge. A *birreria* and a *spaghetteria* are more down-market eating places that sell beer, pasta dishes and snacks; you will mainly find these outside Venice itself. A good *pizzeria* will use wood-fired ovens for the pizza; if this is the case it will normally be open only in the evenings.

If you do not want to eat a full meal at lunchtime you can always stop in a bar or café for a snack. For further information on light meals see page 246.

OPENING TIMES AND CLOSING DAYS

OPENING TIMES are virtually the same throughout Venice and the Veneto: from noon to 2:30pm for lunch, and from 7:30pm to 10:30pm for dinner. Under Italian law all restaurants close one day a week and some close for an additional evening as well; closing days are staggered so there is always somewhere open in the area. Individual restaurants' closing days are given in the listings.

The main bar of the historic Caffè Pedrocchi *(see p178)*

VEGETARIAN FOOD

ITALIANS FIND it difficult to understand vegetarianism, but if you eat fish you should have no difficulty eating well. If not, there is still a variety of meatless dishes since many starters *(antipasti)*, soups and pasta sauces are vegetable-based. Salads and vegetables are always good, and most places will be happy to serve an omelette *(frittata)* or a selection of cheese.

FIXED-PRICE MENUS

IN THE DAYS when Italy was building its tourist industry all restaurants had to supply a fixed-price menu. This has largely fallen into abeyance, particularly outside the main tourist centres. Restaurants may often have the so-called *menu turistico* pinned up in the street, but not on offer inside. Such menus, if you do find them, are usually boring and offer no opportunity to sample the wonderful variety of the local cuisine. If money is tight it is far better to have a good pasta dish and some salad, which is acceptable in all but the grandest places.

The *menu gastronomico* is a fixed-price menu consisting of six or seven courses, which allows you to sample the full range of a chef's specialities.

HOW MUCH TO PAY

TRANSPORT CHARGES can add as much as 30 per cent to the price of basic commodities coming into Venice, which partly explains the high cost of eating. In cheaper eating places and *pizzerie* you can have a two-course meal with half a litre of wine for around €10–15. Three-course meals average about €18–25, and in up-market restaurants you can easily pay €50–70. In the Veneto, prices are lower, except for stylish restaurants in Verona and along Lake Garda during the summer.

Nearly all restaurants have a cover charge *(pane e coperto)*, usually €1–3. Many also add a 10 per cent service charge *(servizio)* to the bill *(il conto)*, so always establish whether or not this is the case. Where leaving a tip is a matter of your own discretion, 12–15 per cent is acceptable.

Restaurants are obliged by law to give you a receipt *(una ricevuta fiscale)*. Scraps of paper with an illegible scrawl are illegal, and you are within your rights to ask for a proper bill. The preferred form of payment is cash, but many restaurants will accept payment by major credit cards. Check which cards are accepted when booking.

Making Reservations

Whatever the price range, Venice's best restaurants are always busy, so it is best to reserve a table, especially if you are making a long boat trip to get there. If restaurants do not accept bookings, try to arrive early to avoid queuing.

Dress Code

Italians like to dress up in general, and dining out is no exception. However, this does not mean that women have to wear evening attire at a restaurant, or that men have to wear a tie, and you will rarely feel under-dressed without a jacket. Smart casual clothes are the general rule for both men and women.

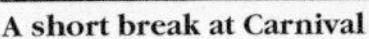

A short break at Carnival

Eating under the loggia of Treviso's Palazzo dei Trecento *(see p174)*

Reading the Menu

Both lunch and dinner in a restaurant follow the same pattern and usually start with an *antipasto*, or hors d'oeuvres (seafood, olives, beef carpaccio, ham, salami), followed by the *primo* (soup, rice or pasta). The main course, or *secondo*, will be fish or meat, either served alone or accompanied by vegetables *(contorni)* or a salad *(insalata)*. These are never included in the price of the main course.

To finish, there will probably be a choice of fruit *(frutta)*, a pudding *(dolce)* or cheese *(formaggio)*, or a combination of all three. Coffee – Italians always have an *espresso*, never a *cappuccino* – is ordered and served right at the end of the meal, often with a *digestivo*. In cheaper restaurants, the menu *(il menu)* may be chalked up or the waiter may simply recite the day's special dishes at your table.

Choice of Wine

House wines will usually be local *(see pp238–9)*. Cheaper restaurants will have a limited wine list, but at the top of the scale there should be a wide range of Italian and local wines and a selection of foreign vintages.

Children

Children are welcome in restaurants, particularly in simple, family-run ones. Smart places may be less welcoming, particularly in the evenings. Special facilities such as high chairs are not commonly provided. Most restaurants will prepare a half-portion *(mezza porzione)* if requested, and some charge less for these smaller helpings.

Smoking

A new law was passed in 2003 requiring all restaurants to provide their patrons with a non-smoking area.

Wheelchair Access

Very few restaurants make special provision for wheelchairs, though a word when booking should ensure a conveniently situated table and assistance on arrival.

Using the Listings
Key to the symbols in the listings on pp240–45.

fixed-priced menu
jacket and tie required
tables outside
air conditioning
good wine list
★ highly recommended
credit cards accepted. Check which cards are accepted when booking.

Price categories for a three-course meal for one including a half-bottle of house wine, cover charge, tax and service.
€ under €25
€€ €25–€40
€€€ €40–€55
€€€€ €55–€70
€€€€€ over €70

What to Eat in Venice and the Veneto

Young globe artichoke

TRADITIONAL VENETIAN specialities rely on the freshest of seasonal produce, meat and cheese from the mainland, and a huge variety of fish and seafood. Pasta is eaten here, as all over Italy, but more typical is polenta, made from maize flour, and also the many types of risotto. The mainland produces some renowned salamis. In the mountainous north, game and wild mushrooms provide the basis for some wonderful dishes, while Lake Garda is noted for *coregone*, a firm pink-fleshed fish rather like trout. The long red radicchio from Treviso is famous all over Italy, while Bassano del Grappa and Sant'Erasmo provide wonderful asparagus.

Baccalà Mantecata
This is dried salted cod, mixed to a paste with olive oil, parsley and garlic.

Fiori di Zucchini
Courgette flowers stuffed with fish mousse, fried in a light batter, are a seasonal dish.

Antipasto di Frutti di Mare
The seafood selection is dressed with olive oil and lemon juice. It may include exotic shellfish rarely found outside the Lagoon.

Risotto alle Seppie
Cuttlefish ink colours the rice in this traditional risotto.

Carpaccio
Wafer-thin slices of raw beef dressed with oil are served here with rocket and parmesan cheese.

Risi e Bisi
Made with fresh peas and flavoured with bacon, this risotto is soft and liquid.

Brodo di Pesce
Fish soup, a classic Venetian dish, is sometimes flavoured with saffron.

Zuppa di Cozze
This is a delicious way of cooking mussels, with white wine, garlic and parsley.

Spaghetti alle Vongole
Fresh clams are served with spaghetti in a piquant sauce made with hot chilli peppers.

Polenta
Made from maize, polenta may be yellow or a more delicate white.

Sardine in Saor
A traditional Venetian way of serving fish is with a sweet and sour sauce.

Anguille in Umido
These eels are cooked in a light tomato sauce with white wine and garlic.

Fegato alla Veneziana
Tender calf's liver is lightly cooked on a bed of onions in this traditional speciality.

Faraona con la Peverada
The sauce for this succulent guinea fowl is based on an ancient Arabian recipe.

Insalata Mista
Wild young leaves of many shapes and colours make up this summer salad.

Radicchio alla Griglia
These red endive leaves from Treviso are grilled over a hot fire.

Tiramisù
This dessert is made with coffee-soaked sponge cake and mascarpone cheese.

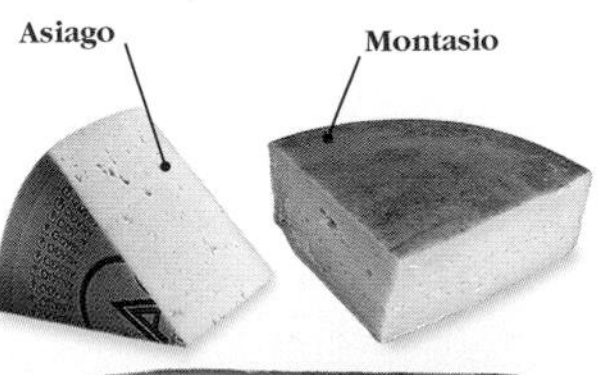

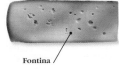

Gelati
In summer, ice cream is made with fresh seasonal fruits.

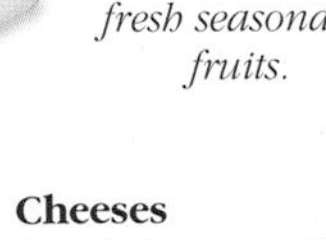

Cheeses
Local cheeses such as asiago, fontina and montasio may be included on the cheese board.

What to Drink in Venice and the Veneto

Italy has been making wine for over 3,000 years, and production in the Veneto reflects this, with the largest output in Italy of superior DOC wines. The area produces an abundance of different wines, which include not only well-known names such as Soave, Valpolicella and Bardolino, but many others which are also excellent value for money. Although Italians tend to drink lighter wines with their food, the area is also noted for some excellent strong wines. Italy's famous *digestivo*, grappa, originated in this corner of the country, and meals are often preceded by an *aperitivo* or a glass of sparkling local Prosecco.

Grapes drying in Valpolicella

Red Wine

Red wines in the Veneto are produced mainly near Bardolino and Valpolicella between Verona and Lake Garda *(see pp208–9)*. Made predominantly from the Corvina grape, they are usually light and fruity, but quality can vary so it is worth looking for reliable names.

Valpolicella comes in several forms. In addition to the normal easy-drinking wine, it is available as a *ripasso*, boosted in colour and strength by macerating the skins of the grapes before pressing. Recioto della Valpolicella is very different, a rich, sweet wine made from selected air-dried grapes. Some Reciotos undergo further fermentation to remove the sweetness, producing the strong, dry Recioto Amarone. These are some of the strongest naturally alcoholic wines in the world and are delicious but expensive.

Excellent red wines are also made by producers such as Venegazzù and Maculan from the Cabernet Sauvignon and Merlot grapes.

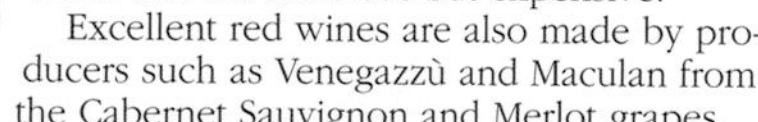

Red Venegazzù

Masi's ripasso

Bardolino wine is light, fruity and garnet-red in colour.

Amarone is full-bodied, rich, full of fruit and very alcoholic.

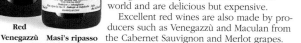

Reading Wine Labels

Italian wines are classified by four quality levels. Starting at the top, DOCG status *(Denominazione di Origine Controllata e Garantita)* has been awarded to a small number of Italian growing areas, none of which are in the Veneto. Most quality wines – more than 250 in the whole of Italy – are in the DOC category (as above but without the "guarantee") and these can be relied on as good value, quality wines. IGT *(Indicazione Geografica Tipica)* is a category new to Italy, corresponding to the popular French Vin de Pays. The final classification is *vino da tavola*, or table wine, but due to the inflexible Italian wine laws many superb wines appear in this category.

No vintage recommendations are given in the chart because almost all Veneto wines are made for young drinking.

Wine Type	Recommended Producers
White Wine	
Soave	**Anselmi, Bertani, Col Baraca (Masi), Boscaini, CS di Soave, Masi, Pieropan, Scamperle, Tedeschi, Zenato, Zonin**
Bianco di Custoza	**Cavalchina, Le Tende, Le Vigne di San Pietro, Pezzini, San Leone, Tedeschi, Zenato**
Breganze di Breganze	**Maculan**
Gambellara	**CS di Gambellara, Zonin**
Red Wine	
Bardolino	**Alighieri, Bertani, Bolla, Boscaini, Guerrieri-Rizzardi, Masi, Tedeschi**
Valpolicella	**Alighieri, Allegrini, Bertani, Bolla, Boscaini, Guerrieri-Rizzardi, Masi, Tedeschi, Zenato**
Ripasso Valpolicella (non-DOC)	**Serègo Alighieri, Jago (Bolla), Le Cane (Boscaini), Le Sassine (Le Ragose), Campo Fiorin (Masi), Capitel San Rocco (Tedeschi)**
Recioto and Recioto Amarone della Valpolicella	**Serègo Alighieri, Allegrini, Masi, Quintarelli, Le Ragose, Tedeschi**

White Wine

Bianco di Custoza

White Recioto

The Veneto produces more white wine than red, and most of the region's whites are from vineyards around the hilltop town of Soave *(see p190)*. These wines can be dull, but increasing numbers of producers are trying to raise Soave's image. Bianco di Custoza, a creamy, richer tasting "super Soave" from the eastern shores of Lake Garda, is well worth trying. Breganze is a name to look out for, with Maculan a leader in making fresh, clean, inexpensive wines and world-class dessert wines. Gambellara is made mainly from Soave's Garganega grape and is seldom of poor quality. Venegazzù is another producer you can trust for good quality white wines.

Pieropan is a top quality producer of Soave. The single-vineyard wines from here are superb.

Venegazzù's Pinot Grigio wine is dry and goes well with Venetian seafood.

White vino da tavola wines range from pale and dry to sweet and golden coloured.

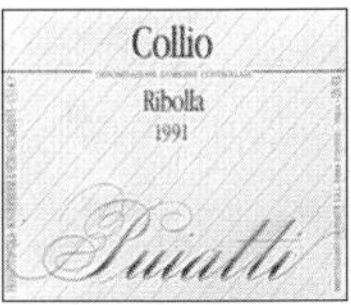

Puiatti's white Ribolla wine is fruity but dry. It is made in neighbouring Friuli.

Aperitifs and Other Drinks

Grappa

Crodino

Italian aperitifs tend to be wine-based, bitter, herb-flavoured drinks such as Martini and Campari. Less familiar are the herbal Punt e Mes, Cynar (made from artichokes), and the vivid orange Aperol, which is good mixed with white wine and soda. Crodino is a popular non-alcoholic choice. For settling the stomach after a good meal there are *amari* (bitters) and *digestivi*. Montenegro and Ramazzotti are well worth trying, and grappa, distilled from wine lees *(see Bassano del Grappa p166)*, is another favourite. A local speciality, Trevisana, is mixed with an extract of the long red radicchio from Treviso. Italian brandy can be rather oily, but Vecchia Romagna is a reliable name.

Prosecco

The Veneto's own sparkling wine, Prosecco is perfect as either a refreshing light *aperitivo* or with a meal. It originates in Conegliano *(see p175)*, the home of Italy's greatest wine school, and comes in both *secco* (dry) or *amabile* (medium-sweet) forms, and as *frizzante* or *spumante* (semi and fully sparkling). An excellent accompaniment to both fruit and seafood, it is also the traditional base for Bellini, a delicious *aperitivo* of wine mixed with fresh white peach juice *(see p92)*. This drink has bred several variants, such as Mimosa (with orange) and Tiziano (with red grape juice).

Prosecco

Bellini cocktail

Soft Drinks

Italian bottled fruit juices are good, and come in delicious flavours such as pear, apricot and peach. Many bars will squeeze you a *spremuta* of fresh orange *(arancia)* or grapefruit *(pompelmo)* juice on the spot. A *frullato* is an ice-cold mix of milk and fresh fruit.

Spremuta di arancia

Coffee

Coffee is an essential part of Italian life. Milky *cappuccino* with chocolate powder is drunk at breakfast time, and tiny cups of strong black *espresso* throughout the day. If you like your coffee with milk, choose a *caffè con latte*, or with just a dash of milk, *caffè macchiato*. Black coffee that is not too strong is *caffè lungo*; a *doppio* has an extra kick and a *corretto* has a good measure of alcohol.

Espresso

Cappuccino

VENICE

SAN MARCO

Al Conte Pescaor

Piscina San Zulian, San Marco 544. **Map** 7 B1. *041 522 14 83.* *Sun.* €€€

It is worth seeking out this little restaurant for its superb fish. Despite its position, the clientele are mainly local, which guarantees the quality of the food.

Da Arturo

Calle degli Assassini, San Marco 3656. **Map** 7 A2. *041 528 69 74.*

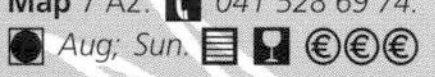

Aug; Sun. €€€

This high-quality, wood-panelled restaurant is unique in Venice in that it serves no fish or seafood dishes. Interesting antipasti include aubergines *"in saor"* (a vinegary sweet and sour sauce), and there are red wines of great distinction. Vegetarians are also well catered for at this establishment.

Al Graspo de Ua

Calle Bombaseri, San Marco 5094. **Map** 7 A1. *041 520 01 50.* *Mon.* €€€€

Housed in three small rooms that were once part of the old sacristy of the church of San Bartolomeo, the Venetian food here is good, but pricey. Worth sampling are the antipasto of prawns, artichokes and rocket, while main courses include fillet of John Dory.

Antico Martini

Campo San Fantin, San Marco 1983. **Map** 7 A2. *041 522 41 21.* www.anticomartini.com *Tue; Wed lunch.* ★ €€€€

The terrace of this smart restaurant used to overlook the Fenice theatre. The cooking is based on regional specialities; breast of duck with black truffles is recommended. Puddings include an iced mousse with raspberry sauce. The wine list features more than 300 labels. Meals are served until 1am.

Le Bistrot de Venise

Calle del Fabbri, San Marco 2159. **Map** 7 B2. *041 523 66 51.* www.bistrotdevenise.com ★ €€€€

This excellent restaurant serves traditional Venetian cuisine and has a very good wine list. There is also a non-smoking room. A meeting place for local artists and poets, it holds cultural events in the afternoons and in the evenings.

La Caravella

Calle Larga XXII Marzo, San Marco 2397. **Map** 7 A3. *041 520 89 01.* ★ €€€€

One of two restaurants in the Hotel Saturnia, the Caravella is decorated to resemble the interior of a 16th-century Venetian galley. The food is outstanding, with a range of imaginative dishes that includes a smooth lobster soup, bigoli and scampi in champagne.

Do Forni

Calle dei Specchieri. San Marco 468. **Map** 7 B2. *041 523 21 48.* www.doforni.it €€€€

A large "show business" establishment, the Do Forni has two dining rooms furnished in contrasting styles; one rustic but smart and the other more elegant. The mixed grilled fish is a house speciality that should not be missed.

La Locanda dell'Europa e Regina

Calle Larga XXII Marzo, San Marco 2159. **Map** 7 A3. *041 520 04 77.* ★ €€€€

This beautiful hotel restaurant is in a 16th-century palace on the Grand Canal and has a waterside terrace. The food lives up to the setting, featuring dishes such as seafood salad, porcini mushrooms with parmesan cheese, *fegato alla veneziana,* raspberry crêpes and tiramisù. The wine list is excellent.

Grand Canal

Monaco Hotel, Calle Vallaresso, San Marco 1332. **Map** 7 B3. *041 520 02 11.* €€€€€

Perfect for stylish dining all year round, the Grand Canal has a winter dining room and a summer terrace with views over the island of San Giorgio Maggiore. The menu features traditional Venetian cuisine, including pasta made freshly every day, and wonderful fish and meat dishes. Because of its popularity with locals, it is advisable to book in advance.

Harry's Bar

Calle Vallaresso, San Marco 1323. **Map** 7 B3. *041 528 57 77.* €€€€€

People eat at Harry's Bar because of its fame. The food is expensive, but can certainly be good. Prawns with oil and lemon, baked tagliolini with prosciutto and *carpaccio alla Cipriani* (raw marinated beef) are among the more interesting dishes. The wine list is good and the cocktails are justifiably world renowned.

Hotel Gritti

Campo Santa Maria del Giglio, San Marco 2467. **Map** 6 F3. *041 79 46 11.* ★ €€€€€

The dining room of this famous hotel is in the Venetian Gothic building. The terrace overlooks the Grand Canal and the church of Santa Maria della Salute. Classic dishes include cuttlefish with black ink risotto, *pasta e fagioli* (pasta and beans), sole with saor sauce and fried scampi.

SAN POLO AND SANTA CROCE

Antica Bessetta

Calle Savio, Santa Croce 1395. **Map** 2 E5. *041 72 16 87.* *Tue, Wed lunch.* €€

This simple family-run restaurant offers real Venetian home-cooking, including *risi e bisi* (fresh spring pea risotto) in season, fresh pasta and good scampi.

Antica Trattoria Poste Vecie

Rialto Pescheria, San Polo 1608. **Map** 3 A5. *041 72 18 22.* *Tue.* ★ €€

This stylish restaurant, situated near the fish market, claims to be the oldest in Venice. Dishes include home-made ravioli and tagliolini, baked turbot and brill, and there is also an impressive dessert trolley.

Trattoria alla Madonna

Calle della Madonna, San Polo 594. **Map** 7 A1. *041 522 38 24.* *25 Dec–31 Jan, 5–20 Aug.* ★ €€

This big, lively fish restaurant is a perennial favourite with Venetians and tourists alike. The seafood risotto and fish soup are excellent, and the fried and grilled main fish courses all highly recommended.

Da Fiore

Calle dello Scaleter 2202a, San Polo. **Map** 6 D2. *041 72 13 08.* *2 weeks in Dec, 3 weeks in Aug; Sun & Mon.* €€€€€

The excellent fish specialities on offer at Da Fiore include a wonderful seafood antipasto, grilled fish and *fritto misto* (mixed seafood in batter). The restaurant has a good wine list, but the house white is also well worth a try.

CASTELLO

Arcimboldo

Calle dei Furlani, Castello 3219. **Map** 8 D1. 041 528 65 69. *Tue.* €€

This restaurant takes its name from 16th-century painter Arcimboldo, who used vegetables and fruit to create portraits of people. It offers equally diverse interpretations on the Venetian culinary theme. Try sea-bass with tomatoes or a delicious marinated salmon with citrus fruit and herbs.

Corte Sconta

Calle del Pestrin, Castello 3886. **Map** 8 E2. *041 522 70 24.* *7 Jan–7 Feb, 21 Jul–16 Aug; Sun & Mon.* ★ €€€

The Proietto family have built up this restaurant from a simple eating house to one of the city's top dining spots. It is rather difficult to find, but worth the effort for the superb fish dishes and home-made pasta, served in the pretty garden in summer.

Hostaria da Franz

Fondamenta San Giuseppe, Castello 754. **Map** 8 D1. *041 522 08 61.* *Jan; Tue.* ★ €€€

Situated behind the Public Gardens, the Gasparini's restaurant with its canalside terrace serves some of the best seafood in Venice. When you visit, try the baby octopus or *spaghetti alla busara* (scampi, tomato and chilli).

Danieli Terrace

Riva degli Schiavoni, Castello 4196. **Map** 8 D2. *041 522 64 80.* ★ €€€€€

The panorama over St Mark's Basin from this stylish hotel restaurant is magnificent, as are the food and service. The risotti are very good and the excellent wine list features solely Italian wines.

Do Leoni

Riva degli Schiavoni, Castello 4171. **Map** 8 D1. *041 520 05 33.* €€€€€

A hotel restaurant with a good reputation, Do Leoni has a terrace right on the Riva. The cooking is Venetian; the *scaloppina* with fresh artichokes being particularly good. The desserts' highlight is the *gelato al mascarpone* with hot spicy quince 'mostarda'.

DORSODURO

Taverna San Trovaso

Fondamenta Priuli, Dorsoduro 1016. **Map** 6 E3. *041 520 37 03.* *Mon.* €

This cheerful, bustling restaurant on two floors is between the Accademia and the Zattere. The cooking is straightforward, serving pizzas and pasta dishes.

Locanda Montin

Fondamenta Eremite, Dorsoduro 1147. **Map** 6 D3. *041 522 71 51.* *Wed.* ★ €€

This famous restaurant, with its artistic and literary connnections, can be variable in quality and service, but the garden is a delight and the atmosphere lively. It also contains a commercial art gallery.

Agli Alboretti

Rio Terrà Antonio Foscarini, Dorsoduro 884. **Map** 6 E4. *041 523 00 58.* *Jan; 3 weeks in Aug; Wed & Thu lunch.* €€€

Named after the trees outside, Agli Alboretti is welcoming inside and refreshing in summer, when you can eat outside under the pergola. The cooking has innovative touches – try saffron risotto with scampi and mussels, monkfish tails or veal with cherries.

Ai Gondolieri

San Vio, Dorsoduro 366. **Map** 6 F4. *041 528 63 96.* *Tue.* ★ €€€

Housed in a restored old inn, this restaurant is owned by Giovanni Trevisan. The menu is dedicated to regional cooking and its specialities include many excellent dishes, such as the radicchio from Treviso and *sformati* of wild leaves.

Cantinone Storico

Fondamenta Bragadin 660, Dorsoduro 774. **Map** 6 E4. *041 523 95 77.* *Nov; Sun.* €€€

Situated near the Accademia, this pleasant trattoria serves a wonderful *risotto terra mare* (a mix of seafood, vegetables and porcini mushrooms), complemented by a good selection of house wines.

Da Silvio

Calle San Pantalon, Dorsoduro 3748. **Map** 6 D2. *041 520 58 33.* *Sat lunch & Sun.* €€€€

This genuine neighbourhood restaurant has a lovely garden in which to eat outside during the summer. The menu has no surprises, but the food is all fresh and home-made.

CANNAREGIO

Ostaria da Rioba

Fondamenta delle Misericordia, Cannaregio 2553. **Map** 2 3F. *041 524 43 79.* *Mon.* €

At this pleasant restaurant, specialities include *Baccalà alla Vicentina* and fish risotto. The wine list is small but excellent.

Ostaria al Bacco

Fondamenta delle Cappuccine, Cannaregio 3054. **Map** 2 D2. *041 71 74 93.* *2 weeks in Jan, 2 weeks in Aug; Mon.* €€

This rustic restaurant serves mainly fish, with first courses including spaghetti with black cuttlefish sauce and *frittura di pesce* (lightly fried fish). *Baccalà* is also on the menu.

Vini Da Gigio

Fondamenta San Felice, Cannaregio 3628/a. **Map** 3 A4. *041 528 51 40.* *15 Jan–1st week Feb, 15 Aug–early Sep; Mon.* €€

Traditional Venetian food with a modern twist is prepared here. The *gnocchetti* with scampi and radicchio is excellent, and puddings include *crema fritta alla veneziana*. Booking is recommended.

Fiaschetteria Toscana

San Giovanni Grisostomo, Cannaregio 5719. **Map** 3 B5. *041 528 52 81.* *mid-Jul–mid-Aug; Mon lunch, Tue.* €€€

This restaurant offers many Venetian dishes. The warm salad of lagoon fish is a delicious antipasto, and main dishes include eels and turbot with black butter and capers.

THE LAGOON ISLANDS

Ai Pescatori

Via Galuppi 371, Burano. *041 73 06 50.* *1–15 Jan; Wed.* ★ €€€

All the food at Ai Pescatori is good, but some of the more interesting dishes include lobster and tagliolini with local artichokes or cuttlefish. In winter the menu is known for its game dishes. The wine list is extensive.

For key to symbols *see p235*

Antica Trattoria alla Maddalena

Mazzorbo 7/b, Burano. *041 73 01 51. Thu.* €€€

Close beside the *vaporetto* stop on Mazzorbo is this modest local bar and eating house. Venetians and visitors flock here to dine in tranquillity and savour the famous wild duck with fettuccine or polenta.

Do Mori

S. Eufemia, Giudecca 588. *041 522 54 52. 20 Dec–20 Jan, 1 week in Aug; Sat lunch, Sun.* ★ €€€

This rustic-style restaurant, on the Giudecca waterfront, is run by the former chef from Harry's Bar, but the prices at this establishment are much lower. The cooking is homely Venetian, featuring good antipasti, home-made pasta and fine fish dishes. The delicious puddings are also home-made.

Osteria al Ponte del Diavolo

Fondamenta Borgognoni 11, 30012 Torcello. *041 73 04 01. Wed in winter.* ★ €€€

The Osteria gets its name from the graceful bridge across Torcello's now neglected main canal. It was founded by a breakaway trio of staff from Cipriani, so the traditional fish-based menu is of a very high standard. The large terrace makes this an attractive spot.

Da Romano

Piazza Galuppi 221, Burano. *041 73 00 30. mid-Dec–early Feb; Tue.* €€€€

Founded in the 1930s, this pretty restaurant with its shady terrace on Burano's main street is now run by the original owner's son. It serves a selection of excellent fish dishes at lower prices than you would find in Venice.

Harry's Dolci

S. Eufemia, Giudecca 773. **Map** 5 C5. *041 522 48 44. late Mar–Oct. Tue.* ★ €€€€€

What started as a bar and tearoom is now a restaurant serving many of the specialities of the main establishment *(see p240)*. You can enjoy *pasta e fagioli* (pasta and beans), *carpaccio* (marinated slivers of raw beef) and liver, preceded by a Bellini and followed by the house chocolate cake. They also sell the range of Cipriani foodstuffs.

Hotel Cipriani

Giudecca 10. **Map** 7 C5. *041 520 77 44.* ★ *evenings. Nov–Mar.* €€€€€

The setting and style alone almost justify the prices of the Hotel Cipriani. The mirror-lined dining room reflects the lagoon and the summer terrace is an oasis of calm. The food is creative and the wine list good. Sample the antipasti buffet before moving on to the other specialities, which include a fish "surprise" in pastry.

Locanda Cipriani

Piazza Santa Fosca 29, Torcello. *041 73 01 50. Jan; Tue.* €€€€€

The most far-flung of the Cipriani establishments was transformed from a fishermans' inn in the 1930s. Dishes include *fritto misto*, and risotto made with fresh greens from the Locanda's picturesque kitchen garden. Lunch here makes a good outing, and the restaurant's launch will collect you from Piazza San Marco.

THE VENETO PLAIN

Asiago

Ristorante Casa Rossa

Road map C3. Via Kaberlaba 19, 36012. *0424 46 20 17. early Jun; Thu.* ★ €

Situated in the hills of the Sette Comuni (Seven Communities), this simple restaurant is noted for its regional cooking. Try the savoury cake with wild salad leaves, the duck breast and the wild berry tart. You can eat outside in the garden.

Asolo

Villa Cipriani

Road map D3. Via Canova 298, 31011. *0423 95 21 66.* FAX *0423 95 20 95.* ★ €€€€

This 16th-century villa houses one of the grand hotels of the Veneto *(see p231)*. The restaurant serves innovative and creative food, using local ingredients in such dishes as pappardelle (broad flat pasta) with scampi, tomatoes and basil, and veal medallions with asparagus and artichoke hearts.

Brenta Canal

Alla Posta

Road map D4. Via Ca' Tron 33, Dolo. *041 41 07 40. 1–15 Jan, 2 weeks Jun– Jul; Mon.* €€€€

The Modena family run this superb fish restaurant, which is housed in an old Venetian staging posthouse. The anchovy and potato tart is particularly good. There is also a good wine list.

Castelfranco

Barbesin

Road map D3. Via Montebelluna 41. *0423 49 04 46. 1–7 Jan, 7–21 Aug; Wed eve and Thu.* €

This restaurant is very good value indeed. It serves a variety of regional specialities, for example the risotto of porcini mushrooms and duck breast with rosemary.

Chioggia

El Gato

Road map D4. Campo San Andrea 653, 30015. *041 40 18 06. Jan–mid-Feb; Mon, weekday lunch.* ★ €€€€

It is the classic cooking in a restrained setting that makes this restaurant special. As you would expect in a fishing port, the emphasis is on seafood. The cuttlefish is cooked in the traditional Chioggian way and served with polenta.

Conegliano

Al Salisà

Road map D3. Via XX Settembre 2, 31015. *0438 242 88. Aug; Tue pm, Wed.* ★ €€

This elegant little restaurant is set in an old house and has a pretty veranda where diners can eat outside on warm evenings. Among the interesting dishes on offer here are home-made fettuccine served with a sauce of radicchio and chicken livers, and turbot cooked wrapped in spinach leaves. For a memorable finale, try the superlative cold zabaglione for pudding.

Euganean Hills

Trattoria da Piero Ceschi

Road map C4. Piazza Trento 16, 35042 Este. *0429 28 55.* *Thu.* €€

Located right in the historic centre of Este, this friendly little restaurant serves tripe soup, dark bigoli pasta with duck or sardines, stewed eel and other home-style regional dishes. The excellent wine list is from local producers.

La Montanella

Road map C4. Via Costa 33, 35032 Arqua Petrarca. *0429 71 82 00.* *Jan–mid-Feb, mid-Aug; Tue eve & Wed.* €€€

Petrarch spent the last years of his life at Arquà Petrarca, the prettiest of the Euganean spa towns *(see p184)*. Eating at La Montanella is a pleasure in itself, however, with a menu that includes asparagus tortelloni and guinea-fowl among its many treats. Dishes are served with local seasonal vegetables.

Mestre

Dall'Amelia

Road map D4. Via Miranesi 113, 30171 Mestre. *041 91 39 51.* *Wed.* €€€

This restaurant is considered to be one of the finest specializing in classic Venetian cooking. That there is a separate area for those eating fried fish is indicative of high standards delivered by this establishment. Among the house specialities are tagliolini with prawns and fresh seasonal vegetables, and porcini mushrooms with rocket. There is also an excellent choice of fresh fish recipes and mouth-watering puddings to be sampled here. The wine list is exceptional.

Ristorante Marco Polo

Road map C4. Via Forte Marghera 67, 30173 Mestre. *041 98 98 55.* *3 weeks in Aug; Sun.* €€€

Familiar dishes are given a personal interpretation in the Ristorante Marco Polo. John Dory with wild fennel, and swordfish with capers are recommended choices, while meat-eaters will not fail to enjoy the veal served with porcini mushrooms.

Oderzo

Gambrinus Parco

Road map E3. Località Gambrinus 22, 31020 San Polo di Piave. *0422 85 50 43.* *1–15 Jan; Mon (exc. public hols).* ★ €€€

This restaurant is faithful to the regional culinary tradition. Two of the outstanding fish dishes served here are the freshwater crayfish alla Gambrinus and the sturgeon cooked with coarse salt. The comprehensive wine list can provide the perfect accompaniment to the wonderful food served in this restaurant.

Padua

Osteria L'Anfora

Road map D4. Via dei Soncin 13, 35122. *049 65 66 29.* *1–6 Jan, 2 weeks in Aug; Sun.* €

This enticing restaurant serves traditional Venetian cuisine enlivened by influences originally brought to Venice by travelling Renaissance merchants.

La Braseria

Road map D4. Via N Tommaseo 48, 35100. *049 876 09 07.* *evenings in Aug; Sat lunch, Sun.* €€

This is a friendly restaurant where guests can enjoy good straightforward cooking at a very reasonable price. In particular the penne with porcini mushrooms and the smoked ham, called *speck*, are both highly recommended.

Belle Parti El Toulà

Road map D4. Via Belle Parti 11, 35100. *049 875 18 22.* *3 weeks in Aug; Sun.* €€€

This comfortable and distinguished restaurant is housed in a 16th-century *palazzo*. The selection of vegetable recipes, especially the mouthwatering aubergine *sformato*, is particularly good.

Boccadoro

Road map D4. Via della Resistenza 49, 35100 Noventa Padovana. *049 62 50 29.* *2–12 Jan, 4–27 Aug; Tue eve & Wed.* €€€

Good Paduan food is served in this family-run restaurant. There is an excellent radicchio soup and the goose is worth sampling.

Portogruaro

Duilio

Road map E3. Via Strada Nuova 19, 30021 Caorle. *0421 810 87.* *mid-Jan, Mon in winter.* ★ €€

In this roomy and very attractively priced restaurant, fish-based regional recipes are given an imaginative modern slant. Turbot is gently poached in champagne or used as a filling for the lightest of savoury pancakes.

Alla Botte

Road map E3. Viale Pordenone 46, 30026. *0421 76 01 22.* *Sun in winter.* ★ €€€

This cosy hotel restaurant serves good seasonal, local food, and the menu usually includes some recipes from the neighbouring area of Friuli, close to the Austrian border. The gnocchi flavoured with nettles are well worth trying.

Treviso

Agnoletti

Road map D3. Via della Vittoria 190, Giavera del Montello. *0422 77 60 09.* *1–15 Jul; Tue.* €€

The pretty hillside location north of Treviso and the lovely garden alone make this restaurant well worth a visit. Seasonal antipasti and the gnocchi are recommended.

Osteria dalla Pasina

Road map D3. Via Marie 3, Dosson di Casier. *0422 38 21 12.* *1 week at Christmas; Sun eve, Mon.* €€

This *osteria* offers tasty dishes that make the most of fresh, seasonal produce. The risotto with scampi and asparagus makes a good prelude to a main course of tender rabbit cooked with herbs, and there are deliciously light mousses and sorbets for pudding.

Toni del Spin

Road map D3. Via Inferiore 7, 31100. *0422 54 38 29.* W www.ristorantetonidelspin.com *Aug; Sun, Mon lunch.* €€

A homely restaurant offering good value, Toni's serves hearty regional fare. Typical house specialities include *pasta e fagioli* (pasta and beans), baked tripe and a rich tiramisù for dessert.

Ristorante alle Beccherie

Road map D3. Piazza Ancillotto 10, 31100. *0422 54 08 71.* *15–30 Jul; Sun eve & Mon.* €€€

The Beccherie, one of Treviso's oldest restaurants, is housed in an old Venetian-style building with period furniture. The guinea fowl with pepper sauce, served with a risotto of radicchio, is delicious.

Ristorante Enoteca Marchi

Road map D3. Via Castellana 177, Montebelluna. *0423 238 75.* *Mon.* ★ €€€

This restaurant is worth patronizing for the choice of wines alone – there are over 500 Italian and foreign wines. Try the lamb cooked in Prosecco or the spaghetti with radicchio and pomegranate.

Vicenza

Al Torresan

Road map C3. Via Zabarella 1, 36042 Breganze. *0445 87 32 60.* *end Jul–25 Aug; Thu.* €€

In the autumn locals flock here to enjoy the wild mushroom dishes. The cooking is hearty and is complemented by the local wines.

Ristorante Storione

Road map C4. Strada Pasubio 64, 36100. *0444 56 62 44.* *Sun.* €€

The Zorzo family run this charming restaurant with its pretty garden. Sturgeon *(storione)* is among the many fish specialities available here. Parents are encouraged to bring children.

Taverna Aeolia

Road map C4. Piazza C. Da Schio 1, 36023 Costozza di Longare. *0444 55 50 36.* *1–15 Nov; Tue.* €€

Luca Chemello, chef-patron at this elegant villa, creates wonderful dishes to complement the charm of the frescoed dining room. The menu changes monthly, but constant features include the delicious home-made filled pasta.

Trattoria Leoncino

Road map C4. Via Tavernelle 72, 36077 Altavilla Vicentina. *0444 57 20 32.* *27 Dec–10 Jan, Aug; Sun & Mon.* €€

This rustic restaurant just outside Vicenza is run by the Tecchio family. Good local dishes include the famous *bolliti misti* (boiled meats) served with a delicious herby sauce. There is also a buffet.

Cinzia e Valerio

Road map C4. Piazzetta Porta Padova 65/67, 36100. *0444 50 52 13.* *25 Dec–5 Jan, 3 weeks in Aug; Sun eve & Mon.* ★ €€€

This stylish restaurant within the old city walls serves nothing but fish. Featured on the menu are a myriad of culinary treats including marinated raw salmon, prawn risotto, delicate fillets of sole and lobster, mussels and clams.

Antica Trattoria Tre Visi

Road map C4. Corso Palladio 25, 36100. *0444 32 48 68.* *Jul; Sun eve & Mon.* €€€€

Housed in an old inn dating from the 1500s, this restaurant is in the historic town centre. Diners can see into the busy kitchen, where Luigi cooks good Vicentine dishes.

Verona and Lake Garda

Lake Garda South

Antica Locanda Mincio

Road map A4. Via Buonarroti 12, 37067 Valeggio sul Mincio. *045 795 00 59.* *2 weeks in Nov, 2 weeks in Feb; Wed & Thu.* €€€

The Locanda was once a staging post and is now a delightful dining spot with frescoed walls and open fireplaces. The "rustic" hors d'oeuvres are a good choice for a starter, and many of the main courses have a regional emphasis.

Trattoria Vecchia Lugana

Road map A4. Piazzale Vecchia Lugana 1, 25019 Lugana di Sirmione. *030 91 90 12.* *1 Jan–15 Feb; Mon & Tue.* ★ €€€€

Meat is cooked on the old open fire in the kitchen of this charming restaurant. You can sample a good range of local dishes, including lake fish and tender young kid served with polenta. The wine list is strong on Garda labels.

Esplanade

Road map A4. Via Lario 10, 25015 Desenzano del Garda. *030 914 33 61.* *Wed.* ★ €€€€€

At this waterside restaurant diners find imaginative food with firmly regional roots. Courgette flowers stuffed with scampi or a light lake-fish terrine make tempting first courses, while main courses include lamb with onions, potatoes and a rosemary sauce. The wine list has some interesting dessert wines.

Lake Garda West

Alla Campagnola

Road map A3. Via Brunati 11, 25087 Salò. *0365 221 53.* *3 weeks in Jan; Mon & Tue lunch.* €€

At this mother-and-son establishment, Elisa Dal Bom has revived some interesting traditional recipes. She serves an array of vegetables as an antipasto, and pasta stuffed with pumpkin or aubergine.

Capriccio

Road map A3. Piazza San Bernardo 6, Frazione Montinelle, 25080 Manerba del Garda. *0365 55 11 24.* *Jan–Feb; Tue.* €€€€

The terrace here has a fine view over the lake and hills and the menu offers a good choice of fish. Puddings include a delicate muscat-grape jelly with a peach sauce.

La Tortuga

Road map A3. Via 24 Maggio, Porticciolo di Gargnano, 25084 Gargnano del Garda. *0365 712 51.* *Jan–Feb; Mon eve (winter only) & Tue.* ★ €€€€€

La Tortuga has a charming lakeside location and light, imaginative food. Try the lake fish, such as *coregone*, served with tomatoes and capers.

Villa Fiordaliso

Road map A3. Corso Zanardelli 132, 25083 Gardone Riviera. *0365 201 58.* *Dec–Jan; Mon & Tue lunch.* ★ €€€€€

This stylish restaurant is housed in the villa that was the love-nest of Mussolini and Clara Petacci. In summer you can eat in the garden, which sweeps down to the lake, and enjoy creative cuisine from the best local ingredients.

Lake Garda East

Locanda San Vigilio Regina

Road map A3. Località San Vigilio, 37016 Garda. 045 725 66 88. *Nov–Mar.* ★ €€€

This restaurant is part of one of the loveliest hotels on Lake Garda. There is an antipasto buffet and an astounding range of fish dishes.

Verona

Al Bersagliere

Road map B4. Via Dietro Pallone 1, 37100. *045 800 48 24.* *Sun.* ★ €

An old wood-lined dining room makes a pleasant setting for some traditional Veronese cooking, such as mixed boiled meats and polenta with wild mushrooms.

El Cantinon

Road map B4. Via S Rochetto 11, 37100. *045 59 52 91.* *Wed.* €

The varied menu here changes frequently, but always features meats, seafood and goats' cheeses. Service in the wood-beamed dining room is excellent, as is the wine selection.

Ciccarelli

Road map B4. Via Mantovana 171, 37100. *045 95 39 86.* *3 weeks in Aug; Sat.* ★ €€

Ten minutes' drive from Verona, Ciccarelli's has been renowned for over 40 years. There are excellent grilled, roast and boiled meats, home-made pasta, and superb *crème caramel all'amaretto.*

Baba-jaga

Road map B4. Via Cabalao 11, 37030 Montecchia di Crosara. *045 745 02 22.* *Jan, 2 weeks in Aug; Sun eve & Mon.* €€€

This is a good choice in the Soave wine-producing area. The lengthy menu includes black truffle risotto, and fillet of sea bass.

Ristorante ai Teatri

Road map B4. Via S. Maria Rocca Maggiore 8. *045 801 2181.* *late.* ★ €€€€

Located just a few minutes walk from the Piazza Erbe, the Ai Teatre is a local favourite serving innovative food with excellent service. Menu changes seasonally.

Bottega del Vino

Road map B4. Via Scudo di Francia 3, 37100. *045 800 45 35.* *Tue (out of opera season).* €€€€€

A haunt of local wine-producers, the Bottega offers more than 800 wines. The food is good – specialities include a selection of antipasti.

Il Desco

Road map B4. Via dietro San Sebastiano 5/7, 37100. *045 59 53 58.* *25 Dec–10 Jan, 15–30 Jun; Sun, Mon (exc. Jul & Aug).* ★ €€€€€

Recognized as one of Italy's best, this restaurant, in a 16th-century *palazzo,* pays great attention to detail. The imaginative menu is full of temptations: potato cake with truffles, lobster risotto, leeks and glazed onions, and a delicious range of puddings.

THE DOLOMITES

Belluno

Antica Locanda al Cappello

Road map D2. Piazza Papa Luciani 20, 32026 Mel. *0437 75 36 51.* *2 weeks in Jul; Tue eve, Wed (exc. Aug & Christmas).* ★ €

Antique furniture complements the frescoed rooms of this stylish restaurant, which is situated on a beautiful late-Renaissance piazza. The selection of interesting dishes includes poppy-seed gnocchi and ravioli stuffed with wild spinach. Game is often on the menu too.

Dolada

Road map D2. Via Dolada 21, 32010 Pieve d'Alpago, Località Lois. *0437 47 91 41.* *Mon, Tue lunch (exc. Jul & Aug).* ★ €€€

An obscure village on the slopes of Monte Dolada is home to one of Italy's great restaurants. Enzo and Rossana de Pra's reputation is well-founded. Deer in red wine and contrefilet of beef with thyme are served with imaginative vegetables and superb wines.

Locanda San Lorenzo

Road map D2. Via IV Novembre 79, 32015 Puos d'Alpago. *0437 45 40 48.* *2 weeks Jan–Feb; Wed (exc. Aug).* ★ €€€€

Trout, rabbit, duck and pigeon are served at this hotel restaurant in a hillside village above the lake of Santa Croce. The Dal Farra brothers are the chefs and take justifiable pride in their regional cooking with a modern slant.

Cadore Area

Al Capriolo

Road map D1. Via Nazionale 108, 32040 Vodo di Cadore. *0435 48 92 07.* *May–mid-Jun, Oct; Tue (exc. Jul & Aug); Wed lunch in winter.* ★ €€

You will find excellent game, including venison and elk, at this restaurant which is situated in stunning surroundings in the heart of the Dolomites. As a bonus, truffles are used for flavouring.

Dal Cavalier

Road map E1. Località Cima Gogna, 32041 Auronzo di Cadore. *0435 98 34.* *Wed (exc. Jul), Aug & Christmas.* ★ €€

The Munerin family run this mountain restaurant, which has period furniture and a large collection of copper pots. Good dishes include braised venison with wild mushrooms. The wine list is very strong on hard-to-find regional wines.

Cortina d'Ampezzo

Ristorante El Zoco

Road map D2. Via Cademai 18, 32043. *0436 86 00 41.* *May, Nov; Mon (low season).* ★ €€€

Game, particularly chamois meat, features in the culinary repertoire here. The vegetable dishes are of a high standard, especially the *sformato* of Trevisan radicchio and the grilled wild mushrooms.

El Toulà

Road map D1. Via Ronco 123, 32043. *0436 33 39.* *Easter–mid-Jul, mid-Sep–mid-Dec; Mon.* ★ €€€€€

You can eat on the terrace of this rustic but chic restaurant, which was originally a hay barn. The food is sophisticated and good, and includes dishes such as basil crêpes, veal, duck, and a range of delicious puddings. Wine is only available by the bottle.

For key to symbols *see p235*

Bars and Cafés in Venice

Many bars in Venice draw their trade from tourists and are busy throughout the day, as visitors ease their aching feet and consult their guide-books. Custom is swelled mid-morning and around lunchtime as the Venetians drop in for a drink or snack. Cafés range from basic one-room bars patronized by local workmen, to opulent coffee houses in old-world style, such as **Caffè Quadri** and **Caffè Florian**. Even the humblest establishment provides a continuous range of refreshments and you can enjoy anything from a morning coffee or lunchtime beer, to an aperitif or a final brandy before bed. Bars also serve snacks throughout their opening hours: freshly baked morning pastries and lunchtime sandwiches, rolls, cakes, biscuits and sometimes home-made ice cream. Wine bars often have a wide range of traditional Venetian snacks, and so make good places to stop for lunch.

Bars

Italians will often stop for breakfast in a bar on their way to work. This normally consists of a *cappuccino* (milky coffee) and a *brioche* (a plain, jam- or cream-filled pastry). **Pasticceria Dal Mas**, on the main route from the station to the Rialto, is much favoured by early morning commuters.

A wide range of alcoholic drinks is on offer, and you can ask for a glass of wine or beer on tap. Beer from the keg is called *birra alla spina* and comes in three different sizes: *piccola, media* and *grande.* Italian and imported bottled beers are also available, though the latter can be expensive. All bars serve glasses of mineral water and it is acceptable to request a glass of tap water *(acqua del rubinetto),* which will be free. Most bars also serve delicious freshly squeezed fruit juices *(una spremuta)* and milk-shakes made with fruit *(un frullato).* Italian bottled juices are good and are available in delicious flavours such as apricot and pear.

All bars serve a range of sandwiches *(tramezzini)* and filled rolls *(panini),* and often have toasted sandwiches and pizzas as well. Some double as cake-shops *(pasticceria),* and these have a tempting range of calorie-filled delights on display to eat in or take away. If you are near the Accademia, seek out the tiny **Pasticceria Vio** for wonderful cakes, or for an expensive treat, go to **Harry's Dolci** on the Giudecca *(see p241).*

Bear in mind that sitting down to drink in a bar or café can cost a lot more than standing at the bar, as there is a table charge, which can be high. This rises proportionally as you draw nearer San Marco. Some bars, particularly in the less tourist-frequented areas, have a stand-up counter only. All have a lavatory *(il bagno* or *il gabinetto),* though you may have to ask at the desk for the key. It is also worth noting that bars and cafés tend to shut earlier here than in other parts of Italy, particularly in winter.

The normal procedure is to choose what you want to eat or drink, then ask for it and pay at the cashdesk. You will be given a receipt *(lo scontrino)* which you present at the bar. If they are busy, a small tip will usually speed things up. If you decide to sit down, either inside or at an outside table, your order will be taken by a waiter who will bring the bill when he delivers the drinks. You should expect to pay double or more for this, but you can stretch your drink out for as long as you like.

Wine Bars

There is an old tradition in Venice called *cichetti e l'ombra,* meaning "a little bite and the shade". The little bite ranges from a slice of bread and *prosciutto crudo* (raw cured ham), meatballs or fried vegetables, to sardines and *baccalà* (salt cod). The shade is a glass of wine, so called because the gondoliers used to snatch a glass in the shade away from the glare of the sun on the water. Wine bars serving these snacks and a range of wines are numerous and heavily populated by locals. Many, such as **Do Mori**, are in the crowded alleys off the Rialto, but one of the nicest is the **Cantina del Vino già Schiavi** near the Ponte San Trovaso.

Cafés and Ice Cream Parlours

Coffee houses have played their part in the history of the Veneto – notably Padua's Caffè Pedrocchi *(see p178)* – and a visit to Venice would not be complete without a drink at the historic **Caffè Florian** or **Caffè Quadri**. It is a hard decision whether to take a table outside and watch the crowds or to experience the elegant charm of the interior rooms, with their atmosphere of past eras. The prices are sky-high, but you can take your time and be entertained by the resident orchestras.

Harry's Bar *(see p92),* is another world-famous bar and café. In summer it is crammed with foreigners and the prices are always high, but for a treat, sip a Bellini, a mixture of Prosecco and fresh white peach juice, in the place where it was invented.

The cafés along the Zattere, with their lovely views across the Giudecca Canal, make good places to pause, and the prices are much lower. Many Venetian squares have cafés with tables outside. There are several in the Campo Santo Stefano, or try **Bar Colleoni** in Campo Santi Giovanni e Paolo (San Zanipolo). **Il Caffè** is the nicest in Campo Santa Margherita.

Venetian ice cream is definitely among the best in Italy, with ice cream shops *(gelaterie)* serving a wide selection of seasonal flavours, some unique to Venice. The Venetians eat ice cream all year round, often instead of pudding or as the finale to the evening stroll, or *passeggiata.* It comes as either a cone *(un cono)* or a cup *(una coppa)* and it is normal to have at least three flavours. **Paolin** on Campo Santo Stefano is one of the best ice cream shops. You could also try **Il Doge**, which is in Campo Santa Margherita, and **Nico** on the Zattere, where you will find *gianduiotto,* a rich chocolate-based Venetian speciality. Make certain you buy ice cream made on the premises, *artigianato* or *produzione propria,* and experiment with what is clearly seasonal; the high-summer fruit ices such as melon, peach and apricot are refreshing and mouthwatering.

Directory

San Marco

Bar Gelateria Paolin
Campo Santo Stefano, San Marco 2962A. **Map** 6 F3.

Caffè Florian
Piazza San Marco, San Marco 56/59. **Map** 7 B2.

Caffè Quadri
Piazza San Marco, San Marco 120–24. **Map** 7 B2.

Harry's Bar
Calle Vallaresso, San Marco 1323. **Map** 7 B3.

Hostaria ai Rusteghi
Campiello del Tentor, San Marco 5513. **Map** 7 B1.

Osteria Terrà Assassini
Rio Terrà degli Assassini, San Marco 3695. **Map** 7 A2.

Rosa Salva
Calle Fiubera, San Marco 951. **Map** 7 B1.

Vino Vino
Ponte delle Veste, San Marco 2007. **Map** 7 A3.

San Polo and Santa Croce

Al Prosecco
C. San Giacomo dell'Orio, S. Croce 1503. **Map** 2 E5.

Bar Dogale
Campo dei Frari, San Polo 3012. **Map** 6 E1.

Do Mori
Calle Do Mori, San Polo 429. **Map** 3 A5.

Castello

Bar Colleoni
Campo Santi Giovanni e Paolo, Castello 6811. **Map** 3 C5.

Bar Gelateria Riviera
Ponte de la Pietà, Riva degli Schiavoni 4153. **Map** 8 D2.

Bar Mio
Via Garibaldi, Castello 1820. **Map** 8 F3.

Bar Orologio
Campo Santa Maria Formosa, Castello 6130. **Map** 7 C1.

Caffè al Cavallo
Campo Santi Giovanni e Paolo, Castello 6823. **Map** 3 C5.

La Boutique del Gelato
Campo San Lio, Castello 5727. **Map** 7 B1.

Snack & Sweet
Salizzada San Lio, Castello 5689. **Map** 7 B1.

Dorsoduro

Accademia Foscarini
Rio Terra A Foscarini, Dorsoduro 878/C. **Map** 6 E4.

Ai do Draghi
Calle della Chiesa, Dorsoduro 3665. **Map** 6 F4.

Al Chioschetto Zattere
Dorsoduro 1406A. **Map** 6 D4.

Bar Gelateria Causin
Campo Santa Margherita, Dorsoduro 2995. **Map** 6 D2.

Bar Gelateria Il Doge
Campo Santa Margherita, Dorsoduro 3058A. **Map** 6 D2.

Bar Gelateria Nico
Zattere ai Gesuati, Dorsoduro 922. **Map** 6 D4.

Bar Pasticceria Vio
Rio Terrà della Toletta, Dorsoduro 1192. **Map** 6 D3.

Cantina del Vino già Schiavi
Ponte San Trovaso, Dorsoduro 992. **Map** 6 E4.

Il Caffè
Campo Santa Margherita, Dorsoduro 2963. **Map** 6 D3.

Soto Sopra
Calle San Pantalon, Dorsoduro 3740. **Map** 6 D2.

Cannaregio

Alla Bomba
Calle dell'Oca, Cannaregio 4297. **Map** 3 A5.

Bar Algiubagio
Fondamente Nuove, Cannaregio 5039. **Map** 3 C4.

Bar Gelateria Solda
Campo Santi Apostoli, Cannaregio 4440. **Map** 3 B5.

Caffè Pasqualigo
Salizzada Santa Fosca, Cannaregio 2288. **Map** 2 F4.

Enoteca Boldrin
San Canciano, Cannaregio 5550. **Map** 3 B5.

Il Gelatone
Rio Terrà Maddalena, Cannaregio 2063. **Map** 2 F3.

Osteria da Alberto
Calle Larga Giacinto Gallina, Cannaregio 5401. **Map** 3 C5.

Pasticceria Dal Mas
Lista di Spagna, Cannaregio 150/A. **Map** 2 D4.

The Lagoon Islands

Bar della Maddalena
Mazzorbo.

Bar Ice
Campo San Donato, Murano. **Map** 4 F2.

Bar La Palanca
Fondamenta Santa Eufemia, Giudecca 448. **Map** 6 D5.

Bar Palmisano
Via Baldassare Galuppi, Burano.

Bar Trono di Attila
Torcello.

Harry's Dolci
Fondamenta San Biagio, Giudecca 773. **Map** 6 D5.

Lo Spuntino
Via Baldassare Galuppi, Burano.

Shops and Markets

THE NARROW STREETS of Venice are lined with beautifully arranged windows that cannot fail to tempt shoppers, and the city has the additional bonus of being truly pedestrianized. Few cities of similar size have such a wide variety of goods to browse through as you explore the fascinating and diverse neighbourhoods. There is still a strong artisan tradition in Venice, and alongside glass and lace you will find high-quality fashion and leather goods, antiques and jewellery. In the Veneto, which is one of Italy's most prosperous regions, every town boasts a wide range of shops, and many have seasonal speciality markets. In country areas you can buy wine and olive oil direct from the producers.

Piece of traditional Murano glass

Display of jewellery in a shop window in the Frezzeria

When to Shop

GENERALLY, SHOPS open around 9 or 9:30am and close for lunch at 12:30 or 1pm, with the exception of food shops and markets, which are in business from 8am. In the afternoon stores are open from 3:30pm to 7:30pm in winter, and 4pm to 8pm in summer. In Venice, many stores aimed directly at tourists are open all day and even on Sundays, as are big out-of-town supermarkets and hypermarkets – useful if you are self-catering in the region.

Monday is usually the traditional closing day in northern Italy though, again, this does not apply to all shops in Venice itself. The smaller towns in the Veneto often have very variable opening hours, with perhaps food shops closing on Mondays but ironmongers and clothes shops closing on Wednesdays. Shops and markets in the Veneto are often closed for two or three weeks during the national holiday time in August.

The best time for finding bargains is during the January and July sales: look out for window signs with the words *saldi* or *sconti*.

Where to Shop in Venice

THE GLITTERING Mercerie *(see p95)*, which runs from Piazza San Marco to the Rialto, has been the main shopping street since the Middle Ages and, together with the parallel Calle dei Fabbri, is still a honey pot for the crowds. West of San Marco, the zigzagging Frezzeria is full of interesting and unusual shops. The main route from the Piazza to the Accademia Bridge is lined with up-market speciality stores, while the streets north of Campo Santo Stefano *(see p93)* are another excellent trawling ground for quality souvenirs and gifts.

Across the Grand Canal, the narrow streets from the Rialto southwest towards Campo San Polo *(see p101)* are lined with a wide variety of less expensive stores, while near the station the bustling Lista di Spagna and the route along the Strada Nova towards the Rialto cater for the everyday needs of ordinary Venetians.

The islands of Murano and Burano *(see pp150–51)* are *the* places to buy traditional glass and lace.

A colourful display of T-shirts with the "Venezia" logo

How to Pay

MAJOR CREDIT cards are usually accepted in the main stores for larger purchases, but cash is preferred for small items, and smaller shops will want cash. Travellers' cheques are also accepted, though the rate that you will get is less favourable than at a bank.

By law, shopkeepers should give you a receipt *(ricevuta fiscale)*, which you should keep until you are some distance away from the store (legally this is 600 m). If a purchased item is defective, most shops will change the article or give you a credit note, as long as you show the till receipt. Cash refunds are not usually given.

VAT Exemption

VISITORS FROM non-European Union countries can reclaim the 19 per cent sales tax (IVA) on goods exceeding €160 from the same shop. Ask for an invoice when you buy the goods and inform the shop that you intend to reclaim the tax. The invoice must be stamped at customs as you leave Italy. The shop will reimburse the tax in euros once they have received the stamped invoice.

Designer clothes shop in Treviso

Fashion and Accessories

In Venice, the big names in fashion are all found near San Marco. **Armani**, **Laura Biagiotti**, **Missoni** and **Valentino** all have stylish shops just off the Piazza. For really innovative and outrageous designs visit **Fiorella** in Campo Santo Stefano. The stalls at the foot of the Ponte delle Guglie on Strada Nuova sell a range of good value leather shoes and a wide variety of traditional Venetian slippers in a stunning range of colourful velours. For a genuine gondolier's shirt, take a look in **Emilio Ceccato**.

A typical Venetian mask

Fabrics and Interior Design

Venice has long been famed for sumptuous brocades, fine silks and figured velvets. **Trois** sells silks by the metre, including the gossamer-fine pleated silks invented by Fortuny for his Delphos dresses *(see p94)*, and **Valli** has wonderful designer silks and other fabrics in its shop in the Mercerie. The famous house of **Rubelli** has a shop on Campo San Gallo. Here you will find a variety of rich brocades and velvets. **Color Casa**, in San Polo, has equally lovely textiles at slightly lower prices, and **Jesurum**, not far from the Bridge of Sighs, is the place to go for beautiful fine linens. They also sell seductive lingerie. The Lido's Gran Viale has a number of stylish shops that are devoted to modern interior design and which sell beautiful objects for the home.

Masks and Costumes

You can buy cheap, mass-produced masks all over the city, but a genuine one is a good souvenir, and you will be spoilt for choice. **Laboratorio Artigiano Maschere** in Castello revived traditional mask-making and their designs are absolutely stunning. Near Campo San Polo **Tragicomica** sells costumes and masks, as well as Commedia dell'Arte figures. You will find these at **Leon d'Oro** on the Frezzeria too, where they also make string puppets. Dorsoduro has several workshops; **Mondonovo**, just off Campo Santa Margherita, has a marvellous selection of masks and costumes.

In the weeks leading up to Carnival, maskmakers are, of course, extremely busy, but at other times of the year many workshops welcome visitors and are pleased to show you their craft *(see p31)*.

Glass

The best place to buy glass is on the island of Murano, where it has been made since the 13th century *(see p151)*. All the main manufacturers have their furnaces and showrooms here, catering to mainstream taste. Some manufacturers also have showrooms in Venice itself.

On Murano, **Seguso** and **Barovier e Toso** make glass to traditional designs with good simple lines. You will find similarly attractive pieces in Venice at **Paolo Rossi**, where they specialize in reproductions of antique glass. **Pauly** and **Venini** both have shops near San Marco; they represent the top end of the market and some of their designs are very pleasing.

Jewellery

Venice's smartest jewellers are **Missiaglia** and **Nardi**, both in the arcades of Piazza San Marco. Shops on the Rialto Bridge sell cheaper designs, and this is a good place to find bracelets and chains, whose price is determined by the weight of the gold. For inexpensive, pretty Venetian glass earrings, necklaces and bracelets try **FGB** in Campo Santa Maria Zobenigo.

Wide range of fruit and vegetables for sale in the Rialto market

A typical general food store in the San Marco area

Department Stores

Department stores are not as common in Italy as in many other countries. The main chain store in Venice is Coin, which sells everything from umbrellas to tableware. Oviesse and Upim are cheaper supermarket-style options. You will find branches of these in other towns in the Veneto.

Treasure trove in one of the art shops on Murano

Books and Gifts

The best general bookshop in Venice is **Goldoni**, which also sells maps. **Filippi Editori Venezia** stocks facsimile editions of old books and books about Venice. **Fantoni** is a specialist art bookshop, and English books are sold at **Cafoscarina 2**, **Libreria Serenissima** and **Libreria Emiliana**.

Hand-made marbled and dragged paper are typically Venetian, and used as book covers and made up into writing desk equipment. The **Legatoria Piazzesi** sells stationery items. **Paolo Olbi** has a wide range of papers, while **Alberto Valese-Ebru** uses a distinctive marbling technique on fabrics as well as paper. For watercolour views of Venice, try the stalls in Campo dei Santi Apostoli.

The San Barnaba area has several art and craft shops where you can buy unusual gifts and souvenirs. **Signor Blum** on the Campo San Barnaba has charming carved and painted wooden objects and toys. Another carver, **Livio de Marchi**, makes large whimsical wooden ornaments. **La Bottega dell'Arte** sells interesting paper objects and masks. For unusual soaps and other toiletries browse in **Il Melograno**, a herbalist in Campo Santa Margherita.

Markets and Food Shops

One of the delights of Venice is a morning spent exploring the food markets and shops around the Rialto. Fruit and vegetable stalls sprawl to the west of the bridge and the Pescheria, or fish market, lies right beside the Grand Canal *(see p100)*. The neighbouring streets are full of unusual and excellent food shops. Olive oil, vinegar and dried pasta, which comes in many colours, shapes and flavours, are all good choices if you are looking for food to take home. **Aliani (Casa del Parmigiano)** is a superlative cheese shop right by the vegetable market, where you can also buy a selection of fresh pasta, salamis and ready-made dishes for a picnic.

Round the corner, on Ruga Rialto, the **Drogheria Mascari** has a fine range of coffees, teas, dried fruits, and nuts. **Pasticceria Marchini** is Venice's best pasticceria, selling traditional sweetmeats as well as cakes and biscuits.

Viale Santa Maria Elisabetta, the main shopping street of the Lido

DIRECTORY

FASHION AND ACCESSORIES

Emilio Ceccato
Sottoportico di Rialto, San Polo 16/17. **Map** 7 A1.
041 522 27 00.

Emporio Armani
Calle dei Fabbri, San Marco 989. **Map** 7 B2.
041 523 78 08.

Fiorella Gallery
Campo Santo Stefano, San Marco 2806. **Map** 6 F3.
041 520 92 28.

Laura Biagiotti
Calle Larga XXII Marzo, San Marco 2400–2401. **Map** 7 A3.
041 520 34 01.

Missoni
Calle Vallaresso, San Marco 1312. **Map** 7 B3.
041 520 57 33.

Valentino
Salizzada San Moisè, San Marco 1473. **Map** 7 A3.
041 520 57 33.

Stalls at the foot of Ponte delle Guglie
Strada Nuova, Cannaregio. **Map** 2 D3.

FABRICS AND INTERIOR DESIGN

Annelie
Calle Lunga San Barnaba, Dorsoduro 2748. **Map** 6 D3.
041 520 32 77.

Color Casa
Calle della Madonneta, San Polo 1990. **Map** 6 F1.
041 523 60 71.

Jesurum
Mercerie del Capitello, San Marco 4857. **Map** 7 B2.
041 520 61 77.

Rubelli
Campo San Gallo, San Marco 1089. **Map** 7 B2.
041 523 61 10.

Trois
Campo San Maurizio, San Marco 2666. **Map** 6 F3.
041 522 29 05.

Valli
Merceria San Zulian, San Marco 783. **Map** 7 B1.
041 522 57 18.

MASKS AND COSTUMES

Balo Coloc
Santa Maria Mater Domini, San Croce 2134. **Map** 2 F5.
041 524 05 51.

Laboratorio Artigiano Maschere
Barbaria delle Tole, Castello 6657. **Map** 4 D5.
041 522 31 10.

Leon d'Oro
Frezzeria, San Marco 1770. **Map** 7 A2.
041 520 33 75.

Mondonovo
Rio Terrà Canal, Dorsoduro 3063. **Map** 6 D3.
041 528 73 44.

Tragicomica
Calle dei Nomboli, San Polo 2800. **Map** 6 F1.
041 72 11 02.

GLASS

Barovier e Toso
Fondamenta Vetrai 28, Murano. **Map** 4 E3.
041 73 90 49.

Paolo Rossi
Campo San Zaccaria, Castello 4685. **Map** 8 C2.
041 523 00 90.

Pauly
Calle Larga, Ponte dei Consorzi, San Marco. **Map** 7 C2.
041 520 98 99.

Seguso
Fondamenta Vetrai 143, Murano. **Map** 4 E2.
041 73 94 23.

Venini
Piazzetta dei Leoncini, San Marco 314. **Map** 7 B2.
041 522 40 45.

JEWELLERY

FGB
Campo Santa Maria Zobenigo, San Marco 2514. **Map** 7 C1.
041 523 65 56.

Missiaglia
Procuratie Vecchie, San Marco 125. **Map** 7 B2.
041 522 44 64.

Nardi
Procuratie Nuove, Piazza San Marco, San Marco 69/71. **Map** 7 B2.
041 522 57 33.

BOOKS AND GIFTS

Alberto Valese-Ebru
Campiello Santo Stefano, San Marco 3471. **Map** 6 F3. *041 523 88 30.*

Cafoscarina 2
Calle Foscari, Dorsoduro 3259. **Map** 6 D2
041 522 18 65

Cartoleria Accademia
Rio Terrà Carità, Dorsoduro 1044. **Map** 6 E3.
041 520 70 86.

Cartoleria Testolini
Fondamenta Orseolo, San Marco 1744. **Map** 7 A2.
041 522 30 85.

Daniela Porto
Rio Terrà dei Nomboli, San Polo 2753. **Map** 6 E1.
041 523 13 68.

Erborista Il Melograno
Campo Santa Margherita, Dorsoduro 2999. **Map** 6 D2. *041 528 51 17.*

Fantoni
Salizzada San Luca, San Marco 4119. **Map** 7 A2.
041 522 07 00.

Filippi Editori Venezia
Calle Casselleria, Castello 5284. **Map** 7 C1.
041 523 69 16.

Goldoni
Calle dei Fabbri, San Marco 4742. **Map** 7 A1.
041 522 23 84.

La Bottega dell'Arte
Ponte San Barnaba, Dorsoduro 2806. **Map** 6 D3.
041 523 08 25.

Legatoria Piazzesi
Campiello della Feltrina, San Marco 2511. **Map** 6 F3. *041 522 12 02.*

Libreria Emiliana
Calle Goldoni, San Marco 4487. **Map** 7 A2.
041 522 07 93.

Libreria Serenissima
Calle delle Bande, Castello 5377. **Map** 7 B1.
041 520 09 19.

Libreria della Toletta
Sacca della Toletta, Dorsoduro 1214. **Map** 6 D3. *041 523 20 34.*

Livio de Marchi
Salizzada San Samuele, San Marco 3157/A. **Map** 6 E2. *041 528 56 94.*

Paolo Olbi
Calle della Mandola, San Marco 3653. **Map** 6 F2.
041 528 50 25.

Signor Blum
Campo San Barnaba, Dorsoduro 2840. **Map** 6 D3.
041 522 63 67.

FOOD SHOPS

Aliani (Casa del Parmigiano)
Erberia Rialto, San Polo 214/5. **Map** 3 A5.
041 520 65 25.

Drogheria Mascari
Ruga Rialto, Calle dei Spezieri San Polo 381. **Map** 3 A5. *041 522 97 62.*

Pasticceria Marchini
Spadaria, San Marco 676. **Map** 6 F3.
041 522 91 09.

What to Buy in the Veneto

GLASS IS THE MOST POPULAR Venetian souvenir, but there are many other possibilities, ranging from Carnival masks and ceramics to fabrics and lace. For food lovers there is a wide selection of local olive oils, honey, wines and preserves. In the Veneto many food producers sell direct to the public, while different craft and food specialities are found in individual towns and islands.

Modern vase of opaque glass

Traditional glass with gold overlay

Two-coloured goblet

Venetian Glass

In traditional rich colours of blue and claret, or in striking modern designs, you will find anything from scent bottles to chandeliers.

Gift box covered in marbled paper

Address book

Venetian Marbled Paper

Marbled paper is a Venetian speciality. The sheets of paper are dipped into liquid gum before adding the paint. You can buy a large range of stationery items covered in the paper, as well as paper by the individual sheet. Each sheet of marbled paper is unique.

Pretty trinket box

Sheets of marbled paper

Decorated ceramic vase from Bassano

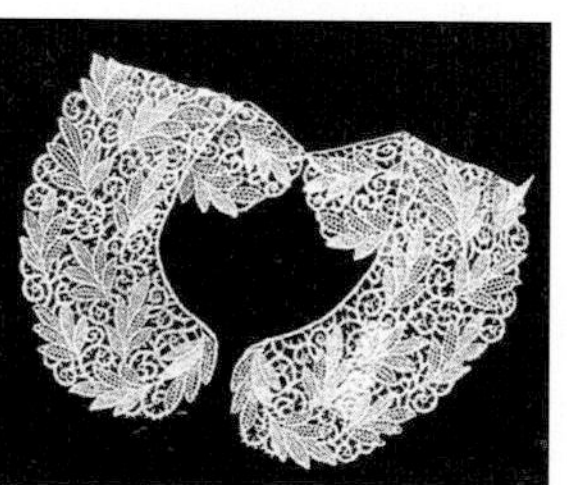

Delicate lace collar from Burano

Crafts from the Veneto

The ancient patterns of Burano lace are used to great advantage on table linen and to trim exquisite lingerie. Hand-painted vases, plates and bowls are produced in the picturesque old town of Bassano del Grappa.

Silver spoon with Venetian lion finial

Red and gold mask

Masks *(see pp30–31)*
Mask designs range from Commedia dell'Arte motifs to modern abstracts from young designers, and many are intricate and colourful. They are available all year, but at Carnival time you can buy them from street stalls.

Carnival mask

Colourful child's sweater

Velvet slippers

Clothing
As everywhere in Italy, stylish designer shops abound. Clothes for children are particularly bright and inventive. Velvet slippers, which are made in rich jewel-like colours, are worn at home as well as to dress up in at Carnival time.

Pasta
Attractively packaged dried pasta comes in many colours, shapes and flavours. Tomato, herb and spinach are the most popular varieties, but beetroot, garlic, artichoke, salmon, squid, and even chocolate can also be found in many shops.

Artichoke

Beetroot

Squid

Pasta shapes

Balsamic vinegar and extra virgin olive oil

Panettone

Amaretto biscuits

Delicacies from the Veneto
Panettone is the light yeast cake, flavoured with vanilla and studded with currants and candied peel, that is traditionally eaten at Christmas. Other local delicacies include olive oil from the shores of Lake Garda, vinegars, mountain honey from Belluno, fruit-flavoured liqueurs, grappa from Bassano (see p166)*, and after-dinner Amaretto biscuits.*

Orange liqueur

Lime liqueur

Pear liqueur

Entertainment in the Veneto

Venice was once one of Europe's liveliest night-time cities, and today it still has an impressive range of special events throughout the year. At every season there are some splendid festivals unique to Venice, and in late summer the normal city diet of opera, theatre and concerts is augmented by the International Film Festival and the Biennale, which rank among the best world-class cultural events. The day-to-day evening entertainment in Venice itself now tends to be far less frenetic than in the heyday of the Republic *(see pp46–7)*, but there are a few clubs and discos, and many more across the causeway in Mestre. Or you could have a little flutter at the casino.

Poster advertising the Film Festival

Whatever you choose, your enjoyment will be enhanced by the idyllic backdrop of Venice itself. The ultimate and quintessential Venetian romantic experience is, of course, a gondola ride by moonlight *(see p276)*. However, an evening's entertainment could more usually comprise the traditional stroll, or *passeggiata*, followed by a drink at a bar or café in one of the squares or amid the floodlit splendours of the Piazza San Marco.

Practical Information

Information about what's on in Venice can be found in *Leo Bussola*, a free bilingual Italian and English booklet published quarterly by the Tourist Board. Another publication, *Un Ospite di Venezia* (A Guest in Venice), is produced by the Hotels' Association. This comes out fortnightly during the summer and monthly in the winter, and is available from most hotels. The Venetian newspaper *Il Gazzettino* also lists cinema performances, rock concerts and discos under *Spettacoli*. Posters advertising forthcoming cultural events are displayed all over town.

For details of events and festivities in the other towns and cities in the Veneto, ask at the local tourist offices. Regional newspapers also often have listings of what is on in their area.

Music and coffee at Florian's café, Piazza San Marco *(see p246)*

Booking Tickets

Booking in advance is not part of the Italian lifestyle, where decisions are made on the spur of the moment. If you want to be certain of a seat you will have to visit the box office in person, as they usually do not take bookings over the telephone. You may also have to pay an advance booking supplement, or *prevendita,* which is usually about 10 per cent of the price of the seat.

The price of a theatre ticket starts at about €16, though prices are likely to be five times as much for star-name performances. Tickets for popular music concerts are normally sold through record and music shops whose names are displayed on the publicity posters.

Whereas tickets for classical concerts are sold on the spot for that day's performance, opera tickets are booked months ahead. There are very few ticket touts, so it is almost impossible to obtain tickets when the box office has sold out. The **Goldoni** box office is open 10am–1pm and 3–7pm.

La Fenice opera house before the 1996 fire *(see p93)*

Cinema and the Film Festival

There are four cinemas in Venice, mainly showing dubbed versions of international films. These are known as *prima visione* (first run). The **Rossini** and the **Giorgione Movie d'Essai** show "art-house" films and Giorgione also shows films in English. You will find these listed in *Il Gazzettino.*

The annual Film Festival, which takes place in August and September, is one of the major world cinema showcases and has been running since 1932. Screenings are held in the **Palazzo del Cinema** on the Lido, and in several cinemas in Venice itself. Tickets are sold to the public direct from the cinema on the day of performance. Programmes can be obtained in advance from the tourist office, and you will see posters for the festival all over the city.

Gondolier serenading on the Grand Canal

Music and Theatre

Like many Italian cities, Venice makes good use of the most magnificent churches as concert halls. La Pietà *(see p112)* was Vivaldi's own church and is still used for concerts, as are the churches of the Frari *(see pp102–3)* and Santo Stefano *(see p93).*

Other concerts are held from time to time in Scuola di San Giovanni Evangelista *(see p104)* and the Palazzo Prigioni Vecchie, the old prison attached to the Doge's Palace *(see pp84–9).* In the summer, the garden of Ca' Rezzonico *(see p126)* is also used as an outdoor concert hall, as is the Doge's Palace's courtyard, albeit occasionally.

Outdoor entertainment in the courtyard of the Doge's Palace

Unfortunately, La Fenice *(see p93),* one of Italy's most charming opera houses and the main local venue for major operas, suffered a disastrous fire in early 1996. Rebuilding is well under way but, in the meantime, opera can be seen at **PalaFenice**, a marquee-like theatre at the island of Tronchetto, or at **Teatro Malibran**.

Venice's principal theatre is **Teatro Goldoni** where, not surprisingly, the repertoire is mainly drawn from the 250 or more comic works written by the Venetian dramatist Carlo Goldoni (1707–93). Most performances are staged in Italian and run from November to June.

At Carnival time in February *(see pp30–31),* the whole city takes on a party atmosphere as it is invaded by merry-makers in fancy dress. Many theatrical and musical events take place, both in theatres and in the streets and *campi.*

Facilities for the Disabled

Access for disabled people is difficult everywhere in Venice, and theatres are no exception, although concerts are often held in easily accessible churches. PalaFenice and Teatro Malibran guarantee obstacle-free entrance for the disabled if contacted one week in advance (fax: 041 786 50). For more advice, see page 261.

Masked reveller at Carnival time *(see pp30–31)*

The Biennale and Other Exhibitions

Venice is without doubt one of the leading art exhibition centres in Europe, offering shows on themes ranging from art history to photography, and frequently playing host to the world's major travelling exhibitions. There are excellent facilities for such exhibitions, and these include the Doge's Palace, the Museo Correr, the Palazzo Grassi, the Querini-Stampalia, the Peggy Guggenheim and the Fondazione Cini. *Un Ospite di Venezia* will give details, as will the tourist office and posters around the city.

One of the best and largest exhibitions is the Biennale, an international display of contemporary and avant-garde art which was first begun in 1895. It is held from June to September in odd-numbered years. The main site is the Giardini Pubblici *(see p121)*, where the specially built pavilions represent about 40 different countries. Another branch of the exhibition showing the work of less established artists, takes place around the city in venues such as the old rope factory in the Arsenale *(see p119)*. The Biennale also organizes architecture, theatre, dance and music festivals.

Exhibit by Larry Rivers at the 1992 Biennale exhibition

Casinos, Clubs and Discos

If you want to gamble or play roulette during your visit to Venice, there is a magnificent casino housed in the **Palazzo Vendramin-Calergi** on the Grand Canal *(see p61)* and you can sweep up to the stately entrance by gondola.

The **Antico Martini** is the best-known late-night club. Open until 2am, it has live music in smart surroundings. A few other bars also feature live bands, including the **Paradiso Perduto** in Cannaregio. Discos are few and far between in Venice. You could try **Piccolo Mondo**, near the Accademia, **Casanova**, near the railway station, or go to the mainland, where Mestre has numerous discos. You will find these advertised in the *Spettacoli* listings in *Il Gazzettino.*

Placido Domingo singing at the Verona Festival

Sport and Children

Venetians are very keen on rowing and sailing. There are several clubs in the city, and the tourist office will be able to give you information. Most of the other sporting facilities are on the Lido, where you can ride, swim, cycle, and play golf or tennis.

In the city itself, there are few attractions for young children, but the mainland is more promising. Around Lake Garda there are plenty of watersports and a theme park, Gardaland *(see p205)*.

Music and Theatre in Verona

Verona has two exceptional venues for theatre and music: the superb Arena *(see p195)*, and the 1st-century Teatro Romano *(see p202)* on the far side of the River Adige. Both stage open-air performances during the summer months.

The Arena is a popular site for rock concerts, and is internationally renowned for its summer opera season. The Teatro Romano stages a succession of ballets and drama, including a Shakespeare Festival, in Italian translation. Tickets for the Teatro can be ordered by post; they are also sold at the box office at the Arena. Tickets to some events are free. Information about all the entertainment is given in the Verona newspaper, *L'Arena.*

Opera at the Arena

Almost everyone will enjoy the experience of hearing opera in the magnificent open-air setting of the Arena. Real opera buffs should be aware, however, that Verona performances are very much "opera for all".

You should be prepared for less-than-perfect acoustics, noisy audiences, and even small children running about. The opera season runs from the first week in July until the beginning of September, and every year features a lavish production of Verdi's *Aida.* Performances start at 9pm, as dusk is falling, and it is customary to buy one of the little candles that are on sale. Ten minutes before the "curtain

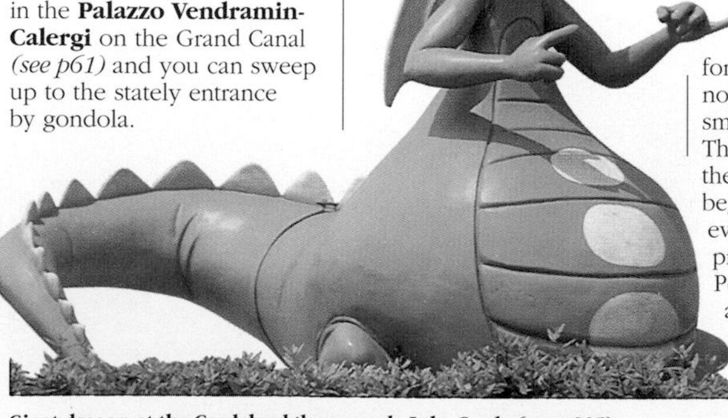

Giant dragon at the Gardaland theme park, Lake Garda *(see p205)*

Aida, **performed annually in Verona's Roman Arena**

goes up", the whole Arena becomes a breathtaking sight, with a sea of flickering lights.

During the intervals, most people eat the picnics they have brought with them, or buy *panini* and ice creams. Glass bottles are not allowed in the Arena, so if you are taking a drink make sure it is in a plastic bottle. Be warned that toilets are few and far between and are most likely to have lengthy queues during the intervals.

Ticket prices are high, though there are some concessions. An unreserved, un-numbered, backless seat in the *gradinata*, or tiers, is €21, while the *poltrone*, literally "armchairs", either on the steps or in the stalls, range from €85 to €160. If you decide to get a cheap seat, arrive at least two hours before the performance and sit halfway down the tiers, where the acoustics are better. You can hire an air cushion for about €3. Numbered seats are more comfortable, but seats lower in the Arena can be very hot and airless and the view of the stage can be restricted. You may well prefer to sacrifice comfort for fresh air and a bird's-eye view. Unless you have a seat in the best stalls with the glitterati, there is no need to dress up.

Visitors flock to Verona to attend the opera season, so you need to book accommodation well in advance.

DIRECTORY

MUSIC AND THEATRE

PalaFenice
Isola Nuova di Tronchetto.
041 520 40 10.
Ticket agents
Vela sales points: Piazzale Roma, Santa Lucia Station, Calle dei Fuseri (San Marco).

Teatro Goldoni
Calle Goldoni, San Marco 4650/B.
Map 7 A2.
041 240 20 11.

Teatro Malibran
Corte del Milion, San Marco.
Map 7 B1.
041 78 65 75.
Ticket agents
See PalaFenice.

CINEMAS

Giorgione Movie d'Essai
Rio Terra dei Franceschi, Cannaregio 4612. **Map** 7 A2. *041 522 62 98.*

Palazzo del Cinema
Lungomare G Marconi, Lido. *041 272 65 01.*

Rossini
Fondamenta Teatro, San Marco 3988. **Map** 7 A2.
041 523 03 22.

CASINOS, CLUBS AND DISCOS

Antico Martini
Campo San Fantin, San Marco 1980. **Map** 7 A2.
041 522 41 21.

Casanova
Lista di Spagna, Cannaregio 158/a. **Map** 1 C4.
041 275 01 99.

Piccolo Mondo
Calle Corfù, Dorsoduro 1056/A. **Map** 6 E3.
041 520 03 71.

Paradiso Perduto
Fondamenta della Misericordia, Cannaregio 2540.
Map 1 C4.
041 72 05 81.

Palazzo Vendramin-Calergi
Strada Nuova, Cannaregio 2040.
041 529 71 11.

SPORTS

Cycling
Bruno Lazzari
21/B Gran Viale, Lido.
041 526 80 19.

Golf
Alberoni
Lido.
041 73 10 15.

Rowing
Canottieri Bucintoro
Punta Dogana, Dorsoduro 15. **Map** 7 B4.
041 522 20 55.

Tennis
Tennis Club Venezia
Lungomare G Marconi 41/d, Lido. *041 526 03 35.*

VERONA OPERA

Main box office
ENTE Arena
Piazza Brà 28, 37121 Verona. *045 800 51 51.*
FAX *045 801 32 87.*
www.arena.it

Ticket agent
Vertours
Galleria Pelliciai 13, 37121 Verona.
045 800 51 12.
FAX *045 59 54 54.*
info@vertours.com

Survival Guide

Practical Information

THE ENORMOUS WEALTH of art and architecture found in Venice and the historic cities of Padua, Verona and Vicenza can dazzle and overwhelm. The best way to avoid cultural overload is to concentrate on sights in the morning, when they are most likely to be open, relax over your lunch as the Italians do, and leave any shopping or sightseeing of churches until the late afternoon or early evening. The inconsistency of museum opening hours and the fact that some sights or large sections of them are closed for years for restoration can be frustrating. This is particularly true of Venice, where you may often see scaffolding and the signs *chiuso per restauro* (closed for restoration), so it is best to check opening hours with individual museums in advance. However, on the plus side, the principal sights are all within easy walking distance of one another, and exploring by boat and on foot is an exciting experience.

Tourist Board logo

Tourists crossing the white stone Ponte della Paglia

Tourist Information

MOST TOWNS in the Veneto have tourist offices, and in season Verona and Padua each have two. The offices in smaller towns may be of limited help. In contrast, the Verona offices publish a useful free booklet, *Agenda di Verona*, with information on what to see and do. Travel agents can supply information on city and other tours on offer. Tourist offices in Venice provide city maps, lists of accommodation, *vaporetto* maps and other literature. Tourist offices and hotels also have leaflets on local entertainment and events *(see pp32–5)*. To obtain information prior to travel, contact **ENIT** (Italian State Tourist Board) in your home country, or write to the **Azienda di Promozione Turistica di Venezia**.

AZIENDA PROMOZIONE TURISTICA

A Tourist Information sign

The **Forum per la Laguna**, a cultural association promoting the lagoon area, also has an information service on Venice and the surrounding area.

Guided Tours

CITY TOURS in Venice with English-speaking guides (by foot or motorboat) can be booked through many agencies, including **American Express**, **Venicescapes** and **Bucintoro**. In Verona and Padua half-day tours are organized in the tourist season by each town's tourist office. Boat trips along the Brenta Canal *(see pp182–3)* between Venice and Padua are available from March to late October. **Avventure Bellissime**'s tours of the hills of the Veneto depart from Venice daily. They also offer walking holidays in the Dolomites.

Museums and Monuments

THE OPENING HOURS of museums, galleries and palaces change frequently. Ask at the local tourist office for a list of opening times or, if in Venice, consult the free booklets *Leo Bussola* or *Un Ospite di Venezia*. Civic museums are often shut on Mondays, otherwise there is no pattern to opening times. Many places shut at 1pm or 2pm and do not re-open in the afternoon. Most museums charge an admission fee, but there may be concessions for children, students and, in a few cases, senior citizens. In Venice, a "Museum Card" is available, givng one year's entrance to many museums. Churches are often open in the mornings from around 9am until noon, then again from mid-afternoon until 6 or 7pm.

A selection of local tourist information publications

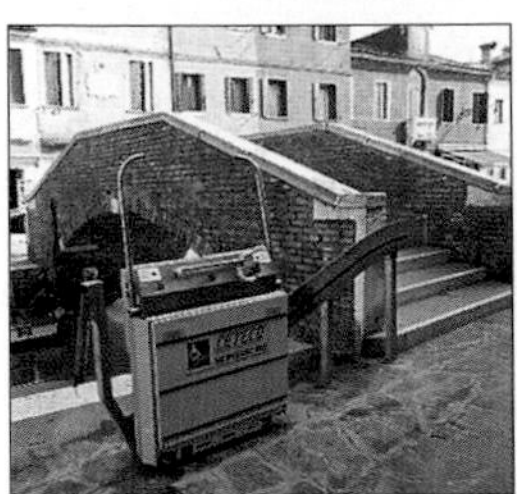

A mechanically operated wheelchair ramp across a bridge

Venice for the Disabled

The stepped bridges of Venice make it almost impossible for the disabled to get around the city – it is difficult enough for a parent with a pushchair. A further problem are the *vaporetti*, particularly the *motoscafi*, which are especially hazardous for those confined to wheelchairs.

One of the few aids for the disabled is the plan of the city prepared by the Tourist Board. This shows places of interest which can be visited by the disabled, and how to reach them by *vaporetto* or by streets avoiding any bridges. Few of the sights have special facilities for the disabled, but a few important bridges have now been fitted with mechanically operated ramps. The key is available from the tourist office.

The Venice tourist office brochure that lists available accommodation also indicates which hotels are suitable for disabled guests.

Etiquette

Any attempt by visitors to speak Italian is always appreciated by local people. Few people speak English in the Veneto, but hotel receptionists are usually helpful and will readily offer to make any enquiries and reservations on your behalf.

To avoid offence always dress decently, particularly for churches, and make sure that you are never drunk in a public place. Smoking is very common in restaurants and bars, but is banned on the *vaporetti*.

Visiting Churches

Bare shoulders and shorts are frowned upon in Italian churches and those unsuitably dressed may well be refused entry. Church interiors tend to be very dark but there are usually coin-operated light meters to illuminate works of art. Make sure you take plenty of coins. Machines that provide recorded information on the church and its artifacts are available to hire, but the commentaries are sometimes inaudible. The majority of churches charge an entrance fee or encourage contributions. Photography is forbidden in most churches.

Pedestrians shopping in Verona

Tipping

Always keep a few euros handy for porters, chambermaids, restaurant staff and custodians of churches. Italian taxi drivers do not expect a tip and there is no need to tip a gondolier.

WCs

There are few public toilets in the Veneto, although Venice is better served. Those in Venice are usualy signposted and cost about 50 cents. You can also use those at the station, or toilets in cafés, bars, or museums. Ask for *il bagno* or *il gabinetto*. The toilets are always short of paper, so it is a good idea to carry tissues with you.

Useful Addresses

Agenzia Bucintoro & Viaggi
Campo San Luca, San Marco 4267/c, Venice. **Map** 7 A2.
041 521 06 32.
www.bucintoroviaggi.com

American Express
Salizzada San Moisè, San Marco 1471, Venice. **Map** 7 A3. *041 520 08 44.*

Avventure Bellissime
Fondamenta delle Ostreghe, San Marco 2442A, Venice.
041 520 86 16.
www.venice-day-tours.com

Azienda di Promozione Turistica di Venezia
Castello 4421, Venice. **Map** 7 C1. *041 529 87 11.*

ENIT UK
1 Princes Street, London W1R 8AY. *020 7408 1254.*
www.enit.it

ENIT US
630 Fifth Avenue, New York, NY 10111. *212 245 4822.*

Forum per la Laguna
Calle Vitturi 2923, 30124 San Marco, Venice. **Map** 6 E3.
041 521 28 30.

Uffici Informazioni (Tourist Information)
Palazzina Selva, Giardinetti Reali, Venice. **Map** 7 B3.
041 529 87 11.
www.turismovenezia.it

Marco Polo Airport.
041 524 15 87.

Ferrovia Santa Lucia, Venice. **Map** 1 B4. *041 529 87 27.*

Piazza San Marco 71, Venice. **Map** 7 B2. *041 529 87 40.*

Gran Viale 6, Lido, Venice.
041 526 57 21.
summer only.

Piazzale Roma, Venice.
041 241 14 99.

Via Degli Alpini 9, Verona.
045 806 86 80.
www.tourism.verona.it

Piazzale della Stazione, Padua.
049 875 20 77.
www.turismopadova.it

Piazza Matteotti 12, Vicenza.
0444 32 08 54.
www.vicenzae.org

Venicescapes
Castello 4954, Venice.
041 520 63 61.
www.venicescapes.org

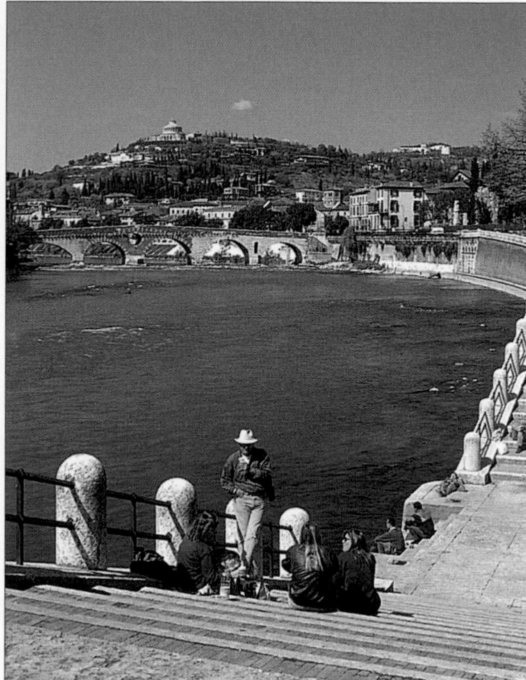

Students relaxing in the sun in Verona

Immigration and Customs

European Union (EU) residents and visitors from the United States, Canada, Australia and New Zealand do not need visas for stays of up to three months. However, all visitors need to bring a full passport. A visa is needed for stays longer than three months. It is advisable for all visitors to check their requirements before travelling.

All visitors to Italy should, by law, register with the police within three days of arrival. Most hotels will register visitors when they check in. If in doubt, contact a local police department or phone the **Questura**.

In 1999, the intra-EU Duty and Tax Free Allowances, better known as Duty-free, were abolished. However, for EU residents the amount of these goods that can be imported for personal use has increased. Consulates can provide information on customs regulations. To find out what you can take back from Italy to non-EU countries, contact that particular country's customs office.

The refund system for Value Added Tax (IVA in Italy) for non-EU residents is complicated and is worth reclaiming only if you have spent at least €160 in one single establishment.

Student Information

An international Student Identity Card (ISIC) or a Youth International Educational Exchange Card (YIEE) will usually get reductions on museum admissions and other charges. Venice Municipality's Rolling Venice card for 14- to 29-year-olds offers, for a small fee, a package of useful information on the city. It includes alternative itineraries, fashionable haunts, and lists of shops, hotels, theatres and restaurants offering card-holder discounts.

Discount rail tickets are sold at Favola Tours, next to Venice railway station, and at CTS, near the university.

Educational Courses

In Venice, the **Società Dante Alighieri**, the **Istituto Venezia** and the **Venice University Centro Linguistico** organize Italian courses for foreigners. In Padua the **Istituto Linguistico Bertrand Russell** organizes Italian language courses that run throughout the year.

The **Venice European Centre for the Trades and Professions of Conservation**, on the island of San Servolo, offers standard three-month or intensive two-week courses to Italian and foreign craftspeople. The **Scuola Internazionale di Gràfica** in Venice specializes in short summer courses in painting, printing and sketching.

Newspapers, Radio and TV

The local newspapers are the *Gazzettino* and the *Nuova Venezia*. European and American newspapers and magazines are available at the main news kiosks, normally a day or two after publication. The state TV channels are RAI Uno, RAI Due and RAI Tre. Satellite and cable TV transmit European channels in many languages, as well as CNN news in English. BBC World Service is broadcast on radio on 15.070 MHz (short wave) in the mornings and 648 KHz (medium wave) at night.

Newspaper stall selling a variety of national publications

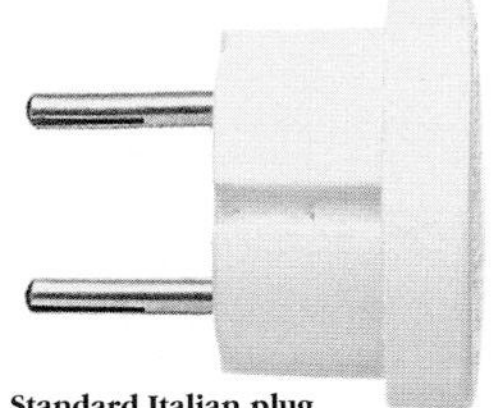

Standard Italian plug

Embassies and Consulates

If you lose your passport or need other help, contact your national embassy or consulate as listed in the directory below.

Electrical Adaptors

Electrical current in Italy is 220V AC, with either two- or three-pin, round-pronged plugs. It is probably better to purchase an adaptor before leaving for Italy. Most hotels graded above three star have electrical points for shavers and hairdryers in all bedrooms.

Italian Time

Italy is one hour ahead of Greenwich Mean Time (GMT). The time difference between Venice and other cities is: London: –1 hour; New York: –6 hours; Perth: +7 hours; Auckland: +11 hours; Tokyo: +8 hours. Daylight saving time is between April and October. For all official purposes the Italians use the 24-hour clock.

The clock of San Giacomo di Rialto in San Polo, Venice

Conversion Table

Imperial to Metric
1 inch = 2.54 centimetres
1 foot = 30 centimetres
1 mile = 1.6 kilometres
1 ounce = 28 grams
1 pound = 454 grams
1 pint = 0.6 litres
1 gallon = 4.6 litres

Metric to Imperial
1 centimetre = 0.4 inches
1 metre = 3 feet, 3 inches
1 kilometre = 0.6 miles
1 gram = 0.04 ounces
1 kilogram = 2.2 pounds
1 litre = 1.8 pints

Directory

Police (Questura)

Venice
Santa Croce 500.
041 271 55 11.

Vicenza
Viale Mazzini 213.
0444 33 75 11.

Padua
Via Riviera Ruzzante 9/11.
049 83 31 11.

Verona
Lungadige Galtarossa 11.
045 809 06 11.

Student Information

Comune di Venezia
San Marco 1529, Venice. **Map** 7 A3. 041 274 76 45. www.comune.venezia.it/citta.htm

CTS
Calle Foscari, Dorsoduro 3252, Venice. **Map** 6 D2. 041 520 56 60.

Favola Tours
Fondamenta Scalzi, Cannaregio 54 ABC, Venice. 041 71 74 33

Ufficio Informativo Rolling Venice
Ferrovia Santa Lucia, Venice. **Map** 1 B4. 041 524 29 04. Jul–Sep.

Educational Courses

Venice European Centre for the Trades and Professions of Conservation
Isola di San Servolo, 30100 Venice. 041 526 85 46.

Istituto Linguistico Bertrand Russell
Via Filiberto 6, 35122 Padua. 049 65 40 51.

Istituto Venezia
Campo Santa Margherita, Dorsoduro 3116/a, Venice. **Map** 6 D2. 041 522 43 31.

Società Dante Alighieri
c/o Istituto Tecnico Commerciale Paolo Sarpi Fondamenta S Giustina, Castello 2821, Venice. **Map** 4 D5. 041 528 91 27.

Scuola Internazionale di Gràfica
Calle del Cristo, Cannaregio 1798, Venice. **Map** 2 E4. 041 72 19 50. www.scuolagrafica.it

Venice University Centro Linguistico
Palazzo Bonvicini, S. Croce 2161 041 234 9711

Embassies and Consulates

Australia
Via Alessandria 215, Rome. 06 85 27 21.

Canada
Riviera Ruzzante 25, Padua. 049 876 48 33.

New Zealand
Via Zara 28, Rome. 06 441 71 71.

United Kingdom
Palazzo Querini Accademia, Dorsoduro 1051, Venice. **Map** 6 E3. 041 522 72 07.

US
Via Principe Amedeo 2/10, Milan. 02 29 03 51.

Religious Services

Anglican
St George's Anglican Church, Campo San Vio, Dorsoduro, Venice. **Map** 6 F4. 041 520 05 71.

Greek Orthodox
Greek Orthodox Church Ponte dei Greci, Castello 3412, Venice. **Map** 8 D2. 041 523 95 69.

Jewish
Sinagoga, Ghetto Vecchio, Cannaregio, Venice. **Map** 2 D3. 041 71 53 59.

Lutheran
Chiesa Evangelica Luterana, Campo Santi Apostoli, Cannaregio 4448, Venice. **Map** 3 B5. 041 522 71 49.

Methodist
Chiesa Evangelica Valdese e Metodista, Campo Santa Maria Formosa, Castello 5170, Venice. **Map** 7 C1. 041 522 75 49.

Personal Security and Health

VENICE IS ONE of the safest cities in Europe. Violent crime is very rare and petty crime minimal in comparison with other main cities. Nevertheless, it is wise to take a few simple precautions, particularly against pickpockets, both in Venice and elsewhere in the Veneto. Leave valuables and any important documents in the hotel safe and carry only the minimum amount of money necessary for the day.

Make sure you take out adequate travel insurance before leaving for Italy, as it is very difficult to obtain once you are in the country.

Venice by night, not always well-lit but safe

Looking After Your Property

TRAVELLERS' CHEQUES are the safest way to carry large sums of money. Always keep your cheques and your cheque receipts separately to be on the safe side, and keep a photocopy of all vital documents such as your passport.

Safeguard against attracting the attention of pickpockets and bagsnatchers, particularly at railway stations, markets and on the buses. In Venice take extra care while waiting at the *vaporetto* landing stages; be especially vigilant when crowds are jostling to get on to the boats.

If you drive while in the Veneto, always remember to lock the car before you leave it and never leave valuables on display inside. Hired cars or those with foreign number plates are favourite targets of car thieves.

Personal Safety

VENICE IS UNEVENTFUL by night and you can stroll through the streets without any threat. There is no red light quarter or any area that could be described as unsavoury. Women alone in Venice are unlikely to encounter anything more troublesome than the usual Latin roving eye. Elsewhere in the Veneto, in the less touristy towns particularly, unescorted females are likely to attract more attention.

Avoid unauthorized taxi drivers, who may not be insured and almost invariably overcharge. Airports are their favourite haunts. Make sure you take only official taxis which have the licence number clearly displayed *(see p278)*.

Police

THE VIGILI URBANI, or municipal police, are most often seen in the streets regulating traffic and enforcing local laws. They wear blue uniforms in winter and white during the summer. The *carabinieri*, with red striped trousers, are the armed military police, responsible for public law and order. *La polizia*, or state police, wear blue uniforms with white belts and berets. They specialize in serious crimes. Any of these should be able to help you.

In the event of theft go straight to the nearest police station *(polizia* or *carabinieri)* to make a statement. If there is a language problem, you should consult your nearest consulate *(see p263)*, which you should also do in the case of a lost passport.

Emergency Numbers

Ambulance
Venice
☎ *118.*
Verona
☎ *118.*
Padua
☎ *118.*
Vicenza
☎ *118.*

Automobile Club d'Italia
☎ *116.*
Car accident and breakdown.

Fire
☎ *115.*

General SOS
☎ *113.*

Medical Emergencies
☎ *118.*

Police (Carabinieri)
☎ *112.*

Traffic Police
Venice
☎ *041 274 70 70.*
Verona
☎ *045 807 84 11.*
Padua
☎ *049 820 51 00.*
Vicenza
☎ *0444 54 53 11.*

Medical Precautions

VISITORS FROM the European Union (EU) are entitled to reciprocal state medical care in Italy. Before you travel, pick up form E111 from the post

A group of Venetian Carabinieri on the Riva degli Schiavoni

office, which covers you for emergency medical treatment. You may wish to take out additional medical insurance, as E111 does not cover repatriation costs for yourself or anyone travelling with you. Australia has a reciprocal medical agreement with Italy, but other visitors from outside the EU should take out a comprehensive medical insurance policy. If you are taking prescribed medication, take supplies or prescriptions with you.

Inoculations are not needed for the Veneto, but take sunscreen and mosquito repellent in the summer. Because of the canals, mosquitoes can be irksome in Venice. An electric gadget, from pharmacies or department stores, will repel insects in your room for up to 12 hours. Tap water is safe, but locals often prefer mineral water, either fizzy *(con gas)* or still *(naturale)*.

Electric mosquito deterrent

Medical Treatment

If you are in need of urgent medical attention, go to the *Pronto Soccorso* (First Aid) department of the nearest main hospital. Standards of health care are generally better than those in the south of Italy, although not as high as in Britain or the US. There are usually queues at the emergency departments and many hospitals expect the patient's family or friends to help with his or her nursing.

Should you require a consultation with a doctor, ask the advice of your hotel or look in the yellow pages of the telephone directory, under *medici*. (A *dottore* is not necessarily a doctor of medicine.) If you have a serious medical complaint or allergy you should bring a letter, preferably translated, from your doctor at home.

Pharmacy sign

Many doctors in the region speak at least a little English. There are first aid facilities with the services of a doctor at airports and at most railway stations.

Dentists are expensive in Italy. You can find the nearest one in the yellow pages of the telephone directory, listed under *dentisti medici chirurghi*, or ask your hotel receptionist for his or her recommendation.

For insurance claims, make sure you keep all receipts for medical treatment and any medicines prescribed.

Pharmacies are open during the summer months from 8:30am to 12:30pm and 4pm to 8pm Monday to Friday, and from 9am to noon on Saturday. Winter hours are slightly shorter. All towns offer a 24-hour pharmacy service, with a night-time and Sunday rota. You will find the rota posted on the doors of pharmacies. Opening times can also be found in the local newspapers or, if you are in Venice, the booklet *Un Ospite di Venezia*.

Italian pharmacists are well-trained to deal with minor ailments and can prescribe many drugs without needing a doctor's prescription. The majority of pharmacies do not stock quantities of foreign medicines but can usually supply the local equivalent. Many of the words for minor complaints and remedies are similar in Italian, for example *lassativo* (laxative), *aspirina* (aspirin) and *tranquillante* (tranquillizer).

Useful Information

Venice Hospital
Ospedale Civile,
Campo Santi Giovanni e Paolo.
Map 3 C5.
041 529 41 11.

Verona Hospital
Ospedale Borgo Trento
Piazzale Stefani 1.
045 807 11 11.

Padua Hospital
Ospedale Civile
Via Giustiniani 2.
049 821 11 11.

Vicenza Hospital
Ospedale di Vicenza
Via Rodolfi 37.
0444 99 31 11.

Lost Property Offices
Ferrovia Santa Lucia,
Venice. **Map** 1 B4.
041 78 52 38.
Railway Station, Verona.
045 802 38 27.
Railway Station, Padua.
049 822 43 86.

Missing Credit Cards
American Express
06 72 90 03 47.
Diners Club
800 86 40 64 (freephone).
Eurocard
800 87 08 66 (freephone).
MasterCard (Access)
800 87 08 66 (freephone).
VISA
800 87 72 32 (freephone).

Missing Travellers' Cheques
American Express
800 87 20 00 (freephone).
Thomas Cook
800 87 20 50 (freephone).
VISA
800 87 41 55 (freephone).

An ambulance boat on the Grand Canal

Banking and Local Currency

VISITORS TO THE VENETO have a number of options available to them for changing money. Banks tend to give more favourable rates than bureaux de change, hotels and travel agents, but the paperwork is usually more time consuming. Alternatively, credit cards can be used for purchasing goods. When changing travellers' cheques you will need to show some form of identification.

Cash dispenser which also accepts VISA and MasterCard (Access)

Changing Money

BANKING HOURS can be erratic, especially the day before a public holiday, so it is safest to acquire some local currency before you arrive in Italy. Exchange rates will vary from place to place. For the best rates, try a bank (look for the sign *cambio*) or the American Express office *(see p261)*. Hotels tend to give poor rates, even if they charge modest commissions.

A more convenient way to change money is to use the electronic exchange machines. These are found at Marco Polo airport, Venice railway station and at several banks in the city. All major towns in the Veneto have foreign exchange machines. These machines have multilingual instructions and the exchange rate is displayed on screen. You simply feed in notes of the same foreign currency, and you will get euros in return.

Travellers' Cheques

TRAVELLERS' CHEQUES are probably the safest way to carry large sums of money. Choose a name that is well known, such as American Express, or cheques issued through a major bank. Always record the travellers' cheques numbers and keep this information separate from the cheques themselves, in case they are stolen.

There is usually a minimum commission charge, which may make changing small sums of money uneconomical. Some establishments will charge you for each cheque.

Check the exchange rates before you travel and decide whether sterling, dollar or euro travellers' cheques are more appropriate for your trip. Bear in mind that it may be more difficult to cash euro travellers' cheques, especially in hotels, because they are not very profitable for the exchanger.

Credit Cards

CREDIT CARDS are widely accepted throughout Italy and it is worth bringing one with you, particularly for hotel and restaurant bills, shopping, car hire and booking tickets by telephone. VISA and Access (MasterCard) are the most popular, with American Express and Diners Club trailing well behind. Some banks and cash dispensers accept VISA or Access for cash advances, although interest is payable once the money is withdrawn. In Venice, cash dispensers accepting credit cards can be found throughout the city, although they may not be so evident in the quieter areas.

Some establishments require a minimum expenditure to accept credit card payment. Always make sure that you have enough cash in case your card is not accepted.

Banking Hours

BANKS ARE USUALLY open from 8:30am to 1:30pm, Monday to Friday. Most also open for an hour in the afternoon from about 2:35pm until 3:35pm. They close at weekends and for public holidays, and they also close early the day before a major holiday. Exchange offices stay open longer, but the rates are less favourable. The exchange offices at Venice airport and railway station stay open until the evening and at weekends.

Using Banks

CHANGING MONEY at a bank can at times be a frustrating process, as it involves endless form-filling and queuing.

Plaque of the Cassa di Risparmio in Campo Manin

You must apply first at the window displaying the *cambio* sign, then move to the *cassa* to obtain your euros. If in doubt, ask someone in order to avoid waiting in the wrong queue.

For security reasons, most banks have electronic double doors with metal detectors, allowing one person in at a time. Metal objects and bags should first be deposited in lockers situated in the foyer. Press the button to open the outer door, then wait for it to close behind you. The inner door then opens automatically.

If you need to have money sent to you in Italy, banks at home can telex money to an Italian bank, but it takes about a week. American Express, Thomas Cook and Western Union all provide swifter money transfer services.

The Euro

Twelve countries have replaced their traditional currencies, such as the Italian lire, with the euro. Austria, Belgium, Finland, France, Germany, Greece, Ireland, Italy, Luxembourg, Netherlands, Portugal and Spain chose to join the new currency; the UK, Denmark and Sweden stayed out, with an option to review their situation.

Euro notes and coins came into general circulation on 1 January 2002. Each country using the euro produces their own coins, which have one common European side and one national side, but these, like the notes which are all uniform in design, can be used anywhere inside the twelve participating member states.

Bank Notes

Euro bank notes have seven denominations. The 5-euro note (grey in colour) is the smallest, followed by the 10-euro note (pink), 20-euro note (blue), 50-euro note (orange), 100-euro note (green), 200-euro note (yellow) and 500-euro note (purple). All notes show the 12 stars of the European Union.

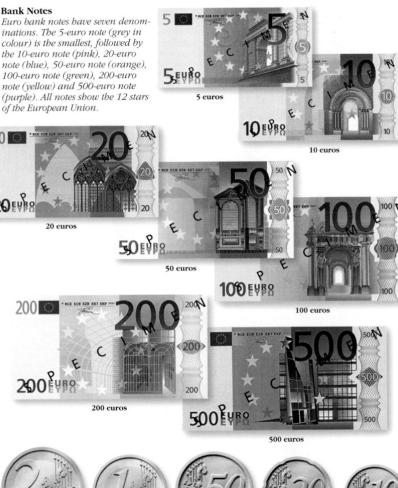

5 euros

10 euros

20 euros

50 euros

100 euros

200 euros

500 euros

2 euros

1 euro

50 cents

20 cents

10 cents

Coins

The euro has eight coin denominations: 1 euro and 2 euros; 50 cents, 20 cents, 10 cents, 5 cents, 2 cents and 1 cent. The 2- and 1-euro coins are both silver and gold in colour. The 50-, 20- and 10-cent coins are gold. The 5- , 2- and 1-cent coins are bronze.

5 cents

2 cents

1 cent

Using the Telephone

YOU CAN FIND PUBLIC TELEPHONES on the streets of all the main towns in the Veneto, as well as at bars and post offices. In Venice there are public phones in most of the main squares and at virtually every *vaporetto* landing stage. Many of these now accept prepaid phonecards, so it is far easier and more convenient for visitors to make long-distance calls.

Call Charges

THE CHEAPEST TIMES to phone within Italy are between 6:30pm and 8am from Monday to Friday, after 1:30pm on Saturday and all day on Sunday. International calls worldwide are cheapest between 10pm and 8am Monday to Saturday and all day Sunday. Although Telecom Italia phones are still the most common on the streets of Venice, phones by other companies are slowly creeping in, each with its own pre-paid phonecard, available from tobacconists or newsagents.

In general, it is much cheaper to dial direct for international calls from a payphone rather than going through the operator or making collect or credit card calls. Telephoning from hotel rooms is usually expensive and is sometimes marked up by as much as several hundred per cent. In general, it is more expensive to phone abroad from Italy than, for example, from the US or the UK.

Telephone sign

Telephone Offices

THE OLD-STYLE *Telefoni* (telephone offices) run by the Italian telecommunications companies Telecom Italia and ASST are no longer found in the Veneto. These operator-assisted, metered telephone booths have been replaced by banks of the same card- and coin-operated public telephones that can be found on the streets of Venice and throughout the Veneto region. Each of the main towns also has a number of centrally located payphones, which can be found at the following addresses:

Telephone company logo

Venice
Ferrovia Santa Lucia. **Map** 1 B4.
Piazzale Roma. **Map** 5 B1.

Verona
Ferrovia Porta Nuova.

Padua
Riviera Ponti Romani 40.

Vicenza
Via Vescovado.

If you want to send a telegram anywhere in Italy or abroad, you can go to any post office or call 186 for assistance.

Using a Telecom Italia Card Telephone

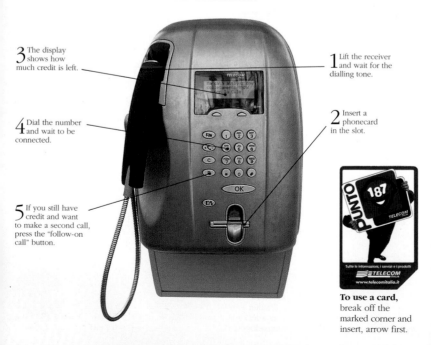

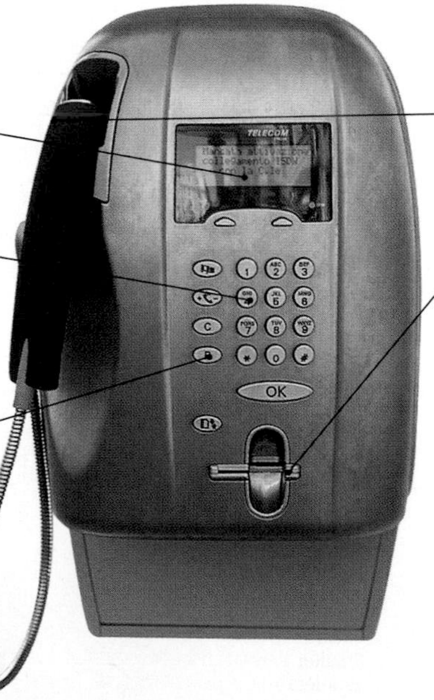

1 Lift the receiver and wait for the dialling tone.

2 Insert a phonecard in the slot.

3 The display shows how much credit is left.

4 Dial the number and wait to be connected.

5 If you still have credit and want to make a second call, press the "follow-on call" button.

To use a card, break off the marked corner and insert, arrow first.

Using Public Telephones

You can dial long-distance and international calls from public telephones. When making long-distance calls, always make sure that you have plenty of change ready. If you don't put enough coins in to start with, the telephone disconnects you and retains your money. Coin-operated phones are slowly being phased out in favour of pay-phones which take telephone cards *(carta* or *scheda telefonica)*. You can buy these from post offices, newspaper kiosks and tobacconists *(tabacchi)* that display the black-and-white T sign.

Tabacchi sign

Any Italian number you dial in Italy must now be prefixed by its area code, even if you are making a local call. When dialling Italian numbers from abroad, do not drop the zero from in front of the area code.

E-mail

The internet has made e-mail a viable and popular way to communicate from abroad. You can e-mail from the following Internet points:

Venice Connection
San Polo 2898/a, San Tomà, Calle Campaniel, Venice. **Map** 6 E2.
041 244 02 76.
10am–10pm daily (winter), 10am–midnight (May–Sep.
info@veniceconnection.com

Net House Internet Café
Campo Santo Stefano, San Marco 2967-2968, Venice. **Map** 6 F3.
041 277 11 90. 24 hours
www.venicepages.com

Venetian Navigator
Calle delle Bande, Castello 5269, Venice. **Map** 7 C1. 041 522 60 84.
10am–10pm daily.
www.venetiannavigator.com
vn@venetiannavigator.com

VeNice
Lista di Spagna, 149 Cannaregio, Venice. **Map** 2 D4.
041 275 82 17.
9am–11pm daily.
www.ve-nice.it
info@ve-nice.it

Reaching the Right Number

To ring Italy from the UK, and Ireland dial 00 39 then the number, including the full area code. From the US and Canada, dial 0 11 39 and from Australia, dial 00 11 39.

- Dialling code for
  - Venice 041
  - Verona 045
  - Vicenza 0444
  - Padua 049
  - Treviso 0422
- International directory enquiries 176
- International operator assistance 170
- Telegrams and cables in Italy and abroad 186

To reach the operator in your own country to place a reverse charge or credit card call dial 172 followed by: 0044 for BT, UK; 0544 for CWC, UK; 1011 for AT&T, US; 1022 for MCI, US; 1001 for Canada; 1061 for Telstra, Australia and 1161 for Optus, Australia.

- *See also* Emergency Numbers, *p264*.

Sending Letters

The Italian postal service is notoriously inefficient. Expect anything sent abroad to take some time, especially during the August holiday season. Postcards to the UK can take up to a month if sent during the summer, and letters sent within Italy can take up to a week to reach their destination. For urgent or important communications, it is better to use the more expensive *Posta Prioritaria* system, which has replaced Air Mail.

You can buy stamps *(francobolli)* from any tobacconist which has the black-and-white T sign, as well as from post offices. Post office hours are usually 8:30am to 2pm, Monday to Friday and 8:30am to noon on Saturday and the last day of the month. Main offices stay open until early evening.

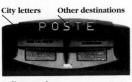

City letters **Other destinations**

Italian post box

Post Office sign

Sending Parcels

Sending parcels from Italy can be extremely difficult. Unless certain rules are adhered to, it is unlikely that your package will be sent. Large items must be in a rigid box, wrapped in brown paper and bound with string and a lead seal. You will need to fill in a customs declaration form. Smaller items can be sent as a letter in a padded envelope.

Poste Restante

Letters and parcels should be sent care of (c/o) Fermo Posta, Ufficio Postale Principale, followed by the name of the town in which you wish to pick them up. Print the surname clearly in block capitals to make sure the letters are filed correctly. To collect your post, you need to show some form of identification and pay a small fee.

Main Post Offices

Fondaco dei Tedeschi 5554, Venice. **Map** 7 B1.
041 271 71 11.

Piazza Viviani 7, Verona.
045 59 09 55.

Piazza Garibaldi, Vicenza.
0444 33 20 77.

Corso Garibaldi 33, Padua.
049 877 21 11.

Travel Information

The easiest way to reach the Veneto is by air. Direct flights link Venice to major European cities, and there are a few direct intercontinental flights. However, visitors from outside Europe usually transfer at Milan or Rome. Venice's Marco Polo airport, 10 km (6.5 miles) north of the city, receives both domestic and European flights as well as some charter flights. The airport is relatively small, but a new terminal is being built to help it handle the high volume of traffic. Treviso and Verona have their own small airports, both of which receive flights from the UK. Car drivers who plan to tour the Veneto must bear in mind toll charges on European motorways. Visitors to Venice itself will have to leave their cars in one of the large car parks on the outskirts of the city because there are no streets for cars in the centre. Parking fees are heavy, and owners run the risk of leaving their cars unattended for the length of their stay. However, the region's rail network is good, and Venice railway station links the city to towns of the Veneto, and major European cities.

Alitalia aircraft

The quayside at Venice's Marco Polo airport

Arriving by Air

Venice is served by two airports: Marco Polo for scheduled flights and Treviso for charter flights. The city is linked to London, Paris and all other major European cities by direct flights. It is now possible to fly from New York to Venice with **Delta Airlines**. Alternatively, visitors from outside Europe can take a budget flight to London, Paris, Amsterdam or Frankfurt, and then a connecting flight to Venice from there.

Daily scheduled flights to Venice are operated by **British Airways** and **Alitalia** (not direct) from London. Low-cost airline **easyJet** offers departures from Bristol, East Midlands and London Stansted. The lowest fares are usually available only to those who avoid peak periods and book well in advance; booking via the Internet also saves money.

Many charter flights operate to Venice (Treviso) as does low-cost airline **Ryanair** from London Stansted. Ryanair also serves Treviso (via London) from Glasgow, Dublin, Oslo, Stockholm, Malmo and Tampere.

If you wish to book flights during your stay, travel agents such as **American Express** or **Agenzia Bucintoro** in Venice offer a good service.

Package Holidays

Taking a package holiday to the Veneto is more convenient but not always cheaper than going independently of a tour operator. It is always worth comparing the costs, particularly if you are intending to travel off-season when charter flights are at their cheapest. For visitors who prefer the convenience of a package holiday, Venice is offered as a single destination or as part of a two- or three-centre holiday with Florence and Rome. Transfer from the airport on arrival is usually included in the holiday price. Most tour operators tend to concentrate on Venice as a centre, though some offer packages to Verona or touring trips of the Veneto taking in the popular villas, museums and art galleries.

Useful Numbers

Alitalia
Venice. *848 86 56 41 (domestic flights); 848 86 56 42 (international flights); 848 86 56 43 (information).*
www.alitalia.it

British Airways
Venice. *848 81 22 66.*
www.britishairways.com

Delta Airlines
800 221 1212 (US only).
www.delta.com

easyJet
www.easyjet.com

Ryanair
www.ryanair.com

American Express
See p261.

Agenzia Bucintoro
See p261.

Airport Information
Venice. *041 260 92 60.*
www.veniceairport.it
Verona. *045 809 56 66.*
Treviso. *0422 31 51 11.*

Marco Polo Airport (Venice)

Facilities are limited at the airport, but there is a hotel reservations office and a currency exchange office that

Verona airport check-in desk

is open all day. There are also several banks, a self-service restaurant and a post office.

The most dramatic entry from the airport into Venice is by boat. The Alilaguna public water launch to San Marco and the Lido departs at hourly or two-hourly intervals depending on the time of day. Tickets are available from the office close to the exit of the arrivals hall. The journey to Venice takes about an hour and costs €9 per person. The boat stops near the San Marco, Murano and Lido *vaporetto* stops. Water taxis operating from the airport to San Marco only take 20 minutes but will cost around seven times as much as the public launch. Beware of water taxi touts who will charge you a good deal more than the official fare.

The less spectacular but quicker and cheaper alternative to the lagoon crossing is the ATVO bus to Piazzale Roma. The service meets all scheduled flights and costs around €4. Cheaper still, but stopping along the way, is the public bus to Piazzale Roma, which departs every 30 minutes. There is also a land taxi rank at the front of the airport. The journey takes 15 minutes and the drop-off point is Piazzale Roma.

Treviso Airport

This is a small airport which receives charter flights from London (Stansted) twice a day. An exchange office is open when flights are in operation. The coach service to Piazzale Roma in Venice, which connects with flights, costs about €4 and takes approximately 45 minutes. Alternatively, you can take the public bus No. 6 which runs to Treviso station, where there is a regular rail service to Venice. For those on package tours the transport to Venice is pre-arranged and normally included in the overall price of the holiday.

Verona Airport

Verona airport receives flights from London (Gatwick), Frankfurt and Paris. There is a currency exchange office which is open daily. The bus service from the airport to Verona, which links up with scheduled flights, costs about €5.

Porters in Venice

Unless you are staying very close to your arrival point, you will have to take a *vaporetto* to the landing stage nearest to your hotel. Porters are very expensive; you will have to pay for the porter's boat fare, as well as for each piece of luggage – each piece costs the same as an adult. The cost of a porter handling two suitcases, including your *vaporetto* fare, could amount to nearly €10. If there are no porters available, which is often the case, call your hotel and ask for a porter to meet you.

Arriving by Car

To drive your own car in Italy you will need an international Green Card (for insurance purposes) and your vehicle registration documentation. EU nationals who do not have the standard pink licence will need an Italian translation of their licence, available from most motoring organizations and Italian tourist offices. Requirements vary for visitors from non-EU countries; check with your insurance company before leaving for Italy. Insurance can always be bought at the border. This is also required to hire a car. *(See also p278.)*

Car Hire Numbers

In addition to those below, each major car hire company has an office at Venice, Treviso and Verona airports.

Piazzale Roma, Venice
Expressway *041 522 30 00.*
Avis *041 522 58 25.*
Hertz *041 528 40 91.*

Padua Railway Station
Maggiore *049 875 28 52.*
Avis *049 66 41 98.*
Hertz *049 865 22 02.*

Verona Railway Station
Maggiore *045 800 48 08.*
Avis *045 800 66 36.*
Hertz *045 800 08 32.*

Vicenza Railway Station
Maggiore *0444 54 59 62.*
Avis *0444 32 16 22.*
Hertz *0444 23 17 28.*

Boat from Venice's Marco Polo airport into the city

Travelling by Train

ITALY'S STATE RAILWAY (Ferrovie dello Stato or FS) runs an extensive and efficient rail network throughout the Veneto. Services are regular, trains tend to be punctual and the cost of travel is very reasonable. The variety of trains ranges from the painstakingly slow *locale*, which stops at almost every station, through various levels of fast intercity services to the high-speed Italian Eurostar, which links Venice with Rome and the rest of Italy.

FS train in Verona station

Eurostar – Italy's fastest train

Arriving by Train

SANTA LUCIA railway station in Venice is the terminus for trains from Paris, Munich, Innsbruck, Vienna, Geneva, Zurich and other European cities. Passengers travelling from London have to change in Paris or Ostend. Fast intercity trains link Venice with Verona, Bologna, Milan, Rome and other major Italian cities.

Europe-wide train passes such as Eurail (US) or InterRail for those under 26 (Europe) are accepted on the FS network. You will have to pay a supplement, however, to travel on Italian Eurostar trains.

Santa Lucia Station, Venice

STANDING AT the west end of the Grand Canal, Ferrovia Santa Lucia is a modern, well-equipped station. There are *vaporetti* landing stages below the steps of the station with boats going to San Marco and all stops en route. There is also a water taxi and gondola service. Porters are not so easy to find, however. The bus and coach terminal and the only land taxi rank in Venice are in Piazzale Roma nearby (follow yellow signs).

Automatic ticket machines in the station are easy to use and display instructions in six languages. Notes, coins and some credit cards are accepted. Tickets can be booked free of charge in advance through travel agents.

Multilingual display screens give information on arrivals, departures, costs of travel and details about city services and tours. A tourist office offers to make hotel reservations, but queues are long in summer. There is also a Rolling Venice office *(see p262)*, a bank and currency exchange, a left luggage facility, a cafeteria and bar, and a shop that sells international newspapers and magazines. There is also a number of telephones. Another useful facility is the *albergo diurno*. This is a daytime hotel where you can rest in a private room with an en-suite shower.

Orient Express

FROM MARCH to November the *Venice Simplon-Orient-Express* runs between London and Venice with stops at Paris, Düsseldorf, Cologne, Frankfurt, Zurich, St Anton, Innsbruck and Verona. A one-way journey with cabin from London to Venice can cost ten times the price of a charter flight. However, if you opt for the return trip, ticket prices are more reasonable.

Santa Lucia station in Venice – gateway to the Veneto

The Orient-Express logo

Verona Stations

VERONA LIES at the intersection of the main railway lines from Venice to Milan and Bologna to Munich. The main station, Porta Nuova, lies south of the centre, connected to it by frequent bus services. Train information is available at the ticket office and automatic help points give information in English. Other facilities include a left luggage office, a bar, an automatic exchange machine and a newspaper shop which sells bus tickets.

The small Porta Vescova station, serving local stations to the east of Verona, is used mainly by locals.

Padua Station

PADUA IS ONLY 30 minutes by train from Venice. The station is in the north of the town (10 minute's walk from the centre), and buses for the centre leave from outside the station. The main bus terminal, with services to Venice and other towns of the Veneto is at Piazzale Boschetti, 10 minutes' walk from the station.

Padua's tourist office is within the station building. There is also a left luggage office, a restaurant, a tobacconist, a counter selling bus tickets and a bureau de change open 9am to noon and 3pm to 5:30pm Monday to Saturday; 9am to noon Sunday.

Vicenza Station

VICENZA, 55 minutes from Venice, is on the main railway line between Verona and Padua. The station is south of the city centre. Facilities include a bar and offices for left luggage, tickets, information and currency exchange open 8am to 12:30pm and 2pm to 6:30pm Monday to Saturday, 8:30am to noon and 2pm to 6pm Sunday.

Train Travel

IF YOU PLAN to travel around, there are passes which allow unlimited travel on the FS network for a determined period of time, such as the Italy Rail Card and the Italy Flexi Rail Card. Available only to non-residents, the cards can be purchased from the station. The *biglietto chilometrico* allows up to 20 trips totalling under 3,000 km (1,865 miles) for up to five people over two months. This is available from international and local **CIT** offices and from any travel agent selling train tickets. For more information on passes, visit the FS's website (www.fs-on-line.com).

There are facilities for disabled travellers on some intercity services.

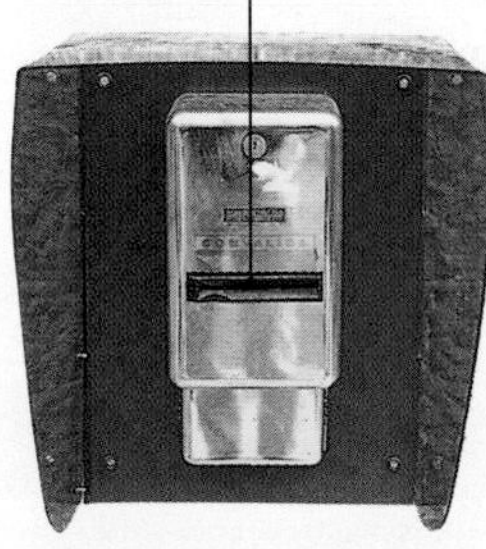

Machine for validating tickets

Machines for FS Rail Tickets

These machines are easy to use, and most have instructions in six languages on screen. They take coins, notes and credit cards.

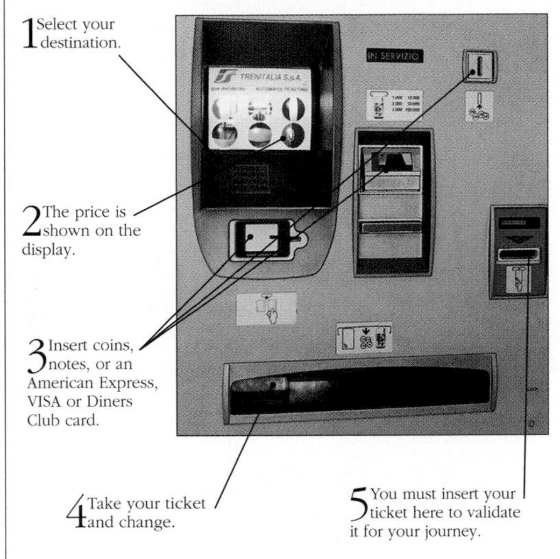

1 Select your destination.
2 The price is shown on the display.
3 Insert coins, notes, or an American Express, VISA or Diners Club card.
4 Take your ticket and change.
5 You must insert your ticket here to validate it for your journey.

Tickets

ON ALL INTERCITY trains a supplement is charged, even if you have a rail card. Booking is often obligatory on the Eurostar and some other intercity services, and it is also advisable on other trains if you wish to travel at busy times.

If you are travelling less than 200 km (125 miles), a short-range ticket *(biglietto a fasce chilometriche)* is available. The ticket is stamped with the destination you require and it must then be validated in one of the machines at the entrance to the platforms. Both outward and return portions of a ticket must be used within three days of purchase. Tickets can be bought on the train but these are liable to a flat rate surcharge *and* a supplement based on the ticket price.

Railway Information Offices

☎ *89 20 21. (Use this national number for all rail enquiries in Italy.)*

Telephone bookings

Venice
☎ *041 275 04 92.*

Verona
☎ *045 800 81 79.*

Booking Agents

CIT

Via Giacomo Matteotti 12, Padua.
☎ *049 66 33 33.*
Piazza Bra 2, Verona.
☎ *045 59 17 88.*
3–5 Lansdown Rd, Croydon CR9 1LL, United Kingdom. ☎ *020 8686 5533.*

Orient Express

c/o Royal Tour, Castello 3476, Venice.
☎ *041 522 17 46.*
@ royal.tour@galactica.it

Multilingual information board showing train departures

Getting Around Venice by Boat

For visitors to Venice, the *vaporetti* or waterbuses provide an entertaining form of public transport, although most journeys within the city can usually be covered more quickly on foot. The main route through the city for the *vaporetti* is the Grand Canal, and these waterbuses also supply a useful service connecting outlying points on the periphery of Venice and linking the city with the islands in the lagoon. The best value service from a visitor's point of view is the No. 1. This operates from one end of the Grand Canal to the other and travels sufficiently slowly for you to admire the parade of palaces at the waterside *(see pp56–71)*.

Vaporetto* stop at the Giardini Pubblici** ***(see pp120–21)

A *vaporetto* pulling into San Marco

The smaller, sleeker *motoscafo*

A two-tier *motonave* on its way to Torcello

The Boats

The original *vaporetti* were steam-powered (*vaporetto* means little steamer); today they are diesel-run motor boats. Although all the boats tend to be called *vaporetti*, strictly speaking the word applies only to the large wide boats used on the slow routes, such as No. 1. These boats provide the best views. The *motoscafi* are the slimmer, smaller and faster boats, such as No. 52. Some of them might look old and rusty, but they go at quite a pace. The two-tier *motonavi*, which look huge in comparison to the *vaporetti* or *motoscafi*, are used on routes to outlying islands and the Lido.

Types of Ticket

Tickets for travel on the waterbuses are the same price for any length of journey. This makes the service very easy to use, although there are a huge number of different types of ticket which, if applicable, could gain you a saving over the standard single ticket price.

If you only want to cross the Grand Canal, you can buy a crossing ticket for less than 2 or a return for just under 3. For other return trips to and from the same destination, a return ticket will cost about 6.

There are also 12-hour, 24-hour or 72-hour tickets that entitle the holder and/or group to unlimited travel on most lines.

For visits of more than a few days, you can buy a monthly season ticket *(abbonamento)*, available from the Piazzale Roma or San Marco ticket offices. Holders of Rolling Venice cards *(see p262)* can buy a *Tre Giorni Giovane*, or three-day youth pass, for 13.

Many of the lagoon islands can also be visited with a special ticket, available on the Northern Lagoon Line. Some island services, however, such as Lineablu, Clodia Line and Alilaguna Line, are not covered by any of the special tickets.

Hours of Service

The main routes run every 10 to 20 minutes until the early evening. Services are reduced at night, particularly after 1am, when a night-route operates. Details of main lines are given in the ACTV timetable, available at most landing stages.

Sightseeing from a *vaporetto* on the Grand Canal

The Main Routes

(1) This is the slow boat down the Grand Canal, stopping at every landing stage. The route starts at Piazzale Roma, travels the length of the Grand Canal, then from San Marco it heads east to the Lido.

(82) The No. 82 is the faster route down the Grand Canal. The whole route goes in a loop, starting at San Zaccaria, continuing westwards along the Giudecca Canal to Tronchetto and Piazzale Roma, then down the Grand Canal back to San Zaccaria and from there out to the Lido (summer only).

(51) (52) The 51 and 52 skirt the periphery of Venice and have also been extended to the Lido. The circular "Giracittà" route provides a scenic tour of Venice, though to do the whole circuit you have to change boats at Fondamente Nuove.

(41) (42) Circular "Giracittà" lines taking in Murano. No. 41 runs anticlockwise, while No. 42 goes clockwise.

(12) Departing from the Fondamente Nuove, the 12 serves the main islands in the northern lagoon: Murano, Mazzorbo, Burano and Torcello, ending at Punta Sabbioni.

(14) The 14 goes to Punta Sabbioni from San Zaccaria, via the Lido.

(61) (62) These "Giracittà" routes take in much of Venice, from the Lido to Piazzale Roma.

(71) (72) The 71 and 72 operate only between 1 April and 31 October. The 71 travels from San Zaccaria via Murano to Tronchetto; the 72 is the reverse route, starting at Tronchetto.

Vaporetto Information

ACTV (Information Office)
Piazzale Roma, Venice.
Map 5 B1. 041 528 78 86.
www.actv.it

Using the Vaporetti

The service is run by **ACTV** *(Azienda Consorzio Trasporti Veneziano)*. The waterbus system is constantly being modified, and thus, while every effort is made to keep the map on the inside back cover of this guide up-to-date, it may not reflect the most recent changes made to the lines. If you are not sure which boat to take to reach your destination, check with the boatman – the *vaporetti* crew tend to be very helpful.

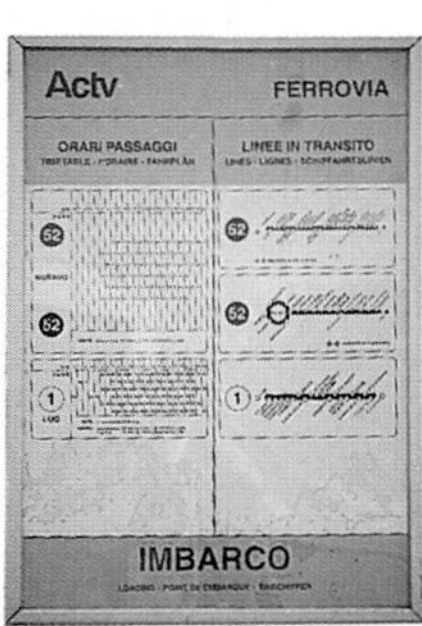

Timetable and routes at a *vaporetto* boarding point

1 Tickets are available at most landing stages, some bars, shops and tobacconists displaying the ACTV sign. The price of a ticket remains the same whether you are going one stop or doing the whole circuit, although a few routes are more expensive. There are also a variety of special tickets available *(see* Types of Ticket*)*.

2 Signs on the landing stage tell you at which end you should board the boat.

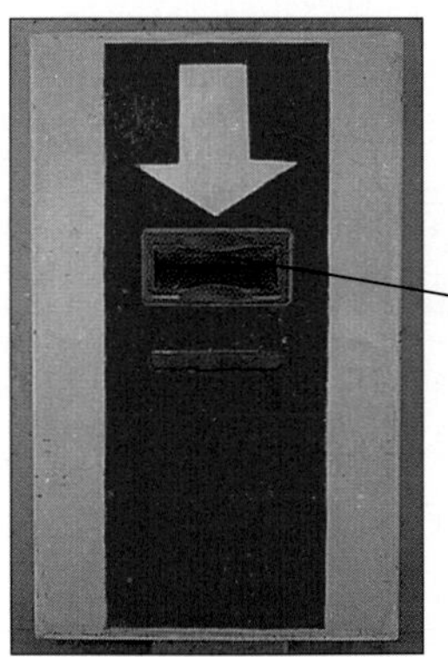

3 Tickets should be punched at the automatic machines on the landing stages before each journey. Inspectors rarely board the boats and this makes it surprisingly easy for tourists (and Venetians) to hop on and off the boats without a validated ticket. However, there are steep fines for passengers without tickets, and there are notices in English to this effect in all the boats.

4 An indicator board at the front of each boat gives the line number and main stops. (Ignore the large black numbers on the side of the boat.)

5 Each landing stage has its name clearly marked on a yellow board. Most stops have two landing stages and it is quite easy, particularly if it is crowded and you can't see which way the boat is facing, to board a boat travelling in the wrong direction. It is helpful to watch which direction the boat is approaching from; if in doubt, check with the boatman on board.

Finding Your Way in Venice

VENICE IS SURPRISINGLY SMALL and most of the sights can be covered comfortably on foot. However, to avoid losing your way in the maze of little alleys, make sure you have the Street Finder *(see pp280–93)* handy. The gondola is the most romantic way to see the city, but prices are high, while the water taxi is the fastest means of travelling through the city and out to the islands.

GONDOLAS

GONDOLAS ARE a luxury form of transport used only by tourists (apart from Venetians on their wedding day). There are a number of gondola ranks throughout the city and plenty of gondoliers waiting for business.

Before boarding, check the official tariffs and agree a price with the gondolier. Prices are in the booklet *Un Ospite di Venezia (see p260)* and should also be available at gondola ranks. Official costs are around 60 for 45 minutes, rising to 80 after 8pm, but Gondoliers are notorious for overcharging; sometimes by double the official price. Try bargaining, whatever the cost quoted. During the low season, or when business looks slack, you may be able to negotiate a fee below the official rate and a journey shorter than the minimum of 45 minutes. Another way of cutting costs is to share a gondola – five is the maximum number of passengers.

Gondoliers all speak a smattering of English and have taken basic exams in Venetian history and art. Do not expect your gondolier to burst into *O Sole Mio*, however; the most you are likely to hear are the low melodious cries of *Oe,* *Premi* and *Stai* – the warning calls that have been echoing down the canals of Venice for centuries. If you want to go on a serenaded tour, join an evening flotilla with accompanying musicians, organized regularly from May to October. Hiring a gondola independently is more romantic, but will cost considerably more. Details are available from any local travel agent.

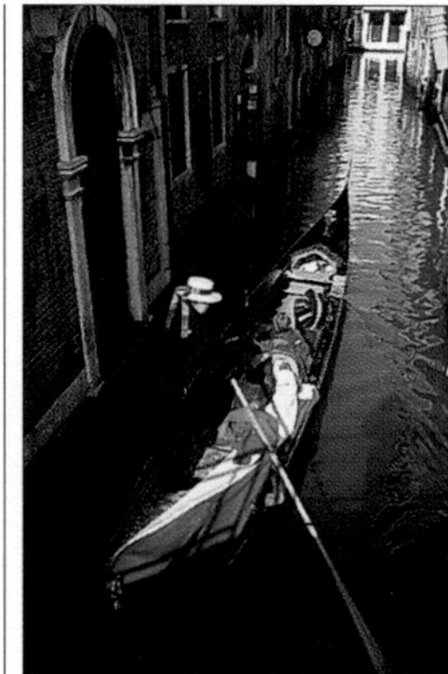

The romance of an early evening gondola ride

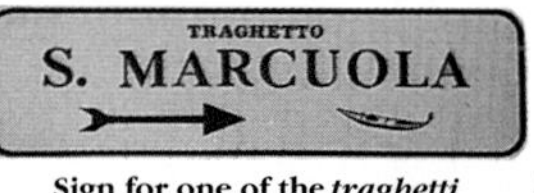

Sign for one of the *traghetti* across the Grand Canal

TRAGHETTI

TRAGHETTI are gondola ferries that cross the Grand Canal at seven different points, providing an invaluable service for pedestrians. Surprisingly, few tourists make use of this cheap, constant service. The points where the *traghetti* cross the Grand Canal are marked on the Street Finder maps *(see pp280–93)*. Yellow street signs show the way to the *traghetti*, illustrated with a little gondola symbol.

Crossing the Grand Canal by *traghetto*

WATER TAXIS

FOR THOSE with little time and sufficient funds, the fastest and most practical means of getting from A to B is by water taxi. The craft are sleek, white or polished wood motorboats, all equipped with a cabin. They zip to and from the airport in only 20 minutes. There are 16 water taxi ranks, including one at the airport and at the Lido. Telephone numbers and official tariffs are listed in the booklet *Un Ospite di Venezia (see p260)*. Extra is charged for luggage, waiting, night service and for calling out a taxi. If the *vaporetti* are on strike, which is extremely rare, water taxis are like gold dust.

A water taxi

GONDOLA STANDS

San Marco (Molo)
041 520 06 85.

Rialto (Riva Carbon)
041 522 49 04.

Railway Station (San Simeone Piccolo)
041 71 85 43.

WATER TAXI STANDS (serving all of Venice)

Consorzio Motoscafi Piazzale Roma
041 71 69 22.

Consorzio Motoscafi Rialto
041 522 23 03.

Serenissima San Marco
041 522 85 38.

Walking in Venice

One of the great pleasures of exploring Venice is walking. In the absence of traffic you soon get used to crossing streets and squares without so much as a glance to left or right. What you do have to contend with is the constant flow of tourists. The narrow alleys, particularly in the *sestiere* of San Marco, become extremely congested. To avoid pedestrian congestion keep to the right and avoid stopping on bridges and in narrow streets. However, the vast majority of tourists never venture beyond San Marco and it will be little more than a matter of minutes before you find yourself with only a few locals for company.

When sightseeing in Venice you will inevitably do a lot of walking, and a day taking in the sights can be extremely tiring. You need to allow only 35 minutes to cross the city from north to south on foot – provided you do not lose your way. Most visitors do, and this is, of course, part of the fun of exploring, but sensible shoes are a must, however short you think your journey may be.

Venice is so compact that you are never very far from the yellow signs that give directions to the key points of the city.

The city has countless *campi*, or squares, which open out

Venice, city of bridges

from the narrow alleys. Most of these are equipped with public benches, and footsore tourists can also sit at an open-air café. However, you will be expected to buy a drink, and drinks are expensive. Many of the main sights are concentrated in the *sestiere* of San Marco, either in Piazza San Marco *(see pp74–5)* or close by. Even the main sights in the *sestieri* beyond San Marco are, for most people, within comfortable walking distance of the main square. Apart from the Accademia and San Marco, the sign-posting is not very impressive, but the maps in this guide will help you find your way around.

An ornate Venetian door knocker

In July and August, when temperatures are at their highest, it is wise to avoid walking around midday. You should also be prepared, particularly at this time of year, for nasty smells which waft from some of the canals.

From October there is always the risk of high tides *(acqua alta)*, which cause flooding in the city. The first area to flood is Piazza San Marco. Duck-boards are laid out in the square, however, and along main thoroughfares. If you are not equipped with wellington boots you can always buy cheap knee-high plastic shoe covers from local shops.

Addresses in Venice

For any newcomer to the city of Venice, the system of addresses is initially very confusing. All buildings are numbered by the *sestiere* (administrative district) in which they fall rather than by the street. Hence a typical address would merely give the name of the *sestiere* followed by the number of the building, for example San Marco 2517 or Cannaregio 3499.

To locate an address it is, therefore, essential for you to establish the name of the street or square or, failing that, the nearest landmark. The Venetians resort to a book called *Indicatore Anagrafico*, which lists all the numbers in Venice and their corresponding streets. More useable, perhaps, is the more recent publication, *Calli, Campielli e Canali*, which also provides detailed maps of the city and islands.

You will find translations of Venetian words commonly used in place names in the Street Finder *(see p280)*.

A plethora of confusing signs in Cannaregio

Getting Around the Veneto

Taxi in Verona

Day trips can be made from Venice by train or bus, and the city centres can be covered easily on foot or by local bus. Although the train and bus networks are excellent, the most practical and pleasant means of travel is by car, allowing total independence to explore the countryside. However, some of the roads between towns tend to be very congested in the summer, city centres are banned to tourist traffic, and the cost of petrol is high.

A city bus in central Verona

On Foot and by Bus

All the cities of the Veneto are small enough to get around reasonably comfortably on foot. Limited traffic zones means that walking is pleasant and there are plenty of squares where you can sit and watch the world go by.

City buses are cheap and regular. Tickets, which must be bought prior to travel, are available from news-stands, bars, tobacconists and shops which display the bus company sign. There are also ticket vending machines in the streets, usually near stops, which take coins and notes. A flat fee is charged for rides within the city and the suburbs. The ticket becomes valid only when you time-stamp it in the machine at the front or rear of the bus.

It is normally cheaper and quicker to travel between towns by train. In some cases the bus will take twice as long as the train, but there are a few towns such as Asolo where your only choice is a bus. In most cases the bus departure point is near the train station. You can usually buy a ticket valid for one, two or more hours of travel.

The city of Venice has excellent rail and bus connections. The most popular routes connect nearby towns such as Mestre, Mira, Marghera and Stra.

Taxis

Travelling by taxi in the Veneto is not cheap. Meters show a fixed starting charge, then clock up every kilometre. There are extra charges for luggage, trips to the airports and journeys taken between 10pm and 7am, on Sundays and public holidays. Taxi drivers do not necessarily expect a tip – Italians give small tips or none at all.

Take taxis only from the official ranks, not from touts at railway stations and airports. In Venice the taxi rank is in Piazzale Roma; in the Veneto towns of Verona, Vicenza and Padua, taxis can be found at the main piazzas.

Car Hire

If you book your car within the Veneto, local Italian firms such as Maggiore *(see p271)* tend to be cheaper than the international ones. Whichever company you choose, make sure that quoted prices include collision damage waiver, theft, breakdown service and IVA (Italian VAT, currently 19 per cent). Insurance against theft is usually an extra. To hire a car you must be over 21 and have held a licence for at least a year. Visitors from outside the EU need an international licence, though in practice hire firms may not insist on this.

Driving and Parking

Cities in the Veneto have limited traffic zones and normally only residents and taxis can drive into the centre. Visitors can unload at their hotel, but must then park on the outside of town and come in by foot or bus. Some hotels have a limited number of parking permits, but this is no guarantee of a space. Your

Rules of the Road

Drive on the right and, generally, give way to the right. Seat belts are compulsory in the front and back, and children should be properly restrained. You must also carry a warning triangle in case of breakdown. In town centres, the speed limit is 50 km/h (30 mph); on ordinary roads 90 km/h (55 mph); and on motorways 110 km/h (70 mph) for cars up to 1099cc, and 130 km/h (80 mph) for more powerful cars. Penalties for speeding include spot fines and licence points, and there are drink-driving laws as elsewhere in the EU.

One-way street

Speed limit (on minor road)

End of speed restriction

Pedestrianized street – no traffic

Give way to oncoming traffic

Give way 320 m (350 yd) ahead

Danger (often with description)

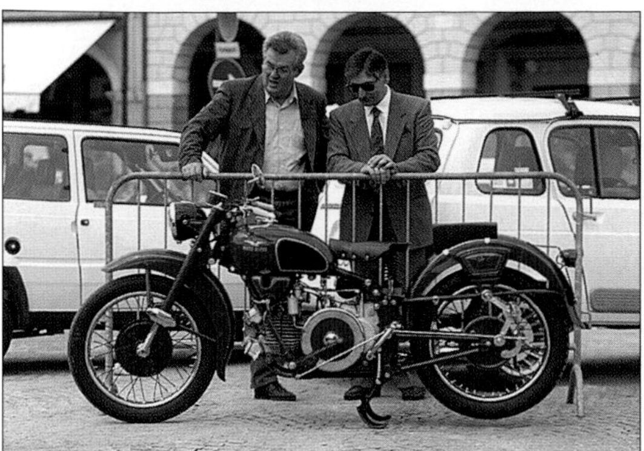

Moto Guzzi's classic Gambalunga in the market place at Montagnana

best bet is to telephone in advance and warn the hotel of your arrival.

Official parking areas are marked by blue lines, usually with meters or an attendant nearby. The *disco orario* system allows free parking for a limited period in certain areas. The cardboard discs, which you place on your windscreen, are provided by car hire companies, or can be purchased at petrol stations and also at supermarkets in the cities of the Veneto.

If you have your car towed away, phone the **Polizia Municipale**, or Municipal Police.

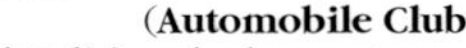

***Disco orario* parking disc**

In Venice parking is prohibitively expensive. The closest car parks to the centre are at Piazzale Roma, where space is at a premium. There is a huge car park on the Isola del Tronchetto, linked to Venice by *vaporetto* and bus. There are cheaper car parks at Fusina and San Giuliano in Mestre.

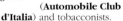

Many of the main roads are old, with only a couple of lanes, and traffic can be heavy. What looks like a short trip on the map may take much longer than you expect. For more details on road conditions contact **CIS** (Centro Informazione Stradale). *Autostrada* tolls, levied on the motorways, are expensive. Payment can be made in cash or by pre-paid magnetic cards called Viacards. These are available from ACI offices (**Automobile Club d'Italia**) and tobacconists.

The picturesque but hair-raising Gardesana *(see p204)*

Petrol

Motorway service stations are open 24 hours a day. Petrol stations are scarce in the countryside and most do not accept credit cards. Many are closed all afternoon, all day Sunday and the whole of August. However, you will find some self-service petrol stations with automatic pumps that accept notes.

Breakdowns

The ACI provides an efficient 24-hour service also available to foreign visitors. The organization has reciprocal arrangements with affiliated associations in other countries such as the AA or RAC in Britain.

Directory

Bus Information

Belluno
Dolomiti Bus,
Via Col da Ren 14.
☎ *0437 94 11 67.*

Padua
Autobus,
ACAP Office Ferrovia.
☎ *049 824 11 37.*

Verona
Azienda Municipalizzata Trasporti.
Via Torbido 1.
☎ *045 887 11 11.*

Vicenza
Aziende Industriali
Municipalizzate
Via Fusineri 83.
☎ *0444 39 49 09.*

Road Information

CIS
☎ *15 18 (Italian only).*

Breakdown

Automobile Club d'Italia
Emergencies
☎ *116.*

Via Ca' Marcello 67/d, Mestre.
☎ *041 531 03 62.*

Via Valverde 34, Verona.
☎ *045 59 53 33.*

Via degli Scrovegni 19, Padua.
☎ *049 65 49 35.*

Viale della Pace 260, Vicenza.
☎ *0444 51 33 71.*

Towing Away

Polizia Municipale (Municipal Police)
Venice
☎ *041 274 70 70.*

Padua
☎ *049 820 51 00.*

Verona
☎ *045 807 84 11.*

Vicenza
☎ *0444 54 53 11.*

Venice Street Finder

All the sights, hotels, restaurants, shops and entertainment venues in Venice have map references which refer you to this section of the book. The key map below indicates the areas of the city covered by the Street Finder, and includes the colour coding specific to each area. Following the map section is a complete index of street names *(see pp290–93)*. The standard Italian spelling has been used on the maps throughout this book, but when exploring the city you will find that the street signs are often printed in Venetian dialect. Sometimes this means only a slight variation in the spelling (see the word Sotoportico/Sotoportego below), but some names look completely different. For example, Santi Giovanni e Paolo *(see Map 3)* is often signposted as "San Zanipolo". Major sights are labelled in Italian.

Recognizing Street Names

The signs for street *(calle)*, canal *(rio)* and square *(campo)* will soon become familiar, but the Venetians have a colourful vocabulary for the maze of alleys which makes up the city. When exploring, the following may help.

FONDAMENTA S.SEVERO

Fondamenta A street that runs alongside a canal, often named after the canal it follows.

RIO TERRA GESUATI

Rio Terrà A filled-in canal. Similar to a *rio terrà* is a *piscina*, which often forms a square.

SOTOPORTEGO E PONTE S.CRISTOFORO

Sotoportico or Sotoportego A covered passageway.

SALIZADA PIO X

Salizzada A main street (formerly a paved street).

RIVA DEI PARTIGIANI

Riva A wide *fondamenta*, often facing the lagoon.

RUGAGIUFFA

Ruga A street lined with shops.

CORTE DEI DO POZZI

Corte A courtyard.

RIO MENUO O DE LA VERONA

Many streets and canals in Venice often have more than one name: *o* means "or".

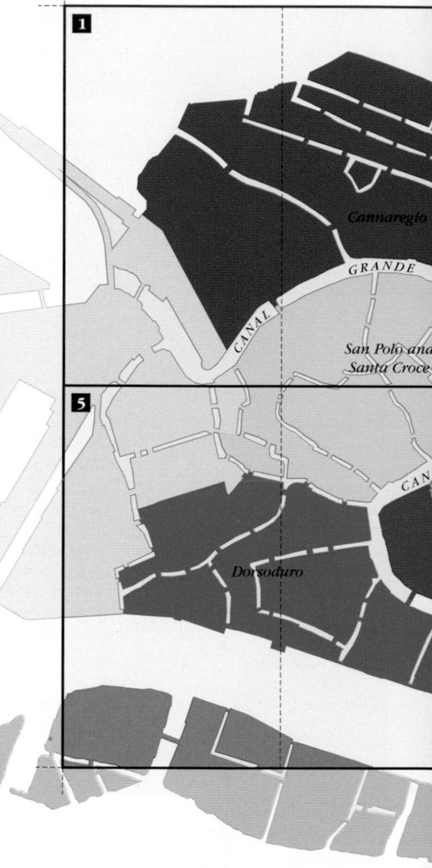

0 metres 500

0 yards 500

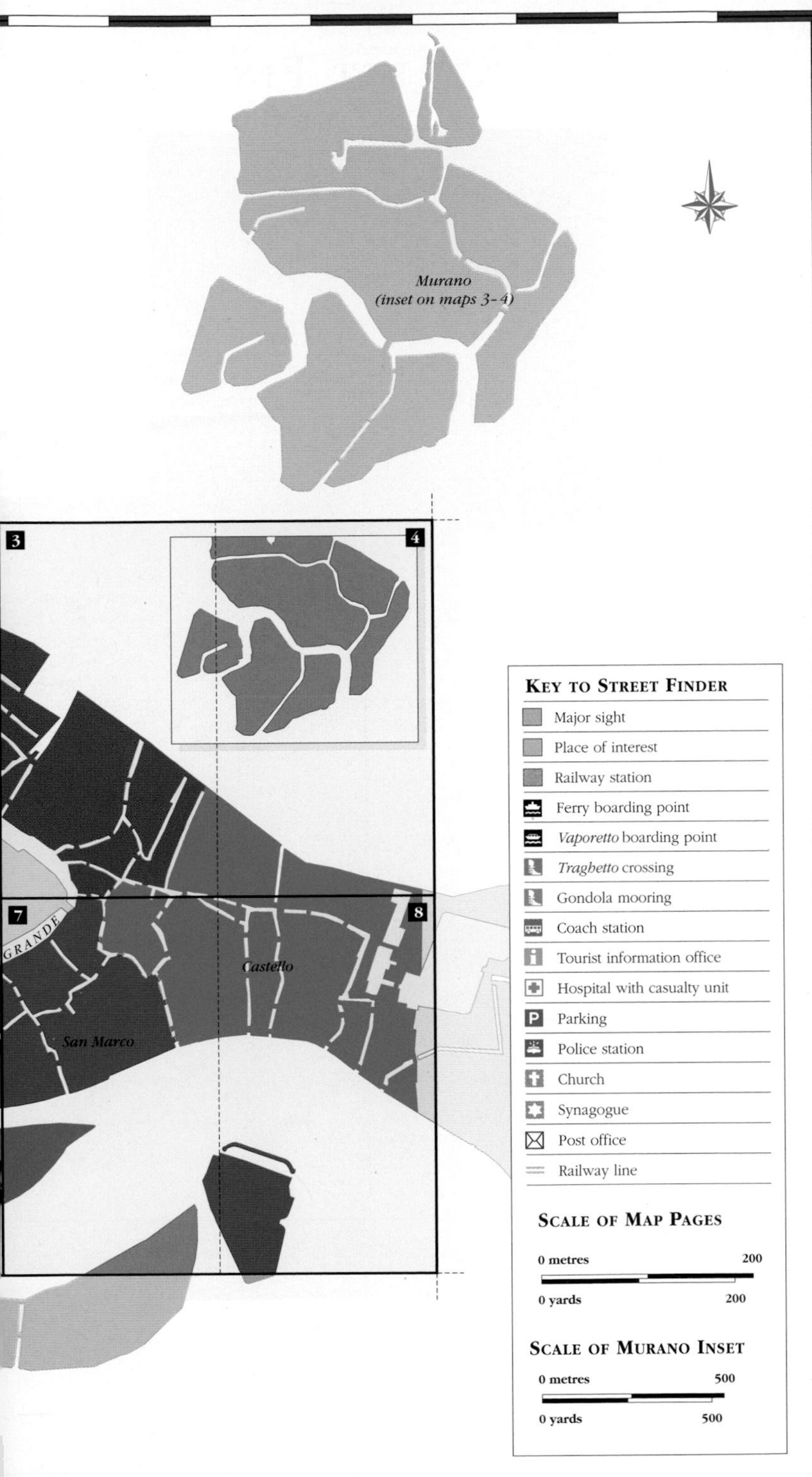

KEY TO STREET FINDER

- Major sight
- Place of interest
- Railway station
- Ferry boarding point
- *Vaporetto* boarding point
- *Traghetto* crossing
- Gondola mooring
- Coach station
- Tourist information office
- Hospital with casualty unit
- Parking
- Police station
- Church
- Synagogue
- Post office
- Railway line

SCALE OF MAP PAGES

0 metres 200

0 yards 200

SCALE OF MURANO INSET

0 metres 500

0 yards 500

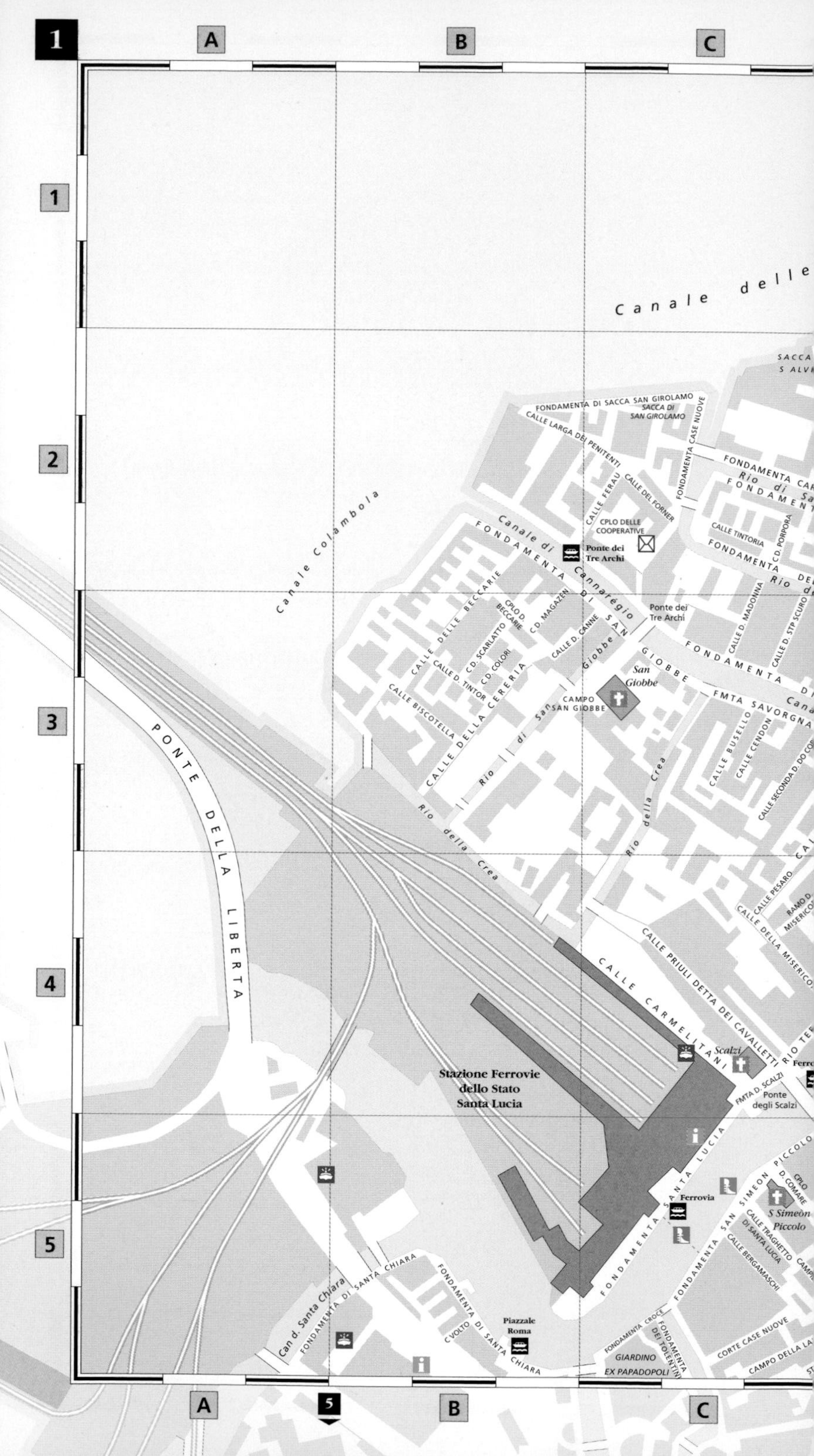
1
A
B
C
1
2
3
4
5
Canale delle
SACCA S ALV
FONDAMENTA DI SACCA SAN GIROLAMO
SACCA DI SAN GIROLAMO
CALLE LARGA DEI PENITENTI
FONDAMENTA CASE NUOVE
CALLE FERAU
CALLE DEL FORNER
CPLO DELLE COOPERATIVE
Canale Colambola
Canale di Cannaregio
FONDAMENTA DI SAN GIOBBE
Ponte dei Tre Archi
Ponte dei Tre Archi
CALLE TINTORIA
C.D. PORPORA
CALLE D. MADONNA
CALLE D. STP SCURO
CALLE DELLE BECCARIE
CPLO D. BECCARIE
C.D. MAGAZEN
C.D. SCARLATTO
CALLE D. CANNE
CALLE D. TINTOR
C.D. COLORI
CALLE DELLA CERERIA
CALLE BISCOTELLA
San Giobbe
CAMPO SAN GIOBBE
FMTA SAVORGNA
CALLE BUSELLO
CALLE CENDON
CALLE SECONDA D. DO CO
Rio di San Giobbe
Rio della Crea
Rio della Crea
PONTE DELLA LIBERTA
CALLE PESARO
RAMO D. MISERICO
CALLE DELLA MISERICO
CALLE PRIULI DETTA DEI CAVALLETTI
CALLE CARMELITANI
Scalzi
Ferr
FMTA D. SCALZI
Ponte degli Scalzi
Stazione Ferrovie dello Stato Santa Lucia
FONDAMENTA SANTA LUCIA
Ferrovia
FONDAMENTA SAN SIMEON PICCOLO
CPLO D. COMARE
S Simeon Piccolo
CALLE TRAGHETTO DI SANTA LUCIA
CALLE BERGAMASCHI
CAMPI
Can d. Santa Chiara
FONDAMENTA DI SANTA CHIARA
FONDAMENTA DI SANTA CHIARA
C VOLTO
Piazzale Roma
FONDAMENTA CROCE
FONDAMENTA DEI TOLENTINI
GIARDINO EX PAPADOPOLI
CORTE CASE NUOVE
CAMPO DELLA LA
A
5
B
C

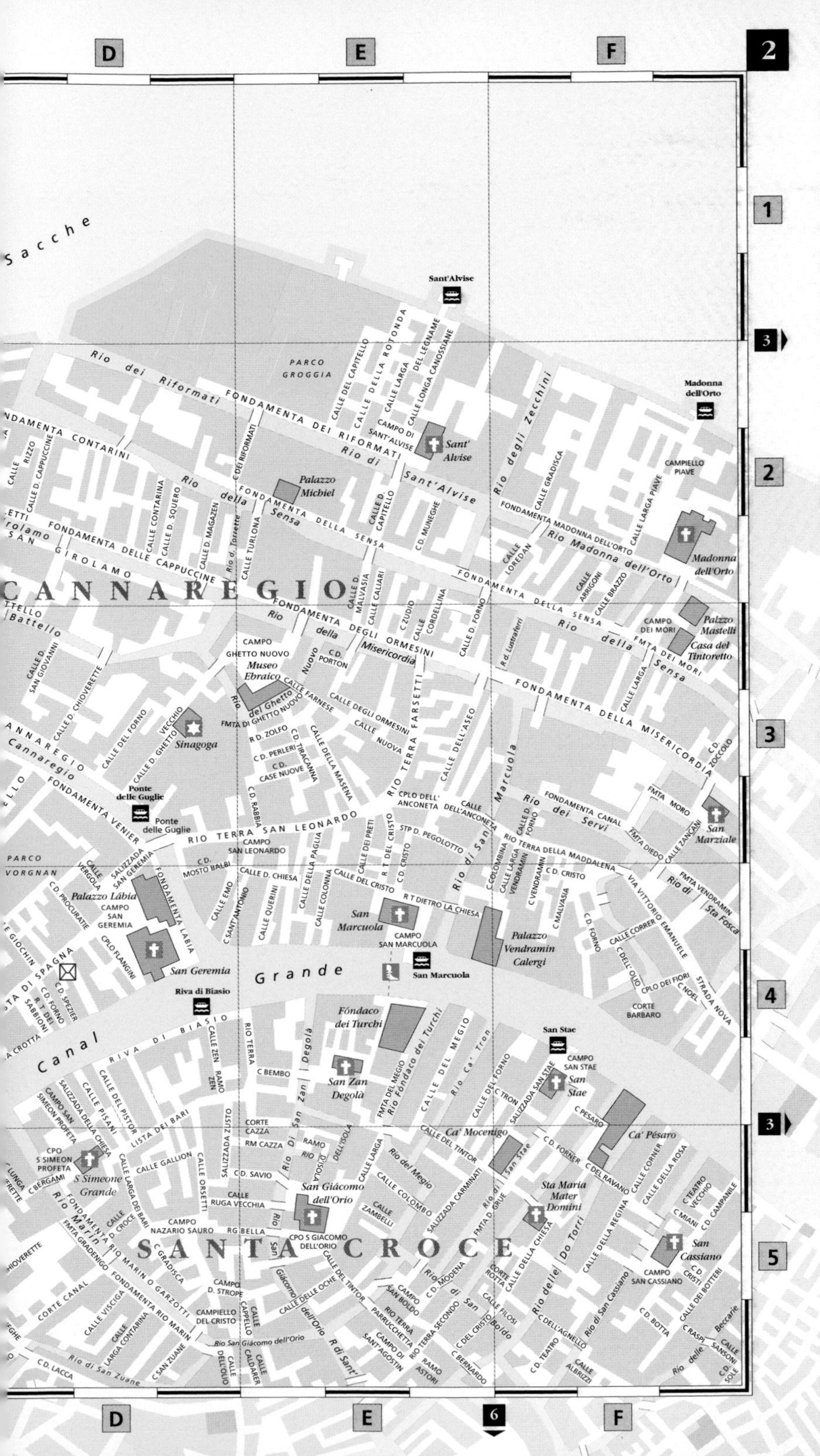
D
E
F
2
1
3
4
5
6
Sacche
Sant'Alvise
PARCO GROGGIA
Rio dei Riformati
FONDAMENTA DEI RIFORMATI
FONDAMENTA CONTARINI
CALLE DEL CAPITELLO
CALLE DELLA ROTONDA
CALLE LARGA
DEL LEGNAME
CALLE LONGA CANOSSIANE
CAMPO DI SANT'ALVISE
Sant' Alvise
Rio di Sant'Alvise
Rio degli Zecchini
Madonna dell'Orto
CAMPIELLO PIAVE
CALLE GRADISCA
CALLE LARGA PIAVE
FONDAMENTA MADONNA DELL'ORTO
Rio Madonna dell'Orto
Madonna dell'Orto
Palazzo Michiel
Rio della Sensa
FONDAMENTA DELLA SENSA
CALLE RIZZO
CALLE D. CAPPUCCINE
CALLE CONTARINA
CALLE D. SQUERO
CALLE D. MAGAZEN
Rio d. Torrette
CALLE TURLONA
C. DEI RIFORMATI
CALLE D. CAPITELLO
C.D. MUNEGHE
FONDAMENTA DELLE CAPPUCCINE
SAN GIROLAMO
CANNAREGIO
CALLE LOREDAN
CALLE ARRIGONI
CALLE BRAZZO
FONDAMENTA DELLA SENSA
CAMPO DEI MORI
Palazzo Mastelli
Casa del Tintoretto
FMTA DEI MORI
Rio della Sensa
CALLE D. MALVASIA
CALLE CALIARI
C. ZUDIO
CALLE CORDELLINA
CALLE D. FORNO
R d. Lustraferri
FONDAMENTA DEGLI ORMESINI
Rio della Misericordia
CALLE LARGA
FONDAMENTA DELLA MISERICORDIA
Battello
CAMPO GHETTO NUOVO
Museo Ebraico
Nuovo
C.D. PORTON
CALLE D. SAN GIOVANNI
CALLE D. CHIOVERETTE
Rio del Ghetto
CALLE FARNESE
FMTA DI GHETTO NUOVO
CALLE DEGLI ORMESINI
CALLE NUOVA
RIO TERRA FARSETTI
CALLE DELL'ASEO
Marcuola
C.D. ZOCCOLO
CALLE DEL FORNO
CALLE D. GHETTO VECCHIO
Sinagoga
R.D. ZOLFO
C.D. PERLERI
C.D. CASE NUOVE
C.D. TIRACANNA
CALLE DELLA MASENA
CANNAREGIO
Rio di Cannaregio
FONDAMENTA VENIER
Ponte delle Guglie
C.D. RABBIA
CPLO DELL' ANCONETA
CALLE DELL'ANCONETA
Rio dei Servi
FONDAMENTA CANAL
FMTA MORO
San Marziale
RIO TERRA SAN LEONARDO
CAMPO SAN LEONARDO
STP. D. PEGOLOTTO
RIO TERRA DELLA MADDALENA
FMTA DIEDO
CALLE ZANCANI
PARCO VORGNAN
CALLE VERGOLA
SALIZZADA SAN GEREMIA
FONDAMENTA LABIA
C.D. MOSTO BALBI
CALLE D. CHIESA
CALLE DEI PRETI
R.T. DEL CRISTO
C.D. CRISTO
Rio di San Marcuola
C. COLOMBINA
CALLE LARGA VENDRAMIN
C. VENDRAMIN
C.D. CRISTO
VIA VITTORIO EMANUELE
FMTA VENDRAMIN
Rio di Sta Fosca
C.D. PROCURATIE
Palazzo Làbia
CAMPO SAN GEREMIA
CALLE EMO
C. SANT'ANTONIO
CALLE QUERINI
CALLE DELLA PAGLIA
CALLE COLONNA
CALLE DEL CRISTO
R T DIETRO LA CHIESA
San Marcuola
C. MALVASIA
C.D. FORNO
CALLE CORRER
CPLO FLANGINI
San Geremia
CAMPO SAN MARCUOLA
Palazzo Vendramin Calergi
C. DELL'OLIO
CPLO DEI FIORI
C. NOEL
STRADA NOVA
San Marcuola
Grande
LISTA DI SPAGNA
C.D. SPEZIER
C.D. FORNO
R.T. DEI SABBIONI
Riva di Biasio
CORTE BARBARO
Canal
RIVA DI BIASIO
CALLE ZEN
RAMO ZEN
RIO TERRA
Fóndaco dei Turchi
Degolà
San Stae
CAMPO SAN STAE
San Stae
C. BEMBO
San Zan Degolà
FMTA DEL MEGIO
Rio Fondaco dei Turchi
CALLE DEL MEGIO
Rio Ca' Tron
CALLE DEL FORNO
C. TRON
SALIZZADA SAN STAE
C. PESARO
Ca' Pésaro
SALIZZADA SAN SIMEON PROFETA
CAMPO SAN SIMEON PROFETA
SALIZZADA DELLA CHIESA
CALLE PISANI
CALLE DEL PISTOR
LISTA DEI BARI
SALIZZADA ZUSTO
CORTE CAZZA
RM CAZZA
Rio di San Zan Degolà
RAMO RIO
DELL'ISOLA
CALLE LARGA
Ca' Mocenigo
CALLE DEL TINTOR
Rio del Megio
Rio di San Stae
C.D. FORNER
C. DEL RAVANO
CALLE CORNER
CALLE DELLA ROSA
CPO S SIMEON PROFETA
C. BERGAMI
S Simeone Grande
CALLE GALLION
CALLE ORSETTI
C.D. SAVIO
Rio di San Giacomo
RAMO ISOLA
San Giácomo dell'Orio
CALLE COLOMBO
CALLE ZAMBELLI
SALIZZADA CARMINATI
FMTA D. GRUE
Sta Maria Mater Domini
C. TEATRO VECCHIO
C. MIANI
C.D. CAMPANILE
Rio Marin
FONDAMENTA RIO MARIN
FMTA GRADENIGO
CALLE D. CROCE
CALLE LARGA DEI BARI
CAMPO NAZARIO SAURO
CALLE RUGA VECCHIA
RG BELLA
CPO S GIACOMO DELL'ORIO
SANTA CROCE
CALLE DELLA CHIESA
Rio delle Do Torri
CALLE DELLA REGINA
San Cassiano
CHIOVERETTE
C. GRADISCA
FONDAMENTA RIO MARIN O GARZOTTI
CAMPO D. STROPE
CALLE DELLE OCHE
CALLE DEL TINTOR
CAMPO SAN BOLDO
Rio di San Boldo
C.D. MODENA
CORTE ROTTA
CALLE FILOSI
CAMPO SAN CASSIANO
C.D. CRISTI
CALLE DEI BOTTERI
CORTE CANAL
CALLE VISCIGA
CALLE LARGA CONTARINA
CAMPIELLO DEL CRISTO
CALLE CAPPELLO
Rio di Sant'Agostin
Rio San Giácomo dell'Orio
RIO TERRA PARRUCCHETTA
CAMPO DI SANT'AGOSTIN
RIO TERRA SECONDO
RAMO ASTORI
C. DEL CRISTO
C. BERNARDO
C. DELL'AGNELLO
Rio di San Cassiano
C.D. BOTTA
C. RASPI
CALLE SANSONI
Beccarie
Rio delle
C.D. SOLE
C.D. LACCA
Rio di San Zuane
C. SAN ZUANE
CALLE DELL'OLIO
CALLE CALDARER
C.D. TEATRO
CALLE ALBRIZZI

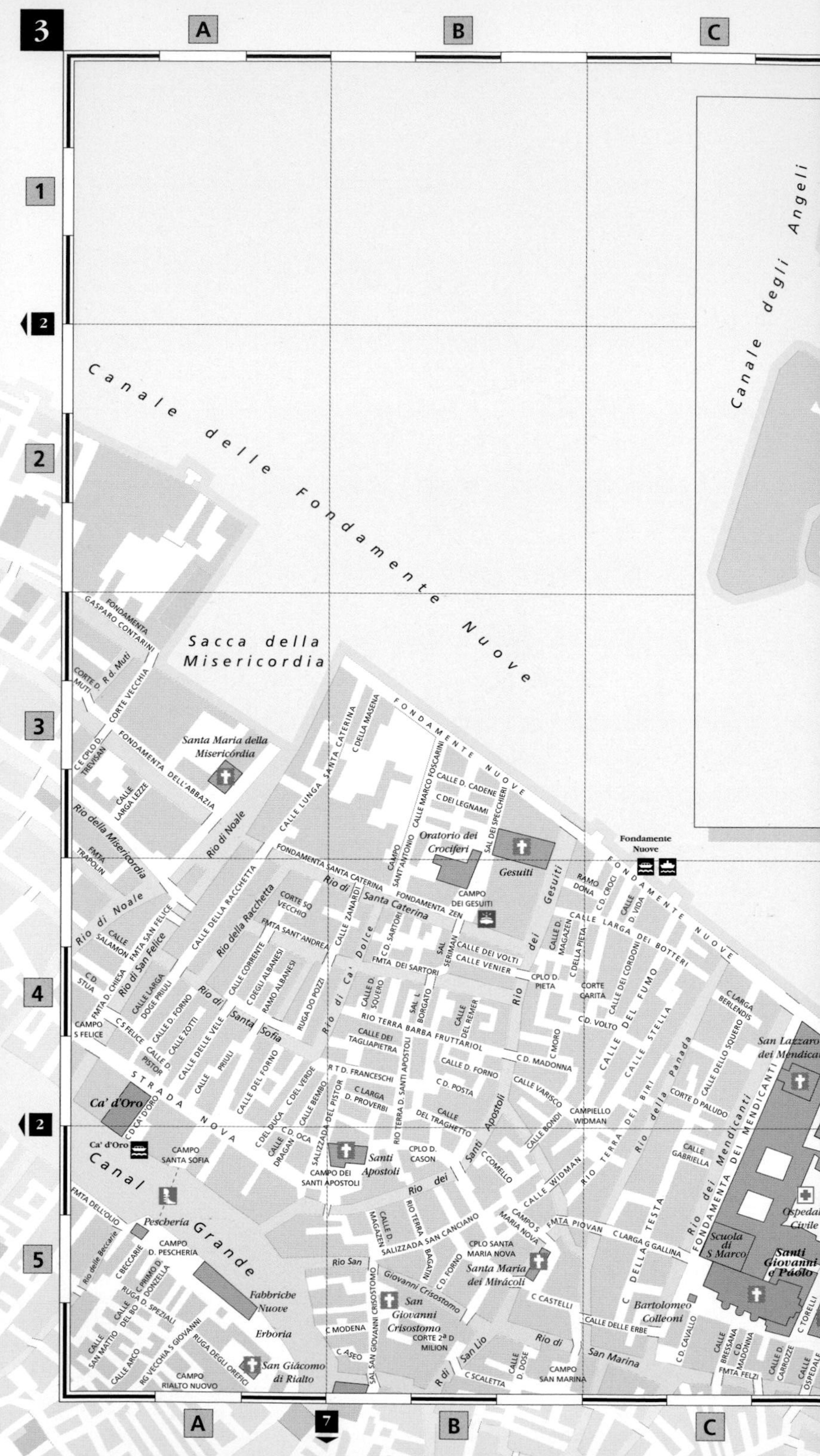

3
A
B
C
1
2
3
4
5
2
2
7
Canale delle Fondamente Nuove
Canale degli Angeli
Sacca della Misericordia
Santa Maria della Misericórdia
FONDAMENTA GASPARO CONTARINI
CORTE VECCHIA
FONDAMENTA DELL'ABBAZIA
CALLE LARGA LEZZE
Rio della Misericordia
Rio di Noale
FMTA TRAPOLIN
CALLE DELLA RACCHETTA
Rio della Racchetta
CALLE LUNGA SANTA CATERINA
C DELLA MASENA
FONDAMENTE NUOVE
CALLE D. CADENE
C DEI LEGNAMI
CALLE MARCO FOSCARINI
SAL DEI SPECCHIERI
Oratorio dei Crociferi
Gesuiti
CAMPO DEI GESUITI
Fondamente Nuove
FONDAMENTA SANTA CATERINA
Rio di Santa Caterina
FONDAMENTA ZEN
CORTE SQ VECCHIO
FMTA SANT'ANDREA
CALLE ZANARDI
Rio di Ca' Dolce
CALLE DEI VOLTI
CALLE VENIER
FMTA DEI SARTORI
Rio dei Gesuiti
CALLE LARGA DEI BOTTERI
CALLE DEI CORDONI
CALLE DEL FUMO
CORTE CARITÀ
CPLO D. PIETÀ
Rio di San Felice
CALLE SALAMON
FMTA SAN FELICE
CALLE LARGA DOGE PRIULI
CAMPO S FELICE
Rio di Santa Sofia
RUGA DO POZZI
RIO TERRA BARBA FRUTTARIOL
CALLE DEI TAGLIAPIETRA
C D. MADONNA
CALLE DEL FORNO
CALLE DELLA STELLA
C LARGA BERLENDIS
San Lazzaro dei Mendicanti
STRADA NOVA
Ca' d'Oro
CALLE DEL FORNO
C DEL DUCA
C DEL VERDE
CALLE BEMBO
SALIZZADA DEL PISTOR
C LARGA D. PROVERBI
CALLE DEL TRAGHETTO
Rio dei Santi Apostoli
CAMPIELLO WIDMAN
Rio della Panada
CORTE D PALUDO
Rio dei Mendicanti
FONDAMENTA DEI MENDICANTI
Ca' d'Oro
CAMPO SANTA SOFIA
Canal Grande
Santi Apostoli
CAMPO DEI SANTI APOSTOLI
CPLO D. CASON
C COMELLO
CALLE WIDMAN
RIO TERRA DEI BIRI
CALLE GABRIELLA
Ospedale Civile
FMTA DELL'OLIO
Pescheria
CAMPO D. PESCHERIA
Rio delle Beccarie
SALIZZADA SAN CANCIANO
CPLO SANTA MARIA NOVA
Santa Maria dei Miràcoli
FMTA PIOVAN
C LARGA G GALLINA
C DELLA TESTA
Scuola di S Marco
Santi Giovanni e Pàolo
Fabbriche Nuove
Erboria
Rio San Giovanni Crisostomo
San Giovanni Crisostomo
C CASTELLI
Bartolomeo Colleoni
CALLE DELLE ERBE
C MODENA
CORTE 2ª D MILION
Rio di San Marina
San Lio
RUGA DEGLI OREFICI
RG VECCHIA S GIOVANNI
CAMPO RIALTO NUOVO
San Giàcomo di Rialto
SAL SAN GIOVANNI CRISOSTOMO
C SCALETTA
CAMPO SAN MARINA
FMTA FELZI
C TORELLI

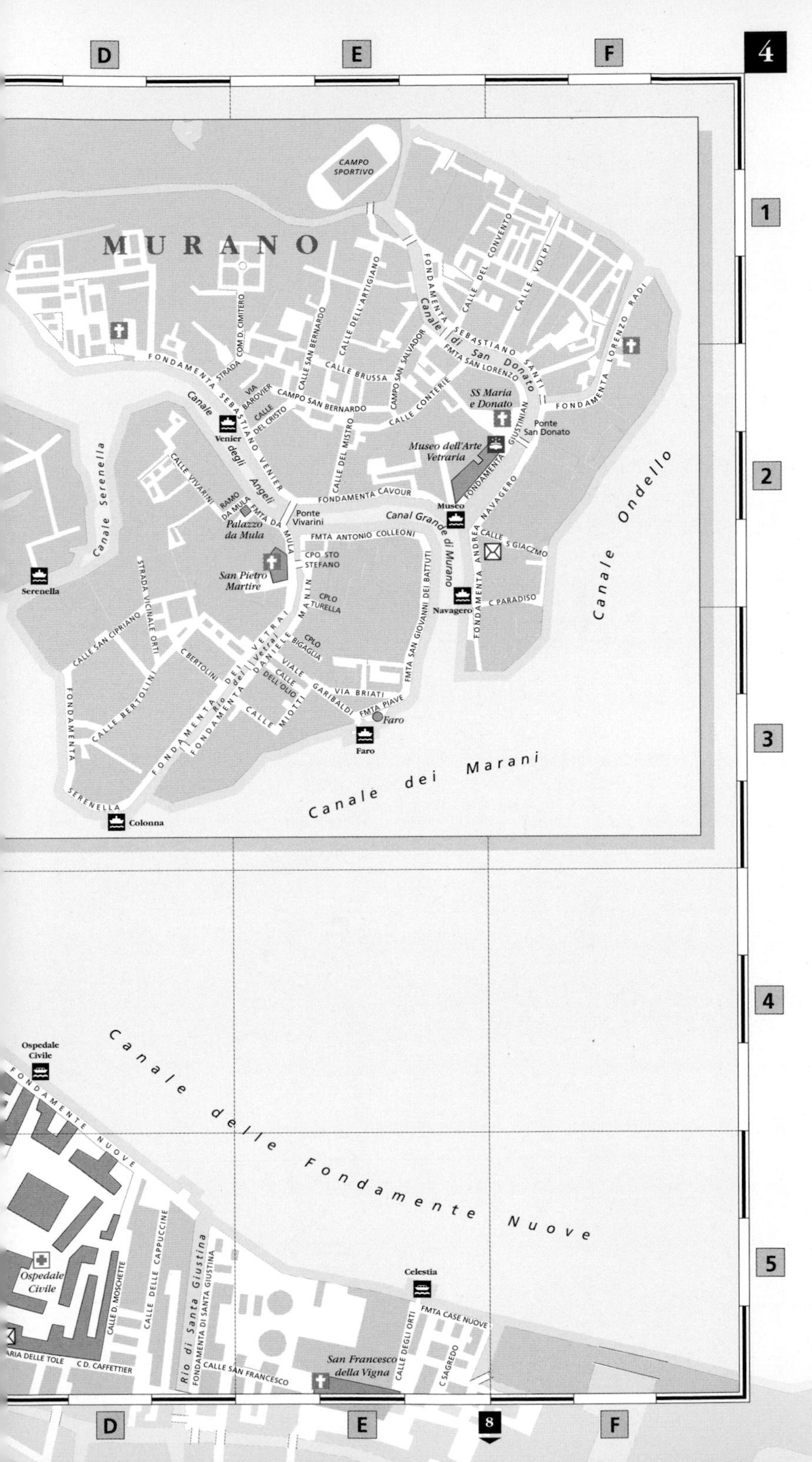
D
E
F
1
2
3
4
5
MURANO
CAMPO SPORTIVO
Canale di San Donato
Canale degli Angeli
Canale Serenella
Canal Grande di Murano
Canale Ondello
Canale dei Marani
Canale delle Fondamente Nuove
SS Maria e Donato
Ponte San Donato
Museo dell'Arte Vetraria
Museo
Venier
Ponte Vivarini
Palazzo da Mula
San Pietro Martire
Serenella
Navagero
Faro
Colonna
Ospedale Civile
Celestia
San Francesco della Vigna
FONDAMENTA SEBASTIANO VENIER
FONDAMENTA CAVOUR
FMTA ANTONIO COLLEONI
FMTA DA MULA
FONDAMENTA ANDREA NAVAGERO
FONDAMENTA GIUSTINIAN
FONDAMENTA LORENZO RADI
FMTA SAN LORENZO
FONDAMENTA SEBASTIANO SANTI
CALLE DEL CONVENTO
CALLE VOLPI
CALLE DELL'ARTIGIANO
CALLE SAN BERNARDO
CAMPO SAN BERNARDO
CALLE BRUSSA
CAMPO SAN SALVADOR
CALLE CONTERIE
CALLE DEL MISTRO
STRADA COM.D. CIMITERO
VIA BAROVIER
CALLE DEL CRISTO
CALLE VIVARINI
RAMO DA MULA
CPO STO STEFANO
CPLO TURELLA
CPLO BIGAGLIA
MANIN
FMTA SAN GIOVANNI DEI BATTUTI
CALLE S GIACZMO
C PARADISO
STRADA VICINALE ORTI
CALLE SAN CIPRIANO
C BERTOLINI
CALLE BERTOLINI
FONDAMENTA SERENELLA
FONDAMENTA DEI VETRAI
Rio dei Vetrai
FONDAMENTA DANIELE MANIN
VIALE GARIBALDI
CALLE DELL'OLIO
CALLE MIOTTI
VIA BRIATI
FMTA PIAVE
FONDAMENTE NUOVE
CALLE DELLE CAPPUCCINE
CALLE D. MOSCHETTE
Rio di Santa Giustina
FONDAMENTA DI SANTA GIUSTINA
CALLE SAN FRANCESCO
CALLE DEGLI ORTI
FMTA CASE NUOVE
C SAGREDO
C D. CAFFETTIER
RIA DELLE TOLE
8

5
A
B
C
1
2
3
4
5
SANTA CROCE
DORSODURO
GIUDECCA
PIAZZALE ROMA
CAMPO SANT'ANDREA
GIARDINO EX PAPADOPOLI
Canale di Santa Chiara
Canale Scomenzera
Canale di Santa Maria Maggiore
FONDAMENTA SANT'ANDREA
San Nicolò da Tolentino
CAMPO DEI TOLENTINI
Rio delle Burchielle
FONDAMENTA DELLE BURCHIELLE
Rio Nuovo
RIO TERRA DEI PENSIERI
Rio della Cazziola
FONDAMENTA RIZZI
FONDAMENTA DELLE PROCURATIE
FMTA DI SANTA MARIA MAGGIORE
FONDAMENTA DEI CERERI
Rio del Tintor
CALLE DEI GUARDIANI
Rio Briati
FONDAMENTA ROSSA
FONDAMENTA SANTA MARTA
RIO TERRA DEI SECCHI
Rio dell'Arziere
Rio delle Terese
Rio dei Carmini
FONDAMENTA DEL SOCCORSO
Santa Maria dei Carmini
Collegio Armeno
Rio dell'Angelo Raffaele
CAMPO SAN NICOLÒ
San Nicolò dei Mendicoli
Rio di San Nicolò
FONDAMENTA DI PESCHERIA
FONDAMENTA BARBARIGO
Angelo Raffaele
CPO ANGELO RAFFAELE
Rio di San Sebastiano
San Sebastiano
Rio dell'Avogaria
CPLO D. STENDARDO
CORTE LARDONA
Stazione Marittima
SALIZZADA SAN BASEGIO
BANCHINA DEL PORTO COMMERCIALE
BANCHINA DI SAN BASEGIO
FMTA ZATTERE PONTE LUNGO
San Basilio
Canale di Fusina
Sacca Fisola
FONDAMENTA BEATA GIULIANA
CALLE DELLA SCUOLA
CALLE DEI FIGHERI
CALLE DEL VAPORETTO
CALLE FISOLA
CALLE DELLA SACCA
CALLE RIMINI
CAMPO DELLA CHIESA
CALLE LARGA DEI LAVRANERI
Canale dei Lavraneri
Mulino Stucky
Rio di San Biagio
CAMPIELLO PRIULI
Rio delle Convertite
FMTA DELLE CONVERTITE
FMTA SAN GERARDO SAGREDO
Can Sacca Fisola San Biagio

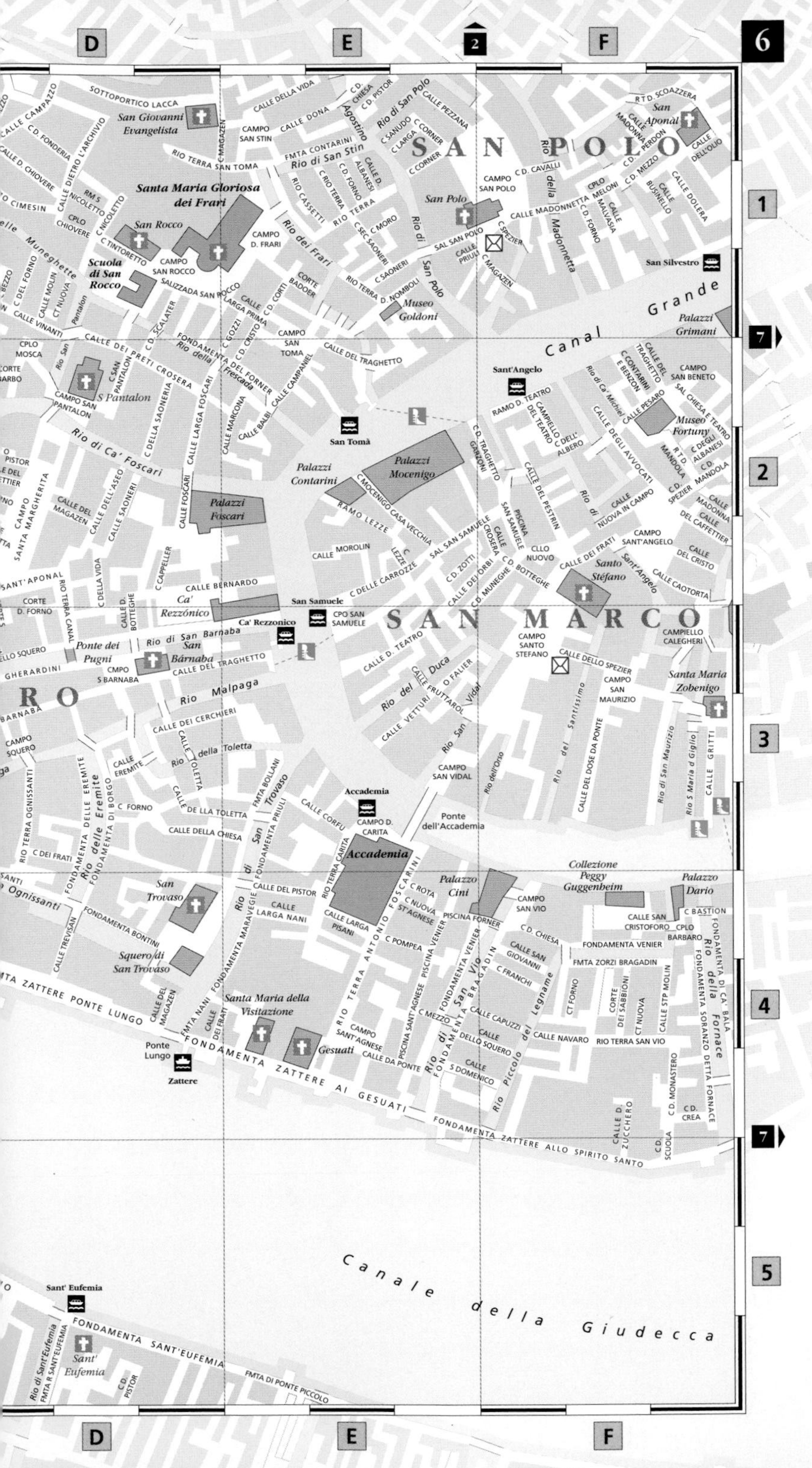
SAN POLO
SAN MARCO
Canal Grande
Canale della Giudecca
Santa Maria Gloriosa dei Frari
San Giovanni Evangelista
San Rocco
Scuola di San Rocco
San Polo
San Aponal
San Silvestro
Museo Goldoni
Palazzi Grimani
Sant'Angelo
Museo Fortuny
San Tomà
Palazzi Contarini
Palazzi Mocenigo
Palazzi Foscari
S Pantalon
Ca' Rezzónico
San Samuele
Santo Stéfano
San Bárnaba
Ponte dei Pugni
Santa Maria Zobenigo
Accademia
Ponte dell'Accademia
Collezione Peggy Guggenheim
Palazzo Cini
Palazzo Dario
San Trovaso
Squero di San Trovaso
Santa Maria della Visitazione
Gesuati
Ponte Lungo
Zattere
Sant' Eufemia
FONDAMENTA ZATTERE AI GESUATI
FONDAMENTA ZATTERE ALLO SPIRITO SANTO
FONDAMENTA SANT'EUFEMIA

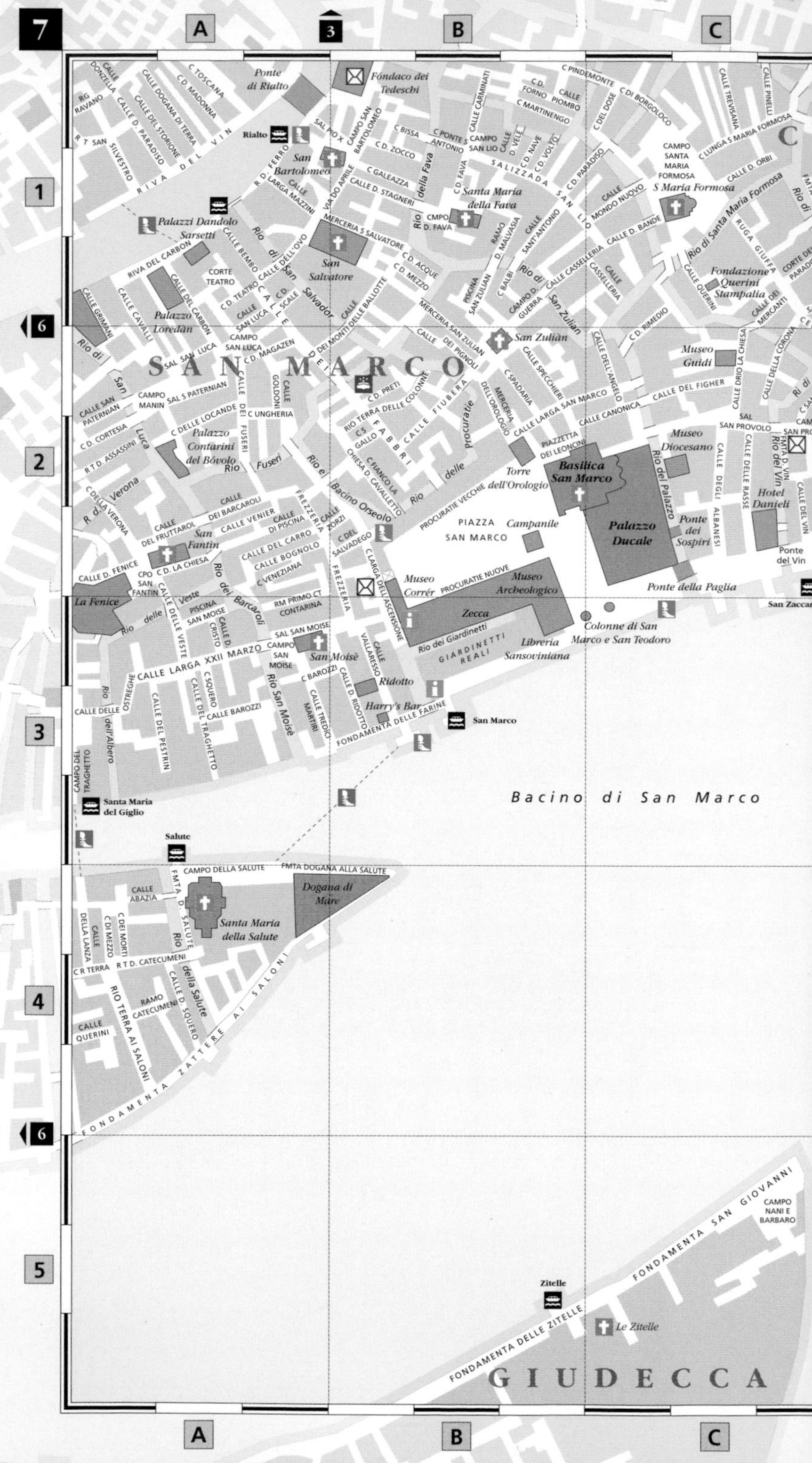

7
A
B
C
1
2
3
4
5
SAN MARCO
GIUDECCA
Bacino di San Marco
Ponte di Rialto
Fóndaco dei Tedeschi
Rialto
San Bartolomeo
Palazzi Dandolo Sarsetti
San Salvatore
Santa Maria della Fava
S Maria Formosa
Fondazione Querini Stampalia
San Zulian
Museo Guidi
Palazzo Loredan
Palazzo Contarini del Bóvolo
San Fantin
La Fenice
Torre dell'Orologio
Basilica San Marco
Palazzo Ducale
Campanile
PIAZZA SAN MARCO
Museo Diocesano
Ponte dei Sospiri
Hotel Danieli
Ponte del Vin
Ponte della Paglia
San Zaccaria
Museo Corrér
Museo Archeologico
Zecca
Libreria Sansoviniana
Colonne di San Marco e San Teodoro
GIARDINETTI REALI
San Moisè
Ridotto
Harry's Bar
San Marco
Santa Maria del Giglio
Salute
Dogana di Mare
Santa Maria della Salute
Zitelle
Le Zitelle

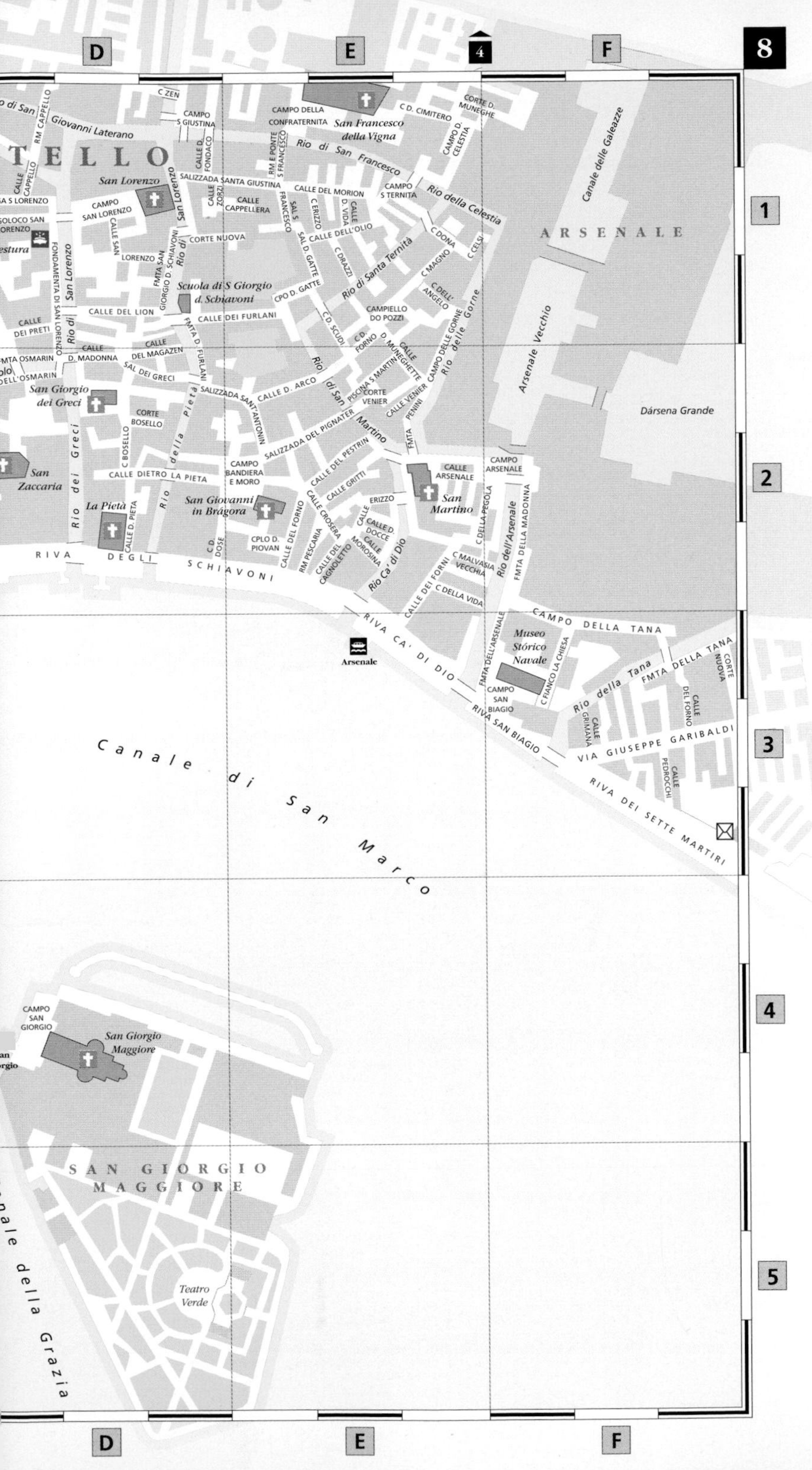

D
E
4
F
1
2
3
4
5
San Francesco della Vigna
Rio di San Francesco
Rio della Celestia
Canale delle Galeazze
ARSENALE
San Lorenzo
Scuola di S Giorgio d. Schiavoni
Rio di Santa Ternita
Arsenale Vecchio
Rio delle Gorne
Dársena Grande
San Giorgio dei Greci
Rio di San Martino
San Zaccaria
La Pietà
Rio della Pietà
Rio dei Greci
San Giovanni in Brágora
San Martino
Rio dell'Arsenale
Rio Ca' di Dio
RIVA DEGLI SCHIAVONI
RIVA CA' DI DIO
Arsenale
CAMPO DELLA TANA
Museo Storico Navale
Rio della Tana
RIVA SAN BIAGIO
VIA GIUSEPPE GARIBALDI
RIVA DEI SETTE MARTIRI
Canale di San Marco
CAMPO SAN GIORGIO
San Giorgio Maggiore
SAN GIORGIO MAGGIORE
Teatro Verde
Canale della Grazia

Street Finder Index

Key to Abbreviations Used in the Street Finder

C	Calle	**d.**	di, del, dell', dello, della, dei, delle, degli	**R**	Rio	**Sta**	Santa
Can	Canale			**R T**	Rio Terrà	**Sto**	Santo'
Cpo	Campo			**Rg**	Ruga/Rughetta	**SS**	Santi/Santissimo
Cplo	Campiello	**Fmta**	Fondamenta	**Sal**	Salizzada	**Stp**	Sottoportico
Ct	Corte	**Rm**	Ramo	**S**	San/Sant'		

T

U

V

W

Z

General Index

A

B

D

H

I

J

Q

R

S

T

W

Y

Z

Acknowledgments

DORLING KINDERSLEY would like to thank the many people whose help and assistance contributed to the preparation of this book.

MAIN CONTRIBUTORS
Susie Boulton studied languages and history of art at the University of Cambridge. She has been visiting Venice for over 20 years and is the author of several guide books on the city.

Christopher Catling has been visiting Italy for over 25 years since his first archaeological dig there while he was a student at Cambridge University. He is the author of several guide books on Italian cities and regions, including *The DK Travel Guide to Florence and Tuscany*.

ADDITIONAL CONTRIBUTOR
Sally Roy first got to know Venice while at school in Rome and has been returning to the country ever since. She read medieval history at St Andrew's University, Edinburgh and has contributed to several books on Italy.

ADDITIONAL ILLUSTRATIONS
Annabelle Brend, Dawn Brend, Neil Bulpitt, Richard Draper, Nick Gibbard, Kevin Jones Associates, John Lawrence, The Maltings Partnership, Simon Roulstone, Sue Sharples, Derrick Stone, Paul Weston, John Woodcock.

DESIGN AND EDITORIAL ASSISTANCE
Gaye Allen, Douglas Amrine, Michael Blacker, Dawn Brend, Lucinda Cooke, Felicity Crowe, Stephanie Driver, Michael Ellis, Gadi Farfour, Irena Hoare, Annette Jacobs, Steve Knowlden, Erika Lang, Ian Midson, Gillian Price, Steve Rowling, Sands Publishing Solutions, Janis Utton, Lynda Warrington, Fiona Wild.

RESEARCH ASSISTANCE
Jill De Cet, Hans Erlacher, Paolo Frullini, Oscar Gates, Marinella Laini, Elizabetta Lovato, Fabiola Perer, Alan Ross, Sarah Sole, Jo-Ann Titmarsh.

INDEX
Indexing Specialists, 202 Church Road, Hove, East Sussex, UK.

SPECIAL ASSISTANCE
Comune di Vicenza; Arch. Gianfranco Martinoni at the Assessorato Beni Culturali Comune di Padova; Ca' Macana; Cesare Battisti at the Media Tourist Office, Venice; Curia Patriarcale Venezia; D.ssa Foscarina Caletti at the Giunta Regionale di Venezia; Jane Groom, Brian Jordan; Alexandra Kennedy; Joy Parker; Frances Hawkins, Lady Frances Clarke and John Millerchip of the Venice in Peril Fund; the staff of the APT offices throughout the Veneto, in particular Anna Rita Bisaggio in Montegrotto Terme, Stephano Marchioro in Padua; Anna Maria Carlotto, Virna Scarduelli and Christina Erlacher in Verona, Anselmo Centomo in Vicenza; Heidi Wenyon.

PHOTOGRAPHY PERMISSIONS
DORLING KINDERSLEY would like to thank the following for their kind permission to photograph at their establishments:

VENICE: Amministrazione Provinciale di Venezia (Museo dell'Estuario, Torcello); Ca' Mocenigo; Ca' Pesaro; Ca' Rezzonico; Caffè Quadri; Collegio Armeni; Fondazione Europea Pro Venetia Viva, San Servolo; Fondazione Giorgio Cini (San Giorgio Maggiore); Peggy Guggenheim Museum; Hôtel des Bains; Libreria Sansoviniana; Museo Archeologico; Museo Correr; Museo Diocesano d'Arte Sacra; Museo Fortuny; Museo Storia Navale; Museo Storico Naturale; Museo Vetrario, Murano; Arch. Umberto Franzoi and staff at the Palazzo Ducale; Procuratie di San Marco (Basilica San Marco); Santi Giovanni e Paolo; San Lazzaro degli Armeni; Santa Maria Gloriosa dei Frari; Scuola Grande dei Carmini; Scuola Grande di San Rocco. **VENETO:** Arena Romano, Verona; Basilica, Vicenza; Caffè Pedrocchi, Padua; Duomo, Padua; Duomo, Vicenza; Giardini Giusti, Verona; Museo Archeologico, Verona; Museo di Castelvecchio, Verona; Museo Civico, Malcésine; Museo Civico, Vicenza; Museo Concordiese, Portogruaro; Museo degli Eremitani, Padua; Museo Lapidario Maffeiano, Verona; Museo dei Storia Naturale, Verona; Ossuario di San Pietro, Solferino; Sant'Anastasia, Verona; San Fermo Maggiore, Verona; San Giorgio, Monsélice; San Giorgio in Braida, Verona; San Lorenzo, Vicenza; Santa Maria in Organo, Verona; San Pietro in Malvino, Sirmione; San Severo, Bardolino; San Stefano, Verona; San Zeno Maggiore, Verona; Santuario di Monte Berico, Vicenza; Teatro Olimpico, Vicenza; Università di Padova; Contessa Diamante Luling-Buschette, Villa Barbaro, Masèr; Conte Marco Emo, Villa Emo, Fanzolo di Vedelago.

PICTURE CREDITS
t = top; tc = top centre; tr = top right; cla = centre left above; ca = centre above; cra = centre right above; cl = centre left; c = centre; cr = centre right; clb = centre left below; cb = centre below; crb = centre right below; bl = bottom left; bc = bottom centre; br = bottom right.

Every effort has been made to trace the copyright holders, and we apologize in advance for any unintentional omissions. We would be pleased to insert the appropriate acknowledgments in any subsequent edition of this publication. Works of art have been reproduced with the permission of the following copyright holders:
© ADAGP, Paris and DACS, London 1995: Intérieur Hollandais II (1928) by Joan Miró, *Maiastra* by Constantin Brancusi, 134cr.

The publishers are grateful to the following museums, companies, and picture libraries for permission to reproduce their photographs:
ACCADEMIA OLIMPICA, VICENZA: 172tr, 173crb; ACE PHOTO/AGENCY TORE GILL: 254b; ACE/MAURITIUS: 257t; ANCIENT ART & ARCHITECTURE COLLECTION: 38c, 40br, 40tl; APT DEL BRESCIANO: 35b; ARCHIV FÜR KUNST UND GESCHICHTE: 26tl/c/cr, 30bl, 36, 43br, 44crb, 45bl, 45t, 46tl, 46tr, 48cla, 49clb, 50b, 54br, 130b, 131b, 131c, 132b, 133t, 30/31c; ARCHIVIO RAIMONDO ZAGO 49cl. ARCHIVIO VENEZIANO: Sarah Quill 29br, 51crb, 67cl, 106tr, 144t.

BENETTON: 51tl; BIBLIOTECA CIVICA DI TRIESTE (FOTO HALUPCA): 119b; BRIDGEMAN ART LIBRARY, LONDON: *Madonna and Child and Saints* (triptych altarpiece) by Giovanni Bellini (c.1431–1516), Santa Maria dei Frari, Venice 27tl/tr; *The Siege of Antioch* 1098 by William of Tyre. Bibliothèque Nationale, Paris 40cla; *Marco Polo with Elephants and Camels* from Livre des Merveilles, Bibliothèque Nationale, Paris, 42cb; *View of Venice* by Bernardo von Breitenbach, from Opusculum Sanctarum Peregrinationum in Terram Sanctam, Bibliothèque Nationale, PARIS, 8–9; *Family Tree of the Cornaro Family*, Italian School (18th century), Palazzo Corner Ca' Grande, Venice, 69tr; *Salome* by Gustav Klimt (1862–1918) Museo d'Arte Moderna, Venice, 105br; *The Nuns' Visiting Day* by Francesco Guardi (1712–93), Museo Ca' Rezzonico, Venice, 112bl; *St George Killing the Dragon* by Vittore Carpaccio (c.1460/5–1523/6), Scuola di San Giorgio degli Schiavoni, Venice, 118tl; *The Stealing of the Body of St Mark* by Tintoretto (1518–94), Accademia, Venice, 131t; *The Rape of Europa* by Francesco Zuccarelli, Accademia, Venice, 133c; *Marco Polo dressed in Tartar costume* (c.1700) Museo Correr, Venice/Giraudon, 4tr/115br; OSVALDO BÖHM: 20b, 20cl, 29bl, 41crb, 63tl, 79tl, 132c, 132t, 144c.

DEMETRIO CARRASCO: 124b, 139br, 141t, 227tr, 274t; CEPHAS PICTURE LIBRARY: Mick Rock, 35cra and 238tr; CIGA HOTELS: 70tl; CLAIRE CALMAN: 55cr; GIANCARLO COSTA: 47clb; CORBIS: royalty-free 146; JOE CORNISH: 15b, 209c, 216bl; STEPHANIE COLASANTI: 56, 195br.

CHRIS DONAGHUE THE OXFORD PHOTO LIBRARY: 3 (inset), 5tl, 76t, 156br, 280t; MICHAEL DENT: 82b, 252tl; DRAUGHTSMAN: 268tr.

E.T. ARCHIVE: Sala dei Prior Siena, 41tl; Baroque Hall of Mirrors, Palazzo Papadopoli, Venice, 64tl; *The Apothecary's Shop* by Pietro Longhi, Accademia, Venice, 130c; ELECTA, MILAN: 180cr, 181t/cl; ERIZZO EDITRICE SRL: 105clb; MARY EVANS PICTURE LIBRARY: 7 (inset), 9 (inset), 24tl, 39clb, 44bl, 47br, 47t, 53 (inset), 58cra, 58tr, 63c, 64c, 69ca, 143tr, 159 (inset), 221 (inset), 259 (inset), 32c.

FERROVIA DELLO STATO: 272tl.

JACKIE GORDON: 273t; GRAZIA NERI: 41b, 49tl, 50crb, 50tr, 65br, 92tl, 157b, 254t; Marco Bruzzo, 5tr, 32t, 35clb, 40tr, 166t; Cameraphoto 71tr, 115bl, 42/43c; Graziano Arici 100tr; Roberta Krasnig 268bl; PEGGY GUGGENHEIM MUSEUM, VENICE: 134b; THE RONALD GRANT ARCHIVE: 50cla.

HOTEL EXCELSIOR, VENICE LIDO: 48crb; ROBERT HARDING PICTURE LIBRARY: 216cl; THE HULTON DEUTSCH COLLECTION: 38br, 38tr, 39br, 43clb, 46br, 48bc, 49br, 61tr, 66b, 66cra, 69cl, 101c, 140bl, 181br, 199b

IMAGE BANK: Guido A. Rossi, 11 (inset); IMAGE SELECT: Ann Ronan, 44cl. LONDRA PALACE: 226br

HUGH MCKNIGHT PHOTOGRAPHY: 71tl; MAGNUM PHOTOS/DAVID SEYMOUR: 48tr; MARKA: 37b, L Baldissin 237bcb; L Barbazza 249br; Roberto Benzi 276cl; Enrico Cerretelli 150bl; M Motta 277cl; Ubik 237bcla, Ubik/Pizzo 237bcar; MORO ROMA: 30cl, 48/49c; MUSEO ARCHEOLOGICO, VERONA: 38bl; MUSEO CIVICO AGLI EREMITANI: 179t/c/b; MUSEO CIVICO DI ODERZO: 39t; THE MANSELL COLLECTION: 46crb, 47bl.

NHPA/GERARD LACZ: 217b; NHPA/LAURIE CAMPBELL: 217c; NHPA/SILVESTRIS FOTOSERVICE: 217crb; THE NATIONAL GALLERY, LONDON: 29t.

OLYMPIA/SELECT: 34b, 51br, 51clb, 157t, 255t; OLYMPIA/SELECT/LARRY RIVERS: 256t.

PERFORMING ARTS LIBRARY/GIANFRANCO FAINELLO: 256c.

THE ROYAL COLLECTION ©1994 HER MAJESTY QUEEN ELIZABETH 11: 46/47c.

JOHN FERRO SIMS: 167t; SCALA, FIRENZE: *Madonna di Ca' Pesaro* by Titian (1477/89–1576), S. Maria Gloriosa dei Frari, Venice 27, c/cr; *Ultimi Momenti del Doge Marin Faliero* by Francesco Hayez (1791–1881), Pinacoteca di Brera, Milan, 43t; *Banquet of Antony and Cleopatra* by Giambattista Tiepolo (1692–1770), Palazzo Labia, Venice, 60t; *Ultimi Momenti del Doge Marin Faliero* by Francesco Hayez (1791–1881), Pinacoteca di Brera, Milan, 68cra; *Crocifissione* by Tintoretto (1518–94), Scuola Grande di S. Rocco, Venice, 106c/cb; *S Michele* by Giambono (15th century), Accademia, Venice, 123b; *Il Trasporto della Santa Casa di Loreto* by Giambattista Tiepolo (1692–1770), Accademia, Venice, 130tr; *Presentazione al tempio* by Titian (1477/89–1576), Accademia, Venice,133b; *Intérieur Hollandais II* by Joan Miró (1928), Museo Guggenheim, Venice, 134c; *Madonna col Bambino* by Filippo Lippi (1406–69), Cini Collection, Venice 134t; *Annunciazione* by Vittore Carpaccio (1460 c.–1526), Ca' d'Oro, Venice,144b; Pala di San Zeno by Andrea Mantegna (1431–1506), San Zeno, Verona, 200cl; SCIENCE PHOTO LIBRARY: Earth Satellite Corporation, 10 (inset); SETTORE BENI CULTURALI, PADUA: 180t/cla/clb; SPECTRUM COLOUR LIBRARY: 28b; STUDIO PIZZI: 45cla, 47crb; TONY STONE IMAGES: 214cla, 216t, 50/51c.

JACKET
Front: DK PICTURE LIBRARY: John Heseltine clb; crb; Roger Moss bl; ROBERT HARDING PICTURE LIBRARY: Simon Harris main image. Back: DK PICTURE LIBRARY: John Heseltine br; Roger Moss t. Spine: ROBERT HARDING PICTURE LIBRARY: Simon Harris.

Phrase Book

In Emergency

Help!	**Aiuto!**	eye-**yoo**-toh
Stop!	**Fermate!**	fair-**mah**-teh
Call a doctor.	**Chiama un medico**	kee-**ah**-mah oon **meh**-dee-koh
Call an ambulance.	**Chiama un' ambulanza**	kee-**ah**-mah oon am-boo-**lan**-tsa
Call the police.	**Chiama la polizia**	kee-**ah**-mah lah pol-ee-**tsee**-ah
Call the fire brigade.	**Chiama i pompieri**	kee-**ah**-mah ee pom-pee-**air**-ee
Where is the telephone?	**Dov'è il telefono?**	dov-**eh** eel teh-**leh**-foh-noh?
The nearest hospital?	**L'ospedale più vicino?**	loss-peh-**dah**-leh pee-**oo**vee-**chee**-noh?

Communication Essentials

Yes/No	**Si/No**	**see**/**noh**
Please	**Per favore**	pair fah-**vor**-eh
Thank you	**Grazie**	**grah**-tsee-eh
Excuse me	**Mi scusi**	mee **skoo**-zee
Hello	**Buon giorno**	bwon **jor**-noh
Goodbye	**Arrivederci**	ah-ree-veh-**dair**-chee
Good evening	**Buona sera**	**bwon**-ah **sair**-ah
morning	**la mattina**	lah mah-**tee**-nah
afternoon	**il pomeriggio**	eel poh-meh-**ree**-joh
evening	**la sera**	lah **sair**-ah
yesterday	**ieri**	ee-**air**-ee
today	**oggi**	**oh**-jee
tomorrow	**domani**	doh-**mah**-nee
here	**qui**	**kwee**
there	**la**	**lah**
What?	**Quale?**	**kwah**-leh?
When?	**Quando?**	**kwan**-doh?
Why?	**Perchè?**	pair-**keh**?
Where?	**Dove?**	**doh**-veh

Useful Phrases

How are you?	**Come sta?**	**koh**-meh stah?
Very well, thank you.	**Molto bene, grazie.**	**moll**-toh **beh**-neh **grah**-tsee-eh
Pleased to meet you.	**Piacere di conoscerla.**	pee-ah-**chair**-eh dee coh-**noh**-shair-lah
See you soon.	**A più tardi.**	ah pee-**oo tar**-dee
That's fine.	**Va bene.**	va **beh**-neh
Where is/are ...?	**Dov'è/Dove sono ...?**	dov-**eh**/doveh **soh**-noh?
How long does it take to get to ...?	**Quanto tempo ci vuole per andare a ...?**	**kwan**-toh **tem**-poh chee voo-**oh**-leh pair an-**dar**-eh ah ...?
How do I get to ...?	**Come faccio per arrivare a ...?**	koh-meh **fah**-choh pair arri-**var**-eh ah..?
Do you speak English?	**Parla inglese?**	**par**-lah een-**gleh**-zeh?
I don't understand.	**Non capisco.**	non ka-**pee**-skoh
Could you speak more slowly, please?	**Può parlare più lentamente, per favore?**	pwoh par-**lah**-reh pee-**oo** len-ta-**men**-teh pair fah-**vor**-eh
I'm sorry.	**Mi dispiace.**	mee dee-spee-**ah**-cheh

Useful Words

big	**grande**	**gran**-deh
small	**piccolo**	**pee**-koh-loh
hot	**caldo**	**kal**-doh
cold	**freddo**	**fred**-doh
good	**buono**	**bwoh**-noh
bad	**cattivo**	kat-**tee**-voh
enough	**basta**	**bas**-tah
well	**bene**	**beh**-neh
open	**aperto**	ah-**pair**-toh
closed	**chiuso**	kee-**oo**-zoh
left	**a sinistra**	ah see-**nee**-strah
right	**a destra**	ah **dess**-trah
straight on	**sempre dritto**	**sem**-preh **dree**-toh
near	**vicino**	vee-**chee**-noh
far	**lontano**	lon-**tah**-noh
up	**su**	**soo**
down	**giù**	**joo**
early	**presto**	**press**-toh
late	**tardi**	**tar**-dee
entrance	**entrata**	en-**trah**-tah
exit	**uscita**	oo-**shee**-ta
toilet	**il gabinetto**	eel gah-bee-**net**-toh
free, unoccupied	**libero**	**lee**-bair-oh
free, no charge	**gratuito**	grah-**too**-ee-toh

Making a Telephone Call

I'd like to place a long-distance call.	**Vorrei fare una interurbana.**	vor-**ray far**-eh oona in-tair-oor-**bah**-nah
I'd like to make a reverse-charge call.	**Vorrei fare una telefonata a carico del destinatario.**	vor-**ray far**-eh oona teh-leh-fon-**ah**-tah ah **kar**-ee-koh dell dess-tee-nah-**tar**-ree-oh
I'll try again later.	**Ritelefono più tardi.**	ree-teh-**leh**-foh-noh pee-oo **tar**-dee
Can I leave a message?	**Posso lasciare un messaggio?**	**poss**-oh lash-**ah**-reh oon mess-**sah**-joh?
Hold on.	**Un attimo, per favore**	oon **ah**-tee-moh, pair fah-**vor**-eh
Could you speak up a little please?	**Può parlare più forte, per favore?**	pwoh par-**lah**-reh pee-**oo for**-teh, pair fah-**vor**-eh?
local call	**la telefonata locale**	lah teh-leh-fon-**ah**-ta loh-**kah**-leh

Shopping

How much does this cost?	**Quant'è, per favore?**	kwan-**teh** pair fah-**vor**-eh?
I would like ...	**Vorrei ...**	vor-**ray**
Do you have ...?	**Avete ...?**	ah-**veh**-teh.. ?
I'm just looking.	**Sto soltanto guardando.**	stoh sol-**tan**-toh gwar-**dan**-doh
Do you take credit cards?	**Accettate carte di credito?**	ah-chet-**tah**-teh **kar**-teh dee **creh**-dee-toh?
What time do you open/close?	**A che ora apre/ chiude?**	ah keh **or**-ah **ah**-preh/kee-**oo**-deh?
this one	**questo**	**kweh**-stoh
that one	**quello**	**kwell**-oh
expensive	**caro**	**kar**-oh
cheap	**a buon prezzo**	ah bwon **pret**-soh
size, clothes	**la taglia**	lah **tah**-lee-ah
size, shoes	**il numero**	eel **noo**-mair-oh
white	**bianco**	bee-**ang**-koh
black	**nero**	**neh**-roh
red	**rosso**	**ross**-oh
yellow	**giallo**	**jal**-loh
green	**verde**	**vair**-deh
blue	**blu**	bloo
brown	**marrone**	mar-**roh**-neh

Types of Shop

antique dealer	**l'antiquario**	lan-tee-**kwah**-ree-oh
bakery	**la panetteria**	lah pah-net-tair-**ree**-ah
bank	**la banca**	lah **bang**-kah
bookshop	**la libreria**	lah lee-breh-**ree**-ah
butcher's	**la macelleria**	lah mah-chell-eh-**ree**-ah
cake shop	**la pasticceria**	lah pas-tee-chair-**ee**-ah
chemist's	**la farmacia**	lah far-mah-**chee**-ah
delicatessen	**la salumeria**	lah sah-loo-meh-**ree**-ah
department store	**il grande magazzino**	eel **gran**-deh mag-gad-**zee**-noh
fishmonger's	**la pescheria**	lah pess-keh-**ree**-ah
florist	**il fioraio**	eel fee-or-**eye**-oh
greengrocer	**il fruttivendolo**	eel froo-tee-**ven**-doh-loh
grocery	**alimentari**	ah-lee-men-**tah**-ree
hairdresser	**il parrucchiere**	eel par-oo-kee-**air**-eh
ice cream parlour	**la gelateria**	lah jel-lah-tair-**ree**-ah
market	**il mercato**	eel mair-**kah**-toh
news-stand	**l'edicola**	leh-**dee**-koh-lah
post office	**l'ufficio postale**	loo-**fee**-choh pos-**tah**-leh
shoe shop	**il negozio di scarpe**	eel neh-**goh**-tsioh dee **skar**-peh
supermarket	**il supermercato**	su-pair-mair-**kah**-toh
tobacconist	**il tabaccaio**	eel tah-bak-**eye**-oh
travel agency	**l'agenzia di viaggi**	lah-jen-**tsee**-ah dee vee-**ad**-jee

Sightseeing

art gallery	**la pinacoteca**	lah peena-koh-**teh**-kah
bus stop	**la fermata dell'autobus**	lah fair-**mah**-tah dell **ow**-toh-booss
church	**la chiesa**	lah kee-**eh**-zah
	la basilica	lah bah-**seel**-i-kah
closed for the public holiday	**chiuso per la festa**	kee-**oo**-zoh pair lah **fess**-tah
garden	**il giardino**	eel jar-**dee**-no
library	**la biblioteca**	lah beeb-lee-oh-**teh**-kah
museum	**il museo**	eel moo-**zeh**-oh
railway station	**la stazione**	lah stah-tsee-**oh**-neh
tourist information	**l'ufficio turistico**	loo-**fee**-choh too-**ree**-stee-koh

Staying in a Hotel

Do you have any vacant rooms?	**Avete camere libere?**	ah-**veh**-teh **kah**-mair-eh **lee**-bair-eh?
double room	**una camera doppia**	oona **kah**-mair-ah **doh**-pee-ah
with double bed	**con letto matrimoniale**	kon **let**-toh mah-tree-moh-nee-**ah**-leh
twin room	**una camera con due letti**	oona **kah**-mair-ah kon **doo**-eh **let**-tee
single room	**una camera singola**	oona **kah**-mair-ah **sing**-goh-lah
room with a bath, shower	**una camera con bagno, con doccia**	oona **kah**-mair-ah kon **ban**-yoh, kon **dot**-chah
porter	**il facchino**	eel fah-**kee**-noh
key	**la chiave**	lah kee-**ah**-veh
I have a reservation.	**Ho fatto una prenotazione.**	oh **fat**-toh oona preh-noh-tah-tsee-**oh**-neh

Eating Out

Have you got a table for ...?	**Avete una tavola per ... ?**	ah-**veh**-teh oona **tah**-voh-lah pair ...?
I'd like to reserve a table.	**Vorrei riservare una tavola.**	vor-**ray** ree-sair-**vah**-reh oona **tah**-voh-lah
breakfast	**colazione**	koh-lah-tsee-**oh**-neh
lunch	**pranzo**	**pran**-tsoh
dinner	**cena**	**cheh**-nah
The bill, please.	**Il conto, per favore.**	eel **kon**-toh pair fah-**vor**-eh
I am a vegetarian.	**Sono vegetariano/a.**	**soh**-noh **veh**-jeh-tar ee-**ah**-noh/nah
waitress	**cameriera**	kah-mair-ee-**air**-ah
waiter	**cameriere**	kah-mair-ee-**air**-eh
fixed price menu	**il menù a prezzo fisso**	eel meh-**noo** ah **pret**-soh **fee**-soh
dish of the day	**piatto del giorno**	pee-**ah**-toh dell **jor**-no
starter	**antipasto**	an-tee-**pass**-toh
first course	**il primo**	eel **pree**-moh
main course	**il secondo**	eel seh-**kon**-doh
vegetables	**il contorno**	eel kon-**tor**-noh
dessert	**il dolce**	eel **doll**-cheh
cover charge	**il coperto**	eel koh-**pair**-toh
wine list	**la lista dei vini**	lah **lee**-stah day **vee**-nee
rare	**al sangue**	al **sang**-gweh
medium	**al puntino**	al poon-**tee**-noh
well done	**ben cotto**	ben **kot**-toh
glass	**il bicchiere**	eel bee-kee-**air**-eh
bottle	**la bottiglia**	lah bot-**teel**-yah
knife	**il coltello**	eel kol-**tell**-oh
fork	**la forchetta**	lah for-**ket**-tah
spoon	**il cucchiaio**	eel koo-kee-**eye**-oh

Menu Decoder

l'acqua minerale gasata/naturale	lah-kwah mee-nair-ah-leh gah-**zah**-tah/nah-too-**rah**-leh	mineral water fizzy/still
l'agnello	lahn-**yell**-oh	lamb
al forno	al **for**-noh	baked
alla griglia	ah-lah **greel**-yah	grilled
l'anguilla	lahng-**gwee**-lah	eel
l'aragosta	lah-rah-**goss**-tah	lobster
arrosto	ar-**ross**-toh	roast
il baccalà	eel bahk-kah-**lah**	dried salted cod
la birra	lah **beer**-rah	beer
la bistecca	lah bee-**stek**-kah	steak
il brodetto	eel-broh-**det**-toh	fish soup
il burro	eel **boor**-oh	butter
il caffè	eel kah-**feh**	coffee
i calamari	ee kah-lah-**mah**-ree	squid
il carciofo	eel kar-**choff**-oh	artichoke
la carne	la **kar**-neh	meat
carne di maiale	**kar**-neh dee mah-**yah**-leh	pork
i fagioli	ee fah-**joh**-lee	beans
il fegato	eel **fay**-gah-toh	liver
il formaggio	eel for-**mad**-joh	cheese
le fragole	leh **frah**-goh-leh	strawberries
il fritto misto	eel free-toh **mees**-toh	mixed fried fish
la frutta	la **froot**-tah	fruit
frutti di mare	**froo**-tee dee **mah**-reh	seafood
i funghi	ee **foon**-ghee	mushrooms
i gamberi	ee **gam**-bair-ee	prawns
il gelato	eel jel-**lah**-toh	ice cream
l'insalata mista	leen-sah-lah-tah **mees**-tah	mixed salad
l'insalata verde	leen-sah-lah-tah **vehr**-day	green salad
il latte	eel **laht**-teh	milk
i legumi OR i contorni	ee leh-**goo**-mee ee kon-**tor**-nee	vegetables
il manzo	eel **man**-tsoh	beef
la melanzana	lah meh-lan-**tsah**-nah	aubergine
la minestra	lah mee-**ness**-trah	soup
il pane	eel **pah**-neh	bread
il panino	eel pah-**nee**-noh	bread roll
le patate	leh pah-**tah**-teh	potatoes
le patatine fritte	leh pah-tah-**teen**-eh **free**-teh	chips
il pepe	eel **peh**-peh	pepper
la pesca	lah **pess**-kah	peach
il pesce	eel **pesh**-eh	fish
il pollo	eel **poll**-oh	chicken
il prosciutto cotto/crudo	eel pro-**shoo**-toh **kot**-toh/**kroo**-doh	ham cooked/cured
il riso	eel **ree**-zoh	rice
il sale	eel **sah**-leh	salt
la salsiccia	lah sal-**see**-chah	sausage
le seppie	**leh sep-pee-eh**	cuttlefish
secco	**sek**-koh	dry
la sogliola	lah **soll**-voh-lah	sole
i spinaci	ee spee-**nah**-chee	spinach
succo d'arancia/ di limone	**soo**-koh dah-**ran**-chah/ dee lee-**moh**-neh	orange/lemon juice
il tè	eel **teh**	tea
la tisana	lah tee-**zah**-nah	herbal tea
il tonno	eel **ton**-noh	tuna
la torta	lah **tor**-tah	cake/tart
la trippa	lah **treep**-pah	tripe
vino bianco	**vee**-noh bee-**ang**-koh	white wine
vino rosso	**vee**-noh **ross**-oh	red wine
il vitello	eel vee-**tell**-oh	veal
le vongole	leh **von**-goh-leh	clams
lo zucchero	loh **zoo**-kair-oh	sugar
gli zucchini	lyee dzu-**kee**-nee	courgettes
la zuppa	lah **tsoo**-pah	soup

Numbers

1	**uno**	**oo**-noh
2	**due**	**doo**-eh
3	**tre**	treh
4	**quattro**	**kwat**-roh
5	**cinque**	**ching**-kweh
6	**sei**	**say**-ee
7	**sette**	**set**-teh
8	**otto**	**ot**-toh
9	**nove**	**noh**-veh
10	**dieci**	dee-**eh**-chee
11	**undici**	**oon**-dee-chee
12	**dodici**	**doh**-dee-chee
13	**tredici**	**tray**-dee-chee
14	**quattordici**	kwat-**tor**-dee-chee
15	**quindici**	**kwin**-dee-chee
16	**sedici**	**say**-dee-chee
17	**diciassette**	dee-chah-**set**-teh
18	**diciotto**	dee-**chot**-toh
19	**diciannove**	dee-chah-**noh**-veh
20	**venti**	**ven**-tee
30	**trenta**	**tren**-tah
40	**quaranta**	kwah-**ran**-tah
50	**cinquanta**	ching-**kwan**-tah
60	**sessanta**	sess-**an**-tah
70	**settanta**	set-**tan**-tah
80	**ottanta**	ot-**tan**-tah
90	**novanta**	noh-**van**-tah
100	**cento**	**chen**-toh
1,000	**mille**	**mee**-leh
2,000	**duemila**	**doo**-eh **mee**-lah
5,000	**cinquemila**	**ching**-kweh **mee**-lah
1,000,000	**un milione**	oon meel-**yoh**-neh

Time

one minute	**un minuto**	oon mee-**noo**-toh
one hour	**un'ora**	oon **or**-ah
half an hour	**mezz'ora**	medz-**or**-ah
a day	**un giorno**	oon **jor**-noh
a week	**una settimana**	oona set-tee-**mah**-nah
Monday	**lunedì**	loo-neh-**dee**
Tuesday	**martedì**	mar-teh-**dee**
Wednesday	**mercoledì**	mair-koh-leh-**dee**
Thursday	**giovedì**	joh-veh-**dee**
Friday	**venerdì**	ven-air-**dee**
Saturday	**sabato**	**sah**-bah-toh
Sunday	**domenica**	doh-**meh**-nee-kah

Vaporetto Routes Around Venice

The Vaporetto Routes
The ACTV network runs regular services around the city and out to most of the islands. Some services are circular for part of their route; others extend their routes during the high season. Full details of the different types of vaporetti *and how to use them are given on pages 274–5.*

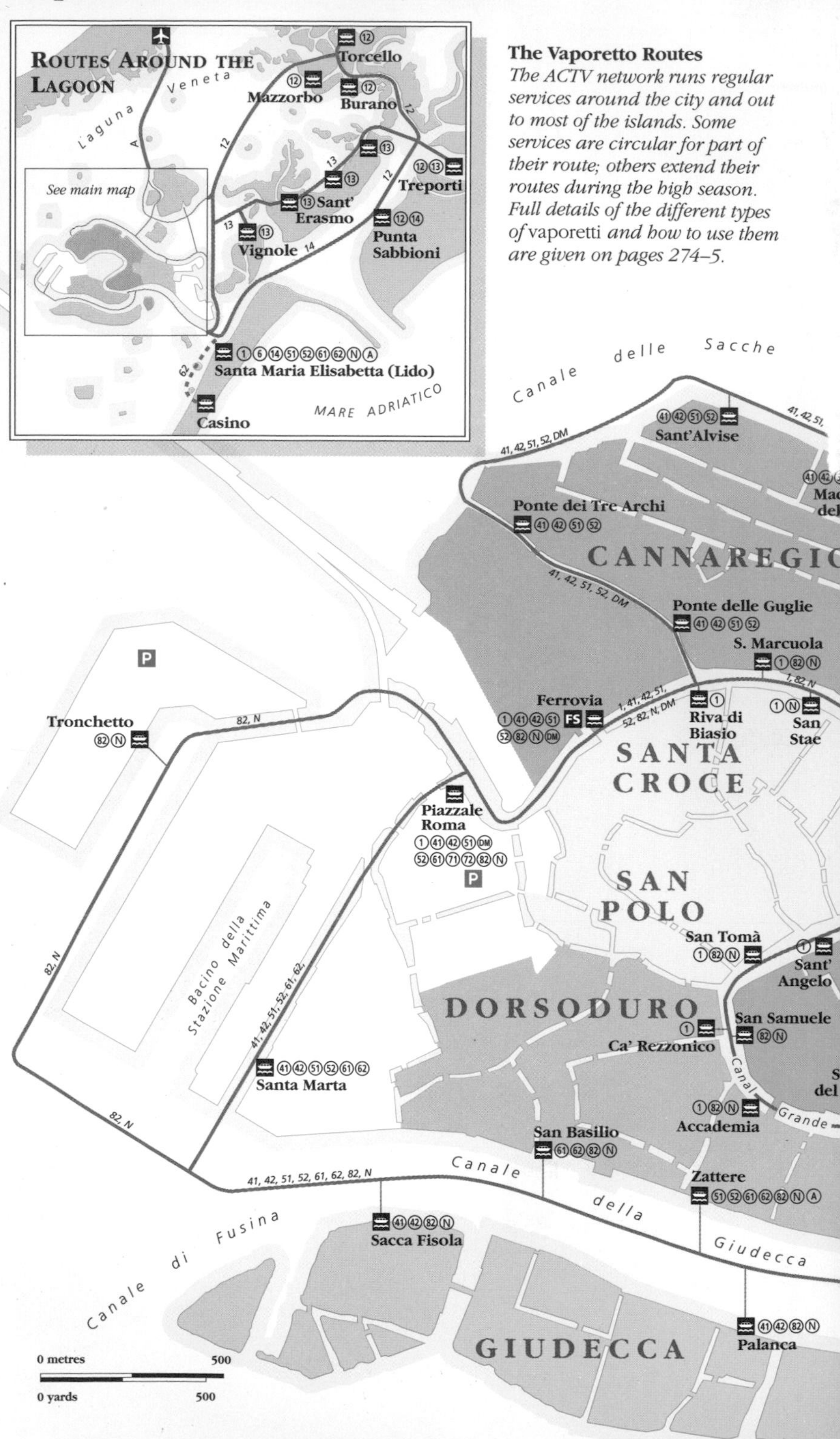